# Poverty and Wealth: Comparing Afro-Asian Development

**CONTEMPORARY STUDIES IN
ECONOMIC AND FINANCIAL ANALYSIS, VOLUME 75**

*Editors:* Robert J. Thornton and J. Richard Aronson
*Lehigh University*

To my colleagues and students at Kansas State University

# Contemporary Studies in Economic and Financial Analysis

## An International Series of Monographs

### Edited by Robert J. Thornton and J. Richard Aronson

Volume 1 - *Hunt, L.* - Dynamics of Forecasting Financial Cycles

Volume 2 - *Dreyer, J.S.* - Composite Reserve Assets in the International Money System

Volume 3 - *Altman, E.I., et al.* - Application of Classification Techniques in Business, Banking and Finance

Volume 4 - *Sinkey, J.F.* - Problems and Failed Institutions in the Commercial Banking Industry

Volume 5 - *Ahlers, D.M.* - A New Look at Portfolio Management

Volume 6 - *Sciberras, E.* - Multinational Electronic Companies and National Economic Policies

Volume 7 - *Allen, L.* - Venezuelan Economic Developement: A Politico-Economic Analysis

Volume 8 - *Gladwin, T.N.* - Environment Planning and the Multinational Corporation

Volume 9 - *Kobrin, S.J.* - Foreign Direct Investment, Industrialization and Social Change

Volume 10 - *Oldfield, G.S.* - Implications of Regulation on Bank Expansion: A Simulation Analysis

Volume 11 - *Ahmad, J.* - Import Substitution, Trade and Development

Volume 12 - *Fewings, D.R.* - Corporate Growth and Common Stock Risk

Volume 13 - *Stapleton, R.C. and M.G. Subrahmanyam* - Capital Market Equillibrium and Corporate Financial Decisions

Volume 14 - *Bloch, E. and R.A. Schwartz* - Impending Changes for Securities Markets: What Role for the Exchange

Volume 15 - *Walker, W.B.* - Industrial Innovation and International Trading Performance

Volume 16 - *Thompson, J.K.* - Financial Policy, Inflation and Economic Development: The Mexican Experience

Volume 17 - *Omitted from Numbering*

Volume 18 - *Hallwood, P.* - Stabilizationof International Commodity Markets

Volume 19 - *Omitted from Numbering*

Volume 20 - *Parry, T.G.* - The Multinational Enterprise: International Investment and Host-Country Impacts

Volume 21 - *Roxburgh, N.* - Policy Responses to Resource Depletion: The Case of Mercury

Volume 22 - *Levich, R.M.* - The International Money Market: An Assessment of Forecasting Techniques and Market Efficiency

Volume 23 - *Newfarmer, R.* - Transnational Conglomerates and the Economics of Dependent Development

Volume 24 - *Siebert, H. and A.B. Anatal* - The Political Economy of Environmental Protection

Volume 25 - *Ramsey, J.B.* - Bidding and Oil Leases

Volume 26 - *Ramsey, J.B.* - The Economics of Exploration for Energy Resources

Volume 27 - *Ghatak, S.* - Technology Transfer to Developing Countries: The Case of the Fertilizer Industry

Volume 28 - *Pastre, O.* - Multinationals: Bank and Corporation Relationships

Volume 29 - *Bierwag, G.O.* - The Primary Market for Municipal Debt: Bidding Rules and Cost of Long Term Borrowing

Volume 30 - *Kaufman, G.G.* - Efficiency in the Municipal Bond Market: The Use of Tax Exempt Financing for "Private" Purposes

Volume 31 - *West, P.* - Foreign Investment and Technology Transfer: The Tire Industry in Latin America

Volume 32 - *Uri, N.D.* - Dimensions of Energy Economics

Volume 33 - *Balabkins, N.* - Indigenization and Economic Development: The Nigerian Experience

Volume 34 - *Oh, J.S.* - International Financial Management: Problem, Issues and Experience

Volume 35 - *Officer, L.H.* - Purchasing Power Parity and Exchange Rates: Theory Evidence and Relevance

Volume 36 - *Horwitz, B. and R. Kolodny* - Financial Reporting Rules and Corporate Decisions: A Study of Public Policy

Volume 37 - *Thorelli, H.B. and G.D. Sentell* - Consumer Emancipation and Economic Development

Volume 38 - *Wood, W.C.* - Insuring Nuclear Power: Liability, Safety and Economic Efficiency

Volume 39 - *Uri, N.D.* - New Dimensions in Public Utility Pricing

Volume 40 - *Cross, S.M.* - Economic Decisions Under Inflation: The Impact of Accounting Measurement Error

Volume 41 - *Kaufman, G.G.* - Innovations in Bond Portfolio Management: Immunization and Duration Analysis

Volume 42 - *Horvitz, P.M. and R.R. Pettit* - Small Business Finance

Volume 43 - *Plaut, S.E.* - Import Dependence and Economic Vulnerability

Volume 44 - *Finn, F.J.* - Evaluation of the Internal Processes of Managed Funds

Volume 45 - *Moffitt, L.C.* - Strategic Management: Public Planning at the Local Level

Volume 46 - *Thornton, R.J., et al.* - Reindustrialization: Implications for U.S. Industrial Policy

Volume 47 - *Askari, H.* - Saudi Arabia's Economy: Oil and the Search for Economic Technology Transfer in Export Processing Zones

Volume 48 - *Von Pfeil, E.* - German Direct Investment in the United States

Volume 49 - *Dresch, S.* - Occupational Earnings, 1967-1981: Return to Occupational Choice, Schooling and Physician Specialization

Volume 50 - *Siebert, H.* - Economics of the Resource-Exporting Country Intertemporal Theory of Supply and Trade

Volume 51 - *Walton, G.M.* - The National Economic Policies of Chile

Volume 52 - *Stanley, G.* - Managing External Issues: Theory and Practice

Volume 53 - *Nafziger, E.W.* - Essays in Entrepreneurship, Equity and Economic Development

Volume 54 - *Lea, M. and K.E. Villani* - Tax Policy and Housing

Volume 55 - *Slottje, D. and J. Haslag* - Macroeconomic Activity and Income Inequality
in the United States

Volume 56 - *Thornton, R.F. and J.R. Aronson* - Forging New Relationships Among Business,
Labor and Government

Volume 57 - *Putterman, L.* - Peasants, Collectives and Choice: Economic Theory and
Tanzania's Villages

Volume 58 - *Baer, W. and J.F. Due* - Brazil and the Ivory Coast: The Impact of International
Lending, Investment and Aid

Volume 59 - *Emanuel, H., et al.* - Disability Benefits: Factors Determining Applications
and Awards

Volume 60 - *Rose, A.* - Forecasting Natural Gas Demand in a Changing World

Volume 61 - *(Omitted from Numbering)*

Volume 62 - *Canto, V.A. and J.K. Dietrich* - Industrial Policy and Industrial Trade

Volume 63 - *Kimura, Y.* - The Japaneese Semiconductor Industry

Volume 64 - *Thornton, R., Hyclak, T. and J.R. Aronson* - Canada at the Crossroads:
Essays on Canadian Political Economy

Volume 65 - *Hausker, A.J.* - Fundamentals of Public Credit Analysis

Volume 66 - *Looney, R.* - Economic Development in Saudi Arabia: Consequences of
the Oil Price Decline

Volume 67 - *Askari, H.* - Saudi Arabia's Economy: Oil and the Search for
Economic Development

Volume 68 - *Godfrey, R.* - Risk Based Capital Charges for Municipal Bonds

Volume 69 - *Guerard, J.B and M.N. Gûltekin* - Handbook of Security Analyst Forecasting
and Asset Allocation

Volume 70 - *Looney, R.E.* - Industrial Development and Diversification of the
Arabian Gulf Economies

Volume 71 - *Basmann, R.L., et al.* - Some New Methods for Measuring
and Describing Economic Inequality

Volume 72 - *Looney, R.E.* - The Economics of Third World Defense Expenditures

Volume 73 - *Thornton, R.J. and A.P. O'Brien* - The Economic Consequences of
American Education

Volume 74 - *Gaughan, P.A. and R.J. Thornton* - Litigation Economics

Volume 75 - *Nafzinger, E. Wayne* - Poverty and Wealth: Comparing Afro-Asian Development

Volume 76 - *Frankurter, George and Herbert E. Phillips* - Forty Years of Normative Portfolio
Management: Issues, Controversies, and Misconceptions

# Poverty and Wealth:
# Comparing Afro-Asian Development

*by* E. WAYNE NAFZIGER
*Department of Economics*
*Kansas State University*

 JAI PRESS INC.

*Greenwich, Connecticut*                    *London, England*

**Library of Congress Cataloging-in-Publication Data**

Nafziger, E. Wayne.
    Poverty and Wealth  :  comparing Afro-Asian development  /  by E.
Wayne Nafziger.
        P.   cm.—(Contemporary studies in economic and financial
analysis  ;  75)
    Includes bibliographical references and index.
    ISBN 1-55938-761-0
    1.  Africa—Economic policy. 2.  Africa—Economic conditions—1960-
3.  Asia—Economic policy. 4.  Asia—Economic conditions—1945-
5.  Development economics.  I.  Title.  II.  Series.
HC412.N237   1994
338.96—dc20                                              94-40381
                                                            CIP

*Copyright © 1994 JAI Press Inc.*
*55 Old Post Road No. 2*
*Greenwich, Connecticut 06836*

*JAI PRESS LTD.*
*The Courtyard*
*28 High Street*
*Hampton Hill*
*Middlesex TW12 1PD*
*England*

*ISBN: 1-55938-761-0*

*Library of Congress Catalog Number: 94-40381*

*Manufactured in the United States of America*

# CONTENTS

List of Figures                                                                      xv

List of Tables                                                                       xvii

Abbreviations                                                                        xix

Glossary                                                                             xxi

Acknowledgements                                                                     xxv

Abstract                                                                             xxvii

Introduction                                                                         xxix

## PART I.   APPROACHES TO COMPARATIVE
## ECONOMIC DEVELOPMENT

I.  **A Critique of Anglo-American
    Development Economics**                                                          **3**
    Inaccurate or Insufficient
        Sociopolitical Analysis                                                      4
    An Ethnocentric Approach to U.S. and
        Western International Involvement                                            6
    Insufficient Consideration of Domination and
        Subordination within the International
        Economic System                                                             6
    The Concept of "Traditional"
        Society and Economy                                                          10
    An Inadequate Perspective on Marxism                                             12
    Skewed Premises on Inequality                                                    19
    Conclusion                                                                       22

II. **Afro-Asian Development in
    Comparative Perspective**                                                        **25**
    Capitalism and Modern Western Economic
        Development                                                                  25

The West and Afro-Asia: The
   Nineteenth-Century and Today          28
The Colonial Legacy and Post-Colonial
   Transnational Economic Linkages          28
Economic Modernization by Japan          29
Problems of Economic Reform in China          31
Recent Economic Growth in Afro-Asia          35
Human Development and Human Freedom          38
Oil Exporters and Importers          39
Comparing Nigeria and Indonesia          41
Population Growth          42

## PART II. DEVELOPMENT, DISTRIBUTION, AND DECENTRALIZATION

III. **Inequality in Africa**          **47**
Rising Poverty and Malnutrition          47
Elites and the State          49
Colonialism and Neocolonialism          49
Foreign Trade, Investment and Debt          50
African Socialism          51
Elite Stability and Instability          51
Africanization          52
Education and Class Reproduction          52
Urban Bias          53
Nigerian Disease          54
Conclusion          56

IV. **The Debt Crisis in Africa**          **59**
The U.S. Banker's Perspective          59
The LDC Perspective and DC Interdependence          60
The World Bank-IMF Approach          62
The UNICEF Critique          64
The ECA's Alternative Framework          64
Other Criticisms of the World
   Bank-IMF Approach          66
Major LDC Debtors          67
Indicators of Debt          67
The Burden of Debt
   Net Transfers          68
A Rising Balance on Goods and Services Deficit          70
Stagnation, Inequality, and External Imbalance          71
Trade Dependence          71
Oil Shocks and Their Aftermath          73
Primary-product Export Glut          73
Foreign Capital Dependence          74
Debt and Capital Flight          75
The Baker Plan          75

Toronto Terms 76
The Brady Plan 76
Trinidad Terms 76
Global Competion for Funds 77
Emphasis on International
Development Association-Eligible
Countries 78
Debt Reductions 78
Concerted Action 79
Breaking up the Policy Cartel 80

V. **African Capitalism, State Power, and**
**Economic Development** **81**
Colonial Capitalism 81
Peripheral Capitalism since 1960 83
The State and Capitalism 84
A Commercial Triangle 86
Agrarian Capitalism 88
Conclusion 88

VI. **Democracy, Adjustment, and**
**Economic Reform in Africa** **89**
Adjustment and Democratization 89
DC and Bank/Fund Responses 92

## PART III. ENTREPRENEURSHIP
## AND ECONOMIC DEVELOPMENT

VII. **Class, Caste, and Community of**
**Indian Industrialists** **97**
Concepts Methods, Procedures, and
Objectives of the Study 98
The Concept of Caste 98
Caste, Family, and Social Community 99
Birthplace 110
Paternal Economic Status 111
Enterpreneurial and Management
Experience 112
Sources of Initial Capital 112
Firm Survival 113
Conclusion 114

VIII. **Society and the Entrepreneur** **117**
The Relative Importance of Social and
Economic Variables 117
Achievement Motivation and
Enterprepreneurship 118
A Theory of Technological Creativity 124

Religious and Ethnic Origin                                      125
Class and Class Origin                                          129
The Status of Schumpeterian Entrepreneurs                      130
Comparative Data on Socioeconomic Mobility                     131
Innovators and Managers in Socialist Economies                 134
The Family                                                      135
Education                                                       136
Gender                                                          136
Summary                                                         137

## PART IV.   COMPARATIVE DEVELOPMENT

IX.   **Bangladesh and Biafra: The Political**
      **Economy of Secessionist Conflict**                     **143**
      The Colonial Legacy                                       145
      Transitional Economic Linkages After
          Independence                                          148
      Class Formation and Conflict                              152
      Development Planning and Industrial Policy                156
      Regional Economic Competition and Conflict               159
      Summary                                                   163

X.    **India vs. China: Economic Development**
      **Performance**                                          **167**
      China's Policies                                          167
      India's Policies                                          168
      Development Indicators                                    170
      GNP Per Capita                                            170
      Real GNP Per Capita                                       170
      Growth of Real GNP Per Capita, 1950-80                    172
      Income Inequality                                         174
      Poverty                                                   178
      Trends in Poverty and Income Inequality                   179
      Hunger and Food Output                                    180
      Life Expectancy                                           185
      Infant Mortality                                          186
      Literacy and Education                                    186
      The Reform Period after 1978                              188
      Conclusion                                                190

XI.   **Learning from the Japanese: Japan's**
      **Development Model and Afro-Asia**                       **193**
      The Focus of the Study                                    193
      Self-directed Development                                 194
      Borrowing and Modifying Foreign Technology                195
      Product Cycle                                             199
      Education                                                 200

An Indigenous Capitalist Class 201
Financial Institutions 203
Transfer of Agricultural Surplus 205
Low Industrial Wages 210
Industrial Dualism 212
Export Expansion and Import
 Substitution 213
Conclusion 215

XII. **Why Has Japan Succeeded?** **221**
Comparing Japan's and the United
 State's Economic Performance 221
The Japanese Political Economy: From
 Military-Industrial Oligarchy to Liberal
 Democracy 223
Guided Capitalism: Small Government
 and Industrial Targeting 224
Capital Formation: Business and Private
 Saving 225
Education, Science and Technology: The
 World Champion Borrowers 227
Labor-Management Relations:
 Decentralized Decisions, Longterm
 Employment, and Unions 229
Foreign Trade and Investment: The
 New Feedback 235
The Asian Boomerang 239
Japan and the European Community 240
Conclusion 241

XIII. **Concluding Remarks** **243**
Self-directed and Dependent Development
 in Afro-Asia 243
Afro-Asian Capitalism and the State 244
Advantages of Priviledged Backgrounds for
 Entrepreneurs 244
Inequality and Economic Development 245
DC Policies for Low-income Afro-Asia 245

**References** **247**

**Indexes** **267**

# List of Figures

*Introduction*

1. U.S.-Japanese Nominal & Real
   Exchange Rates (1972,1-1991,12)                    xxxi

*Chapter II*

1 World Crude Oil Prices
   (in U.S. dollars a barrell)                        40

*Chapter III*

1. Index of Per Capita Food Production
   1960-1989 (1960-100)                               48

*Chapter IV*

1. Sub-Saharan African Commodity
   and Income Terms of Trade,
   1972-1992 (1970-100)                               72

# List of Tables

## Chapter II

1. Annual Rate of Growth of Real
   GNP per Capita (percent)                                30
2. Development Indicators (by
   Country, LDC Regions, and
   Country Income Groups)                                  36

## Chapter IV

1. Total External Public Debt (EDT)
   Less Developed Countries, 1980-1990
   ($ billions) ($10 billion or more
   in 1989, ranked by 1989 debt)                           68
2. Total External Public Debt (EDT)
   Subsaharan Africa, 1980-1989
   ($ billions) ($1 billion or more
   in 1989, ranked by 1989 debt)                           69

## Chapter VII

1. Caste Origin and Birthplace of
   Entrepreneurs                                          100
2. Frequency Distribution of Hindu
   Entrepreneurs by Caste Ranking                         101
3. Frequency Distribution of Non-
   Vaishya Hindu Entrepreneurs by
   Caste Ranking                                          101
4. Frequency Distribution of Non-
   Vaishya Hindu Entrepreneurs
   Born in Andhra Pradesh by Caste
   Ranking                                                101
5. Frequency Distribution of Hindu
   Entrepreneurs by Paternal Economic
   Status                                                 102

6. Firms and Entrepreneurs                                    103
7. Distribution of Fathers of
   Entrepreneurs in Economic Sector                           111

*Chapter X*

1. Real Gross National Product Per
   Capita, 1979 (adjusted for
   purchasing power)                                          171
2. Average Annual Rates of Real
   Growth of GNP and GNP per
   Capita by Decade                                           173
3. International Comparison of
   Rural-Urban Inequality                                     175
4. International Comparison of
   Urban Income Inequality                                    176
5. International Comparison of
   Rural Income Inequality                                    177
6. International Comparison of
   Overall Income Inequality                                  178
7. Per Capita Income, Population,
   and Poverty, 1975                                          179
8. Foodgrain Output                                           181
9. Annual Growth Rates in
   Foodgrain Output per Person
   (in percentage)                                            182
10. Food Availability, 1977                                   183
11. Life Expectancy at Birth (years)                          186
12. Basic Education in the 1970s (%)                          187
13. Annual Growth Rates in Foodgrain
    per Person (late 1970s-mid
    1980s) (in percentages)                                   189

# *Abbreviations*

**AL(s)**  Adjustment loan(s)—Sectoral adjustment loans (SECALs) of the World Bank or structural adjustment (SALs) loans of the Bank or IMF.

**CFAF**  Communauté financière africaine franc

**DCs**  Developed countries

**EU**  European Union

**ECA**  UN Economic Commission for Africa

**GATT**  General Agreements on Tariffs and Trade—International organization which administers rules of conduct in international trade.

**GDP**  Gross domestic product—A measure of the total output of goods and services, which encompasses income earned within a country's boundaries. This includes income earned by foreign residents and companies, even if it is transferred abroad, and excludes income earned by a country's residents and companies abroad.

**GNP**  Gross national product)—A measure of the total output of goods and services, which encompasses income earned by a country's residents. This includes income by the country's residents abroad, and excludes income earned domestically by foreign residents.

**HDI**  Human Development Index—UN Development Programme index of development based on real GDP per capita, life expectancy at birth, and educational attainment.

**HFI** Human Freedom Index—UN Development Programme index based on civil and legal rights, freedom from torture and censorship, electoral and religious freedom, ethnic and gender egalitarianism, independent media, courts, and trade unions, and related indicators.

**IDA** International Development Association—The World Bank's concessional window, primarily for low-income countries.

**ILO** UN International Labour Office

**IMF** International Monetary Fund—International organization established at Bretton Woods, New Hampshire in 1944 for the initial purpose of providing credit to ease short-term international payments imbalances.

**LDCs** Less developed countries

**MNCs** Multinational corporations

**OAU** Organisation for African Unity

**ODA** Official development assistance—Official aid.

**ODC** Overseas Development Council

**OECD** Organisation for Economic Cooperation and Development—A major bilateral donor group, which includes the U. S., Canada, Western Europe, Japan, Australia, and New Zealand.

**SALs** Structural adjustment loans—World Bank/IMF loans to affect the supply side, which support sectoral, relative price, and institutional reform to improve efficiency and long-term growth.

**SAPs** Structural adjustment programs—World Bank/IMF programs involving policy-based SALs.

**SECALs** Sectoral adjustment loans—World Bank loans emphasizing trade, agricultural, industrial, public enterprise, financial, energy, educational, or other sectoral reforms.

**SOEs** State-owned enterprises

# Glossary

*Balance on current account*—An international balance comprising exports minus imports of goods and services, plus net grants, remittances, and unilateral transfers received.

*Commodity terms of trade* (net barter terms of trade)—The price index of exports divided by the price index of imports. For example, if export prices increase 10 percent and import prices 22 percent, the commodity terms of trade drop 10 percent, that is $1.10/1.22 = 0.90$.

*Concessional lending*—Loans which have at least a 25-percent grant element. The grant element of the loan depends on how much the interest rate is below commercial rates, the length of the grace period in which interest charges or repayments of principal is not required, how long the repayment period is, and the extent to which repayment is in local inconvertible currency. To calculate the grant element, compare the present value of the net income stream forthcoming from the loan to a loan tendered at bankers' standards.

*Conditionality*—Conditions the International Monetary Fund or World Bank sets for lending.

*Debt*—External debt stock owed to nonresidents and repayable in foreign currency, goods, or services.

*Debt service*—The interest and principal payments due in a given year on external debt.

*Economic growth*—The rate of growth of GNP per capita.

*Export purchasing power*—Same as income terms of trade.

*Foreign exchange rate*—Same as price of foreign exchange.

*Gini index on inequality*—A measure of concentration that indicates how far a distribution is from perfect equality. It ranges from a value of 0 representing perfect equality to 1 representing maximum inequality (for example, where the richest individual has all the income).

*GNP per capita*—Gross national product (GNP) divided by the population.

*IDA-eligible countries*—Poor countries eligible for International Development Association concessional loans.

*Import substitution*—Domestic production replacing imports.

*Income terms of trade*—The commodity terms of trade times export volume. For example, if the commodity terms of trade drop 10 percent but export volume increases by 22 percent, the income terms of trade increase by 10 percent, that is $0.90 \times 1.22 = 1.10$.

*International balance of (merchandise) trade*—Exports minus imports of goods.

*International balance on goods and services*—Exports minus imports of goods and services.

*London Club*—Framework for rescheduling official country debt to commercial banks.

*Oligopoly*—An industry with few sellers, with interdependent pricing decisions among the firms in the industry.

*Parastatal enterprises*—Public corporations and statutory boards owned by the state, but responsible for day-to-day management to boards of directors, at least partially appointed by the state.

*Paris Club*—Framework for rescheduling official country debt to governments and international lending agencies.

*Price elasticity of demand*—The absolute value of the percentage change in quantity demanded divided by the percentage change in price. Values more than one are elastic, and less than one inelastic.

*Price of foreign exchange*—The domestic price of foreign currency, for example, the rupee price of the U. S. dollar, Rs. 30 = $1.

*Primary products*—Food, raw materials, and organic oils and fats.

*Real economic growth*—Inflation adjusted growth in GNP per capita (usually expressed per annum).

*Surplus*—Output minus wages, depreciation, and purchases from other firms.

*Total economic growth*—The rate of GNP growth.

# Acknowledgments

These essays span the period 1975 through 1992. I did the research for them during several trips to sub-Saharan Africa, India, China, Japan, and Britain, and received funds from Kansas State University, the International University of Japan, and the American Philosophical Society. Peter Nicholls, Marvin Kaiser, James Ragan, Jarvin Emerson, and numerous other colleagues in North America, Africa, and Asia facilitated my research. Elfrieda, Brian, and Kevin Nafziger provided the love and support I needed for writing. Dedication of this book reflects my thanks for the support and friendship of colleagues and students in the Department of Economics, College of Arts and Sciences, and the community at large at Kansas State University. I am grateful for the strengths they contributed to this work, but I am solely responsible for its errors.

I also thank the following for permission to reproduce copyrighted materials: the World Bank for tables from *World Debt Tables, 1990-91, 1991-92* (Washington, D.C.: World Bank, 1989); the International Monetary Fund for a figure from the *World Economic Outlook–May 1992* (Washington, D.C., 1992); and Fayez Tayyem for a figure, "U.S.-Japanese Nominal and Real Exchange Rates," from his Ph.D. dissertation.

I received permission to reprint from my "A Critique of Development Economics in the United States," *Journal of Development Studies* (October 1976), and "Class, Caste and Community of South Indian Industrialists: An Examination of the Horatio Alger Model," *Journal of Development Studies* (January 1975), from Frank Cass Publishers; "Entrepreneurship, Social Mobility, and Income Redistribution in South India," *American Economic Review* (February 1977), from the American Economic Association; "Society and the Entrepreneur," *Journal of Development Planning* (1988), from the United Nations; "India vs. China: Economic Development Performance," *Dalhousie Review* (Fall 1985), from the *Dalhousie Review*; "The Japanese Development Model," in *The Global Economy: Today, Tomorrow, and the*

*Transition*, ed. Howard F. Didsbury, Jr. (Washington, D.C., 1985), from the World Future Society; and "African Capitalism, State Power, and Economic Development," *Journal of Modern African Studies* (March 1990), and selected portions of *Inequality in Africa: Political Elites, Proletariat, Peasants, and the Poor* (Cambridge, 1988), from Cambridge University Press. "Biafra and Bangladesh: The Political Economy of Secessionist Conflict," written jointly with William L. Richter, in the *Journal of Peace Research* (1976), was reprinted with the publisher's and coauthor's permissions. "The Debt Crisis in Africa," is abstracted from a forthcoming book with the same title from Johns Hopkins University Press. "Why Has Japan Succeeded?" is based on an 5 December 1989 lecture to the Eureka College International Studies Lecture Series. I also received permission from M.E. Sharpe, Inc., for using material from my *Learning from the Japanese: Japan's Pre-War Development and the Third World* (Armonk, NY., 1994).

# *Abstract*

These comparative studies of African-Asian development encompass economies in East, Southeast, and South Asia and sub-Saharan Africa, including China, India, Indonesia, Japan, Nigeria, Bangladesh, Pakistan, and other countries. The essays, which integrate economics, politics, sociology, and history, contrast with the abstract formalism of standard Anglo-American economics in analyzing Africa and Asia. With emphases on U.S.-Japanese competitiveness, the contributors to secessionist conflict, the causes and effects of income inequality, the nature of Africa's economic breakdown and debt overhang, factors influencing the supply and success of entrepreneurs, and an assessment of economic reforms in Africa, India, and China, the themes of the book apply to major current issues in the political economy of development.

# Introduction

This book focuses on comparative case studies of major Afro-Asian economies, including China, India, Indonesia, Japan, Nigeria, Bangladesh, and Pakistan (among the world's 10 most populated countries) and the regions of East, Southeast, and South Asia, and sub-Saharan Africa. I have excluded the only oil exporting region in Afro-Asia, the Middle East, which is considered a region separate from the rest of Asia by the UN. But the study includes DC (developed country) Japan because: its level of economic development was substantially less than that of the west in the mid-nineteenth century, suggesting the rest of Afro-Asia can learn lessons from a rapidly-growing Japan.

Chapter I is based on the criticisms of the Anglo-American neoclassical analysis of Afro-Asia development economics as expressed in textbooks by dissenting political economists in the 1970s. Since the parameters of the debate have not changed much, I have edited but not substantially revised the views I expressed in the 1970s, except for an added section on inequality. Many economists would classify subsequent textbook authors Todaro (1977, 1981, 1985, 1989) and the author, Nafziger (1984, 1990), as dissenters. I am not, however, the appropriate person to evaluate these dissenting views.

The debate between orthodox and dissenting economists continued even after the collapse of Central European and Soviet centralized socialism in the late 1980s and early 1990s. The dissenters I identify with were not defenders of the superiority of Soviet-type systems to western capitalism. They were primarily critics of the inaccurate and insufficient socio-political analysis, ethnocentrism, lack of consideration of domination and subordination of dominance and subordination within the international economic system, fallacious concept of "traditional" society and economy, inadequate perspective on Marxian economic analysis, and skewed premises on inequality by mainstream economics.

Chapter II examines Afro-Asian development in comparison to modern capitalist development, which began in the west. The chapter considers the long-term economic development of Afro-Asia, the effect of colonialism and post-colonial economic ties to the west on Afro-Asia's underdevelopment, economic modernization by Japan, and problems of economic reform in the major socialist developing country, China. The last section includes a bird's-eye view of Afro-Asian development since World War II in comparative perspective.

Chapters III-VI concentrate on economic development, income distribution, and decentralized and democratic decision-making in sub-Saharan Africa, especially since 1972-1973. The poorest countries of the world, primarily in sub-Saharan Africa, have had a slow annual real growth of GNP per capita since 1972-1973 and have experienced negative growth since 1980. In many ways, 1972-1973 is a watershed date for the international economic system when the post-1945 Bretton Woods system of fixed exchange rates broke down. At the same time, raw materials and food prices increased substantially, giving an impetus to cost-push inflation and increased international balance on goods and services especially in oil-importing less-developed countries (LDCs).

The crisis that struck sub-Saharan Africa and parts of (especially South) Asia after 1972-1973 was partly linked to changes in the world economy—that is, the abrupt end of a quarter-century of post-World War II rapid economic growth. The major factors contributing to fast growth in the earlier postwar years were (1) pent-up demand from preceding years, (2) European and Japanese reconstruction, (3) accelerated technical change (partly from an unused stock of wartime innovations), (4) demand management for full employment, (5) increasing international trade and payments liberalization, (6) a stable international economic system under U.S. hegemony, and (7) the concomitant high profit (and investment) rates. These sources of growth for the global economy generally were less important after 1973. Since then, slower growth and greater economic instability resulted from increased raw-materials price uncertainty, oil price shocks, rise in real interest rates worldwide, cost-push inflationary spurred wage increases, declining profit rates, DC exchange-rate instability (Figure 1), and attempts to control state spending (Ghai 1991, 2; Baumol, Blackman, and Wolff 1989).

Growth in Afro-Asia decelerated from slower GNP growth among its dominant trading partners in the Organisation for Economic Cooperation and Development (OECD, the West, Japan, Australia, and New Zealand). When the OECD sneezed (as in 1980-1982 and 1991), low-income Afro-Asia (primarily in the sub-Sahara and South Asia), at the fringe of the international economic periphery, caught pneumonia. These changes made it more difficult to attain both domestic (full employment and price stability) and external (current-account) balances.

Since the mid 1970s, nonfuel primary goods and raw-materials-processing producers have faced declining commodity terms of trade (the price index of exports divided by the price index of imports) and slow growth in income terms

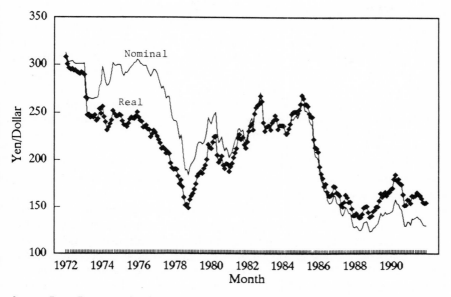

*Source:* Fayex Tayyam, update from "An Empirical investigation of Purchasing Power Parity and the Dynamics of Real Exchange Rates." Ph.D. dissertation, Kansas State University, 1991.

*Figure 1.* U.S.—Japanese Nominal and
Real Exchange Rates (1972, 1—1991, 12

of trade (that is, export purchasing power, or commodity terms of trade times the volume of exports). The pressures faced by *numerous* Afro-Asian LDCs in their adjustment programs in the 1980s and early 1990s to expand exports in primary products increased supply and reduced prices and terms of trade (Nafziger 1992; FAO 1991). Afro-Asian low-income countries' comparative advantage and learning-by-doing gains suggest labor-intensive industries with lower levels of technology and processing, such as the processing of natural-resource-based goods, as potential areas for export expansion. However, World Bank analysis indicates DC *effective* rates of protection, a measure of protection as a percentage of value added by productive factors at each processing stage, highest among the lowest levels of processing and manufacturing value-added (for example, cotton yarn in comparison to higher levels of processing such as cotton fabrics and clothing) (World Bank 1981b, 23; World Bank 1987b, 136-38; World Bank 1988b, 16-17).

Chapter III examines how, in the midst of these shrinking economic pie slices and growing political consciousness, national leaders in the sub-Sahara formed coalitions to govern. The analysis shows regime survival required marshaling elite support at the expense of both egalitarianism and growth. Chapter IV discusses Africa's chronic debt overhang and external deficit, and increasing dependence on International Monetary Fund and World Bank loans of last resort in the 1980s and early 1990s. The chapter argues Bank/Fund conditions for lending exacerbated sub-Saharan stagflation and external deficits. Chapter V asks whether Africa has a potential capitalist class that can spearhead economic modernization and whether African states, highly dependent on DCs and international agencies, have pursued policies creating opportunities for capitalist growth. Chapter VI investigates the relationship between democracy, adjustment, and economic reform in Africa.

Chapters VII-VIII analyze the role of the entrepreneur in Afro-Asian economic development. The rate of economic growth is dependent on the growth of the factors of production and the rate of technical change. In the early 1950s, economists attributed the sources of growth primarily to the increase in capital (Cairncross 1955). However, empirical studies since the late 1950s have undermined growth theories based on the single factor of capital (Solow 1957, 312-20; Abramovitz 1956, 5-23; Robinson 1971, 391-408; and numerous sources cited in Nafziger 1990, 256-59). These studies support the contention major sources of growth are from the combination, organization, and coordination of inputs, attributable by most definitions to the entrepreneur, rather than to the growth of inputs. Chapter VII focuses on the class, caste, and background of Indian entrepreneurs, while Chapter VIII investigates more broadly how society affects Afro-Asian entrepreneurs.

Chapters IX-XII present four studies of comparative economic development. Chapter IX applies the economist's analysis of inequality, deprivation, and competition to the study of political instability. Its major foci are domestic political violence in Nigeria, including the two coups d'etat of 1966, the Biafran secession of 1967, and the civil war of 1967-1970, and in Pakistan, encompassing the civil war in Pakistan (March-December 1971), in which East Pakistan won independence as the Republic of Bangladesh. The chapter looks for patterns in the politico-economic factors contributing to secessionist conflicts in Nigeria and Pakistan.

Chapter X compares the economic development performance of centralized socialist China and democratic socialist India since 1947-1949. The major emphases are comparative growth for the period between the early 1950s and late 1970s, and *levels* of development from the late 1970s to early 1980s, thus generally reflecting policies before China's liberalization reforms and India's reduced government regulation since 1978. Additionally, the chapter analyzes the periods of reform in the two economies since the late 1970s.

Japan has enjoyed the fastest rate of economic growth since 1868, when it abolished feudal property relationships. Chapter XI examines whether contemporary Afro-Asian economies can learn from early Japanese guided capitalist development under the Meiji emperor, 1868 to 1912, and the period through the late 1930s. Chapter XII investigates the reasons for the economic success of Japan, especially during its later period of capitalism. It compares the successes of Japan and the west (especially the United States). Chapter XIII consists of concluding remarks.

Thus, the book includes emphases on U.S.-Japanese competitiveness, the economic factors contributing to civil war, Africa's economic breakdown and debt overhang, and privatization and price decontrol in Africa, India, and China (with particular emphasis on Chinese and Indian economic reforms after 1976-1978). All in all, the themes of the book apply to major current issues in the political economy of development.

# Part I.

*Approaches to Comparative Economic Development*

# Chapter I

# A Critique of Anglo-American Development Economics

The trickle of disaffection with the orthodox (neoclassical) literature on the economics of Africa and Asia in the 1950s and 1960s became an avalanche of discontent in the 1970s, 1980s, and early 1990s. In the later period, even major contributors to the field complained the study of development economics did not add much to the understanding of poverty in LDCs nor to the tools useful for policy (Meier 1970, 59-60).

Several intellectual currents have converged to produce this malaise. Even in the early years of the offerings of development economics in U.S. and British universities, a few economists argued Anglo-American economic principles had only a limited applicability to a comprehension of the problem of economically underdeveloped countries (Singer 1950, 473-85; Prebisch 1962, 1-22; Myrdal 1957; and Seers 1963, 77-98).[1]

Fundamental criticisms of existing conceptions of reality in development studies originated in Latin America, Asia, Africa, and continental Europe, all with some "inside" perspective on the weaknesses of dependent economies, rather than in the United States, where national interests and wealth made available relatively greater funds and intellectual resources for the study of LDCs (Merton 1972, 41-48).[2] Some major themes of these dissenters have been: the disharmony of interests between DCs and LDCs; a rejection of the development goals of ruling elites in both DCs and LDCs; and the explanation of economic underdevelopment of a given country, not merely in terms of domestic factors, but in terms of the international economy as a system.

While I share the discontent with neoclassical development economics by dissident scholars, my purpose is not to construct something new in this chapter, but to illuminate the cracks in the existing edifice; in subsequent chapters I will indicate approaches I think are essential to reorient development economics toward important issues in comparative African-Asian development. To simplify what would otherwise be unmanageable in a single chapter, I pay particular attention to the views of the authors of six of the leading textbooks used in the United States, United Kingdom, and Canada in the 1970s: Everett Hagen, Benjamin Higgins, Gerald Meier, Charles Kindleberger, Henry Bruton, and Theodore Morgan. These six economists enjoyed a wide professional influence throughout much of the post-World War II period, and, despite the appearance of new textbooks, the views they expressed in the 1970s remained as the dominant development paradigm in the 1980s and 1990s. (The men are to be referred to collectively as the authors or the six economists.) Views presented by beginning students in textbooks are generally representative of Anglo-American development economics.

## INACCURATE OR INSUFFICIENT
## SOCIO-POLITICAL ANALYSIS

In much of the orthodox literature on Afro-Asian economic development, the social and political system is taken as given or a constant. Fundamental shifts in socio-political variables and non-quantitative economic ones are frequently conveniently excluded with the phrase, *ceteris paribus* or other things equal. For analytical purposes, development economists generally view the economic sphere as a closed system. Focusing on only a limited number of variables—mostly economic and measurable—facilitates the use of quantitative methods, and the search for determinants of a stable equilibrium. Only a few of the major interrelationships which affect the economic realm are analyzed.

The following statement is indicative of the casual attitude toward social and institutional reality of the orthodox economic analyst viewing LDCs.

> In economic exposition,... it usually makes little or no difference whether the comparisons [of societies] are anthropologically authentic or not. Indeed,... it would seem to be definitely requisite in the teaching of economics to bring out principles affecting our own institutions by means of comparisons between our own and "simpler" societies and at the same time out of the question to make the comparison refer to any particular society or social type as reported by anthropolitical investigations.... 'Authentic' facts are not necessarily more useful than travelers' tales based on superficial and largely false impressions... or even outright fiction or poetry (Knight: 1941, 262).

Contemporary Anglo-American economists in the United States place little more emphasis on institutional accuracy than Knight did. According to Adelman, "One mark of our professional arrogance is the implicit [view] that a plausible model is obviously correct, and... need not be checked thoroughly against a large variety of empirical, historical, and case study evidence" (Adelman 1974, 3). Yet for a science to contribute to understanding and policy, it continually needs to examine prevailing premises and paradigms and provide feedback between hypotheses and data.

An example of such a hypothesis, which has survived without data testing, is the widespread assumption that in Africa and Asia "the organization of much of subsistence farming is such that the produce available to the workers is divided among all the people involved, more or less irrespective of individual contributions to output" (Bruton 1965, 100). There is no empirical evidence for this assumption. In fact, field studies by economic anthropologists contradict the premise that peasant societies have roughly uniform poverty (Hill 1968, 239-60; Dube 1955, 167-84; and essays on Northeast India, Hong Kong, Guatemala, and Mauritius in Firth and Yamey, eds. 1964).

Even where development economists are willing to acknowledge the importance of socio-cultural and psychological variables, they tend to accept political institutions as given (Higgins 1968, 373), and frequently exclude political determinants and determinates of development and stagnation. Political instability is considered a problem, but there is no effort to try to explain it and its relationship to the international economic system and domestic class system (Meier 1970, 116) as in chapter IX below. Higgins is representative of the development economists when he indicates "we shall abstract from the purely political factor in economic development, not because the political factor is unimportant but because social scientists have little to say about it" (Higgins 1968, 227).

The economists do not examine the disparities of economic interests among subgroups within the population when discussing formulating and implementing government development policy. The statement that "past failures [in development planning] are to be found mainly in an inability or unwillingness to implement development plans" (Meier 1970, 744) calls for an analysis of the extent to which it is actually in the interest of the elites to achieve stated goals which indicate a high priority on improvement in the material well-being of the low-income classes.[3] To mention another point, skepticism and resistance by peasants and workers to plans result not only from their misperceptions about the "nature of the development process" (Bruton 1965, 155, 246), but also from underlying conflicts of interest between the privileged and underprivileged.

Perhaps in their attempt to avoid making explicit their personal value presuppositions, the six development economists, five of whom have had substantial experience as consultants to U.S. agencies, the World Bank, the International Monetary Fund, or LDC governments, accept the goals and targets selected by the political, bureaucratic, and business elites. Higgins is explicit in his view of the job of the development economist when he states "there are enough countries where the political power elite does want economic development to keep economists busy for some time to come." At times it is implicit that to discuss targets alternative to those of the "policy makers," that is, those favored by less influential segments of the population, is to enter the domain of normative economics, which is to be eschewed (Higgins 1968, 227, 373, 376-77; Bruton 1965, 362).

## AN ETHNOCENTRIC APPROACH TO U.S. AND WESTERN INTERNATIONAL INVOLVEMENT

The economists surveyed tend to appraise the LDCs from the perspective of U.S. and western standards, achievements, and sympathies, lacking the sensitivity to explaining an alien political economy in terms of its own goals, institutions, values, and character. The authors often view LDCs through the lens of U.S. international political involvement and economic interests.[4] "Stability in underdeveloped areas" is identified with the hegemony of the United States and its allies (Higgins 1968, 197-98). Frequently economists view LDCs as potential recipients of foreign aid, whose main objective, in the case of the United States, as with "other tools of foreign policy, is to produce the kind of political and economic environment in the world in which the United States can best pursue its own social goals" (Chenery 1964, 81). Even Kindleberger (1965, 374-75), among the least patronizing of the authors, is inclined to legitimize rich and powerful donors intervening into the internal political and economic affairs of LDCs. He argues the position that

> [foreign] assistance should be given with no strings attached...is too simple and idealistic by half. Sovereignty is not inviolable, nor are internal politics sacrosanct where they stand in the way of development.... If the sole condition of foreign aid is that it be used effectively, the abridgment of sovereignty which comes from consultations with foreign missions, with the International Bank, or a United Nations agency is supportable. If such outside forces are to be effective, they must take positions on issues which are subjects of internal struggles, and thereby find themselves interfering in internal politics.

## INSUFFICIENT CONSIDERATION OF DOMINATION AND SUBORDINATION WITHIN THE INTERNATIONAL ECONOMIC SYSTEM

The conceptual matrix of Anglo-American development economics is limited in explaining poverty and underdevelopment. Orthodox economists explain underdevelopment primarily in terms of economic factors within a given nation-state, with little reference to the effect of the international economy as a system. The authors regard DC development and LDC underdevelopment as unrelated phenomena. LDC national aspirations for rapid growth are in the interest of, and are encouraged by, DCs (Meier and Baldwin 1957, 13).

Except for Higgins (1968, 161-87, 267-95, 683-93, 800-06), the economic impact of colonialism and post-colonial imperialism on the DCs and LDCs is not considered (cf. Hagen 1975, 73-100). The evidence of economic history, including that of western colonialism, is overlooked, with arguments that "bygones are bygones"—that the present situation determines the future, irrespective of how the present arose historically from the past. In the words of one author: "It is unnecessary to account for a situations presented to the initial conditions by history" (Bruton: 1965, 90. See also Morgan 1975, 143).

Because the authors generally do not consider the history of imperialism, a part of the explanation for development in the west and underdevelopment in most of the non-western world is disregarded. The textbooks virtually omit reference to the economic and geographical expansion of Europe at the expense of non-European peoples, especially after the fifteenth-century. Empire—both formal and informal—may have facilitated the development of the west through the control and stabilization of markets and raw material production needed for industrial growth, and the provision of added profitable outlets for capital investment. At no point do the authors systematically discuss or refute the argument that western economic development benefited at the expense of the non-western world,[5] an argument a comprehensive textbook would be expected to make.

On the other side of the coin, the economists largely overlook the adverse effect of colonialism and informal empire on present LDCs. For Meier (1970, 117), it is not "the intentional or unintentional exploitation of colonialism or neo-colonialism which can have detrimental effects on development efforts." There is little consideration of what might have happened if countries under formal colonial rule or informal political suzerainty of the metropolitan powers had been free to direct their economies themselves—by borrowing from western civilization and economies as a separate autonomous system rather than as peripheral areas integrated into international capitalism. To discuss this, economists must analyze something absent in five of the books—the culture and economy of the LDCs before European domination and colonialism, and the impact of formal and informal empire and post-colonial dependency. Virtually all LDCs experienced past economic and political domination under DC colonialism or informal empire. The crucial relationships of the now DCs with present LDCs have disrupted the pre-existing fabric of these societies, many of which were sophisticated, cultured, or relatively prosperous before European penetration.

There may be a few instances (such as Malaya and the Gold Coast, which both had spare land) where economies responded positively, with widespread benefits, to overseas capitalism; but these are exceptions. On the other hand, India experienced economic stagnation under British colonial rule, with a decline in the output of industrial goods (particularly handicraft articles) per capita from 1757 to 1857, a fall in the export of cotton manufactures in the early nineteenth-century and again at the turn of the twentieth-century as a result of foreign competition, and a drop in agricultural (especially food) output per capita from 1893-96 to 1936-46. Indonesia, a prosperous region at the beginning of the sixteenth-century, suffered a marked decline in per capita material well-being during the period of Dutch suzerainty. In coastal West Africa, the slave trade of the sixteenth through eighteenth centuries brought about the disintegration of central authority, while colonization (primarily in the nineteenth and twentieth-centuries) reoriented trade externally. Within a generation after Spanish penetration of the West Indies, the indigenous economy was ruined, and the native population virtually disappeared (Frank 1969, 41-42; Maddison 1971, 53-63; D. Thorner and A. Thorner 1972, 70-112; Griffin 1969, 38-45; and Amin 1972, 97-121).

Development economists single out Japan as "the only country in recent decades to have 'graduated' from the ranks of ... an underdeveloped country" to an advanced country (Higgins 1968, 617). This dramatic progress has been attributed to adaptation of labor relationships to the "imperatives of Japanese personality," "reactive nationalism," land reform, other institutional reform, government assistance to private enterprise, drastic monetary and fiscal measures to the "efforts of government to transfer and develop a technology suitable to Japanese conditions," and an open economy (Ibid., 717-19; and Hagen 1975, 297-98). The economists fail to point out that these measures and adaptations would probably not have occurred had the Japanese been under western economic domination (chapter 11). Conceivably, similar strategies might have been used by other Afro-Asian countries to develop rapidly had they been free to borrow, adapt, innovate, and plan in light of indigenous goals and strengths.

In the subsequent part of this section, I consider the orthodox view of the benefits LDCs received from foreign trade and investment. One model recommended for emulation by LDCs is Britain in the eighteenth and nineteenth-centuries, at which time international trade was "a leading sector" which served as an engine of growth (Kindleberger 1965, 304). The relevance of the British experience breaks down, however, when we recall international trade and output expanded rapidly during acquisition of informal and formal empire, accompanied by British military strength, political domination, and market power. British suzerainty—which includes British control of imperial tax and tariff policy, preferential treatment of British entrepreneurs in Britain and the colonies, and the promotion of the production of inputs needed for British industry—established an "international division of labor" based on a "comparative advantage in real costs."

Meier asks: "why has not a process of export-induced development followed upon an expansion of the export sector" in LDCs? He rejects the view that integration in an existing international trading network might have inhibited development and increased international inequality. "A more convincing explanation [for the lack of an export-induced development] focuses on the differential effects of the various export goods [on forward and backward linkages, and the structure of demand]...and on market imperfections and socio-cultural impediments within a poor country." Meier argues forgoing the employment of surplus resources in the foreign export-oriented sector would have meant these resources would have been idle, without mentioning the possibility of locally-based development, with part of the capital and technology acquired from DCs.

Foreign investment is considered mutually advantageous to the DCs and LDCs, usually without investigating the evidence on the other side. To Meier, a "central problem...is for the recipient country to devise policies that will succeed in...encouraging a greater inflow of private foreign capital." The major factors accounting for the sub-optimal flow of private capital to LDCs are "controls exercised by the host country over the conditions of entry of foreign capital, regulations of the operation of foreign capital,...restrictions on the remittance of profits and the repatriation of capital,...[and] limitations on the extent of foreign participation in ownership or management." Meier finds it important to raise profits expectations of the prospective foreign investor, partly through public expenditures in "developing the country's infrastructure and in ensuring a supply of trained labor" (Meier 1970, 297-99, 305). Despite the vast literature indicating foreign firms are not significantly influenced by tax incentives (Gordon and Grommers 1962; Mikesell 1962), Higgins stresses LDCs should realize they are "competing for capital against other countries in both the highly developed and the less developed categories." Measures to attract foreign firms include offering tax schemes and incentives and allowing foreign firms to bring their own managers and technicians (Higgins 1968, 567-71).

The authors recommend improving LDC "investment climate" through liberalizing the terms for foreign capital (for example, Meier 1970, 296-98). Yet they do not consider possible distortion in the post-independence ownership structure of industrial assets in LDCs from foreign investment which entered during the colonial period, largely because of policies and rules of the game discriminating in favor of DC firms, or joint foreign-indigenous ventures after colonialism that strengthen politicians, bureaucrats, and middlemen at the expense of the majority of the local population, including small-scale capitalists (chapters 3-5). Moreover, as a result of DC post-colonial pressures, existing legal commitments and regulations permitting foreign capital and entrepreneurship to enter the country freely could not be easily rescinded. Finally, the authors overlook that investing countries often had to threaten economic retaliation and military force to compel LDCs to keep their economies open to foreign capital (Griffin 1972).

The authors neglect a number of arguments. The structure and growth of an LDC open to foreign investment becomes dependent on the expansion of DCs (Rodney 1972; Frank 1969, 3-17). Let us mention more specific arguments. Forgoing the limited gains by foreign investment may be outweighed by increases in returns to the domestic competitors of foreign investors (MacDougall 1960, 13-35). The opportunity costs of local resources used in the foreign sector contribute to a "backwash" effect. The subordination of an LDC acquiring finance, technology and high-level personnel to developments and interests in a metropolitan economy may hamper indigenous efforts to establish a capital market, generate appropriate technology, acquire industrial and business experience, develop a local bourgeoisie, and train and educate skilled industrial labor. Finally, as the next paragraph maintains, a major argument for overseas investment, which centers around the necessity to transfer the knowledge, skills, and techniques of modern production, is of limited validity in most LDCs.

Hagen (1975, 101-29) and Higgins (1968, 203) point out the rarity of technological innovation in the LDCs and the lack of technology available to fit their factor proportions and cultural patterns. But under colonial rule, LDCs did not have the control to experiment, innovate, or build institutions needed to produce or adapt technology appropriate to their economies and cultures. After independence, LDCs have virtually depended on the advanced capitalist countries, where the control of technology is concentrated. Data on patents granted by a group of mixed and capitalist LDCs suggest if the number of patents is weighted by their economic worth (that is, volume of sales or value added), LDCs would find the share of patents thus weighted granted to foreigners to be more than 90 percent (Müller 1973, 151-78). Furthermore, world markets and the incentives of multinational corporations (MNCs) often thwart them from imparting the knowledge and skills on which commercial success is based to indigenous counterparts. MNCs restrict the use of technology and output in Afro-Asia by, for example, banning exports, limiting technology to the period of agreement, preventing modification of a technology, and requiring purchase of intermediate inputs into the technology from the MNC headquarter country (Weisskopf 1973, 48; Streeten 1973, 1-14; Lall 1974, 41-48).

Those who neglect the history of economic subordination assume understanding this history is irrelevant for current policy (Bruton 1965, 90). But as suggested above, the legacy of economic dependence has important implications for current international trade, investment, technological transfer, and political relations, which affect the domestic economy and polity.

# THE CONCEPT OF "TRADITIONAL" SOCIETY AND ECONOMY

The six economists' neglect of LDC history, including colonialism and post-colonial dependency, is consistent with the assumption the present LDCs resemble earlier stages in the history of the DCs. Past economies—"primitive," ancient, and medieval, and present DCs a century or two ago—are placed with present LDCs in a single category, a "traditional economy," in contrast to the "modern economy" of contemporary DCs. Higgins (1968, 175) indicates "it is hard to see how one could identify a traditional society in terms other than its level of economic development."

But you cannot classify today's LDCs with the preindustrial societies of the west under the rubric "traditional society," which implies its underlying socioeconomic features have been shaped by endogenous forces. We need a historical explanation to determine the extent socioeconomic traits are traditional and originate internally and the extent they are products of non-traditional and exogenous forces. Few present LDCs can be considered traditional, since their societies and economies were disrupted by colonialism (or some other dependent relationship to DCs). Many characteristics development economists label as "traditional society" are an outgrowth of the last two centuries or so, when the entire fabric of the LDCs' polity and society was affected by western (and Japanese) intrusion. The replacement of indigenous enterprises with technologically more advanced global subsidiary companies, the formation of an unskilled labor force to work in the factories, mines, and plantations, the attraction of highly educated youths to junior posts in the colonial administrative service, the migration of workers from the villages to the foreign-dominated urban economic complexes, and the opening of the economy to trade with and investment from the DCs are not concomitant with the process of economic modernization, as orthodox economists assume. Instead, the same phenomena, the penetration of modern capitalism into archaic economic structures in the periphery, are the basis for creating underdevelopment.

Identifying societies as traditional rather than disrupted by imperialism distorts the determination of underdevelopment. For Hagen (1975, 81) "traditional societies tend to be hierarchical and more or less authoritarian in political structure. Such structure persisted for centuries and in some societies for several millennia, up to modern times" (cf. Morgan 1975, 37). Doubtless, in some cases. But it is essential to ascertain to what extent the hierarchy was a function of "traditional" culture, on the one hand, or a culture shaped by an era of politico-economic subservience, on the other. In some instances, for example, Northern Nigeria and parts of the Indian subcontinent, colonial support for a compliant indigenous political elite, who held office when it was advantageous to the colonial rulers, eliminated important sources of both external and internal opposition, strengthened the hands of the native elite in dealing with dissidents, and hampered indigenous political development. The role of native chiefs in Nigeria and South Asia inhibited the development of nationalism and a strong local bourgeoisie, and strengthened land concentration among overlords and zamindars. In the post-colonial era, metropolitan nations, with their means of coercion (military, economic, and political power) and superior resources (resulting in aid, investment, and a dominant trade position), can structure their relationships with LDCs so, even though there is a conflict of interest between the rich and poor nations in general, there is a harmony of interest between the elites of these nations. The DC develops a bridgehead in the LDC which enables the former to maintain political and economic hegemony in the latter and in the process support and assist those in the poor country willing to cooperate, that is, those whose interests are in harmony with the rich country.

Of course, the elite of a country can be authoritarian and lack an orientation toward the economic development of the masses, even where the country has never encountered alien control and imperial hegemony. But countries which have experienced foreign economic and political domination, class hierarchy, elite structure, and the formation of ruling ideologies and values cannot be analyzed apart from historically examining transnational interrelationships. A "politically powerful group which has a big stake in maintaining the *status quo*" (Higgins 1968, 195) does not spring from Jove's brow and may have even been created and strengthened during colonialism or post-colonial imperialism. The present elite may be "traditionalistic rather than choice-making" and not imbued with the "idea of progress" (Bruton 1965, 113) as a result of a social structure created by colonialism and supported by neo-imperialism. Even the Indian caste system (Ibid., p. 111; Morgan 1975, 39), though existing in ancient times, was strengthened by British policy in the colonial period (chapter 8).

Hagen finds "the sign of eliteness in a traditional society is that the individual does not demean himself by concerning himself with the details of manual labor." Myrdal (1968 II, 1020-1285, 1369) argues a major barrier to high labor productivity in LDCs is a class system in which the elite are contemptuous of manual work (cf. Hagen 1975, 132; also pp. 115-16, 270-71, 278). The implication is upper-and middle-class westerners, who are more likely to carry their own briefcases, mow the lawns, and repair their automobiles, have different attitudes. However, attitudes toward manual work are primarily related to its remuneration relative to that of intellect work. This relative wage structure is a product of past values, institutions, and history, which, for Afro-Asia, was influenced by imperialism disrupting traditional society.[6]

Those for whom today's "modernized" societies present an image of the future of "traditional societies" envision a movement in history from a "rigid" social structure and underdevelopment economy to a fluid social structure and developed economy, whose archetype is the U.S. and Western Europe. Comparative evidence, however, indicates that the fluidity of the prototypical modern country, the United States, does not vary much from that of India (chapters 8 and 9), with a "caste system...of the ironclad variety" (Bruton 1965, 111).

## AN INADEQUATE PERSPECTIVE ON MARXISM

After 1989, many critics of Marxism proclaimed its death, undoubtedly referring to the state-managed socialism of Central Europe and the Soviet

Union. To this reference to Communist Party-dominated states, Karl Marx might have repeated his disavowal of movements using his name he opposed during his lifetime: "I am not a Marxist." Some major contributions to Marxism include Friedrich Engels' skillful propagation of Marxist thought (from Marx's death 1883 through 1895), Vladimir Ilich Lenin's writing on monopoly capitalism and imperialism before the 1917 Russian revolution, the emphases by Leon Trotsky and Nikolai Bukharin on decentralized socialism and the international class struggle (considered "deviationist" by Joseph Stalin), German social democratic Eduard Bernstein (1850-1932) on the ameliorative trends in capitalism, Oskar Lange's model of market socialism, Bruno Hórvat's and Jaroslav Vanek's insistence that socialism be democratic and decentralized, Paul Sweezy's and Paul Baran's analysis of monopoly capitalism in the United States, Charles Bettelheim's and Sweezy's theories of class conflict under actually existing socialism, as well as the numerous variations of socialist and communist praxis as exemplified in Lenin's and Stalin's decentralized Soviet New Economic Policy (1921-1928), Mao Zedong's stress on education and indoctrination, and recent market reforms by Hungary and China. The evolution of Marxist economic systems is beyond the scope of this book, as the discussion here concentrates on orthodox development economists' analysis of Marxian economics (which focused more on capitalism than socialism) rather than the "Marxism" or socialism practiced in China, Viet Nam, Cuba, the former USSR, and other parts of the world.

The six economists use orthodox standards of theoretical excellence in selecting the relevance and assessing the validity of alternative approaches such as Marxism. Higgins does not evaluate and criticize the Marxist model in terms of its own or some "neutral" paradigm. Rather, the model is forced into a series of equations in a neoclassical general equilibrium model, which, not surprisingly, reduces the Marxian contribution to triviality. The Schumpeterian system differs from the classical Marxist systems, according to Higgins, by its "introduction of the interest rate as a determinant of savings,...[its] separation of autonomous from induced investment and the isolation of 'innovations' as the factor influencing autonomous investment,...[and its] emphasis on entrepreneurship as the vital force in the whole economy." The concern of Higgins is not "to evaluate the Marxist system as a whole" but to "isolate the key propositions of its pure theory of economic development." He examines pure theory in neoclassical terms, with a predisposition toward capitalism and the free market, a selection of only certain relevant variables, and a neglect of class conflict, historical dialectics, and the relationships between social relations and the means of production. Marx's system thus viewed is said not to be as applicable to LDCs as Malthus's theory is (Higgins 1968, 76-87, 100-01).

Higgins's general synthesis of Marx, Schumpeter, Harrod, Domar, and Hansen includes the statement "the key figure in the process of technological advance is the entrepreneur." The equation that synthesizes these general theories is the basis for indicating an effective plan must: encourage a higher level of private investment with the existing rate of resource discovery and technological progress, encourage a "long view" through promotion of confidence, and improve the climate for foreign investment (Ibid., pp. 150, 156).

In reply to these criticisms, Higgins points out he borrowed his equations from Joan Robinson, who is sympathetic to Marxism (Higgins 1979, 245). But Robinson "confined [her] argument to Marx's economic analysis in the narrow sense [theories of value, employment, profit, and effective demand]," while never purporting to analyze the Marxist model of growth and collapse, as Higgins does (Robinson 1942, vi; Higgins 1968, 76-87).

Moreover, Schumpeter considers Marx's pure theory within the classical tradition, as Higgins correctly argues (Higgins 1979, 245), but not Marx's model of capitalist process and historical evolution, left outside the scope of *History of Economic Analysis* (Schumpeter 1954, 390-91). Nevertheless, Schumpeter, *Capitalism, Socialism, and Democracy* (1950, 28), contends since the aim of Marx was not the analysis of "a state of equilibrium which according to him capitalist society can never attain, but on the contrary a process of incessant change in the economic structure," criticism "on the ground on which it is so easy to beat him [the classical framework] is not completely decisive." Higgins's synthesis of five general theories into an equilibrium model expunged Marx's contributions on class conflict and economic breakdown, which are processes of disequilibria.

Meier, in accepting Rostow's stage theory (1971) as an answer to Marx, remarks that Rostow, unlike Marx, does not "reduce the complexities of man to a single economic dimension." Rostow also is said to have a "broader view of human motivation" in contrast to Marx's "narrow view that political behavior is dependent on economic advantage. Furthermore, Meier asserts Rostow's analysis "draws upon a far wider range of historical knowledge, and is thereby more comprehensive and less doctrinaire" (Meier 1970, 92-94). All this is asserted, with no reference to Marx's work, or any attempt to even sketch a part of his theory of economic development and capitalist crisis.

Marx viewed the classical approach as static and unhistorical in contrast to his dialectical approach, which examined a social phenomenon, where it was going, and its process of change. History moves from one stage to another, say, from feudalism to capitalism to socialism, on the basis of changes in ruling and oppressed classes and their relationship to each other. Conflict between the forces of production (the state of science and technology, the organization of production, and the development of human skills) and the existing relations of production (ideology, *Weltanschauung,* and appropriation and distribution of output) provide the dynamic movement in the materialist interpretation of history. The interaction between forces and relations of production shapes politics, law, morality, religion, culture, and ideas (Marx 1904, 11).

Ironically, Hagen, who recognizes the key role of powerful interests in opposing measures that are "economically desirable" and whose own theory attributes economic stagnation and lack of innovation to the hierarchical and authoritarian social system of traditional societies (Hagen 1975, 357, 434; Hagen 1962a), is harsh in attacking a contemporary Marxist analysis of hierarchy, interest groups, and administrative weaknesses. For Hagen, the major ingredients of the theory of Baran, probably the foremost U.S. Marxist in the post-World War II period, are "[a] special version of all of the hypotheses of peculiar barriers" of Nurkse, Singer, and Rosenstein-Rodan, and "[a] political theory [concerning an] alliance between feudal landlords, industrial royalists, and the rising bourgeois capitalist middle classes" (Hagen 1975, 175-76). Since Hagen's characterization of the thesis of Baran is devoid of class interests and conflict, historical dialectics, and the theory of comprador governments, his contribution is reduced to that comprehensible in the standard non-Marxist paradigm. Hagen (1975, 176) has the following to say in his appraisal of Baran's analysis.

> No technical or entrepreneurial problems exist. If the ruling alliance had the will, economic development (and social progress) could proceed without difficulty.
> Beneath the polemics, [Baran's] thesis has a good deal in common with some of the arguments presented [in Hagen's book, viz.] that the market opportunity is not seized because innovation is difficult,...[that] the difficulties are not surmounted ... because insufficient innovative entrepreneurship exists,...[and] that the landed elites of low-income societies do not save and invest productively because their attitudes toward life constrain them. Baran agrees concerning the overt behavior but he will have none of this coddling concerning its causes. The reasons men who might act do not, he states, is that they are evil men. But this [Baran's view] of course, is characterization, not analysis.
> If one regards the propensity of men not to save as evil, one must still ask, if one wishes to gain more than a superficial understanding, why men are evil....His [Baran's] thesis will be unsatisfying except to persons who believe that the devil theory of history is adequate analysis.

From the Marxian viewpoint, these "attitudes" toward life are not themselves primary variables but are determined by the social relations of production corresponding to a definite stage of development of the material powers of production. For example, the attitudes and values of diligence, thrift, and punctuality may be especially emphasized during the early period of industrial capitalism.

To Baran, those concerned about the problems of lack of supply of entrepreneurs have misplaced their emphasis. The entrepreneur is not the major figures accounting for capitalist development, but is, along with the capitalist, a figure that has benefited significantly from the age of modern capitalism. Furthermore, Baran charges that the study of entrepreneurship is ideologically oriented. Much of the literature on entrepreneurship, he contends, extols the "genius" of the entrepreneur in the capitalist system, without trying to explain why his "genius" turned to the accumulation of capital. Additionally, the problem of entrepreneurial ability in LDCs is not its inadequacy but the composition of entrepreneurship between the various sectors of the economy (Baran 1957, 234-37).[7]

Contrary to Hagen, Baran neither attributes a lack of economic development to the actions of "evil men," nor does he lack an explanation for these actions. Instead

> It is fundamental to [Baran's] Marxian approach to the study of man that there is no such thing as an external invariant, "human nature"...[T]he character of man is the product of the social order in which he is born..."[S]ocial order"...encompasses the attained stage of the development of productive forces, the mode and relations of production, the form of social domination prevailing at any given time, all together constituting the *basic* structure of existing organization (Baran 1969, 97-98).8

A ruling coalition whose interests are in conflict with those of the masses may, according to Baran, be exploitative and oppressive. But Baran's explanation of the contribution of the upper classes to the underdevelopment of LDCs, as indicated in the following paragraphs, is far removed from a "devil theory of history."

Furthermore, it is unfair for Hagen to imply that Baran lacks an analysis of the role of the capitalist (entrepreneurial) and landed classes in the inhibition to capital accumulation and economic growth. For Baran, capitalist revolution, homegrown variety, in LDCs was unlikely because of western economic and political domination, especially in the colonial period. Capitalism arose not through the growth of small competitive firms at home, but through the transfer from abroad of advanced monopolistic business. Baran felt as capitalism took hold, the bourgeoisie (business and middle classes) in LDCs, lacking the strength to spearhead thorough institutional change for major capital accumulation, would have to seek allies among other classes.

Thus, in certain instances, the bourgeoisie would ally itself with the more moderate leaders of the workers and peasants to form a progressive coalition with a New Deal orientation (such as the Congress party governments under Prime Minister Jawaharlal Nehru, 1947-64, in India, discussed in chapter 10). At the outset, such a popular movement would be essentially democratic, antifeudal, and anti-imperialist and in support of domestic capitalism. However, the indigenous capitalist middle classes would ultimately be either unwilling or unable to provide the leadership for a sustained economic development that would also greatly reduce poverty and liberate the masses. In time the bourgeoisie, frightened by the threat of labor radicalism and populist upheaval and the possible expropriation of their property, would be forced into an alliance with the landed interests and the foreign bourgeoisie in their midst, whose governments could provide economic and military assistance to stave off impending disaster.

The differences within this counterrevolutionary coalition would not interfere with the overriding common interest in preventing socialism. Even so the coalition would be unable to raise the rate of capital accumulation significantly. A progressive income tax system to eliminate nonessential consumption; channeling savings from the landed aristocracy into productive investment; and undertaking substantial public investment in sectors where private capital does not venture, where monopolistic controls block expansion, or where infrastructure is required would be beyond the coalitions's ability or desire. Thus this conservative alliance thrusts the popular forces even further along the road of radicalism and revolt, leading to further polarization. Finally, Baran theorizes that the only way out of the impasse may be worker and peasant revolution, expropriating land and capital, and establishing a new regime based on the "ethos of collective effort," and "the creed of the predominance of the interests of society over the interests of the selected few" (Baran 1957).[9]

Morgan criticizes Baran for neglecting the possibility that the aims of the ruling group toward power and status could express themselves in a concern for "the general public good.... Some national leaders clearly have a...sense of values...[where] the general public good has been the primary goal" (Morgan 1975, 100). Even if this is the case, the Marxist conceptual scheme, with its emphasis on the economic superstructure as the great moving power of all historic events, and class interest as a basic determinant of behavior and attitudes, would provide a framework for explaining the origin of these values.[10]

Marx's main analysis, of course, was of capitalism, but his discussions of socialism and communism were not well developed. Even his analysis of capitalism, and the transition to socialism, had a number of flaws. He had theorized worker revolt in the industrialized west, but the revolution occurred first in Russia, one of the least developed capitalistic countries in Europe.

Contemporary Marxists indicate reasons why western workers have yet to overthrow capitalism. Having realized the dangers of a rebellious working class at home, the capitalists have developed a tactic of divide and rule that depends on exploitation of workers outside the west. Furthermore, the news media, educational institutions, churches, and synagogues create a false consciousness supporting ruling-class ideologies. And the capitalist state has powerful legal, police, military, and administrative machinery to quell potential resistance.

Marx also overlooked the possibility that the interests of workers and capitalists might not conflict. Thus workers in the west may have supported capitalism because they gained more in the long run by receiving a relatively constant share of a rapidly growing output than by trying to acquire a larger share of what might have been a more slowly growing output under an alternative system.

Regardless of how we view Marxism, it remains a rallying point for discontented people. The irony is that nationalist groups that overthrow their rulers in the name of Marxism are frequently threatened by class antagonisms from those they rule. Almost no other socialist government is willing to go as far as China's Mao, who recognized the existence of classes under socialism, and called for a continuing revolution to oppose the encrusted, socialist, upper classes.

Baran incorporated Lenin's concepts of imperialism and international class conflict into his theory of economic growth and stagnation to bring Marx up to date. Although Baran's approach explains the difficulties that some reformed capitalist LDCs face in spurring economic development, the theory fails to examine a number of economic and political conflicts of interest. Although there are certainly many local agents, managers, merchants, industrialists, bureaucrats, and politicians who benefit considerably from foreign-controlled capital and technology, there are also some local capitalists whose interests compete with foreign business. These capitalists and their allies frequently lead movements for independence. [For example, Côte d'Ivoire cocoa farmers who opposed the formation of French cocoa plantations were major supporters of the nationalist Parti Démocratique de Côte d'Ivoire (PDCI) in the 1950s.] After independence these nationalist elements may become even stronger as colonial economic ties are gradually weakened. Economic policy under a coalition of domestic capitalists, politicians, and bureaucrats may erode the power of foreign capital. The allies and competitors of foreign business people are often locked in economic and political conflict.

Baran also ignores the probability that power is more frequently transferred from one elite to another when revolution occurs, rather than the advantaged classes to the politically dispossessed masses: very few of the Soviet and Chinese revolutionary leaders were workers or poor peasants.

For Baran (1952, 84) the society closest to "a new social ethos [that] will become the spirit and guide of a new age" is the Soviet Union after 1917. He argues that despite the political violence used by Stalin in the 1930s, and the loss of several million lives during this period, the collectivization of agriculture in the Soviet Union was the only possible approach to economic growth, given an irrational and illiterate peasantry. However, he ignores the substantial growth in both agriculture and industry from 1921 to 1928 under the Soviet New Economic Policy of market socialism. This policy consisted of widespread reliance on market prices, limited private ownership (especially in agriculture), and state ownership of most of the largest industrial enterprises. After Stalin began collectivization, agricultural production declined, the peasant's standards of living dropped significantly, and even the savings agriculture contributed to the industrial sector probably did not increase. There were widespread violence, famine, forced labor, and purges during collectivization. Although the performance of Soviet agriculture after that improved, the relatively slow growth in agricultural productivity frustrated Soviet leadership in its attempt to increase average consumption levels to those of DCs.

Baran does not ask whether a more gradual, less-centralized approach to agricultural production would have resulted in more rapid development. But perhaps such a question cannot be resolved. Some historians argue raising living levels, increasing life expectancy, and improving literacy during economic growth have inevitable human costs. The economic transition may be marked by squalor, poverty, unhealthy environment, high infant mortality rate, and a high premature death rate among the working poor, as occurred during Europe's Industrial Revolution, or by the disruption, famine, and death among peasants in the USSR in the 1930s. But in any case, some human costs cannot be avoided.

Several Marxian economists argue that the Russian Revolution of 1917 did not erase divergent class interests. Bettelheim (vol. 1, 1978) contended the USSR abandoned the socialist road, creating a new ruling class—made up of the Communist party, the Praesidium, and the bureaucracy—whose economic interests were antagonistic to those of Soviet workers.

# SKEWED PREMISES ON INEQUALITY

## The Legitimacy of Inequality

Bauer disregards income distribution, stating aid "is likely to be unproductive is evident when its declared objective is redistribution, relief of poverty or some other purpose unrelated to development." In defending inequality, he contends wealth concentration cannot be attributed to differential political and economic power. Indeed "the accumulation of wealth, especially great wealth, normally results from activities which extend the choices of others." Most income inequality is from people differing in "their ability to perceive and utilize economic opportunities.... Economic differences are largely the result of people's capacities and motivation." Equality of opportunity, not results, is important. Bauer (1981, 8-25, 101) points out variations in people's endowment and motivation, but fails to seek their correlation with the advantages of the superior environment, education, and influence those with wealth have.

I show children from upper classes and established business families use the advantages of their parents—property, influence, and status—to acquire education, training, capital, experience and concessions to become disproportionately successful in economic activities, especially business. Wealth and position facilitate the possession of greater opportunities like greater information, superior education and training, and a lower discount of future earning. Afro-Asian political elites use power and wealth to acquire education and investment opportunities to maintain their families' high-status position (chapters 7-8).

At the December 1990 American Economic Association meeting, Lal's conclusion from 13 volumes of comparative studies (not yet published in early 1991) was "that growth does 'trickle down,' whilst growth collapses lead to increasing poverty." Additionally, "direct transfers and social expenditures to alleviate poverty were found not to have made any appreciable dent on poverty." Indeed expanding entitlements have "the effect of 'killing the goose that laid the golden egg'." A part of his finding is the "Director's law" stating "that most politics (except for the Platonic variety) leads to income transfers from the poor and the rich to the middle class." For Lal, "it is not surprising that a common finding of many empirical studies of poverty redressed in countries with the most widespread welfare systems is that these programmes far from relieving absolute poverty have tended to institutionalise it." Lal's conclusions about growth trickling down to the poor and the inefficacy of welfare programs, presented ex cathedra, even contradict studies by the World Bank in 1974, 1980, and 1990 (Chenery, Ahluwalia, Bell, Duloy, and Jolly 1974; World Bank 1980b; World Bank 1990c).

## The Efficiency of Inequality

Economists widely maintain inequality, by spurring high investment rates, benefits the poor, since accumulation raises productivity and average material welfare. Papanek asserts a conflict "between the aims of growth and equality" such that "great inequality of incomes is conducive to increased savings" (Papanek 1967). Ul Haq, an eloquent World Bank spokesperson for meeting LDC basic needs in the 1970s, contended while Pakistani planner in the 1960s: "The underdeveloped countries must consciously accept a philosophy of growth and shelve for the distant future all ideas of equitable distribution and welfare state. It should be recognised that these are luxuries which only developed countries can afford." His conclusion was "additional output should be distributed in favour of the saving sectors." His was "basically a philosophy of growth as opposed to a philosophy of distribution [and] is indispensable in a period of 'take-off' " (ul Haq 1966). In the 1980s, as Pakistani planner, he stated views similar to those he held in the 1960s.

Stolper (1966), head of the Economic Planning Unit preparing Nigeria's first development plan, 1962-68, argued "a very good case can be made that premature preoccupation with equity problems will backfire and prevent any development from taking place." His view is consistent with the neoclassical assumption of Pareto efficiency in a self-regulating capitalist state, where resource allocation is optimal if no other productively feasible allocation can make all individuals in the economy at least as well-off, and at least one person better off, than they were initially. Government intervention to improve the welfare of the homeless by reducing the income of the millionaire violates the neoclassical optimal position stated by Pareto (1971), an early twentieth-century Italian positivist and antidemocrat.[11]

## My Premises on Inequality

Unlike Bauer, most western development economists do not make their value premises clear. Economists frequently accept the premises of sponsors or ruling elites as neutral, and dissenting views as value-laden.

Many economists support elites' maximizing modernization, while waiting for a later stage of development to emphasize income distribution. Yet initial income, physical, and human capital distribution determines the trend in inequality. People owning property, holding an influential position, and receiving a good education are in the best position to profit once growth begins. Thus a society with initial income inequality that begins growth is likely to remain unequal or become more so, whereas one with small disparities may be able to avoid large increases in inequality. A society may not be able to grow first and redistribute later, because early socioeconomic position largely fixes the pattern of distribution, at least until much higher income levels are approached. Reducing inequality requires immediate priority through land reform, mass education, and other means, rather than leaving redistribution until after growth has taken place.

Even if inequality spurs capital accumulation and growth, the prudent LDC poor may not favor inequality, with the risk of their children's health and nutrition, to bequeath prosperity to their grandchildren. Promoting saving through inequality is more costly than using the state to promote both equality and saving (Robinson 1942).

If society tolerates inequality to promote capital formation, a large part of higher incomes is wasted in providing the rich with luxuries. Indeed progressive taxation may stimulate capital accumulation by curbing luxury spending that distorts investment. Before progressivity, too much is invested in industries catering to the rich. Afterwards, some investment shifts from luxuries to necessities. Thus, there are fewer conflicts between African income redistribution and saving than is commonly believed (Kaldor 1975, 29-48) (chapters 3-5, and 10).

How do we evaluate whether inequality is justified? I reject Pareto optimality, assuming rather that society adheres to Rawls' first principle of equality of basic rights and duties. Should we not reward an innovator or risk-taker whose new techniques improve the country's productivity and welfare? For example, the Nigerian government has to pay incomes far above average to spur innovators, researchers, administrators, financiers, and marketing experts to use time and money to develop a safe, effective spray to kill the tsetse fly, thus eliminating trypanosomiasis, a disease attacking people, cattle, goats, and transport animals in southern Nigeria. Suppose poor Nigerians agree that the extra remuneration for tsetse-fly project personnel is preferable to using these funds for alternative wants. This fulfills Rawls' second principle (1971): inequalities of wealth and authority are just if they result in compensating benefits for everyone, particularly the least advantaged.

I accept Rawls' second principle in evaluating income distribution. Yet Afro-Asian elites, like those everywhere, often justify policies furthering their economic interests in terms of compensating benefits for the rest of the population. We must look at whether government's "modernizing" policies, ostensibly in the general interest, may not merely benefit the tiny elite that controls state levers.

One rule of thumb is that a development project should pay for itself in the long run, unless the program creates positive spillover effects or redistributes income in a clearly desirable way. A program that does not pay for itself, where the recipient of the service is not charged an economic price, involves a subsidy to him. Since the alternative to a subsidy is resource allocation to another project, the burden of proof should fall on the subsidy's advocate.[12] The rule would be consistent with, for instance, subsidies to distribute milk or corn to low-income families, but not to provide automobile allowances for senior civil servants in higher-income brackets.

## CONCLUSION

Anglo-American development economics developed largely in isolation from the views of Marxism and other heterodox systems of thought. As a result, the treatment of radical economics by mainstream scholars has been inaccurate and inadequate. Furthermore, orthodox economics has been impoverished by the lack of intellectual ferment that ensues from dialogue and controversy with other paradigms. The insufficient cross-fertilization of orthodox thought by these other views have contributed to the abstraction from politics, the lack of institutional accuracy, the ethnocentric view of international economic and political relations, the relative disregard of imperialism and neocolonialism, the neglect of economic history, the distorted concept of the "traditional" economy, the inaccurate perspective on Marxism, and skewed premises on income redistribution.

These flaws in the orthodox conception of political economy may be responsible for much of the difficulty U.S. and British economists have encountered in adapting successfully to work in LDCs. The following observation regarding western economics graduates working in LDCs is still substantially valid.

> There is so much for economics graduates to unlearn—and unfortunately the abler the student has been in absorbing the current doctrine, the more difficult the process of adaptation (Seers 1963, 79).13

To enhance their comprehension of poverty and underdevelopment in Afro-Asia, Anglo-American economists will need to expand their intellectual horizons beyond their limited universe of discourse to become conversant with the contributors of heterodox views in the United States and the rest of the world. For a major task for development economists is to devise critical tests— capable of being refuted or falsified—to determine the validity and the range of applicability of some hypotheses of orthodox and radical economics mentioned and implied above. But if my contention is correct, those engaged in this task will need a background in and understanding of heterodox conflict and historical approaches, as well as standard economic thought.

# NOTES

1. The Prebisch work was first published in Spanish in 1950.
2. Merton indicates the advantages to scholarship that comes from "truths" perceived by insiders.
3. I discuss reasons for rejecting the development values and plans of the politico-economic elite and their foreign consultants in chapter IX.
4. An author of a development textbook, Enke (1963: vii-viii), is explicit in indicating his interest in economic development is motivated by ideological concerns arising from the gains of the Soviet Union and China in the LDCs during the Cold War.
5. Higgins' discussion (1968, 152-53) of secular stagnation illustrates the blind spot of orthodox economics to the possibility of LDC underdevelopment being related to DC international economic extension. Although the tendency toward stagnation in advanced capitalist economies impels their expansion of international trade and investment, Higgins considers this expansion "irrelevant to the present underdeveloped countries" of contemporary DCs.
6. Hagen and Myrdal overlook Northern Europeans hiring Turkish, Croatian, Slovenian, and Italian "guest workers" for menial jobs, and farmers in southwestern United States employing large numbers of Hispanics to do "stoop" work. And in Afro-Asia, more elites resort to manual work themselves as the minimum wage for cooks, nannies, gardeners, and other servants increases, as in Nigeria during the oil boom of the mid 1970s.
7. Much of the discussion of entrepreneurship (Bruton 1965, 94, 97, 254-59; Hagen 1975, 268-99; Meier 1970, 588; and Higgins 1968, 105, 150.), if not apologetics for ruthless capitalist exploitation as Baran (1957, 254-57) suggests, is a celebration of the virtues of the capitalist entrepreneur in economic growth, without a critical look at his class origins and oligopoly power, or the impact of colonial policies on entrepreneurial supply. For an analysis of the ethnocentric view of U.S. development economists on entrepreneurship, see chapters 7 and 8.
8. Reprinted from *Monthly Review,* October 1959. Author's italics. Compare, for example, Morgan 1975, 357, who states "Businessmen are by nature individualists."
According to Morgan (1975, 100), Baran does not consider the necessity of relying on "the strongest motive (the advantage of individuals and their families)" in order to build effective incentives into any successor system to capitalism. However, Baran, like Marx, does not regard "human nature" as invariant, but expects the selfishness and greed associated with the profit motive to decline with a shift in the ownership and control of the means of production from capitalists to workers. Moreover, implicit in Baran's discussion is the Maoist view that human beings can be socialized, educated, and indoctrinated to place more reliance on "moral incentives" instead of "material incentives" (Baran 1969, 92-111.)
9. His views are more succinctly presented in Baran 1952, 66-84.
10. To Morgan (1975, 343), governing elites utilize and adjust to a pre-existing ideology, the origin of which is not explained. For example, "[governing groups] are impelled ... to cater to

local religions, customs, and patterns of value. They are likely, specifically, to support local economic orthodoxy, whatever it is—private enterprise, socialist, communist, co-operative; or state-directed isolationist." To the Marxist, on the other hand, the existence of an ideology is a product of the material conditions in society, and the class struggle. The effort of a ruling elite to justify and legitimize their position is especially important in creating an ideology.

11. Eatwell, Milgate, and Newman, vol. 3, 799-813, especially B. Lockwood, "Pareto Efficiency," pp. 811-13.

12. Tariffs have a similar effect to subsidies. Government distorts prices, benefiting special interests, through redistributing income from consumers or merchants to industrialists.

13. Krueger et al. (1991, 1038-51) express concern about recent American economics Ph.D.s' lack of: knowledge of economic problems and institutions, real-world connections, creativity, problem-solving ability, and expository skills.

# Chapter II

# *Afro-Asian Development in Comparative Perspective*

## CAPITALISM AND MODERN WESTERN ECONOMIC DEVELOPMENT

Historians hesitate to name a threshold period in history when economic growth took off. Although there were periods of economic growth during ancient and medieval times (including a renaissance of learning in the medieval Arab world), rapid, sustained growth was rare. Living standards remained at a subsistence level for the majority of the world's population. The rapid, sustained increase in real GNP per capita for a century or so began in the west (Western Europe, the United States, Canada, Australia, and New Zealand) more than 150 years ago. Industrialization and sustained growth had begun in Great Britain by the last half of the eighteenth century; in the United States and France in the first half of the nineteenth century; in Germany, the Netherlands, and Belgium by the middle of that century; and in Scandinavia, Canada, Italy, non-western Japan, and perhaps Russia, by the last half of the century.

Why did sustained growth begin in the west? A major reason is the rise of capitalism, the economic system dominant there since the breakup of feudalism from the fifteenth to the eighteenth-centuries. Fundamental to capitalism are the relations between private owners and workers. The means of production—land, mines, factories, and other forms of capital—are privately held; and legally free but capital-less workers lease their labor to employers. Under capitalism production decisions are made by private individuals operating for profit.

Capitalist institutions had antecedents in the ancient world, and pockets of capitalism flourished in the late medieval period. For example, a capitalist woolen industry existed in thirteenth-century Flanders and fourteenth-century Florence, but it died out because of revolutionary conflict between the workers and capitalists. Thus the continuous development of the capitalist system dates only from the sixteenth-century.

Especially after the eleventh century, the growing long-distance trade between capitalist centers contributed to the collapse of the medieval economy. As European trade activity expanded during the next few centuries, certain institutions facilitated the growth of modern capitalism. Among them were private property, deposit banking, formal contracts, craft guilds, merchant associations, joint stock companies (the precursor of the corporation), insurance, international financial markets, naval protection of trade vessels, and government support in opening markets and granting monopoly privileges for inventions.

At the same time, burgeoning industrialization and urbanization further weakened the feudal economy, an agricultural system based on serfs bound to their lord's land. Ultimately these changes in trade, industry, and agriculture transformed the medieval economy into a new society fueled by capitalist endeavors.

Before the twentieth century, only capitalist economies were successful in large capital accumulation and in generating and applying a vast scientific and technical knowledge to production. Why was capitalism first successful in the west?

1. The breakdown of the all-encompassing authority of the medieval Roman Catholic Church during the period of the Protestant Reformation of the sixteenth and seventeenth-centuries stimulated a new economic order. Weber argues that although Protestantism, like Catholicism, was ascetic, manifesting itself in the systematic regulation of the whole conduct of the Christian, the new Protestant ethic translated its "inner-worldly" asceticism into a vigorous activity in a secular vocation, or *calling* (in contrast to the "other-worldly" asceticism of the Catholic monastery). The Protestant ethic, Weber contends, fostered hard work, frugality, sobriety and efficiency, virtues coinciding with the spirit essential for capitalist development. For Weber, acceptance of the Protestant idea of a calling led to the systematic organization of free labor and gave a religious justification for unstinting work even at low wages in the service of God (and incidentally the employer) (Weber 1930, with the first German edition in 1904-05).

It probably was not the "this-worldly" asceticism of Protestantism, but the disruption of the Catholic social system and loss of civil power, the accommodation of the Protestant ethic to the needs of the rising capitalist class, and the secularization and social realism of Protestantism that explain the correlation between the Protestant Reformation and capitalist economic development. Chapter 8 criticizes Weber's explanation of capitalist development in greater detail.[1] For now, it suffices that while medieval Islam was not secular enough to free the spirit of capitalist development, other reform religious ideologies besides ascetic Protestantism (or Puritanism) can be the vehicle for breaking the stranglehold of a theocracy (government by persons claiming divine authority) on the economic, political, and intellectual realms. Furthermore, *Corpus Christianum* or other all-encompassing religious authority might have precluded changes outlined in points 2 through 5 below.

2. Between the sixteenth and nineteenth centuries, Western Europe witnessed the rise of strong national states that created the conditions essential for rapid and cumulative growth under capitalism. The nation-state established a domestic market free of trade barriers, a uniform monetary system, contract and property law, police and militia protection against internal violence, defense against external attack, and basic transportation and communication facilities—all of which fostered capitalism. Initially absolute monarchs wrested power from feudal lords and town authorities and consolidated territory into large political and economic units—the nation-state. The nation-state was necessary for larger markets and economies of scale of capitalist expansion. Eventually monarchy ceded power to the bourgeoisie, the capitalist and middle classes. Where an absolute monarch existed, the bourgeoisie, who enjoyed only a precarious existence under autocratic authority, ultimately stripped the monarch of power and installed representatives more favorable to their economic interests.

3. The declining influence of the church coincided with the Enlightenment, a period of great intellectual activity in seventeenth and eighteenth-century Europe that led to the scientific discoveries of electricity, oxygen, calculus, and so on. These discoveries found practical application in agriculture, industry, trade, and transport and resulted in extended markets, increased efficiency of large-scale production, and enhanced profits associated with capital concentration. Furthermore the rationalism permeating the new science and technology meshed with the spirit of capitalist enterprise.

4. Protestantism's spiritual individualism (the "priesthood of all believers"), coupled with philosophical rationalism and humanism of the Enlightenment, emphasized freedom from arbitrary authority. In the economic sphere, this liberalism advocated a self-regulating market unrestricted by political intervention or state monopoly. These views were tailormade for the bourgeoisie in its struggle to overthrow the old order.

5. Intellectual and economic changes led to political revolutions in England, Holland, and France in the seventeenth and eighteenth centuries that reduced the power of the church and landed aristocracy. The bourgeoisie took over much of this power. Economic modernization in Europe would probably not have been possible without these revolutions.[2]

6. Modern capitalism is distinguished from earlier economic systems by a prodigious rate of capital accumulation. During the early capitalism of the sixteenth and seventeenth centuries, the great flow of gold and silver from the Americas to Europe inflated prices and profits and speeded up this accumulation. Inflation redistributed income from landlords and wage laborers, whose real earnings declined, to merchants, manufacturers, and

commercial farmers, who were more likely to invest in new and productive enterprises.[3]

Capitalism, as an engine for rapid economic growth, spread beyond Europe to the outposts of western civilization—the United States, Canada, Australia, and New Zealand. Indeed during most of the twentieth century, capitalism has been more successful in the United States than in other western economies.

However, modern industrial capitalism was established in the west at great human costs. Physical violence, brutality, and exploitation shaped its early course in England and Belgium, wages dropped and poverty increased markedly during the accelerated industrial growth of the latter eighteenth and early nineteenth centuries. In both countries, it took a half century before the absolute incomes of the poor reached Industrial Revolution levels (Adelman and Morris 1978, 245-73). Charles Dickens portrays the starvation, destitution, overcrowding, and death among the nineteenth century unemployed and working class, in lives fictionalized in *Nicholas Nickleby, A Christmas Carol,* and *Oliver Twist.* Dickens's novels provide insight into English (and western) workers during this time. Although these human costs may not be inevitable, similar problems have not been avoided by newly industrializing countries in subsequent periods. But despite these costs, even Marxist Dobb (1926) concedes capitalism improved the level of living for a large proportion of the western population since the early nineteenth century.

## THE WEST AND AFRO-ASIA: THE NINETEENTH CENTURY AND TODAY

GNP per capita for developed countries in Europe in the late 1980s and early 1990s was roughly 15 to 20 times that of Afro-Asian less developed countries (with DC Japan not included). The gap was not so great 140 to 150 years before, since people could not have survived on one-fifteenth the per capita income of European DCs in the nineteenth-century. Updating a rough assessment by Nobel laureate Kuznets (1971, 23-28) indicates at that time, Western Europe, the United States, Canada, and Australia had an average real income higher than that of most African and Asian countries today. The DC economic growth has been much more rapid during the past century, and of course the DCs are adding to an already substantial economic base.

## THE COLONIAL LEGACY AND POST-COLONIAL TRANSNATIONAL ECONOMIC LINKAGES

Western capitalism, through informal imperialism and late nineteenth- and early twentieth-century colonialism, developed at the expense of Afro-Asia, capturing some of its surplus (output above wages, depreciation, and purchases from other firms) through policies controlling their raw materials, markets, international trade, and planning. Chapter 1 indicated how today's DCs disrupted the pre-existing fabric of Afro-Asian economies. Chapter 3's discussion of British and French policies during the terminal colonial period supporting African elites at the expense of workers and peasants, and the alliances between post-colonial politicians, middlemen, DC international traders, and multinational corporations, together with chapter 5's analysis of the relationship between LDC state power and foreign business, demonstrates the adverse impact of western neo-colonialism in Africa. Substantial debt overhang in sub-Saharan Africa, examined in chapter 4, exacerbates the dependence of poor countries on western banks, aid agencies, the World Bank, and the International Monetary Fund. Moreover, debt and the concomitant dependence on the external economy even threaten Africa's fledgling democracies, as chapter 6 contends.

Colonialism and post-colonial dependence on international trade and capital are major contributors to the weakness of indigenous entrepreneurs in India, Nigeria, and other LDCs (chapters 7-8). The differential impact of British colonial policies in West Punjab and East Bengal (parts of the Indian empire) and Northern and Southern Nigeria, together with the relationships of Pakistani and Nigerian regions to the world economy, contributed to internal political and economic conflicts that triggered secessionist wars by Bangladesh and Biafra (chapter 9). Western imperialism and post-1949 relationships to foreign economic actors had a major impact on the relative economic development performance of India and China discussed in chapter 10.

Japan, which has had the greatest economic success among African and Asian economies since the mid-nineteenth century, was virtually the only country in Afro-Asia with substantial autonomy in economic affairs. Furthermore, Japan's development was aided by a transfer of capital from colonies Korea and Taiwan, 1911-40 (chapter 11).

# ECONOMIC MODERNIZATION BY JAPAN

Capitalism led to modern economic growth in only a few non-western countries, as few had the strong indigenous capitalists and the effective bureaucratic and political leadership essential for rapid economic modernization. One notable exception was Japan, one of the few non-western countries that escaped western colonialism. Despite unequal treaties with the west from 1858 to 1899, Japan had substantial autonomy in economic affairs compared to other Afro-Asia countries (chapter 11).

Japan's level of economic development was much lower than western countries in the middle to late nineteenth-century. However since 1867, when

Japan abolished feudal property relationships, its growth of 3.5 percent per year was the fastest in the world (Table II.1), increasing at a rate of 31 times per century. For about the same period, annual growth rates of real GNP per capita of Sweden, Germany, and Canada also have been at least 2 percent, a rate that multiplies income sevenfold in a 100 years, and has been much more rapid than that of the developing countries, whose growth (with a few exceptions, such as Brazil, Argentina, Mexico, and Malaysia) for the same period was only a fraction of 1 percent per year (Morawetz 1977, 14).

What explains U.K. and the U.S. slow and Japan's (and Germany's) accelerated growth since World War II? Thurow (1985) attributes Japan's superior performance to that of the United States to higher savings rates, higher primary and secondary educational standards, more emphasis on technical and applied science education, a higher propensity to import technology, the

**Table II.1.**   Annual Rate of Growth of Real GNP per Capita (percent)

| Country | *Annual Growth Rates, columns (1)-(5)* | | | | | |
|---|---|---|---|---|---|---|
| | (1) *1860 or1870 to 1910* | (2) *1910 to 1950* | (3) *1950 to 1975* | (4) *1975 to 1986* | (5) *(Long period)* *1860 or* *1870 to* *1986* | *Multiplication of 1860 GNP per capita in 1986* |
| Japan | 2.9 | 1.8 | 7.6 | 3.4 | 3.5 | 76 |
| Sweden | 2.4 | 2.6 | 2.6 | 2.4 | 2.5 | 23 |
| Germany[a] | 2.0 | 0.7 | 4.5 | 2.4 | 2.1 | 14 |
| Canada | 2.2 | 1.3 | 2.4 | 2.2 | 2.0 | 11 |
| Denmark | 1.8 | 1.3 | 2.9 | 2.5 | 1.9 | 11 |
| France[b] | 1.5 | 0.9 | 3.8 | 2.3 | 1.9 | 11d |
| United States | 2.5 | 1.1 | 2.0 | 2.0 | 1.9 | 11 |
| Russia-USSR[c] | 1.0 | 2.0 | 2.7 | 1.9 | 1.8 | 9d |
| Ireland | 1.7 | 1.4 | 2.6 | 1.9 | 1.8 | 9 |
| Italy | 0.8 | 1.3 | 4.3 | 2.2 | 1.8 | 9 |
| United Kingdom | 1.2 | 1.2 | 2.2 | 1.8 | 1.4 | 6 |

*Notes:*   [a] Since World War II, West Germany.
[b]Figures for period (1) and the long period begin in 1840.
[c]The periods are: (1) 1870-1913 and (2) 1913-1950.
[d]Multiplication for period 1960-1986 at same annual growth rate as that in column 5.

*Sources:*   Kuznets 1956: 13; Morawetz 1977, 80; OECD 1988, 44; Ofer 1987, 1778; and U.S. Congress 1988. The 1975 to 1986 rates, (except for the USSR) are estimates based on World Bank 1987a, 6-9.

scientific and technological background of top managers, their longer time horizons, and the "leaner" management bureaucracy. Olson (1982) argues that the growth of special interests in DCs with long periods of stability (without invasion or upheaval) such as Britain and the United States, reduces efficiency and growth. Thus the Allied powers' defeat and occupation of Japan and Germany in the late 1940s abolished special interests that slowed economic growth while encouraging the establishment of highly encompassing interests, and spurred low per capita military spending (especially for Japan) that freed resources for technological innovation. Kennedy (1987) contends great powers emerge because of a strong economic base but decline (for example, Britain in the mid-twentieth century and the United States in the late twentieth-century) from military overcommitment obstructing economic growth. Chapter 12 compares Japanese and American long-term and post-World War II growths, and examines why Japan's growths have been faster.

# PROBLEMS OF ECONOMIC REFORM IN CHINA

European and Asian economies undertaking the transition from centrally managed socialism to mixed capitalism or more decentralized socialism have been plagued with internal inconsistencies and bureaucratic resistance. Since the subject is too vast to cover comprehensively, let me suggest some problems and successes by concentrating on China's economic reforms since 1979, including reforms in agriculture, individual enterprises, and industry.

In December 1978, two years after Mao's death, China's Communist party's Eleventh Central Committee, under Deng Xiaoping, committed itself to market socialism within a framework of national economic planning. In reforms beginning in 1979, China decontrolled (and increased) prices for farm commodities, virtually eliminated compulsory deliveries to the state, reduced multitiered pricing, relaxed interregional farm trade restrictions, encouraged rural markets, allowed direct sales of farm goods to urban consumers, and decollectivized agriculture, instituting household management of farm plots under long-term contracts with collectives and allowing farmers to choose cropping patterns and nonfarm activities. From 1977 to 1984, India's 0.3-percent annual growth in food output per capita was outstripped by China's 2.4-percent growth (Table X.13), which was not so rapid as gains in oilseed, livestock, and cotton output. Instead China reversed its pre-1979 dependence on imported grains, exporting maize, other coarse grains, soybeans, and raw cotton, which competed with exports from the U.S. Midwest and South, especially to Japan. These remarkable gains were achieved without increased farm inputs except for chemical fertilizer (World Bank 1986, 104-06; U. S. Department of Agriculture 1986, U.S. Department of Agriculture 1988; FAO 1991). In the late 1980s and early 1990s, however, agricultural productivity grew more slowly, partly from some inattention to maintaining fertility, drainage, irrigation facilities, and other infrastructure, and less emphasis on soil conservation and practices than under collectivization.

China's individual economy grew rapidly as the number of privately self-employed in cities and towns (primarily in services, commerce, handicrafts, and catering) grew from 150,000 in 1978 to roughly 5-10 million in 1988, increasing industrial output and soaking up underemployed labor. While privately owned and operated proprietorships could employ only five outside the family, vertically and horizontally integrated cooperatives and corporations had higher employment limits that varied by locality. In 1984, Wan Runnan persuaded six Academy of Sciences engineering colleagues to join him in borrowing $5400 and renting a small office to found the Beijing Stone Company, which grossed $85.5 million sales in electronic equipment, earned $6.7 million after taxes, employed 800, and had 15 subsidiaries (including Japan and Hong Kong) by 1987. The Stone Group controlled ownership and provided technical knowledge for joint ventures with Japan's Mitsui in producing an English-Chinese electronic typewriter, word processors, and printers suitable for China, and software. Chinese law and social sanctions limited annual after-tax income of company President Wan to $8500, yet as an entrepreneur, he had independence, prestige and an income five times his academy salary. However, the alliance of Wan with dissident Chinese students and intellectuals, and his going into exile in June 1989 as a leader of the Chinese Democratic Front opposing the Chinese government reversed his success in the individual economy. Indeed, after June 1989, Chinese private enterprise declined with its suppression by the government (Harding 1987, 124-28; Gould 1985, 46-50; Shi 1987; Ignatius 1988, 10; Ignatius 1989, A1; and Goldman 1989, 5-9).

But the key to China's urban reform was not the small industry, services, or informal sectors but state-owned enterprises. The reform of these industrial enterprises has not been so successful as China's agricultural reform. Annual gross industrial output growth, 11.4 percent from 1952 to 1978 (9.4 percent, 1965-78), slowed to 7.0 percent from 1978 to 1982, with no substantial improvements in industrial efficiency the decade after 1978 (Riskin 1987, 368-72). Urban reform entails built-in contradictions, since increased market forces threaten the power and expertise of bureaucrats, who were trained to run a command system.

The reform instituted a responsibility system, in which an enterprise manager's task was to be carefully defined and performance was to determine managers' and workers' pay. The initiative and decisions were to be centered in producing units rather than in government administrations. Under this system, taxes on enterprise bonuses more than a certain level replaced the profits and losses the state absorbed. But rewarding producers with higher pay for higher productivity requires an increase in consumer goods, especially food. And with reduced investment, growth must rely on technical innovation and increased efficiency. Although the early reform period emphasized worker authority in selecting managers, this selection was deemphasized when it increasingly conflicted with the professionalization and responsibility of managers (Lippit 1987, 209-16).

Economists identify several problems with China's industrial reform. A major problem is fragmented administrative control, numerous overlapping authorities for project approval, and multiple levels of controls at different levels of government, what the Chinese call too many mothers-in-law. The Qingdao Forging Machinery Plant, a state enterprise, is responsible to the national Ministry of the Machine Industry, the city materials board, and the county for material supplies, to the municipal machine industry office for plant production, to the county planning agency for output value, to relevant county agencies for supplies from the plant, to two separate county agencies for personnel, and to the county committee for party matters, which is immersed in implementing policies (Zheng 1987, 303-04).

Thus planning is not integrated nor coherent, and enterprises are not treated consistently concerning targets. Investment decisions are bureaucratized and politicized. Moreover, administrative agencies lack enough information about enterprises and commodities to make good decisions. Despite the management responsibility system, in practice management has still been centralized and rigid, with firm managers having limited control over performance. Moreover, decentralization merely substituted interference by local government authorities for that of Beijing (Tidrick and Chen 1987; Lee 1986, 45-71; Riskin 1987, 352-53; Lippit 1987, 215-16; Barnett and Clough 1986, 54-57; and Lichtenstein 1991).

If profits are to guide enterprise behavior, profits must be determined by prices reflecting true relative economic scarcity. If prices are set incorrectly, as in China, they will give the wrong signal, spurring enterprises to produce too little of what is short and too much of what is in surplus.

For the market to have meaning, products of enterprises must be sold on the market rather than delivered to governmental authorities for a fixed price. As of 1988, the prices of 60 products subject to mandatory control outside the market included foodstuffs, all energy sources, most metals, basic raw materials for the chemical industry, important machinery and electrical equipment, and several other items.

Prices are arbitrary and distorted, and are only changed incrementally throughout the system. Setting of multiple prices by regions does not correspond to the cost of distances travelled. Distorted prices means that profits are not linked to supply and demand. Enterprises are spurred to produce overpriced goods regardless of the market. Scarce goods that are priced cheaply become even more scarce. Moreover, the Chinese, who restrict new firm entry and rarely close down inefficient firms, lack the market's creative destruction, in which an industry's old, high-cost producers are replaced by new, low-cost enterprises (Schumpeter 1947, 81-86).

If increasing market forces are to result in higher levels of efficiency, enterprises must compete with each other rather than have monopoly control of particular markets. To be sure, enterprises have more freedom buying and selling, and collective businesses sometimes compete with state enterprises. Yet as long as planners allocate key inputs administratively, competition is limited, at least for intermediate products.

For the market to have meaning, enterprises must be able to buy productive inputs on the market. But prices usually do not show where resources can best be put to use, thus providing false signals to enterprises. In many instances, enterprises are still not allowed to retain profits for capital; indeed much capital is still allocated administratively rather than by interest payment. Additionally the Chinese lack a labor market, which hampers labor adjustments with changes in demand. Enterprise managers have little control over paying or hiring labor, and little discretion in firing unproductive workers. Moreover, the variety and amount of supplies available to a firm do not bear much relationship to output targets. Firms have little scope to search the market for the cheapest combination of input costs.

Firms have a soft budget constraint, meaning that though management and worker bonuses are nominally linked to profits and other targets, virtually no enterprise has lost bonuses for not meeting targets, since firms can negotiate during the output year to reduce quotas. Enterprise managers bargain for profit targets, which often can be changed retroactively. Firms may receive inducements for production, yet not be able to respond because managers do not have meaningful discretionary authority. Norms for firms are too many, and changes too frequent, thus making planning difficult. The norms encourage output of high-value commodities that use a high proportion of materials, and a delinking of production from marketing.

Chinese industry still suffers from the classic Soviet planning approach— using the preceding year's achievement as the minimum target for the current year, known by the Chinese as "whipping the fast ox." Near the end of the year, enterprises overfulfilling quotas deliberately slow down operations in order not to increase targets too much for the subsequent year. From 1979 to 1980, Beijing instituted profit retention and rewards for fulfilling several performance indicators (including profits) in several pilot firms. But the experiment was suspended, since the growth of profits and other performance indicators slowed down to keep future targets down, and local governments objected to the high administrative costs and reduced control associated with enterprise profit retention.

Moreover most enterprises do not receive their quotas until after the beginning of the planning year. Due to dependence on administrative decisions and the cooperation of other firms in receiving inputs, enterprises keep excessive levels of inventory.

Since the state sets few variety, grade, or style targets, the enterprise has little incentive to produce the variety of goods demanded by the market. Price incentives are also lacking for quality improvement.

The emergence of a buyers' market in 1980, partly a result of the substantial increases in the supply of light industry and consumer goods, had more effect, the World Bank and Chinese Academy of Social Sciences point out, than industrial reform in improving industrial performance and quality (Tidrick and Chen 1987).

# RECENT ECONOMIC GROWTH IN AFRO-ASIA

Economic growth in developing Afro-Asia was more rapid after World War II than before. Data before this war are generally poor and lacking altogether. From the start of the twentieth century until independence in 1947, real growth in India, the Afro-Asian LDC with the best estimates, was no more than 0.2 percent yearly compared to an annual 1.7-percent growth from 1950 to 1986. World Bank studies indicate real growth rates for Afro-Asia to be less than 1 percent a year compared to about 2.8 percent per year from 1950 to 1988, a rate that doubles income per head in about 25 years (Morawetz 1977, 12-14; Heston and Summers 1968, 96-101; World Bank 1990c, 178-79; Uppal 1977, 15-17). Even if we plausibly assume that annual growth rates are overstated by 0.5 percentage points during modernization (see Kuznets 1972, 185-209, for a discussion of the reasons why LDC growth rates tend to be overstated relative to DC rates), the rate was still faster than that of developed countries during any comparable period before 1950. If maintained, this rate would be faster than the median growth rate (1.9 percent yearly; see Table II.1) for the last 125-150 years or so for developed countries on which there are data.

The fastest growing LDC region was East Asia, whose annual growth rate, 1965-1988 was 6.7 percent (without China's rapid yearly growth of 5.4 percent). Southeast Asia, which includes Indonesia (see below), Thailand, Malaysia, and Singapore, each with at least 4.0 percent yearly growth rates [counteracting the slow-growing Philippines, Viet Nam, Myanmar (Burma), and Cambodia], also was rapidly growing, with 4.4 percent yearly. The Middle East and Latin America, which had the highest GNPs per capita except for (non-China) East Asia, had intermediate growth rates close to 2 percent annually for the period. The two poorest regions, South Asia and Sub-Saharan Africa, had the lowest GNPs per capita and growth rates (Table II.2) (World Bank 1990c, 178-79). South Asia, comprised primarily of slow-growing India and Bangladesh and moderate-growing Pakistan, is discussed in chapters 9 and 10.

A tragedy is that Afro-Asia's gains do not include sub-Saharan Africa, whose economy has been stagnant, poverty rates high, and life expectancy low. The

**Table II.2.** Development Indicators (by Country, LDC Regions, and Country Income Groups)

| | (1) Population (millions) mid-1990 | (2) GNP Per Capita 1988 ($) | (3) Average Annual Growth rate of GNP per Capita 1965-88 (percent) | (4) Poorest 20% share/ Richest 5-10% share | (5) Percentage Poulation in Poverty— 1985-1990 l\$370 Purchasing Power Adjustment (a) | (6) Life Expectancy at Birth 1990 (years) | (7) Adult Literacy Rate 1985 (%) | (8) Human Development Index (b) | (9) Human Freedom Index (c)6 |
|---|---|---|---|---|---|---|---|---|---|
| *Selected Countries[d]* | | | | | | | | | |
| China | 1,120 | 330 | 5.4 | | 20 | 70 | 68 | 0.614 | 2 |
| India | 853 | 340 | 1.8 | 0.303 | 48 | 59 | 44 | 0.308 | 14 |
| U.S. | 251 | 19,840 | 1.6 | 0.188 | | 76 | 99 | 0.976 | 33 |
| Indonesia | 189 | 440 | 4.3 | 0.332 | 38 | 62 | 72 | 0.499 | 5 |
| Brazil | 150 | 2,160 | 3.6 | 0.052 | | 66 | 79 | 0.759 | 18 |
| Japan | 124 | 21,020 | 4.3 | 0.338 | | 79 | 99 | 0.993 | 32 |
| Bangladesh | 115 | 170 | 0.4 | 0.238 | 86 | 52 | 32 | 0.186 | 7 |
| Pakistan | 115 | 350 | 2.5 | 0.249 | 30 | 58 | 31 | 0.311 | 5 |
| Mexico | 89 | 1,760 | 2.3 | | | 70 | 85 | 0.838 | 15 |
| Nigeria[e] | 86 | 290 | 0.9 | | | 52 | 43 | 0.242 | 13 |
| Philippines | 66 | 630 | 1.6 | 0.171 | 58 | 64 | 88 | 0.613 | 10 |
| Thailand | 56 | 1,000 | 4.0 | | 30 | 66 | 91 | 0.713 | 14 |
| Ethiopia | 52 | 120 | -0.1 | | 61 | 46 | 50 | 0.166 | 2 |
| Korea, South | 43 | 3,600 | 6.8 | | 16 | 70 | 95 | 0.884 | 14 |
| Zaire | 37 | 170 | -2.1 | | 83 | 53 | 66 | 0.299 | 5 |
| Tanzania | 26 | 160 | -0.5 | | | 54 | 52 | 0.266 | 10 |
| Sudan | 25 | 480 | 0.0 | | 81 | 51 | 24 | 0.164 | |
| Kenya | 25 | 370 | 1.9 | | 47 | 60 | 65 | 0.399 | 8 |
| Malaysia | 17 | 1,940 | 4.0 | 0.132 | 5 | 70 | 74 | 0.802 | 9 |
| Ghana | 15 | 400 | -1.6 | 0.223 | 44 | 55 | 53 | 0.311 | 11 |
| Côte d'Ivoire | 13 | 770 | 0.9 | 0.137 | 29 | 53 | 49 | 0.311 | |
| Cameroon | 11 | 1,010 | 3.7 | | 30 | 54 | 67 | 0.351 | 8 |

*LDC regions[f]*

| | | | | | | | |
|---|---|---|---|---|---|---|---|
| Sub-Saharan Africa | 517 | 330 | 0.2 | 0.155 | 47 | 52 | 42 |
| South Asia | 1,192 | 320 | 1.8 | 0.288[g] | 51[g] | 57 | 36 |
| Southeast Asia | 455 | 650 | 4.4 | 0.215 | 20 | 70 | 90 |
| East Asia | 92 | 4,210 | 6.7 | 0.384 | 20 | 70 | 68 |
| China | 1,120 | 330 | 5.4 | 0.227 | 31 | 62 | 42 |
| Middle East | 255 | 1,860 | 2.1 | 0.116 | 19 | 67 | 82 |
| Latin America | 447 | 1,840 | 1.9 | | | | |
| *Country income groups[f]* | | | | | | | |
| LDCs | 4,107 | 750 | 2.7 | 0.198 | 37 | 63 | 55 |
| High-income oil exporters | 21 | 8,380 | 3.1 | | | 63 | |
| DCs | 762 | 17,470 | 2.3 | 0.443 | | 76 | 99 |
| Socialist (pre-1989) | 431 | 10,040 | | | | 70 | |
| World | 5,321 | 3,930 | 2.6 | | 28 | 66 | |

*Notes:* Blank cells indicate data not available, except U.S. and Japanese blanks for poverty rates mean virtually 0% poverty rates (by I$370 standard). Sub-Saharan Africa does not include South Africa. Southeast Asia contains the Philippines. LDCs comprise the low- and middle-income countries in World Bank 1988b. DCs are nonsocialist only. Socialist includes only Soviet and Eastern European. High-income oil exporters consist of the United Arab Emirates, Kuwait, Saudi Arabia, Libya, and Oman.

a. People in poverty include those in households with less then $370 per capita income, with purchasing power adjustment, which is based on converting income in local currency into international dollars by measuring the country's purchasing power relative to all other countries rather than using the exchange rate. See Nafziger 1990, 24-25, 110-13.

b. UN Development Programme 1991, 119-21. Index is based on life expectancy at birth (1990), educational attainment [adult literacy rate (1985) and mean years of schooling (1980)], and real GDP per capita (I$). HDI ranking varies from 0.993 in Japan to 0.048 in Sierra Leone.

c. UN Development programme 1991, 20. Index is based on civil and legal rights, freedom from torture and censorship, electoral and religious freedom, ethnic and gender egilitarianism, independent media, courts, and trade unions, and related indicators. HFI ranking varies from 0 for Iraq to 38 for Sweden.

d. Column (4)—poorest 20% share/richest 10% share in 1980s.

e. Nigerian figures adjusted to reflect November 1991 census.

f. Column (4)—poorest 20% share/richest 5% share c 1970.

g. Includes Southeast Asia (e.g., Indonesia and Malaysia).

*Sources:* Ahluwalia, Carter, and Chenery 1979, 302-03, 312-13; World Bank 1990b, 29, 178-79, 236-37; World Bank 1980b; Population Reference Bureau 1990; UN Development Programme 1991, 20, 119-120, 124-25, 160-61.

Economic Commission for Africa described Africa's economic situation in the 1980s as the worst since the 1930s' great depression, and Africa "the very sick child of the international economy." Recognizing this, the UN devoted its thirteenth special session in 1986 to develop a five-year strategy to safeguard Africa's economic survival. But the UN's 1991 review stated that "Economic and social conditions actually worsened over the five years of the period of the United Nations Programme of Action for African Economic Recovery and Development 1986-1990" (ECA 1986; UN General Assembly 1986; and UN General Assembly 1991, 3).

Growth declined from the 1950s to the 1960s (1.3 percent per annum) to the 1970s (0.8 percent yearly) to the 1980s (-1.2 percent annually) (Morawetz 1977, 12-14; World Bank 1981a, 143; World Bank 1989a, 221; and World Bank 1991b, 3). Sub-Saharan Africa's annual growth, 1965-1988, 0.2 percent, was far below that of Afro-Asia generally, 2.8 percent (Table II.2). Since real growth is overstated as countries modernize, due to the increased proportion of goods and services produced for the market, the Sub-Sahara's overall growth during this period may be zero or negative. All Sub-Saharan African countries with six million or more people (except Cameroon) grew by less than 2 percent yearly for the same period.

## HUMAN DEVELOPMENT AND HUMAN FREEDOM

In 1990 and 1991, the UN Development Programme developed two indices of development, the Human Development Index (HDI) and Human Freedom Index (HFI). HDI (adjusted for gender differences) is based on components longevity (a proxy for health), education, and living standards (adjusted for income distribution) (see Table II.2, note 1) and HFI on civil and legal rights, freedom from torture and censorship, electoral and religious freedom, ethnic and gender egalitarianism, independent media, courts, and trade unions, and related indicators.

Chapter 12 discusses the reason for the success of Japan, ranked first in HDI, with a number of comparisons to the United States, ranked seventh among 160 countries.

Chapter 10 compares the development performance of the two most populated countries, India and China, which both have low figures of nominal GNP per capita. Because of high life expectancy (70) and literacy rate (68 percent), the HDI ranking of China (82) is medium compared to its low income ranking (133) and India's low HDI ranking (123). I compare the planning for resource use from booming exports by three oil exporters—Nigeria (129) and Indonesia (98) below, and neighboring West African countries Cameroon (119) and Nigeria in chapter 3. In contrast to these, the UN ranked human development high for another oil exporter, Malaysia (52), whose life expectancy was 70 years and literacy rate 74 percent. Among Afro-Asian LDCs with 15 or more million people, only the Republic of Korea (35) and Taiwan (not included) ranked higher, and only South Africa (57), Thailand (66), Democratic Republic of Korea (74), Sri Lanka (75), China, and the Philippines (84) are medium-ranking in HDI. Chapter 9 demonstrates how the economic policies of Pakistan (120) hurt East Bengal, which seceded in 1971 as Bangladesh (136). Chapters 4-6 outline sub-Saharan Africa's efforts at economic adjustment and reform to reduce its debt overhand and reverse its stagnation and inflation. Kenya, with a life expectancy of 60 years and an adult literacy rate of 65 percent, ranked 113th. All except two countries ranked 115th through 160th (last) were sub-Saharan African and South Asian. The latter included Nepal (145), Pakistan, India, and Bangladesh. Sizeable sub-Saharan countries included Ghana (120), Zaïre (124), Tanzania (127), Nigeria (129), Uganda (134), Ethiopia (141), and Sudan (143).

While human development is not complete without including freedom, existing measures of freedom (such as HFI) are too crude to incorporate in HDI. However, HDI and HFI are highly correlated, as political freedom unleashes creative energy favorable to development, while abundant resources facilitate fulfilling citizens' rights.

The UN ranked the United States thirteenth and Japan fifteenth (high freedom ranking) in HFI. The next sizeable Afro-Asian countries were South Korea (39), Thailand (41), India (42), Nigeria (44), Sri Lanka (47), and Ghana (50), with medium freedom rankings. For comparison, Brazil ranked 35th and Mexico 38th. Low rankings included the Philippines (53), Tanzania (54), Malaysia (55), Kenya (63), Bangladesh (69), North Korea (76), Indonesia (77), Viet Nam (78), Pakistan (79), Zaïre (80), South Africa (83), China (84), and Ethiopia (85), among 88 countries (UN Development Programme 1991). Chapter 10 shows how, in India, democratic since its 1947 independence except during emergency rule declared by Prime Minister Indira Gandhi, 1975-77, political opposition and media criticism compelled the federal government to address severe regional food deficits, while in authoritarian China, the regime continued disastrous food policies with little political feedback.

## OIL EXPORTERS AND IMPORTERS

The fourfold increase in oil prices over four months from 1973 to 1974 and subsequent increases in the 1970s greatly benefited oil-exporting countries but severely disrupted oil-importing countries. The 1980 commodity terms of trade (price index of exports divided by price index of imports) of Afro-Asian LDC (except Middle Eastern) oil exporters (Nigeria, Indonesia, Malaysia, and Cameroon) were 195 percent of 1973 levels while those of oil-importing Afro-Asia were only 85 percent of 1973.

The 1973 to 1974 oil price shock slowed economic growth and accelerated inflation more in Afro-Asian oil-importing countries than in DCs in the first two to three years. Petroleum accounted for almost one-half of the total energy supply of Afro-Asian LDCs countries in the 1970s. Producers used oil largely to meet basic energy requirements, with only a tiny fraction for powering private automobiles, air conditioning, and other consumer items. Furthermore the energy crisis also affected agricultural output as higher prices for petrochemicals contributed to sharp price increases for fertilizers and pesticides.

Developing countries imported 4.6 million barrels of oil per day in 1973 and 6.2 million barrels per day in 1980, but they paid $7 billion for petroleum imports in 1973 and $67 billion in 1980, almost a tenfold increase. The price per barrel (c.i.f.) rose from $4.20 in 1973 to $29.80 in 1980 (a sevenfold increase), and the real (inflation-adjusted) price increased by about three and one-third times (see Figure II.2).[4]

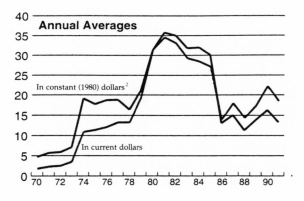

*Notes:* [1] Data 1984 are the unweighted average spot market price of Brent, Dubai, and Alaska North Slope crude oils representing light, medium, and heavier crude oils, respectively, in three different regions. Estimated average prices for earlier years are intended to be comparable with these data.

[2] The deflator used is the index of the export price of manufacturers of the industrial countries.

**Figure II.1.** World Crude Oil Price[1]
(In U.S. Dollars a barrel)

Despite the adverse immediate effect of the oil shock, the medium-run growth impact was less severe, since oil-importing Afro-Asia grew by 3.1 percent yearly from 1973 to 1980, less than oil-exporting Afro-Asia, 4.8 percent annually, but more than the DC yearly growth rate, 2.1 percent. The greater cost of the oil price hike was future debt service (interest and principal payments due in a given year on long-term debt) from the growth of LDC long-term debt, since LDCs were spurred to borrow funds at negative real interest rates (nomi.1al rates less than the inflation rate) from 1973 to 1975, but often had to roll over the debt, or borrow enough to cover debt service and imports, at positive world real rates of interest of 7-12 percent from 1982 to 1988. Oil-importing Afro-Asia's long-term external debt, which increased from $14.7 billion (1970) to $36.7 billion (1973) to $143.9 billion (1980) to $229.3 billion (1984) to $346.4 billion (1989), constrained 1980s' growth, sacrificed, along with other domestic goals of high employment, poverty reduction, and democratization, for external goals (see chapters 4 and 6 on Africa).

From 1980 to 1989, while real oil prices dropped 46 percent, oil-importing Afro-Asian growth was 2.1 percent and oil-exporting Afro-Asia 0.6 percent yearly. The 1989 terms of trade were 50 percent of 1980 (but 120 percent of 1973) for oil-exporting LDCs, and 88 percent of 1980 (and 75 percent of 1973) for oil-importing LDCs. Yet Afro-Asian oil importers, with a 1989 population of 2,812 million, had a GNP per capita of $430, compared to a 321 million population and $520 GNP per person for oil-exporting LDCs.[5]

## COMPARING NIGERIA AND INDONESIA

The oil boom of the 1970s proved a blessing for many oil-exporting countries but a curse for others. In 1976, Nigeria's Head of State General Olusegun Obasanjo, responding to political unrest and an overheated economy, pointed out that petroleum revenue was not a cure-all. "Though this country has great potential she is not yet a rich nation.... Our resources from oil are not enough to satisfy the yearnings, aspirations and genuine needs of our people, development and social services" (Rake 1976, 1263-65; and Nafziger 1983, 187).

Oil revenues increased average material welfare, widened employment opportunities, and increased policy options. But they also altered incentives, raised expectations, distorted and destabilized nonoil output, frequently in agriculture.

Oil-exporters Indonesia, with a 4.3-percent annual growth, and Nigeria, 0.9 percent (Table II.2), which both had more than 40 percent of pre-1973 GNP originating in agriculture, provide a revealing contrast. Nigeria's annual real growth from 1965 to 1973 was 5.3 percent compared to Indonesia's 2.3 percent, 1.2 percent to Indonesia's 6.1 percent, 1973 to 1980, and -4.8 percent to Indonesia's 4.8 percent, 1980 to 1987 (World Bank, *World Bank Atlas,* various issues).

While Indonesia's agricultural output increased 3.7 percent annually, 1973-1983, output in Nigeria declined 1.9 percent and exports 7.9 percent yearly over the same period. Agricultural imports as a share of total imports rose from 3 percent in the late 1960s to 7 percent in the early 1980s in Nigeria, while in Indonesia the share remained unchanged at about 1 percent.

Several differences in agricultural pricing and investment explain Indonesia's more favorable agricultural development. The real value of the naira appreciated substantially from 1970-1972 to 1982-1983, depreciating relative to the dollar only under pressure in 1986, while the Indonesia's rupiah real value increased much more slowly, and depreciated vis-é-vis the dollar, 1978-1983. Additionally, Indonesia invested a substantial amount of government funds in agriculture, especially rice, while less than 10 percent of the Nigerian plan's capital expenditures were in agriculture. The attempt by Nigeria, beginning in the mid 1980s, to increase incentives and investment in agriculture had little initial impact (World Bank 1986, 72). The country will require sustained policy changes to reverse the effects of years of neglect.

## POPULATION GROWTH

From 1950 to 1990, Afro-Asian LDC population grew at 2.1 percent per year, a rate faster than DCs or Afro-Asia at any other time in history. Improvements in food production, nutrition, transport, communication, personal hygiene, health, medical care, the use of insecticides, immunization programs, and drainage and reclamation of land occurred rapidly after World War II. As a result death rates decline. Average life expectancy in Afro-Asia increased from 31 years in the 1930s to 41 years in the 1950s, 48 years in the 1960s, 53 years in the 1970s, 60 years in the 1980s, and 61 in 1991. Couples usually reduce family size only after changes in values, aspirations, social structure, and child-rearing costs associated with a later period of economic, technical and educational development. Correspondingly, birth rates did not decline in Afro-Asia as a whole until the 1970s, and the burden of nonworking dependents, 0-14 years old, until the 1980s. High birth rates requires resources to be diverted to schools, food, health care, and social services for these dependents (Nafziger 1990, 58, 181-212; and Population Reference Bureau 1991).

## NOTES

1. For further criticisms of Weber's thesis, see Nafziger 1965, 187-204, reprinted as chapter 12 in Nafziger 1986, 261-95.

2. Even though capitalism originated in the modern West, much of what contributed to its rise originated in other civilizations. For example, much of its scientific and technical content came from the Middle East and India, the philosophical from ancient Greece, and the legal and political from ancient Greece and Rome.

3.   Much of this section is from Dillard 1967, 72-149; Dillard 1979, 69-76; and North and Thomas 1970, 1-17.

4.   C.i.f. includes the cost of insurance and freight in the price per barrel.

5.   World Bank, *World Development Report* (New York: Oxford University Press, 1978-1991); World Bank, *World Debt Tables* (Washington, D.C., 1971-1991); and International Monetary Fund, *World Economic Outlook* (Washington, D.C, 1980-1991).

When a country's terms of trade shift greatly, growth in GNP in constant price does not accurately reflect changes in purchasing power. The volume of imports that can be bought with a given export volume rises if the terms of trade increase and falls if they decline. There is no generally accepted way of adjusting for shifts in the terms of trade. The main point, however, is that the growth of oil importers is overstated and the growth of oil exporters is understated for the 1970s and vice versa for the 1980s. World Bank 1980b, 158-65.

# *Part II.*

*Development, Distribution
and Decentralization*

# Chapter III

# *Inequality in Africa*

Africans entered the last half of this century with high expectations. Ghana's Kwame Nkrumah prophesied in 1950 that with "self-government, we'll transform the Gold Coast into a paradise in ten years" (Killick 1978). But the annual real growth in GNP per person in the sub-Sahara through 1990 was virtually zero since 1965 (negative since 1980 and since 1986), compared to substantial positive growth (faster than DC growth) in LDCs generally during the same periods.

## RISING POVERTY AND MALNUTRITION

From 1965 to 1985 the percentage of people in poverty in sub-Saharan Africa rose.[1] Additionally, during that period, sub-Saharan Africa had the highest inequality of any world region except Latin America.

Even in the midst of Nigeria's 1970s' oil boom, the International Labour Office (1981) warned:

> Many Nigerians are worse off than before, especially in the rural areas and growing city slums. Even those with increased buying power speak of what they have lost—regular supplies of water, continuous electricity, telephones that worked, and the ability to walk or drive around without fear of road accidents and armed robbery.

Moreover, the yearly growth in food production per person, 1960-89, was 0.5 percent in the third world generally, but -0.9 percent in sub-Saharan Africa (Figure III.1), the only world region where calories, even if equally distributed, were below minimal nutritional standards in the 1980s (U.S. Department of Agriculture 1980). Illustrative of the enormity of the sub-Sahara's difference from other LDCs is that the sub-Sahara and India both produced 50 million tons of foodgrains in 1960, while India produced 150 million tons (after the Green Revolution and other farm technological improvements) and sub-Saharan Africa (with faster population growth) was still stuck at little more than 50 million tons in 1988 (Singer 1990, 178-81). While the roots of Africa's

47

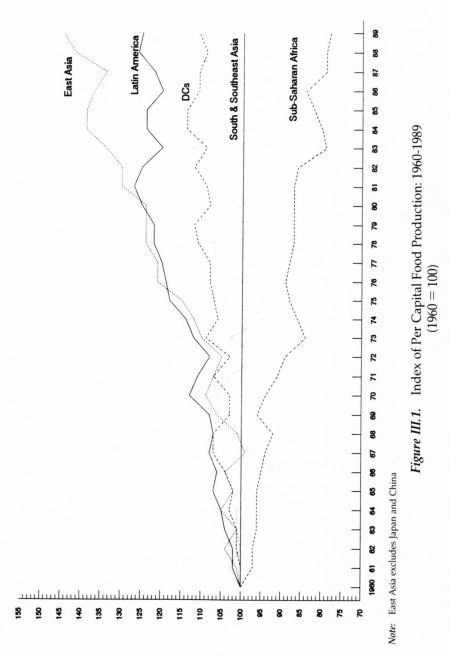

*Figure III.1.* Index of Per Capital Food Production: 1960-1989
(1960 = 100)

*Note:* East Asia excludes Japan and China

48

food crisis began during colonialism, the continuing crisis is due to African governments' neglect of agriculture.

The ECA's projection to 2008 envisions explosive population growth pressing on resources and social services. Maintaining past trends means degrading human dignity for most, rural population surviving on intolerable toil, disastrous land scarcity, and a worsening urban crisis, with more shanty towns, congested roads, unemployed, beggars, crime, and misery alongside the *few* unashamedly consuming conspicuously, shopping at national department stores filled with luxury imports. The consequences of extreme wealth and poverty would be social tensions threatening national sovereignty (ECA 1983).

## ELITES AND THE STATE

The rest of the chapter, which summarizes a larger study (Nafziger 1988), offers explanations for the high and growing inequality in Africa during the 1970s and early 1980s.

In Africa, shrinking economic pie slices and growing political consciousness added pressures to national leaders, whose response was usually not only anti-egalitarian but also anti-growth, hurting small farmers' incentives, taking peasant savings for government industry, building government enterprises beyond management capacity, and using these inefficient firms to give benefits to clients. Regime survival in a politically fragile system required marshaling elite support at the expense of economic growth. Spurring peasant production through market prices and exchange rates interfered with national leaders' ability to build political support, especially in cities.

African leaders advocated a socialist (actually statist) economic approach in the 1980 Lagos Plan of Action (OAU 1980). The Plan's emphasis on detailed state planning, large government firm expansion, heavy-industry development, and increased government intervention in peasant price-setting contributes to inequality and rural poverty. A major theme of this chapter is how the political elites used the state to pursue economic policies that supported their interests at the expense of Africa's poor and working classes.

## COLONIALISM AND NEOCOLONIALISM

African social stratification and political power shows some continuity from the precolonial to the (British and French) colonial to the contemporary period. Inequality was fossilized as colonial regimes protected cooperative native rulers against revolt from rivals or masses.

As colonial rule became expensive by the 1950s, farsighted administrators sought ways to maintain influence without incurring the costs of colonialism. The British and French emphasized policies to meet some demands of the elite-led nationalist movements (Africanizing jobs and African civil-service salaries and allowances comparable to Europeans), steps that eased the colonial burden and helped shape a postcolonial elite favorable to the former colonial power.

Neocolonialism requires that the interests of the political elites are allied to foreign governments (the United States, the United Kingdom, France, and South Africa) and capitalists which uphold their joint economic interests. Between 1960 and 1985, almost half the western foreign investment in Africa was in South Africa, supporting not only apartheid there but also contributing to neighboring countries' underdevelopment (Seidman and Makgetla 1980).

In 1986, the income per person of black South Africans was $590, roughly the same as sub-Saharan Africa as a whole ($530). Yet this low income for 23 million blacks ($1,470 for 3 million other nonwhites) appalls the world community when compared to the $7,400 income per person for the 5.5 million white South Africans, almost as high as Britain's (McGrath 1977; McGrath 1984).

## FOREIGN TRADE, INVESTMENT, AND DEBT

The overwhelming majority of African international trade is with rich countries. Africa is vulnerable to international price instability and decline because of dependence on primary product exports and high export concentration.

Roughly four-fifths of Africa's trade is handled by foreign-based multinational corporations (MNCs), which contribute to inequality. Foreign capital usually enters Africa only if political leaders, civil servants, and private middlemen are rewarded for facilitating the joint venture. Much of this reward is for unproductive activity and is paid for by tariffs, higher consumer prices, or subsidies from tax revenue, the burden of which falls mainly on workers and farmers. Additionally, MNCs tend to use technology designed for capital-abundant rich countries (ECA 1983a; Stewart 1974: 80-93).

The capitalists or government officials allied with foreign investors receive the lion's share of the income from high-tech processes. Also officials and intermediaries in Kenya, Malawi, and other countries depend critically on external aid for increasing income, dispensing patronage, and controlling state power.

Even though in 1987, only one of the top 20 LDC debtors was from sub-Saharan Africa, its debt was probably more burdensome than that for any other world region (World Bank 1990a, vol. 2). Africa's debt crisis has forced many countries to curtail poverty programs, even though much of the external borrowing was for projects to benefit or build patronage for a small elite.

# AFRICAN SOCIALISM

According to Nkrumah (1970), African socialism is a myth as its supporters neglect the fierce class "struggle between the oppressors and the oppressed." While class discrepancies were temporarily submerged during the struggle against colonialism, they returned with increased intensity in independent states embarking on socialist policies.

President Julius K. Nyerere's 1967 Arusha Declaration committed Tanzania to egalitarianism, self-reliance, and African socialism. Ten years later, he admitted that Tanzania had fallen far short of these goals, and had lower average standards of living and higher inequality than in 1967 (Nyerere 1977).

While "socialist" governments proclaimed the elimination of class privilege, nearly all (like the Soviet Union) produced domination by a political and bureaucratic class antagonistic to worker interests. And while African elites lacked centralized planning control, they usually had the power of "life and death" over an enterprise through taxes, subsidies, and access to foreign currency and essential inputs.

Class differences and income inequality do not vary much between African socialism and mixed capitalism. In both systems, the political and bureaucratic elites use the economic levers of the state to enlarge their size and prosperity.

# ELITE STABILITY AND INSTABILITY

Africa's meager economic base and weak business and middle classes resulted in some built-in contradictions. Rapid growth, with the rise of new classes, undermined the position of the existing ruling elites, while slow growth, with less to share with varying economic classes, threatened foreign capital, provided too few incentives for workers, or increased potential mass rebellion.

The smallness of savings and the political expectations and poverty of the African masses exerted revolutionary pressures. The demands from this radical consciousness were directed at the African ruling elites, who could not meet expectations under the existing economic system. Since their stagnating economies gave them little room for maneuvering, they resorted to increased repression to control the masses. But this increased tensions and forced the elites to depend more on foreign support.

In both precolonial and colonial periods, wealth and privilege helped transmit class standing from one generation to another. The sons of African elites were more likely to get jobs and education during colonialism. And during the late colonial and early independence periods, the African upper and middle classes, with greater control, became more self-perpetuating.

Class and ethnic identities cross-pressure African workers and peasants. Indeed elites, especially in Nigeria and Kenya, distribute benefits on an ethnic or regional basis. This distribution of benefits transfers potential hostility from class to ethnic discrepancies.

## AFRICANIZATION

Immediately after independence, African governments relentlessly pursued Africanization of their civil services, catapulting Africans overnight from relatively junior posts to positions of high responsibilities. In Nigeria, the number of federal public service posts occupied by Nigerian citizens increased from 15 percent of 358 on independence day (1 October 1960) to virtually all 4,066 by 1962. In Tanzania, the total established posts in the civil service rose from 65,708 to 295,353, 1966 to 1980, an increase more than three times as fast as economic growth (Adedeji 1981; Ogbuagu 1983, 241-66).

After civil services were Africanized, governments indigenized their national economies so that ruling elites and MNCs became partners, facilitating state capture of resources in the name of the people but for the primary benefit of the political and bureaucratic leadership. This Africanization often increased inequalities. Thus in the early 1970s Nigerianization became an instrument for a few civil servants, military rulers, business people, and professionals to amass considerable wealth through manipulating state power. Ironically, an indigenization policy designed partly to reduce foreign concentration created Nigerian oligopolies, especially among those with the wealth and influence to obtain capital and government loans to purchase foreign shares.

## EDUCATION AND CLASS REPRODUCTION

Africa has the lowest educational enrollment rates of any world region. A large majority of students are enrolled in public schools. State subsidies are substantial, as fees for public education recover only 6 percent of the cost of primary education, 11 percent of secondary education, and 2 percent of higher education (Tan 1985, 103-17).

As African elites took form during the late colonial and early independence periods, they used their wealth and position to get access to education to convey their high status to their children. Class lines began to solidify as the educated first generation read books with children, made sure they attended good schools, and provided tutors for entrance examinations.

Education in Africa increases inequality. In 1980, African children of white-collar families benefited greatly from educational subsidies, receiving 5-10 times as much benefit as farm children.

Primary education can be an exception, favorably affecting equality of opportunity. As primary schooling expands, children in rural areas, the poorest urban children, and girls have more chance to go to school. In general, public expenditures on primary education redistributes income toward the poor, who have larger families and almost no access to private schooling.

Improving income distribution calls for abolishing most subsidies, which increase with educational level. Higher education students are privileged, as the state concentrates its resources on a small number of individuals, primarily from privileged backgrounds, who will enjoy higher incomes than average during their active lives and could afford to reimburse the community later if they received loans rather than scholarships.

The system of allocating school places based on examination scores tends to favor the rich. Rich people can send children to better schools, spend more on books and private tutoring, and are better able to support repeating a year than poor people (World Bank 1980a; Jimenez 1986, 111-29; Mingat and Psacharopoulos 1985,35-38).

## URBAN BIAS

The most significant discrepancies in Africa are industry-agriculture differences in productivity, wider in Africa than other world regions. Industrial incomes in Africa are 4-9 times agricultural incomes, compared to 2-2.5 times in other developing countries. Despite plans proclaiming agriculture's priority, government allocates most resources to cities. African politicians respond to the more powerful and articulate urban dwellers. Thus, ruling elites divert farm land from growing millet and beans for hungry villagers to produce meat and milk for urban middle and upper classes (Lecaillon et al. 1984; Lipton 1977).

Most African states try to keep food prices low to satisfy urban workers and their employers (foreign and government enterprises). Urban unrest from increasing living costs sometimes contributes to governments losing power or even being overthrown. Insecure African ruling classes forgo policies promoting rural innovation and reduced urban-rural income gaps to insure political survival.

Urban policy biases among African governments include high industrial relative to farm prices; concentration of investment in industry; tax incentives and subsidies to industry but rarely to agriculture; tariff and quota protection for industry, which contributes to a cost-price squeeze and reduced incomes in agriculture; more spending for education, health care, and transport in urban areas; and low prices for foreign currency (thus reducing domestic currency receipts from agricultural exports and lowering the costs of industrial inputs).

Why does government pursue urban-oriented policies? State intervention in the market is an instrument of political control and assistance. Government and business pressure political elites for cheap food policies to keep wages down. Unrest by urban workers over erosion of their purchasing power has threatened numerous African governments. Real (inflation-adjusted) wage reductions in Nigeria (1964, 1974-75) and Ghana (1971) contributed to political unrest which precipitated military coups. Chief Obafemi Awolowo's Western Nigerian government, 1954-62, used agricultural export marketing board surpluses to fund industrial programs and build political support.

Farm market-clearing prices, whose benefits are distributed indiscriminately, erode urban political support and secure little support from the countryside. In comparison, project-based policies allow benefits to be selectively apportioned for maximum political advantage. Government makes it in the individual's interest to cooperate in programs harmful to the interest of producers generally.

Why do not rural dwellers organize to oppose anti-rural policies? First, they are politically weak and fear government reprisals. While poor peasants have little tactical power, rich ones have too much to lose from protest. Second, they have less costly options, selling in black markets, shifting resources to other commodities, or migrating to urban areas (Bates 1981; Acharya 1981, 109-47; Nafziger 1983, 75-92).

# NIGERIAN DISEASE

Roemer analyzes Dutch disease, named when the booming North Seas' gas export revenues in the 1970s appreciated the guilder, making Dutch industrial exports more costly in foreign currencies and increasing foreign competition and unemployment. Analogously the United States suffered from a similar disease from 1980 to 1984, experiencing a farm export crisis and deindustrialization from the decline of traditional U.S. export industries (automobiles, capital goods, high technology, railroad and farm equipment, paint, leather products, cotton fabrics, carpeting, electrical equipment and parts, and basic chemicals) during substantial capital inflows strengthening the dollar.

The pathology might better be called the Nigerian disease, a 1970s' economic distortion resulting from dependence on a single booming export commodity, petroleum. As in Roemer's three-sector model, growth in Nigeria's booming exports increased the foreign-exchange price, retarding other sectors' growth by reducing incentives to export other commodities and replace domestic goods for imports, and raising factor and input prices for the non-booming sectors. Moreover, labor moved from the lagging export and import-substitution sectors to the booming and nontradable sectors. Other ill effects of the export boom were relaxed fiscal discipline, increased capital-intensive projects, and wage dualism (Roemer 1985, 234-52; cf Findlay 1985, 218-33; Neary 1982, 825-48).

The contrast is instructive between West African oil-exporting neighbors Cameroon (3.7-percent annual growth) and Nigeria (0.9 percent), the only LDC to fall from the fast-growing group (4 percent annual growth or more), 1965 to 1975, to the slow-growing group (2 percent or less), 1975 to 1986. Nigeria's annual real growth from 1965 to 1975 was 7.0 percent compared to the Cameroon's 3.0 percent, while Nigerian growth from 1975 to 1986 was -2.5 percent yearly compared to Cameroon's 4.7 percent (*World Bank Atlas*, various issues).

Schatz (1978, 47) describes the period of Nigerian planning right after the quadrupling of world oil prices in 1973 to 1974 as euphoric planning.

> Projects involving huge sums were added hastily, with little investigation or appraisal. Issues of project interrelation and coordination were ignored in the belief that rapid economic growth would ensure the utility of whatever was undertaken. Economic reasoning gave way before economic enthusiasm. Problems of executive capacity (the ability to carry out the Plan) were ignored.

The use of state levers by Nigeria's insecure military or civilian political elites (turning over frequently from coups), civil servants, and intermediaries for foreign capital, not to support capitalist production but to further their own private interests (substantially purchasing goods from, and transferring money to, foreign countries), was labeled pirate capitalism by Schatz (1984, 45-57).

Cameroon, which began oil production off its west coast in 1978, avoided much of the Nigerian syndrome. While Cameroon's petroleum output was only one-tenth of Nigeria's, its potential for economic distortion was as great, since most of its export earnings were also from oil and its population was about one-tenth of Nigeria's. But in the 1970s, Cameroon real domestic currency depreciation (inflation-adjusted decline of the CFA franc relative to the U.S. dollar), compared to the naira's real appreciation, made Cameroon's agricultural exports price competitive while Nigeria's traditional exports fell precipitously—cocoa from 24.5 percent of total exports in 1968 to 4.1 percent in 1979, palm kernels from 18.0 percent to 0.1 percent, rubber from 3.0 percent to 0.1 percent, and groundnuts from 18.0 percent, groundnut oil and cake from 6.8 percent, and raw cotton from 1.6 percent, all to 0.0 percent. All these commodities' export values (in constant naira prices) also fell. In fact the aggregate index of the volume of output of Nigerian agricultural export commodities declined from 100 to 1968 to 50.1 in 1978. Nigeria's agricultural exports as a percentage of total LDC agricultural exports declined during the oil boom, falling 5.7 percent annually from 1965 to 1983 (World Bank 1986: 72; Nafziger 1983, 152-53; and Collier 1983, 191-217). (Chapter XI points out that depreciation of the Japanese yen spurred exports in the late nineteenth-century.)

Roemer emphasizes that government can minimize the negative effects of the booming export pathology by investing in the lagging, traded goods sector before the natural resource is exhausted, so the rest of the economy can capture the potential benefits of the boom. The Cameroon government planned better than the Nigerian government, accumulating substantial foreign exchange reserves abroad and avoiding some of the painful adjustments of the 1980s' oil price fall. Moreover Cameroon used much of its oil revenues for manufacturing and agriculture, including maintaining coffee and cocoa producer prices despite softening world prices (Nafziger 1988, 152-59; and Benjamin and Devarajan 1986, 161-88).

The Nigerian disease from the oil boom of the 1970s may seem a mild case of influenza for Nigeria, Mexico, Venezuela, and Iran compared to the reverse disease from the oil bust of the 1980s. For a top Nigerian economic official in 1988, striking it rich on oil in the 1970s was "like a man who wins a lottery and builds a castle. He can't maintain it, and then has to borrow to move out" (F. Lewis 1988, 7. See Evans 1986, 10-13, on reverse Dutch diseases from depressed primary-product prices). Dependence on one or two exports makes these countries especially vulnerable to external price shocks. In the 1980s, reverse Nigerian disease and declining export relative to import prices reduced Nigeria's inequality because the real incomes of elites, business people, middle classes, and urban workers *fell faster than* those of peasants, day laborers, and informal sector workers, not because of egalitarian policies.

# CONCLUSION

Implementing reform and accelerating economic growth depends on changing the composition of the ruling elite. African economic stagnation and income inequality are interconnected, linked to a ruling class whose affluence and political survival are threatened by policies promoting decentralized economic decision-making, increased competition, redistribution to the underprivileged, and narrowing urban-rural incomes. The ruling-class use of the state to transfer resources from peasants, small farmers, unskilled workers, and the poor to parastatal managers, civil servants, intermediaries, farm estate owners, large commercial farmers, and other members of the elite reduces both growth and equality. While this poverty and exploitation of the African majority exerts revolutionary pressures, the ruling class can increase repression and foreign support to maintain control. Moreover, the economically disadvantaged are rarely united since their interests vary; and in most instances, the ruling class can usually reward potentially restive groups who cooperate with it and thus remain in control. Even overthrowing this class merely ushers in another privileged elite rather than workers and peasants, who lack the strength and skill to win control of the state.

Africa is not capable of using comprehensive planning to redistribute income and reduce poverty, as it lacks the strong state and skilled administration needed to manage socialist industry. Indeed African socialism, initiated by a ruling class rather than through revolutionary conflict, is really statism. Government enterprises, used to enrich the political elite and its clients, are plagued by overcapacity, high capital-labor ratios, and inefficiency. A state bureaucracy collectivizing an agriculture which barely produces subsistence reduces farm living standards by acquiring resources for its own use, while lowering productivity through severing the link between individual effort and income. Tanzania's state elite's authoritarian approach in managing collective and cooperative agriculture in the late 1960s and 1970s resulted in farm output declines. In Africa, the state is the major focus for class struggle by the working class against the state bourgeoisie and their allies.

The role of the African state ruling class is not consistent with Huntington's view (1968) of the state as manager of the conflict and above clashes by various special and parochial interests within society. Indeed changing the anti-growth, anti-egalitarian interests of most of Africa's state bourgeoisie requires higher levels of popular mobilization and mass participation in politics, the opposite of Huntington's prescription. (Nafziger 1983, 7-9, 79, 213-15 elaborates).

The nationalist movement for independence of African states was class-based, with workers and farmers uniting under bourgeois leadership to struggle against the colonial power for independence. Most African states, who viewed organized social forces outside government control as potential threats, assumed power over the labor unions. Yet sometimes, as in Nigeria in May 1981, labor struck or protested against government control.

Leaders of the major South African black trade union organizations, the Congress of South African Trade Unions (COSATU), indicated to the African National Congress they will not make the same mistake labor did in other parts of Africa during the struggle for national liberation. They are determined that labor will not lose its independence to the African state bourgeoisie in a democratic South Africa.

Agrarian leadership for change will not come from the most downtrodden or the well established, but from small farm holders and middle peasants, who have tactical power, a secure land holding, and some education. But rural-based groups are not capable of taking power by themselves, and need to form coalitions with labor leaders, students, intellectuals, civil servants, politicians, the military, women's groups, religious communities, and aggrieved ethnic groups who stress redistribution and growth. In Africa, reducing poverty and income inequality requires widening political participation as well as economic control.

# NOTES

1. In 1991, the sub-Sahara, with a population of 557 million, comprised 82 percent of Africa's population, which included 120 million in Arabic Northern Africa (Population Reference Bureau 1991).

# Chapter IV

# *The Debt Crisis in Africa*

Sub-Saharan Africa suffered both from an unfavorable international environment (declining terms of trade, reduced aid and credit, and higher real interest rates) and from government (exchange-rate, import-substitution, foreign-investment, tariff, pricing, and technology) policies that worsened stagnation and international deficits in the 1980s and 1990s. The economic crisis deepened in the 1980s, despite far-reaching African reforms. Economies such as the sub-Sahara that fail to grow are more likely to encounter or prolong external debt crises.

## THE U.S. BANKERS' PERSPECTIVE

The LDC debt crisis has been a dominant factor in relations between DCs and LDCs since 1982. During the 1980s and early 1990s, U.S. commercial banks were vulnerable to default by LDCs, so that a complete writeoff would have wiped out many banks. LDC debts to U. S. banks as a percentage of their capital grew from 110 percent in 1978 to 154 percent in 1982, before falling to 114 percent in 1986 to 63 percent in 1988. In response to nonperforming LDC loans and petrodollar shrinkage from low world oil prices, U. S. banks reduced their loans to non-Organization of Petroleum Exporting Countries developing countries from $120.6 billion in 1982 to $117.6 billion in 1984 to $100.2 billion in 1986, and after 1988 did not plan to resume 1982 lending levels without major loan restructuring. From 1984 to 1988, net commercial bank lending by Japan was double that of the U. S., the world's second-ranking lender (Huizinga 1989, 129-40).

U. S. bank exposure to LDC foreign debt declined in the mid 1980s from loan writeoffs, writedowns, asset sales, and reduced LDC lending. In 1988, Latin American, Philippine, and Polish loans held by U.S. banks sold at a 40-70 percent discount on the second-hand market, indicating market expectation of partial default. Secondary market prices of bank debts to heavily indebted countries ranged from 4 percent for Peru, 6 percent for Côte d'Ivoire, and 24 percent for Nigeria to 64 percent for Chile (Rogoff 1990, 4).

# THE LDC PERSPECTIVE AND DC INTERDEPENDENCE

From 1970 to 1980, LDC total external debt increased from $67.0 billion to $572.2 billion, an eightfold increase, a harbinger of debt-servicing problems of the 1980s; in 1990, total debt was $1220.9 billion. Debt-payment problems are portended by such maladies as arrears on interest and then principal, International Monetary Fund (IMF) borrowing beyond the country's initial contribution of convertible currency, and rescheduling loans. The world press focused on the LDC debt crisis in 1981, when Poland could not meet its obligations to European banks, and in August 1982, when Mexico, facing rapidly falling oil export prices, announced its inability to pay its external debt obligations to banks.

By June 1984, the Group of 7 industrialized countries agreed to resolve debt case by case. Beginning in 1985, several LDCs renegotiated foreign debts through multilateral agreements with official creditor groups, the Paris Club, or with commercial banks, lengthening or modifying repayment terms. In October 1985, U. S. Secretary of the Treasury James Baker announced a plan for expanded lending to middle-income countries in financial trouble (emphasizing Japanese, multilateral-agency, and commercial-bank creditors) rather than debt reduction or loans to low-income sub-Sahara, India, and Bangladesh.

DC banks improved their financial position in the late 1980s; DC governments were less worried debt repudiation would bankrupt commercial banks and threaten banking stability. The main focus then became the fall in living standards of LDCs, where external debt was $937 billion in 1985, increasing to $1135-1155 billion for each of the years 1987-1989. Living standards declined in several indebted countries, especially Latin America, where external debt exceeded $400 million in 1985, increasing to $422 million in 1989, and sub-Saharan Africa, where debt increased steadily from $97 million in 1985 to $147 million in 1989 (World Bank 1990a, First Supplement, p. 1).

Sub-Saharan Africa's debt overhang, without new money or debt reduction, dampened investment and adjustment. African countries, with years of austerity and stagnation, could not afford to reduce spending to effect an external transfer. Large future repayments have acted as a tax on investment. Paying back the debt often meant slowing economic growth to avoid an import surplus (Claessens and Diwan 1989, 213-25). Real GNP per capita fell 3.5 percent yearly in low-income indebted sub-Saharan countries and 0.9 percent in highly-indebted middle-income countries, 1980-88, compared to substantial positive growth rates in other LDCs during the same period.

In early 1987, Nigeria and Zambia imposed a ceiling on the percentage of exports they would pay for debt servicing, and Côte d'Ivoire introduced a debt moratorium to draw attention to its plight. At a meeting of leaders of debtor nations in late 1987, Argentine President Raúl Alfonsin indicated the west must recognize how "current economic conditions impede our development and condemn us to backwardness. We cannot accept that the south pay for the disequilibrium of the north." (Truell 1990, A3; Campbell and Loxley 1989, 8).

The debt problem emerged earlier in Africa than in Latin America. Beginning with Zaïre in 1976, 10 low-income sub-Saharan countries rescheduled official debt claims 19 times and commercial bank claims five times before the first Latin American rescheduling in 1982. In the 1980s and early 1990s, producers in industrialized countries, seeing how slow third-world growth hindered export expansion, joined bankers in pressing Washington, other DC capitals, and international agencies to resolve LDC debt, but the primary focus was the debt problem of middle-income Latin America, whose crisis hurt western and Japanese exports much more than the sub-Sahara's.

External debt in sub-Saharan Africa was small compared to other third-world regions. In the sub-Sahara in 1985-87, only Nigeria and Côte d'Ivoire were among U. S. Secretary of the Treasury James A. Baker, III's 17 severely indebted (all middle income) countries. Some 85 percent of the sub-Saharan debt was owed to official creditors. Still commercial bank claims were a significant problem in some low-income sub-Saharan countries. Indeed the smallness of the 1990 debt of the sub-Sahara, $174 billion (14 percent of third-world debt), compared to Latin America's $431 billion (34 percent) or Asia's $350 billion (27 percent), reflected its low income and poor credit rating, as debt to GNP in the sub-Sahara was higher than for any world region. Furthermore, *actual* debt service (interest and principal payments due in a given year on long-term debt) in the sub-Sahara was 8 percent of GNP and 24 percent of export earnings in 1990, far more than the minimal burden (3 percent of GNP and 15 percent of exports) the depressed region can bear. However, since *actual* debt service was less than 40 percent of *scheduled* debt payment, the latter figure was 22 percent of GNP and 65 percent of export earnings! (World Bank 1990a, vols. 1 2; and Mistry 1991, 3, 36).

The debt overhang limited the sub-Sahara's imports, as their volume, which grew 2.4 percent per annum, 1971-81, and dropped 2.7 percent yearly, 1981-86, increased only 0.6 percent annually, 1986-90. The purchasing power of the sub-Sahara's exports (the value index of exports divided by the price index of imports) fell by 17 percent, 1984-1990.

The sub-Sahara's debt overhang, without new money or debt reduction, restrained investment and adjustment. African countries, with years of austerity and stagnation, could not afford to reduce spending to effect an external transfer. Large future repayments acted as a tax on investment. Paying back debt often meant slowing economic growth to avoid an import surplus.

The rich countries' interest is broader than bankers' and exporters' profits. DCs have motives of humanitarianism and maintaining a stable, global political system. The United States and other OECD countries want an international order that avoids war, widespread hunger, resource depletion, and financial collapse. Aid helps to build a stable world order. By the late 1980s, multilateral agencies and DCs began expressing concern about the adverse effect of Africa's debt on development and democracy.

## THE WORLD BANK-IMF APPROACH

For the World Bank and IMF, fraternal twins established in Bretton Woods in 1944, Africa's economic crisis during the late 1970s and 1980s resulted from a failure of economic management. Yet what appeared to be policy mistakes and mismanagement was actually strategies pursued in the interest of Sub-Saharan elites, but which were not sustainable in the long run. Without debt rescheduling, chronic external deficits and debt overhang require economic adjustment (structural adjustment, macroeconomic stabilization, or economic reform), imposed domestically or (usually) by the IMF or World Bank.

In 1979-81, the World Bank, in response to increased LDC debt from the second oil price shock of the decade, changed from project loans to structural adjustment loans (SALs), policy-based and quick disbursing loans for coping with external balances. The Bank stressed that in low-income sub-Saharan Africa, where all countries have undertaken Bank/Fund adjustment, the supply response to lending is slow because of "inadequate infrastructure, poorly developed markets, rudimentary industrial sectors, and managerial weaknesses in the public and private sector." Structural adjustment (SA) indicates changes in relative prices and institutions to make the economy more efficient, more flexible, and better able to use resources for sustainable long-term growth. SA overlaps with stabilization, which refers to remedying an acute internal (inflation, high unemployment) or external imbalance. Structural adjustment loans (SALs) and sectoral adjustment loans (SECALs) provide support for specific policy reforms, not being linked to specific investment programs, and furnish a basis for Bank discussion with the recipient on its development policy. SALs contained macroeconomic policy understandings and sectoral reforms, while SECALs emphasized trade, agricultural, industrial, public enterprise, financial, energy, educational, or other sectoral reforms. During the 1980s, SALs and SECALs became increasingly important in the Bank's operation, accounting for $19.9 billion, 24.1 percent of 1988 lending.

The IMF was involved in assisting LDC stabilization programs throughout the 1980s and early 1990s, but also included structural adjustment programs (SAPs) in the late 1980s. Bank/Fund lending to avert balance-of-payments crises was usually linked to reducing social (often anti-poverty) programs, decontrolling (especially agricultural) price, privatizing state-owned enterprises, devaluing currency, and opening the economy to foreign investment and trade. Donor governments, multilateral agencies, and commercial banks insisted SALs be in place before debt rescheduling, new lending, or aid expansion. The restrictions on macroeconomic and exchange-rate policies indicated to Nyerere that the Bank and Fund have "usurped the role of 'finance minister of the Third World'" (Mills 1989, 7-9).

The Economist Intelligence Unit (1986, 17-18) characterized the World Bank/IMF position in the following way:

> During the crisis decision-making process, it was determined that the developing countries were suffering from a short-term liquidity as opposed to a long-term solvency crisis, i.e., they needed to realign their spending habits with their shrunken earnings potential. Once this realignment took place balance would be restored and these countries would be able to return to the capital markets.

Since 1979-80, virtually all sub-Saharan countries have undertaken Bank/Fund adjustment. Indeed sub-Saharan economic policy making in the 1980s and early 1990s was primarily shaped by conditions of Bank/Fund loans of last resort in return for requiring adjustment and reform to reduce the external deficit and ameliorate the debt crisis. Some African elites allied with the Bank/Fund, supporting liberalization and becoming (with their accomplices and clients) the emerging economically dominant group, the nouveau riche (Kiondo 1992, 41-45). Bank/Fund cooperation also enabled elites to protect vested interests from threats by reform and its new rules. But declining GNP pie slices meant adjustment came disproportionately at the expense of poverty programs, wages, employment, and public services for working and peasant classes, who received little benefit from the borrowing, rather than the ruling elites and upper classes whose spending had contributed to the external crisis. The popular classes opposed the economic liberalism of the Bretton Woods twins, whose publications emphasized longer-term structural adjustment but whose programs, under constant monitoring, usually carried out demand reduction. To control discussion and opposition, regimes undergoing economic reform in Nigeria, Ghana, the Sudan, Kenya, Malawi, and Tanzania (to say nothing of Liberia and Zaïre) arrested, banned, jailed, deported, and (in some instances even) killed dissenting intellectuals, students, and journalists.

Klein (1991) argues the Bank and Fund, "ideologues of the new economic orthodoxy,... may doom democracies" and make "a bad economic situation worse." The Committee for Academic Freedom in Africa (CAFA) (1991, 2-12), which contends "the most frequent violations of academic rights occur when African governments implement World Bank and IMF policies and meet the protest they generate," even states the Bank's "policy [emphasizing educational cost reduction] is unequivocally exterminist." UNICEF (1985, 21) expresses the view of advocates for the African poor that the Bank/Fund adjustment of the 1980s exacerbated the economic crisis rather than ameliorating it:

> The common aim of these [economic adjustment] measures is to improve the balance of payments, repay debts and reduce inflation. Important national objectives—such as expanding and protecting employment, ensuring a minimum income for households and providing basic public services—have become secondary. Ironically, the result has often been an aggravation of the economic crisis and a parallel human crisis as unemployment rises, incomes of the most vulnerable groups fall, import-dependent industries cut production, public services are curtailed and public discontent and political instability grow.

Africa's economic distress is worsened by depending on the financial support and program strategies of the Bank/Fund and DC donors, who usually coordinate policies on debt and adjustment. Yet I argue, contrary to Klein and CAFA, ruling elites in Africa, who benefit at the expense of the majority of its population, bear much blame for Africa's continuously subordinate relationship to the Bank, the Fund, and the world economic system.

## THE UNICEF CRITIQUE

UNICEF found from 1980 to 1985, during a period of negative growth resulting from external debt limiting social spending, child welfare deteriorated in most of the sub-Sahara; that is, infant mortality rates, child death rates, child malnutrition rates, primary-school dropout rates, illiteracy rates, and non-immunization rates all increased. The fall in birth weight occurring throughout the sub-Sahara also indicated declining welfare. In response, UNICEF advocated the World Bank and IMF emphasize "adjustment with a human face," including restoring growth while protecting the most vulnerable groups, and growth-oriented adjustment implying expansionary monetary and fiscal policies and Bank/Fund loans sufficient to avoid a depressed economy (Cornia, Jolly, and Stewart 1987, 2 vols.; UNICEF 1989).

## THE ECA'S ALTERNATIVE FRAMEWORK

The Lagos Plan of Action, an ECA recommendation adopted by the Organisation of African Unity 28-29 April 1980, stressed a "socialist" (actually statist) approach consisting of comprehensive planning, large parastatal firm expansion, capital-goods and heavy-industry development, increased state intervention in peasant price-setting, and an introverted development strategy. After the Lagos Plan was adopted, the decade of the 1980s was characterized by continuing reductions in food production, a disintegration of the physical infrastructure of the 1960s resulting from poor maintenance and a lack of renovation, and a deterioration in education, health, sanitation, housing, potable water, social services, and welfare, with particularly adverse effect on the most vulnerable groups. While more than 30 countries adopted Bank/Fund structural adjustment programs, few programs contributed to Africa's long-term development objectives, as orthodox financial, credit, exchange-rate, and trade prescriptions had little validity in Africa's poorly structured economies.

In the late 1980s, the ECA searched for an African alternative to SAPs. ECA recognized rescheduling debt in the early to mid 1980s merely postponed debt service payments without reducing the debt's present value. Accordingly, in 1987 ECA's Abuja (Nigeria) statement addressed debt relief, calling for lower interest rates on existing debts, longer repayment and grace periods, conversion of bilateral debts into grants for low-income countries undertaking structural adjustment, repayment of debt in local currency, and conversion of debt into equity.

A series of meetings in early 1989 with senior officials of central banks and ministries of finance and economic planning culminated with the adoption of the African Alternative Framework to Structural Adjustment Programmes for Socio-Economic Recovery and Transformation (AAF-SAP) by ministers of finance and economic planning in Addis Ababa 10 April 1989. AAF-SAP's main thrusts were integrating SAPs and long-term development, designing programs for the characteristics of specific countries, considering human dimensions, democratic decision-making and planning, and inter-country cooperation in planning, implementing, and monitoring national programs.

ECA objected to the World Bank's and IMF's adjustment programs emphasizing deregulating prices, devaluing domestic currency, liberalizing trade and payments, promoting domestic savings, restricting the money supply, reducing government spending, and privatizing production. These programs, ECA argued, fail in economies like Africa with a fragile and rigid production structure not responsive to market forces. Africa's rigidities have resulted in drastic cuts in domestic spending which retard structural adjustment. Indeed the ECA (1989:24) pointed out

> The reduction in public expenditures on education ... necessitated by stabilization and structural investment programmes, has meant a reversal of the process, initiated in the early 1960s, of heavy investment in human resources development ... Today, per capita expenditure on education in Africa is not only the lowest in the world but is also declining.... Thus, Africa may begin the next millennium with a greater proportion of its population being illiterate and unskilled than it did at the beginning of the post-independence era in the 1960s.... All indications are to the effect that structural adjustment programmes are not achieving their objectives.

Empirical studies analyzing the impact of IMF/Bank adjustment programs, while mixed, question whether adjustment programs achieve their goals. Loxley finds little evidence that IMF programs restored growth, bank loans and external balance; Gylfason that the economic performance of LDCs signing IMF standby agreements was not significantly better than other LDCs; King and Robinson that reschedulers attained slower export and GNP growths than non-reschedulers; and Stewart no difference between the fall in GNP per capita between countries undergoing strong and weak Bank/Fund adjustment programs.

ECA called for a holistic alternative to structural adjustment policies, with an emphasis on increased growth enabling an enhanced long-run capacity to adjust, which will aid a socioeconomic transformation facilitating African internal and external balances (Loxley 1986, 96-103; Gylfason 1987, King and Robinson 1989, 110-15; and Stewart 1990, 33-34).

While a 1989 World Bank report perceives "signs of a turnaround" in sub-Saharan Africa, with countries adopting strong SAPs improving markedly, ECA's Adedeji argued "it is only by appreciating the reality—sometimes the bitter reality—that the rest of the international community can continue to rally round with support." It is wrong, he contends, "to portray the economic situation currently prevailing in Africa in rosy terms, to minimize the impact of an adverse external environment, and to depict the effects of structural adjustment programs as having been always positive." Even World Bank economist Ramgopal Agarwala admits it is "time to recognize that we've all failed" in Africa and that new strategies beyond structural adjustment lending are desperately needed (ECA 1987; ECA 1989; and Harsch 1989: 47-50).

## OTHER CRITICISMS OF THE WORLD BANK-IMF APPROACH

Adjustment policies generally shifted internal relative prices from nontradable to tradable goods, promoting exports and "efficient" import substitution. In effect, these policies shifted purchasing power from urban to rural areas, consumption to investment, and labor to capital. Conditions attached to IMF credits provoked urban mass discontent, as in Nigeria's anti-SA "riots" in May-June 1989 (Kahler 1989).

Critics, supported by a commission of 20 diplomats from five continents chaired by former West German Chancellor Willy Brandt, charge the IMF presumes international payments problems can be solved only by reducing social programs, cutting subsidies, depreciating currency, and privatizing public enterprise, similar to a program where Togo relinquished policy discretion in 1988. According to the Brandt report, the Fund's insistence on drastic measures in short time periods imposes unnecessary burdens on low-income countries that reduce basic-needs attainment and may result in the downfall of the existing government. These critics argue the IMF should concentrate on results rather than means (Independent Commission on International Development Issues 1980).

IMF leverage to persuade African austerity in the face of internal political opposition was less in the 1980s than in the 1970s, partly because of the drying up of special funds beyond direct IMF credits for several years in the mid 1980s.

Yet the World Bank's adjustment loans consolidated IMF conditionality in the 1980s. The IMF became gatekeeper for the international financial system, as an IMF standby agreement served as a necessary condition for Bank ALs and commercial bank negotiation. Nyerere contends: "When we reject IMF conditions we hear the threatening whisper; 'Without accepting our conditions you will not get any money, and you will get no other money' " (Nyerere 1986, 8-9). Reducing the linkage between Fund/Bank agreements and official and commercial creditors in Africa, as discussed by the IMF and Bank in the early 1990s, would increase Africa's options.

Sub-Saharan countries resist Bank/Fund adjustment programs because of genuine doubts they will work, fear that the Bank/Fund has a narrow concept of structural adjustment, and the perception that vested interests will resist change. The reasons adjustment programs rarely work are because of a unilateral and doctrinaire design, insufficient coordination between donors and funding organizations, a lack of adaptation of programs to local goals, and a disregard of how volatile international terms of trade can sabotage the adjustment process.

Still the question for an LDC with a major debt problem is not whether to adjust but how to adjust—on their own or with IMF, World Bank, or bilateral assistance and conditions.

## MAJOR LDC DEBTORS

Brazil, Mexico, and Argentina were the three leading LDC debtors in the 1980s, with 1989 debts of $111 billion, $96 billion, and $65 billion respectively (Table 3), accounting for 65 percent of 1989 LDC debt to commercial banks. Moreover, 66 percent of the three countries' external debt was held by commercial banks. Twenty of 27 sub-Saharan African countries listed in Table IV.2 were low-income countries in 1989 compared to only five of the 30 Asian-Latin debtors in Table IV.1.

## INDICATORS OF DEBT

Sub-Saharan Africa's debt comprised 13 percent of 1989 total LDC debt compared to Latin America's 37 percent. The LDC debt-service ratio, figured by dividing interest and principal payments due by the exports of goods and services in a given year, increased from 9 percent in 1970 to 13 percent in 1979 to 18 percent in 1983 to 34 percent in 1987, before decreasing to 27 percent in 1989. This 1987 ratio was 49 percent in Latin America ($89.8 billion exports) and 24 percent in sub-Saharan Africa ($28.5 billion exports), a percentage twice what it would have been if its exports had grown at the rate of LDCs generally rather than falling 14 percent between 1980 and 1987.

***Table IV.1.*** Total External Public Debt (EDT), Less Developed Countries, 1980-1990 ($ billions) ($10 billion or more in 1989, ranked by 1989 debt)

| Year | 1980 | 1982 | 1985 | 1987 | 1989 | 1990 |
|---|---|---|---|---|---|---|
| Brazil | 70 | 93 | 106 | 124 | 111 | 116 |
| Mexico | 57 | 86 | 97 | 109 | 96 | 97 |
| Argentina | 27 | 44 | 51 | 58 | 65 | 61 |
| India | 21 | 27 | 41 | 55 | 63 | 70 |
| Indonesia | 21 | 26 | 37 | 52 | 53 | 68 |
| Egypt | 20 | 29 | 40 | 49 | 49 | 40 |
| China | 5 | 9 | 17 | 35 | 45 | 52 |
| Poland | 0 | 0 | 33 | 43 | 43 | 49 |
| Turkey | 19 | 20 | 26 | 41 | 42 | 49 |
| Korea, Rep. of | 29 | 37 | 47 | 40 | 33 | 34 |
| Nigeria | 9 | 13 | 20 | 31 | 33 | 36 |
| Venezuela | 29 | 32 | 35 | 35 | 33 | 33 |
| Philippines | 17 | 25 | 27 | 30 | 29 | 30 |
| Algeria | 19 | 18 | 18 | 25 | 26 | 27 |
| Thailand | 8 | 12 | 18 | 21 | 23 | 26 |
| Morocco | 10 | 12 | 16 | 21 | 21 | 24 |
| Hungary | 10 | 10 | 14 | 20 | 21 | N.a. |
| Peru | 10 | 12 | 14 | 19 | 20 | 21 |
| Yugdoslavia | 18 | 20 | 22 | 22 | 20 | N.a. |
| Malaysia | 7 | 13 | 20 | 23 | 19 | 20 |
| Pakistan | 19 | 12 | 13 | 17 | 19 | 21 |
| Portugal | 10 | 14 | 17 | 18 | 18 | 20 |
| Chile | 12 | 17 | 20 | 22 | 18 | 19 |
| Colombia | 7 | 10 | 14 | 17 | 17 | 17 |
| Côte d'Ivoire | 6 | 8 | 10 | 14 | 15 | 18 |
| Sudan | 5 | 7 | 9 | 12 | 13 | 15 |
| Ecuador | 6 | 8 | 9 | 10 | 11 | 12 |
| Bangladesh | 4 | 5 | 7 | 10 | 10 | 12 |

*Note:* External public debt also includes government-guaranteed private debt.

N.a. = data not available

*Source:* World Bank, vol. 2, *Country Tables* 1990b; and World Bank, 2 vols. (1991b).
    The following countries, not listed in the World Bank source, had $10 billion or more EDT in 1987: Israel ($34 billion), Greece ($32 billion), Taiwan ($20 billion), Saudi Arabia ($17 billion), Iraq ($16 billion), and Cuba ($10 billion). Romania had $10 billion EDT in 1980 and 1982 but fell to less than $10 billion in subsequent years ($0.5 billion in 1989). OECD 1989: 79-213.

# THE BURDEN OF THE DEBT

The low-income sub-Sahara has been much less creditworthy than anticipated when the original hard loans were made. Its debt problem cannot be solved by marginal adjustments. Additional borrowings, if creditors were prepared to lend, would push future debt service payments to levels in excess of what the sub-Sahara has been able to meet in the past.

***Table IV.2.*** Total External Public Debt (EDT), Subsaharan Africa, 1980-1989 ($ billions) ($1 billion or more in 1989, ranked by 1989 debt)

| Year | 1980 | 1982 | 1985 | 1987 | 1989 |
|---|---|---|---|---|---|
| Nigeria | 9 | 13 | 20 | 31 | 33 |
| Côte d'Ivoire | 6 | 8 | 10 | 14 | 15 |
| Sudan | 5 | 7 | 9 | 12 | 13 |
| Zaïre | 5 | 5 | 6 | 8 | 9 |
| Zambia | 3 | 4 | 5 | 7 | 7 |
| Kenya | 4 | 4 | 4 | 6 | 6 |
| Tanzania | 3 | 3 | 4 | 5 | 5 |
| Cameroon | 3 | 3 | 3 | 4 | 5 |
| Mozambique | 0 | 0 | 3 | 4 | 5 |
| Congo | 1 | 2 | 3 | 4 | 4 |
| Senegal | 1 | 2 | 3 | 4 | 4 |
| Madagascar | 1 | 2 | 2 | 4 | 4 |
| Gabon | 2 | 1 | 1 | 3 | 3 |
| Ghana | 1 | 1 | 2 | 3 | 3 |
| Ethiopia | 1 | 1 | 2 | 3 | 3 |
| Zimbabwe | 1 | 2 | 2 | 3 | 3 |
| Guinea | 1 | 1 | 1 | 2 | 2 |
| Mali | 1 | 1 | 1 | 2 | 2 |
| Somalia | 1 | 1 | 2 | 2 | 2 |
| Mauritania | 1 | 1 | 2 | 2 | 2 |
| Uganda | 1 | 1 | 1 | 2 | 2 |
| Liberia | 1 | 1 | 1 | 2 | 2 |
| Niger | 1 | 1 | 1 | 2 | 2 |
| Malawi | 1 | 1 | 1 | 1 | 1 |
| Togo | 1 | 1 | 1 | 1 | 1 |
| Benin | 0 | 1 | 1 | 1 | 1 |
| Sierra Leone | 0 | 1 | 1 | 1 | 1 |

*Note:* External public debt also includes government-guaranteed private debt.
*Source:* World Bank, vol. 2, *Country Tables*, 1990b.
  Angola, not listed in the World Bank source, had $2 billion EDT in 1987. OECD 1989: 79-213.

Given World Bank assumptions of constant annual OECD real net transfers and 1 percent annual growth in real imports per capita (or 8 percent nominal annual import growth), 1988-95, donors have to increase grants from $5.5 billion in 1987 to $9.5 billion in 1995 for low-income Africa's nonconcessional debt-export ratio (330 percent) to remain constant (Humphreys and Underwood 1989: 45-65).

While only three of the twenty-eight major debtors were from sub-Saharan Africa, its 1989 external debt, only three-fourths of Brazil's and Mexico's total, was probably more burdensome than any other world region. By the end of 1986, two-thirds of the 45 countries under the IMF's African Department had credit outstanding averaging 134 percent of their quotas. In the 1970s and early to mid 1980s, the rulers of Nigeria, Zaïre (most principal and interest from 1971-1974 borrowing), and Ghana squandered their loan funds, sometimes expanding patronage for intermediaries and contractors so fast that they lost track of millions of dollars borrowed from abroad. The countries had to reschedule their debts—Ghana in 1974, after an abrupt decline in the prices of cocoa exports; Zaïre, in 1980-1987 after several years of depressed copper export prices; and Nigeria, in 1983 and 1986, after a prolonged oil-price slump. Compared to Asian-Latin countries, the three African countries have poorer credit ratings among commercial banks because of poor national economic management, as reflected in previous balance-of-payments crises, and a slow growth in output and exports.

## NET TRANSFERS

In sub-Saharan Africa, private debt-service obligations exceeded net transfers of capital by private creditors beginning in 1983, a reversal of the direction of private flows during the 20 years before. However, net private transfers rose from 1985 to 1987 (both negative), not from resumed lending but from falling debt-service payments. Even the IMF received net transfers from the sub-Sahara in 1988 and 1989, as repayment obligations exceeded new loans.

## A RISING BALANCE ON
## GOODS AND SERVICES DEFICIT

Exports minus imports of goods and services equal the international balance on goods and services. Sub-Saharan Africa, largely an importer of oil, experienced global price shocks in 1973-74, resulting in a deficit gradually increasing 1974-1979, falling in 1980, rising during the DC recession in the early 1980s, declining in the mid 1980s, and increasing slowly in the late 1980s.

In the late 1970s, aid (official development assistance) to sub-Saharan Africa fell in real terms, while commercial loans remained sparse, as African countries lacked the creditworthiness to receive many loans at bankers' standards. In the 1980s, donors increased the share of aid to the 41 least-developed countries, designated by the UN on the basis of low per capita income, low share of manufacturing in gross product, and low literacy rates. Since 21 of the 36 sub-Saharan African states are least developed, aid rose gradually during the early to mid 1980s while the trickle of commercial loans almost completely dried up in the late 1980s, although recovering again in 1989.

Sub-Saharan Africa's debt rose from $5 billion in 1970, $14 billion in 1976, $72 billion in 1982, $82 billion in 1984, and $116 billion in 1986 to $148 billion in 1988. The chronic and rising external deficit of sub-Saharan Africa required greater foreign borrowing, thus increasing future external debt. Indeed an

African ministry official commented in 1988 that most external funds Africans obtain are earmarked for paying debt, leaving little scope for adjustment with growth (Mills 1989, 9).

# STAGNATION, INEQUALITY, AND EXTERNAL IMBALANCE

The political survival of existing African political elites depends on their forming coalitions with senior civil servants, government administrators, managers of parastatal corporations, military officers, private capitalists, and other privileged economic interests that place a low priority on growth and equity, and that repress farm prices and foreign-exchange rates. Africa's plight—negative growth and growing poverty rates in the 1980s—contrasts to LDCs generally. When growth or foreign flows fall, African disadvantaged classes usually are hurt the most. While Africa's rulers incur debt partly to expand patronage, they respond to external pressures from debt crises by reducing social programs, especially for small farmers, workers, the unemployed, the sick, and the elderly.

# TRADE DEPENDENCE

Most of Africa's international trade was with DCs. In 1983, 83.3 percent of exports was to DCs, 4.8 percent to developed socialist countries, 11.3 percent to LDCs (3.4 percent to other African countries) and 0.6 percent not specified. The same year 74.2 percent of imports was from DCs, 7.8 percent to socialist, and 18.0 percent to LDCs (3.0 percent to other African countries) (ECA 1985).

Africa's vulnerability is worsened because of high export commodity concentration. The summation of all sub-Saharan African countries' three principal exports as a share of total export earnings was 79.1 percent in 1976-78, an increase from 60.6 percent in 1961. In 1985, six primary commodities accounted for more than 70 percent of sub-Saharan Africa's export earnings (Lancaster and Williamson 1986; Wangwe 1984, 1033-59).

Sub-Saharan Africa, disproportionately producing and exporting primary products, suffered from both fluctuating and declining prices of exports relative to imports (predominantly industrial goods). The sub-Sahara's commodity terms of trade (the price index of exports divided by the price index of imports) plummeted from 100 in 1970 to 77 in 1980 to 53 in 1990, a 47 percent reduction in 20 years! Indeed from 1985 through 1991, the sub-Saharan terms of trade declined every year, falling 34 percent (Figure IV.1). Export volume fell from 100 in 1970 to 86 in 1980, only recovering to 100 for the first time in 1990. Export purchasing power (or income terms of trade), the commodity terms of trade times export volume, dropped from 100 in 1970 to 66 in 1980 to 53

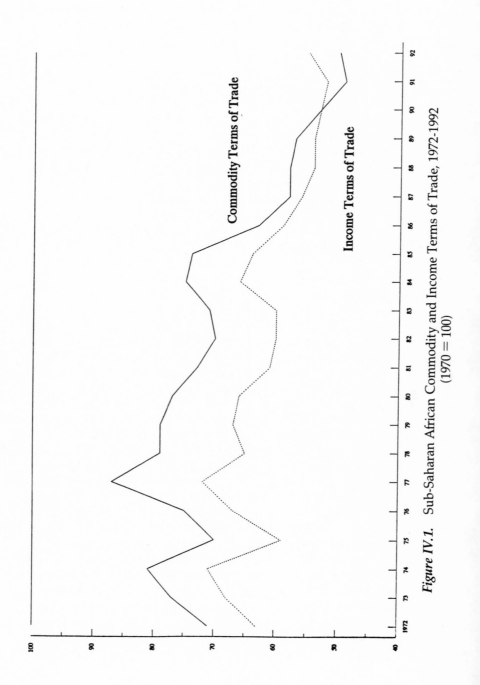

*Figure IV.1.* Sub-Saharan African Commodity and Income Terms of Trade, 1972-1992 (1970 = 100)

in 1990, indicating a reduction of 47 percent during the 20-year period. These declines contributed to a falling goods and services balance and a continually worsening external crisis during the 1980s (calculated from IMF, Oct. 1989, 98, 102; and IMF, Oct. 1990, 139, 141).

The sub-Sahara's international balance on goods, services, and transfers, negative since 1977, exceeded 20 percent of total exports after 1987. Net financial flows to Africa fell the late 1970s and the late 1980s. In 1990 and 1991, one-fourth of Africa's export earnings were for servicing debt (interest and principal) (IMF, *World Economic Outlook*, various issues). Exports were hurt further in the early 1990s by the reduced demand for Africa's primary products from the West's recession.

## OIL SHOCKS AND THEIR AFTERMATH

Sub-Saharan Africa, like U. S. business people and farmers, reacted to the input price hikes of 1973-75 by increased borrowing, lured by abundant funds and negative world real interest rates (the nominal rates of interest minus the inflation rate), which were -7 percent in 1973, -16 percent in 1974, and -5 percent in 1975. The average interest rate for fixed-interest loans (generally subsidized or long-term) rose from 4 percent (1970) to 6 percent (1981) to 7 percent (1986). During the period, 1971-1981, interest rates on floating-interest loans (primarily commercial) increased from 8 percent to 18 percent. The reductions of the average loan maturity from 20 to 16 years and the average grace period from 6 to 5 years from 1970 to 1986 also aggravated the problem of debt service (World Bank 1988b, 260-61; Husain and Diwan 1989, 205).

Additionally, from 1980 to 1985, at the peak of LDC debt expansion, loans at bankers' standards to LDCs fell from $47.1 billion to $28.9 billion. The irony for many LDCs is that commercial-bank debt they assumed in the 1970s to escape IMF discipline compelled them to seek IMF (or World Bank) lending in the 1980s in an even weaker bargaining position.

During the 1970s and early 1980s, many banks made loans so as not to lose business to competing banks. As IMF economist Nowzad (1990, 11-12) argues: "Herd behavior can generate its own momentum." One major lender reducing LDC loan exposure, followed by other banks, can precipitate a debt crisis that can become a self-fulfilling prophecy.

## PRIMARY-PRODUCT EXPORT GLUT

Real world prices for numerous commodities (including bauxite, uranium, cocoa, coffee, sugar, tea, groundnuts, and cotton) peaked in the mid or late 1970s. During the 1980s, the adjustment essential for an export surplus required translating government spending cuts into foreign-exchange earnings and competitive gains, usually necessitating reduced demand and wages, real currency depreciation, and increased unemployment, especially at a time when DC income and import demand growth slowed. Additionally, when many other LDCs go through the same adjustment process, the benefit to a given LDC is less.

Africa is caught in an export trap, as the growth of primary-product exports faces competition from other economies requiring similar expansion for adjustment. Moreover, DC protectionism limits the growth in the export of primary-product processing and light manufacturing in Africa.

Africa's exports were hurt by DC stagnation in the early 1980s and the early 1990s. Each 1 percent change in the DCs' business cycle index is associated with a 2.2 percent change in primary commodity prices, affecting Africa substantially, as 80 percent of their exports are primary goods (Wheeler 1984: 1-23).

## FOREIGN CAPITAL DEPENDENCE

Alliances between foreign capital and domestic political leaders, bureaucrats, and intermediaries are usually maintained even after indigenization decrees, as in Nigeria. The Nigerian government acquired majority equity holdings in the local petroleum extracting, refining, and distribution in the early 1970s, and promulgated the Nigerian Enterprises Promotion Decrees of 1972, 1977, and 1981, which shifted the majority of ownership in manufacturing from foreign to indigenous hands (Ogbuagu 1983, 241-66). But Nigeria's trade was still virtually all with capitalist DCs. In contrast to more diversified exports in the 1960s, petroleum comprised more than 80 percent of export value for the 1970s. Moreover, only 15-20 percent of the petroleum industry's total expenditure on goods and services was spent on locally produced items, which do not include most basic requirements like drilling rigs, platforms, heavy structures, underwater engineering systems, and other advanced technologies. Furthermore, MNC ownership was replaced by MNC-state joint firms, which enriched private middlemen and enlarged the patronage base for state officials, but did little to develop Nigerian administrative and technological skills for subsequent industrialization. Kenya, Tanzania, Zaïre, Malawi, and Côte d'Ivoire made even less progress than Nigeria in using indigenization requirements to reduce neocolonial dependency.

MNCs in Africa contribute to inequality in several ways. Foreign capital usually enters Africa only if political leaders, civil servants, and private middlemen are rewarded for facilitating the joint venture. Much of this reward is for economically unproductive activity, and is paid for by tariff and quota protection, higher consumer prices, or by subsidies from tax revenue. In Africa, where direct taxes like income taxes are not well-developed because of low literacy, poor accounting records, poor administration, and tax avoidance and evasion, the tax structure is usually regressive, meaning that people with lower incomes pay a higher percentage of income in taxes. Any subsidy to inefficiency falls disproportionately on low- to middle-income workers and farmers.

Moreover, MNC-associated enterprises tend to use technology designed for DCs, which have high wages and relatively abundant capital. Estimates based on capital resources available indicate that the appropriate capital stock per person in the United States is 45 times that of Nigeria (Stewart 1974). Additionally, African capital, foreign-exchange, and labor cost distortions that make the actual price of capital cheaper than its market rate encourage MNC high-technology, capital-intensive, and import-intensive processes rather than local modification or adaptation (Nafziger 1990: 226-35; and Langdon 1980).

## DEBT AND CAPITAL FLIGHT

Many African countries not only have difficulty acquiring new loans but also suffer from the flight of their citizens' private assets, sometimes as large as official external liabilities. Bankers may feel it futile to loan funds to LDCs if a large portion flows back through capital flight. Erbe estimates the propensity to flee from additional external debt, 1976-82, was 42 percent in Nigeria (the fifth ranking country in the world), 29 percent in Zambia (eleventh in the world), and 20 percent in Cameroon (fourteenth), the last percentage meaning that 20 cents from a dollar lent by foreign creditors leaves the country through capital flight! (Erbe 1985, 268-75; Cuddington 1986). This flight intensifies foreign-exchange shortages and damages the collective interest of the wealthy classes that buy foreign assets. Reversing capital flight will not eliminate the debt crisis but can reduce debt burdens and commercial bankers' justification for resisting increased exposure to debtor countries (Lessard and Williamson 1987; Williamson and Lessard 1987).

Erbe estimates President Mobutu Sese Seko's·1984 overseas wealth at $4-6 billion, invested in Swiss bank accounts and western real estate, enough to solve Zaïre's debt crisis. Indeed if Mobutu (and his allies) had not taken out of the country a large proportion of funds the Zaïrian government borrowed abroad, Zaïre might not have had a debt crisis (Pound 1990: A4; and Erbe 1985: 268-69).

## THE BAKER PLAN

In 1985, Peruvian President Alan Garcia Paaerez's UN speech posed the debt problem as "democracy or honoring debt." Some U.S. bankers and Treasury officials feared a debtors' cartel. In response, at the 8 October 1985 IMF-World Bank meeting in Seoul, Secretary of the Treasury Baker unveiled a U.S.

proposal that emphasized expanded lending rather than debt writeoffs and writedowns. The plan called for the Inter-American Development Bank, IMF credits and "new techniques" of "enhanced surveillance" (the inspiration for the IMF's beginning SALs in 1986-87), World Bank SALs, contributions from trade-surplus countries like Japan, and additional commercial bank lending, to help the highly indebted middle-income countries. But the Baker initiative did not address how to go from the initial lending package to subsequent inducements for voluntary capital flows. Moreover, the approach stressed saving U.S. banks at the expense of multilateral agencies and Japanese creditors, was vastly underfunded, and neglected the debt burden of the world's poorest countries, primarily from the Sub-Sahara.

## TORONTO TERMS

In 1988, the Toronto Group of Seven (G7) meeting of rich industrialized countries agreed to a "menu" of three options for rescheduling the debt of the world's poorest countries. The U.S. agreed to reschedule sub-Saharan African debt with longer maturities (a lesser writedown than for middle-income Egypt, a "debt for war" swap, and Poland in 1990), while allowing other G7 countries to apply interest rates at below bankers' standards. However, since Toronto terms applied only to debt maturing within 18 months of the consolidation period, the reduction in actual debt service was only $100 million annually in 1989-90. If creditors would have applied the same mix of options, 1989-2000, as they did in 1989-90, the total indebtedness of the low-income Sub-Sahara would have been reduced by just $2 billion, and the savings of principal and interest on debt would have been only 2.5 percent yearly (Mistry 1991, 16-18).

## THE BRADY PLAN

During the 1980's, commercial bank credit to LDCs continually fell. becoming negative, 1983-1989. In 1989, U. S. Secretary of the Treasury Nicholas Brady presented a plan for debt reduction on a voluntary and case-by-case basis, including Bank/Fund and other official support. The Brady Plan asked commercial banks to reduce their LDC exposure through voluntary debt writeoffs or writedowns where banks exchange debt for cash or bonds, and for debtor countries to convert or buy back debt on the secondary market (Huizinga 1989: 130-43).

## TRINIDAD TERMS

In September 1990, at the Commonwealth Conference in Trinidad, British Chancellor of the Exchequer John Major proposed these terms for low-income debt-distressed countries: (1) rescheduling of the entire stock of debt in one stroke instead of renegotiating maturities only as they fall due, (2) increasing the debt cancellation from one-third to two-thirds of outstanding debt stock, (3) setting market interest payments on the remaining one-third debt stock for five years and requiring repayment tied to export and income growth, and (4) stretching repayments of the remaining stock to 25 years with a flexible repayment schedule. The present value of the debt stock of the eligible (poorest) sub-Saharan countries would be reduced by $18 billion (rather than $2 billion under Toronto terms) or $34 billion if all low-income African countries were eligible (Mistry 1991, 18).

The G7 nations at their July 1991 London summit and the Paris Club nations meeting the following September failed to adopt Trinidad terms, largely because of U.S. and Japanese objections. In response, in October 1991 at the Commonwealth conference in Harare, Prime Minister Major announced that Britain would unilaterally cancel, at Trinidad terms, bilateral debt of the poorest nations worth $18 billion. In 1994, the G7 agreed to the terms.

## GLOBAL COMPETITION FOR FUNDS

In the early 1990s, as Germany integrated its eastern states and substantial OECD capital flowed to Central Europe and the former Soviet Union, Africa faced increasing competition for global financial resources. Writing down the 120 million people of Central Europe's 1989 external debt of $101 billion diverted resources from sub-Saharan Africa ($147 billion debt for 427 million people) and from Brazil, Mexico, and Argentina ($272 billion debt for 271 million people). While most OECD members have stressed aid to Central Europe should be additional to aid to LDCs, OECD publics are likely to be more demanding in assessing sub-Saharan recipients' human-rights record, geopolitical importance, and past use of concessional funds. Low-income Africa competes for funds in a capital-short world and would need greater returns on capital to meet higher real interest rates on nonconcessional loans (OECD 1990, 11-12; World Bank 1990b, vol. 1, 105-07).

International agencies and humanitarian lobbies need to keep the food and development requirements of sub-Sahara before the world community. Total U.S. military and economic aid to the sub-Sahara, $1,421 million in 1986, was only 39 percent of Israel's $3,621 million and 56 percent of Egypt's $2,539 million (Sewell, Tucker, and contributors 1988, 244). Donors could switch several middle-income recipients from aid to loans at or near bankers' standards, thus freeing more concessional funding for the sub-Sahara.

# EMPHASIS ON INTERNATIONAL DEVELOPMENT ASSOCIATION-ELIGIBLE COUNTRIES

The low cost of assistance, such that relatively small amounts can avoid substantial deprivation, suggests donors emphasize reducing the debt burden and increasing other funds for countries (mostly sub-Saharan) eligible for concessional IDA loans. World Bank and IMF concessional funds for LDC debtors need to be extended beyond the 17 severely indebted LDCs (mostly middle-income countries) to IDA-eligible countries (29 of 47 of the sub-Saharan countries and seven others). Western bankers advising the UN Secretary-General recommended the Paris Club provide multi-year rescheduling agreements three years long for debt-distressed African countries, in which no interest and principal are to be paid for three years. After that, interest rates are to be written down to IDA levels (Rogoff 1990, 5; UN 1988, 45-47). Moreover, official creditors can have a major role in writing down or off debt, as IDA-eligible Africa owes the majority of its debts to governments and multilateral lending institutions such as the Bank and Fund.

# DEBT REDUCTIONS

World Bank economists Fischer and Husain think countries that have not undertaken realistic economic reform and sustainable adjustment should carry their heavy burden of external debt until they attain the political will to adopt the necessary adjustment. But African finance and planning ministers at a Bank seminar charge Bank/Fund staff with too much emphasis on LDC leaders' political will or courage, reducing the politics of adjustment to an exercise in *machismo*. Sachs argues an LDC in the early 1990s that faces a substantial debt overhang might be better off defaulting on a portion of its debt than undertake timely debt servicing. About 20 countries undertook such unilateral action since 1980. There may be no IMF adjustment program for full debt servicing that makes the LDC better off than foregoing the program by partially suspending debt payments (Fischer and Husain 1990, 24-17; Martens 1988; Mills 1989, 21-23; Sachs 1989a; Devlin 1989, 233).

Bilateral lenders should divide debt into nonperforming and performing parts, and compute the value of the debt as if it included the performing part only (Cohen 1989). Debt that is not to be collected should be converted to concessional aid. Additionally, creditors as a whole, who hold debt highly discounted in the market, benefit by writing off some existing debt, moving debtors back to a higher point on their debt Laffer Curve (an upside-down "U" curve expressing the expected value of the debt as a function of the amount of debt).

Only 12 sub-Saharan countries serviced their debts regularly, while 28 countries rescheduled their official and private debts 113 times, 1980-90.

Nevertheless, sub-Saharan arrears on interest obligations still totalled $5 billion at the end of 1987, half the debt service payments that year.

Results of a World Bank rescheduling model indicate DCs will need to increase real financial flows and the grant component of aid for the sub-Sahara to resume normal debt-servicing capacity in the mid to late 1990s. Partial forgiveness and lower interest rates are more concessional than extending terms under late 1980s' Paris Club practices, which entails both additional concessionality and more rescheduling (World Bank 1988: vol. 1; and Huizinga 1989).

## CONCERTED ACTION

DCs can best support African political leaders by reducing debt so debtor countries have an incentive to undergo reform and offer long-term benefits to their publics. The Bank/Fund or other international agency can assist creditors in establishing an international facility for concerted action to reduce interest rates to debtors. The IMF or Bank can provide technical guidance concerning levels of debt reduction, and expedite concerted bank participation in debt-reduction packages, loans to debtors before banks' resolve debt rescheduling, and financial guarantees through providing collateral on the reduced debt.

Reducing debt without multilateral coordination, as envisioned by the Brady Plan, is not workable. Bilateral arrangements are subject to free-rider problems, where nonparticipating banks benefit from increased creditworthiness and value of debt holdings. Banks are willing to reduce LDC debt, but only if their competitors do likewise (Sachs 1989d, 87-104). Compelling concerted action by creditors and debtors is in the mutual interest of both.

The solution lies in concerted debt reduction, where all banks owed a debt participate jointly on a prorated basis. For debt relief, just as in U.S. bankruptcy settlements (under Chapter 11 of the Bankruptcy Reform Act of 1978), concerted efforts are more effective than individual deals by creditors with debtors, and rebuilding of debtor productive capacity more effective than legalistic solutions. The bankruptcy settlement cuts through the problem of inherent collective inaction and enforces a concerted settlement on creditors. Bankruptcy proceedings (under U.S. law) force individual creditors to give up some legal claims, reducing the contractual obligations of debtors, and thus preserving debtor capacity to function effectively and thereby service as much of the debt as possible.

The world community has had little success in debt reduction. The main channel for debt reduction, debt-equity swaps, is harmful to debtor countries. Through 1989, no commercial bank debt was rescheduled at submarket interest rates, despite widespread recognition that countries such as Bolivia, the Sudan,

Nigeria, and Peru can not fully service their debts on normal market terms. The meager debt-reduction record is intrinsic to the way banks bargain with debtor countries. Bargaining will fail unless creditors undertake concerted agreements to reduce debt. Insistence on voluntary, piecemeal arrangements between individual debtor and bank creditor will frustrate a comprehensive settlement of LDC debt overhang (Sachs 1989c, 239-41).

The inherent barrier to voluntary schemes is that the nonparticipating creditor who holds on to its original claims (which will rise in value) will be better off than those participating in collective debt reduction. Creditor participants pay the cost of debt reduction, while all creditors share the benefits.

Creditors made little attempt to address the problems of debtor countries other than Argentina, Brazil, Mexico, the Philippines, and Venezuela, as settlement with the others provides a damaging precedent for agreement with large debtors. Coordinated debt reduction is the only feasible alternative, as banks, lacking incentives, are becoming increasingly resistant to new-money packages, and debtors lack incentives to undertake tough reform measures designed to increase future debt-servicing payments abroad. DCs can best support moderate political leaders by reducing debt through concerted efforts so debtor countries have an incentive to undergo reform and offer long-term benefits to their publics.

# BREAKING UP THE POLICY CARTEL

Multilateral institutions, primarily the World Bank and IMF, which receive about one-third of the sub-Saharan debt service, do not write down debt. Indeed the IMF, unlike the Bank, received at least an annual $4.5 billion net resource transfer from sub-Saharan countries from 1984 through 1990. The major shareholders of the IMF need to provide it more concessional funds to avoid a sub-Saharan negative transfer when the debt servicing burden already is so high.

The World Bank, donor governments, and commercial banks rely on a Fund "seal of approval" (usually contingent on the borrower reducing demand) before arranging adjustment loans and debt writeoffs for sub-Saharan countries. These countries would benefit from the breaking up of this loan and policy cartel through increasing the resources of UN and other international agencies, strengthening independent financial centers (such as the EU, the Middle East, or East Asia), and delinking commercial bank, World Bank, bilateral, and even African Development Bank lending to IMF approval. Finally, sub-Saharan states should put together their own programs of adjustment and donors should loan on the basis of the financial capability of the borrowers, rather than on meeting conditions on national economic policy.

# Chapter V

# African Capitalism, State Power, and Economic Development

Dependency theorists argue that international capitalist development resulted in peripheral countries (LDCs) specializing in primary products where the scope for technical change there was limited, while the central capitalist countries of the West and Japan (DCs) produced industrial commodities benefiting from rapidly increasing productivity. Rodney (1972) analyzed how Europe expropriated Africa's surplus, Wallerstein (1979) considered stages of African involvement in the world economy, and Amin (1976) examined the social development of Africa's peripheral capitalism.

In chapters 3 and 4, we indicated ECA statements concerning the plight of the African economy. Yet it has been argued by a number of political economists, most recently by John Sender and Sheila Smith, Paul M. Lubeck et al., and Paul Kennedy, that stronger African states are reducing their external economic dependence and creating opportunities for capitalist growth. Except for Kennedy, these scholars depict Africa as making major strides forward, with capitalism providing the impetus for rapid progress (Kennedy 1988; Lubeck 1987; and Sender and Smith 1986).

Sender and Smith (1986, 62-65) emphasize rapid increases in sub-Saharan Africa's life expectancy at birth (from 31 in 1950 to 43 in 1970 to 49 in 1987), literacy, and infant survival rates. Yet other indicators of Africa's quality of life have improved slowly. Only one in four Africans have access to piped water, and child mortality rates, 50 percent higher than the LDC average in the 1950s, were double the LDC average in the 1980s. Most mortal illnesses, especially in rural areas, go undiagnosed. Furthermore, sub-Saharan Africa's food output per capita fell while the LDC figure rose, 1960 to 1989 (chapter 3).

## COLONIAL CAPITALISM

Sender and Smith stress that colonial capitalism resulted in the rising production of consumer goods, more primary-processing industries, increased land and labor markets, enhanced fiscal strength, rapid technical change, expanded social expenditure, an impetus to manufactured exports, and improved education and health for African workers. For Lubeck and contributors, the integration of Nigeria, Kenya, and Côte d'Ivoire into the world market the half century before 1960 contributed to economic growth. Kennedy points out that most social capital budgets were financed from local revenues and that colonial development was uneven and distorted. Yet the economic climate for indigenous enterprise improved during 1940-60, as increased purchasing power spurred capitalist economic growth. Despite European oligopolies and credit and license restrictions, Africans expanded local food and inter-African long-distance trade, transport, contracting, and commercial agriculture. Indeed, Kennedy (1988, 12) argues that "in many parts of Africa colonisation did create the conditions whereby new sources of wealth were generated. The cultivation of cash crops for export increased in an especially dramatic way."

The political economists underestimate the adverse impact of Western imperialism. Africans welcomed the exchange of ideas, inventions, cultures, and commodities, but denied imperialism was needed. The poet Aimé Cesaire (1970, 41) spoke of "societies emptied of themselves, of trampled cultures, undermined institutions, confiscated lands, of assassinated religions, annihilated artistic masterpieces, of extraordinary possibilities suppressed." Africa would have continued its precolonial trade, technical borrowing, and internal innovations without European restrictions.

The majority of colonial investment was in infrastructures primarily designed to promote trade with the mother country. Most of the estimated $6 billion foreign investment (at 1978 prices) in sub-Saharan Africa up to World War II was in mineral-related industries, heavily concentrated in Southern Africa. Foreigners invested funds overwhelmingly in exports, resulting in lopsided development. In addition, the European powers expected African colonies to pay their way even though few could support the bureaucratic superstructure imposed on whatever forms of government existed in precolonial times, let alone a modern military establishment to guard against rebellion (Curtin, Feierman, Thompson, and Vansina 1978; Markovitz 1977). In most of Africa, colonial expenditures were niggardly. British administration in Nigeria has been described as being on a "shoestring" between 1918 and 1948:

> There was no more than 5s per head of population, for all the current needs of central government, for many of the purposes of local government, and for heavy interest charges on loan capital, mostly used to improve the transportation services on which the whole prospect of prosperity and increasing revenues depended....[During] the upheaval of a second World War...the overstretched administrative machinery came very near to collapse (Nicolson 1969, 216, 246, 304-305).

The colonial legacy also contributed to agricultural underdevelopment after independence. (1) Africans were systematically excluded from a number of colonial development schemes, and from producing export crops and improved cattle. British agricultural policy in Eastern Africa benefited European settlers, and discriminated against African farmers, prohibiting Kenyans from growing coffee, for example. (2) Many peasant farmers were compelled to grow selected crops and to maintain roads. (3) Colonialism often changed traditional land-tenure systems from communal to individual control, creating greater inequalities from new affluent farmers and ranchers, and less secure tenants, sharecroppers, and landless workers. (4) Few attempts, if any, were made to train African agricultural scientists and managers. (5) Research and development concentrated on export crops, plantations, and land settlement, neglecting food production and small farmers and herders. (6) Europeans gained most from colonial land grants and agricultural export surpluses (Eicher and Baker 1982, 17-23).

As pointed out in chapter 3, as European rule became expensive by the 1950s, colonial administrators sought ways to create an elite favorable to the metropole by independence. According to Anyang' Nyong'o (1987, 185-86):

> The emergence of ruling classes in postcolonial Africa must be traced to their evolution in colonial times....In the case of the Ivory Coast, it was the small African capitalist class, emergent in the prewar era but consciously nurtured by the colonial state in the postwar era, which ...became the center of [the postcolonial] ruling bloc.

## PERIPHERAL CAPITALISM SINCE 1960

Dependency theorists contend DCs use economic and military power to maintain the former colony as a controlled sources of raw materials, markets, and investment. But Lubeck, Sender and Smith, and Kennedy maintain DC-African relationships do not inhibit indigenous capitalism.

According to Kitching (1987, 43) in the book edited by Lubeck, "a principal weakness of recent Marxist writing...has been to underestimate the variety of forms and sequences of capitalist development that *have* been actualized in the course of the necessarily uneven development of the world system" (italics in original). In other words, a bourgeoisie-proletarian coalition can generate a capitalism, as in Mexico or Brazil, that is independent of foreigners. As Lubeck (1987, 14-15, 21) contends, Côte d'Ivoire's economy, open to foreign trade and investment, experienced an "economic miracle" with one of the highest GDP growth rates for LDCs, 7.3 percent annually, 1960-79.

But the Ivorian "miracle" was transitory, according to predictions by Amin in 1973. First, fast plantation-output growth would be confined to early gains from undeveloped land, cheap Burkinan labor, and improving commodity markets. Second, rapid industrial growth from protecting import substitutes at independence in 1960 would soon be exhausted, because of restricted domestic markets, declining foreign investment opportunities, and increasing repatriation of funds. Third, slower growth would exacerbate interregional, interethnic, Ivorian-immigrant, and capital-labor inequalities (Amin 1973). Indeed, Côte d'Ivoire suffered from a slowdown after 1973.

Langdon emphasizes the vulnerability of Kenya's capitalism, while Swainson (1987, 10) contends that world capitalism, to prevent instability, must allow indigenous capitalist development in countries like Kenya. Overall Lubeck concludes that Kenya's indigenous bourgeois accumulated substantial capital, even in manufacturing. But like Côte d'Ivoire, Kenya fell on hard times so that its real growth after 1973 was slower than low-income countries generally (World Bank 1991b, 204).

Under a subheading, "Nigeria: 'The Brazil of Africa'?," Lubeck (1987, 16) claims that the 1974-82 petroleum boom "initiated a deepening of capitalist social relations of production and an unprecedented expansion of the indigenous bourgeoisie." To be sure, Biersteker (1987, 249-79) argues that, despite Nigerian indigenization, foreign capital still retains managerial control. But Forrest (1987, 307-42) maintains Nigerian capitalism grew with domestic-foreign collaboration.

Sender and Smith (1986, 132), who think the view that African capitalism has been distorted by external forces is "scapegoatism," are correct in attributing slow African export and output expansion to foreign-exchange and marketing-board purchase prices set below market-clearing rates. But they support widespread state protection to promote import-substitution manufacturing, which distorts prices, reduces efficiency, overvalues domestic currency, and increases input prices of other industrial products. Langdon, though, rightly criticizes Kenya's export manufacturing strategy because it relies on large-scale European multinational corporations (MNCs) or joint European-African ventures with inappropriate labor-saving technology.

Kennedy (1988, 106) criticizes the neo-Marxist view that "local business groups in Africa and elsewhere operate primarily in a comprador or 'service' capacity with regard to Western capital." Independent entrepreneurs include wholesale and import-export traders, small financiers, contractors, transporters, commercial farmers, and light industrialists, some running enterprises with more than 100 workers, especially in Nigeria, Kenya, and Ghana. Even public officials who use income or connections to start auxiliary businesses to foreign firms gradually increase their support of local vis-à-vis foreign capitalism.

## THE STATE AND CAPITALISM

Lubeck (1987, 18) indicates in Nigeria, Kenya, and Côte d'Ivoire, described as black Africa's three most developed states, "the drive to 'privatize' industries and inculcate market discipline by center states through international agencies such as the World Bank and even the United Nations, creates opportunities for indigenous capital to invest in directly productive enterprise."

Kenya's "indigenous bourgeoisie inherited a productive base in capitalist agriculture with large units of production and a disciplined state bureaucracy," a base extended by state action, 1960-79. While Lubeck (1987: 23) notes liberal Côte d'Ivoire's rapid growth of the 1960s and 1970s gave way to stagnation in the early 1980s, economic change suggests "a stronger role for the indigenous bourgeoisie in the future, yet one where the state will continue to be the dominant actor and perhaps a social force for increased indigenous accumulation." Indeed, for Lubeck (1987, 9), theorists predicting "stagnation, blocked industrialization, and the impotence of a bourgeois-state technocratic alliance" have difficulty explaining the successful (albeit uneven) transition to capitalism by the three states after the 1960s.

Yet development in sub-Saharan Africa was sluggish, with World Bank figures indicating rapid pre-1973 growth giving way to annual growths in GNP per capita of 1.2 percent (1973-80) and -3.0 percent (1980-87) in Côte d'Ivoire, 1.3 percent (1973-80) and -0.9 percent (1980-87) in Kenya, and 1.2 percent (1973-80) and -4.8 percent (1980-87) in Nigeria, thus dropping to a low-income country in 1987 for the first time (World Bank 1989a, 221). To make matters worse, many of the resources of the new states were devoured by a small ruling elite of high-ranking politicians, military officers, and government administrators, managers of parastatal corporations, top professionals, and traditional authorities, as well as a few private capitalists. The public sector and its average real salaries grew steadily, even when growth was slow or negative.

As indicated in chapter 3, Africa's weak bourgeoisie contributed to some contradictions. Rapid expansion undermined the hegemony of existing political and bureaucratic elites. Yet slow growth, with reduced shares to distribute, endangered ruling coalitions. And since nationalist leaders before independence politicized the masses by stressing self-determination, equality, and modernization to unite against colonialism, the increasing gap between expectation and actuality exerted revolutionary pressures and ruling-class reaction.

For Sender and Smith, the state, through growing public-sector expenditure, played a significant role in increasing investment in Africa. But UN Development Programme and World Bank data (1989, 72) while rough, indicate that in the 1980s public enterprises in sub-Saharan Africa generated no overall profits, implying that the increasing public investment comes from tax revenue rather than internal enterprise earnings.

By the mid 1970s most African countries had taken over mineral extraction, petroleum, banking, insurance, public utilities, and parts of manufacturing. Yet Kennedy sees strong support for indigenous capitalists in Zambia, Côte d'Ivoire, Sierra Leone, and Malawi (see Nafziger 1988, 76-77, 122-23, 147, for a criticism of the widely-held view concerning Malawi's successful capitalist development), but ambivalence (and sometimes hostility) toward local enterprises by most African governments, committed to socialist (actually statist) strategies.

# A COMMERCIAL TRIANGLE

Turner (1978, 166-97) posits a triangular relationship between multinational corporations, indigenous business people and middlemen, and state officials, in which MNCs hire local citizens with privileged access to government officials as a go-between with the state. The middleman may be a public servant or private-company employee who receives concessions, contacts, or retail outlets, or who collects bonuses, commissions, kickbacks, or bribes. But officials directly arranging joint ventures between MNCs and state enterprises may exclude the private middleman.

African governments frequently create industrial monopolies, raise industrial relative to agricultural prices, or protect output through tariffs or quotas, providing rents for parastatal officials, political elites, middlemen, and MNCs, even with no commissions or kickbacks. Thus, in 1969, when Kenya gave Firestone a virtual monopoly of tire production for 10 years, prominent Kenyans, including a former cabinet minister, were appointed managers, while government received the right to choose distributors to share the monopoly profits. The World Bank remarked that Kenya's protection of firms from competition was like a "license to print money" (Bates 1981, 103; World Bank 1975, 298).

After independence in 1963, the Kenyan state supported African capitalists by appropriating land for large commercial farms, and by granting licenses, credit preference, and distribution rights for traders. Indeed, bureaucratic contacts became as important to Kenyan capitalists as production and marketing knowledge. Public office often became the main road to private-sector wealth. African capitalists grew stronger, despite their declining efficiency, because of their symbiotic relationship to the political leadership, bureaucracy and foreign capital (Swainson 1977, 39-55). Officials and intermediaries in Kenya, Malawi, Nigeria, Ghana, Côte d'Ivoire, and other African countries depend critically on external aid and investment for increasing income, dispensing patronage, and controlling state power.

Kitching (1987, 37) contends that, without a national capitalist class, a local political elite, with foreign capital, can promote capitalist development, as in Japan. There industrialization was spurred after 1880 by expenditures on infrastructure and state industrial enterprises (many subsequently sold to private enterprise), as well as business subsidies, protection, loans, and inducements. Yet the bourgeoisie during the Meiji era had much commercial experience, as well as the vision and skills to plan programs to expedite business, and was not so far behind the most technologically advanced economies as Africa today. The irony is that while the weakness of the African bourgeoisie indicates the need for state intervention and skilled planning to induce investment and entrepreneurship, few African bureaucrats can either facilitate the emergence of profitable enterprises in the private sector or manage these in the public sector (chapter XI). While Kitching is correct in doubting that African civil servants can play the Meiji bureaucracy's role, he underestimates Meiji Japan's business experience.

African states have established national trading corporations, as mentioned by Kennedy, which were granted a sizeable share of import licenses, directing business from MNCs to local business. By dominating international trade, these state-owned organizations could control wholesale, retail, and manufacturing enterprises. Kennedy (1988, 65) contends that the state sector created a "parasitic capitalism," where office-holders and politicians exploited privileged access to state resources to acquire private property and business interests.

Indigenization laws in the 1970s in Nigeria, Malawi, Kenya, Senegal, Zaïre, Uganda, Ghana, and Zambia specified minimal local equity shares in foreign enterprises. Except for Côte d'Ivoire, Liberia, and Gabon, each African country nationalized at least one foreign enterprise during this decade, concentrating in banking, insurance, and petroleum distribution. However, only individuals with access to capital or loans were likely to benefit from indigenization programs (Adedeji 1981).

In Nigeria, business people formed an important minority of the political leadership, which used public funds to promote indigenous entrepreneurs. The 1972, 1977, and 1981 indigenization measures expanded the African (especially industrial) capitalist class, but mainly among a privileged few. Yet many entrepreneurs still lacked the capital and skills to replace foreigners, some of whom avoided indigenization by naturalizing, converting equity to debt holdings, or using other loopholes to continue ownership or control. And many Nigerians acquiring shares in indigenized companies were content with the dividends paid to them by foreign managers, so that they increased their share of foreign industries without the enterprising zeal and managerial know-how for higher responsibility (Nafziger 1988, 89-90, 101; and Ogbuagu 1983, 241-66).

In Kenya in the 1960s, land resettlement and Kenyanization of jobs and businesses reduced racial but increased inter-African discrepancies. Those who benefited included high-level managers and technicians, modern urban-sector employees, the few receiving land transfers from European farmers, and the petty bourgeoisie—traders, builders, transporters, small industrialists, and service and repair business people (International Labour Office 1972).

## AGRARIAN CAPITALISM

Industrial productivity relative to agricultural productivity is higher in Africa than in other LDC regions. Despite plans proclaiming agriculture's importance, the state allocates most resources to cities (see chapter 3).

Sender and Smith, as well as Kennedy, stress the state's massive diversion of resources from peasants to industrial parastatals, the excessive taxation of export crops, and the way that overvalued domestic currencies reduce export receipts. Indeed the former are correct in indicating pricing policies are responsible for the fall of sub-Saharan Africa's market shares from the 1960s to the 1980s. However, except for Oculi (1987, 167-84) and Anyang' Nyong'o (1987, 185-86), Lubeck's contributors discuss agricultural production, trade, and exploitation without reference to how the state affects exchange rates and farm prices.

Chapter 3 argues states pursue urban-oriented policies of market intervention to maintain political control and increase political support. Governments provide individual incentives to cooperate in programs harmful to producer interests generally.

## CONCLUSION

Has the African state been able to support a thriving indigenous capitalism? The "yes" by Sender and Smith, and by Lubeck, is based on understating the dependence of ruling classes on MNCs, foreign aid, and Western support for maintaining political strength or expanding state power. African political elites appropriate agricultural surpluses for parastatal industries, often in partnership with foreign capital, and dispense benefits to clients. Political survival in an insecure environment requires marshaling upper-class support at the expense of growth and income distribution. Inducing farm expansion through the market limits the ability of African leaders to build support in the politically dominant urban areas. Disseminating economic power to the multiplicity of petty traders, artisans, and small industrialists, without a quid pro quo, threatens the economic interests of political leaders—the viability and monopoly returns of the public corporations that serve as a basis for patronage, and the large private business interests.

Kennedy thinks an African capitalist class whose emergence depends on state action could build its economic and political strength step by step to reduce its dependence on government and foreign capital, yet he indicates this only occurred in Kenya. In Nigeria and elsewhere in subsaharan Africa, state power was used primarily to amass non-productive private wealth. While few African states have yet created prosperous domestic entrepreneurs, this does not rule out the possibility the growing African bourgeoisie will become increasingly strong at the expense of both state and foreign capital.

# Chapter VI

# Democracy, Adjustment, and Economic Reform in Africa

Roughly half of forty-six sub-Saharan African countries are democratic or strongly or moderately committed to democratic change [*Africa Demo̅s* 2 (February 1992).] With scanty press coverage of Africa, many people have overlooked the political upheavals in the Sub-Sahara, which since 1989 have been as revolutionary as in Central Europe and the former Soviet Union.

The U.S. Agency for International Development announced in 1990 (p. 3): "Within each region of the world, allocation of A.I.D. funds to individual countries will take into account their progress toward democratization. This will place democracy on a comparable footing with progress in economic reforms and the establishment of a market-oriented economy." Some in the U.S. Congress, however, prefer linking aid to the promotion of U.S. exports abroad, especially construction projects.

## ADJUSTMENT AND DEMOCRATIZATION

In an address delivered in July 1991, IMF Managing Director Michel Camdessus (1991, 227) *deplored* the viewpoint "that countries that have recently introduced democracy lack the maturity to manage rigorously [and] that we must facilitate their task by closing our eyes to the abandonment or temporary suspension of the adjustment process." While World Bank economists Fischer and Husain (1990, 27) think that LDCs not undertaking Bank/Fund reform and adjustment should carry their debt burden until they attain the political will, African finance ministers complain that the Bank/Fund neglects the political constraints that operate in countries undertaking adjustment. How does the Bank or Fund expect to persuade African officials to implement adjustment programs that tarnish their prestige as political leaders? (Mills 1989, 21-23; Martens 1988, 15-21).

For vastly different reasons, in a statement published in 1990, the Africa Leadership Forum, OAU, and ECA (1990, 40), jointly representing recipient countries, also rejected donor biases toward multiparty democracies.

> Increasingly there is a tendency of donor countries to introduce a new political conditionality in addition to the existing economic conditionalities for aid and concessionary resource flows to Africa. This new conditionality is unacceptable. Multipartyism is being used as one of the criteria for certification for aid. Yet, multipartyism is no guarantee for democracy. African countries must ensure genuine democracy and popular participation which should be self-induced and sustained rather than externally imposed.

Are economic adjustment and reform compatible with democratization? Sandbrook's survey (1985) of 39 sub-Saharan states shows that authoritarian regimes have no better record on development or integration than liberal democratic regimes, findings generally confirmed by Diamond, et al. (1988). Since other empirical research on Africa's limited democratic experience is sparse, we will use evidence from LDCs generally.

Lal (1983, 33) contends that "a courageous, ruthless and perhaps undemocratic government is required to ride roughshod over...newly-created special interest groups." Democratic governments are viewed by Lal as the source of irrational economic policies to placate interest groups. As a World Bank study (1991, 50, 132-34) points out transitional democratic systems have been remarkably unsuccessful in implementing IMF adjustment programs. Indeed, authoritarian systems appear to be especially successful, the study contends, in controlling rapid inflation in polarized environments. Yet the Bank argues, in opposition to Wilson (1991), that overall political liberties contribute to economic development.

Stedman and Hakim (1989, 166-74) report that in 1982-87, under existing civilian rule, the opposition candidate won seven of eight Latin American presidential elections, primarily because of debt crises and adjustment programs. Although the winning candidates called for higher wages, great social spending, price controls, domestic protection, and sometimes debt suspension or default, no winner ameliorated the economic crisis. Indeed the Acapulco Summit Meeting of Latin American Presidents in 1987 stated: "The economic crisis undermines democracy in the region because it neutralizes the legitimate efforts of our people to improve their living standards."

Haggard and Kaufman (1989, 57-77), examining 25 African, Asian, and Latin American countries in 1978-86, find no difference between the macroeconomic policies of established democratic and authoritarian governments, but countries undergoing transitions to democracy pursued more expansionary central bank credit and expenditures policies than before and after the transition and compared to established regimes. Established governments gave more discretion to national monetary authorities and economic ministries than do countries changing regime types.

Hirschman (1986, 13) agrees, observing that

> When a civilian, democratic government first comes into power after a long period of repressive military rule, it is normal for various, newly active groups of the reborn civil society—particularly the long-repressed trade unions—to stake substantial claims for higher incomes... New inflationary and balance-of-payments pressures are of course likely to result from the granting of such demands ... [I]nflation can nevertheless be a useful mechanism in this situation: it permits newly emerging or re-emerging social groups to flex their muscles, with inflation acting as a providential safety value for accumulated social pressures.

In Nigeria, the repression and control of partisan and ethnic-regional politics under military rule, 1966-79, gave way to demands for increased patronage, income shares, and social spending during the Second Republic, 1979-83. Indeed, in 1979-80, the ports lacked the capacity for imports such as cement going to government agencies controlled by politicians distributing benefits to contractors and other clients. South Korea, though, attained high growth, current-account surpluses, and financial stability before democratic transition, increasing policy flexibility after 1988. As in Korea, coalitional strategies that limit mass appeal and dampen expectations contribute to greater domestic financial and external economic stability. However, in establishing stabilization and adjustment programs, fledgling democratic governments can emphasize the failure of outgoing governments. Moreover, *new* democratic governments, like new authoritarian regimes, provide a fresh supply of ministerial energy and popular credit, facilitating economic reforms; a new broom sweeps the cleanest (Whitehead 1989, 85-86). Still regime instability may continue unless the new government can resist an externally imposed economic stabilization that undermines its legitimacy.

While Africa had fewer open elections than Latin America, heads of state feared that economic mistakes might hasten their removal through irregular power transfers such as coups, assassinations, and military takeovers. The strongest opposition comes from vested interests (mainly upper and middle classes) threatened by privatization, currency devaluation, farm price decontrol, and other reforms (Waterbury 1989, 40-46). Measures helping the poorest third rarely contribute to ruling-class sustainability, except where the poor's interests overlap with those of the middle deciles. Indeed, Nelson's study (1989, 100-05) of five Middle Eastern states plus Pakistan and Turkey showed the most populous group, the peasantry, not to be a part of any politically dominant coalition, and organized labor to be a part of only three of the seven.

# DC AND BANK/FUND RESPONSES

In designing adjustment programs, the IMF cannot neglect domestic political pressures, especially in sub-Saharan Africa when economies are facing declining terms of trade and export purchasing power, as in Nigeria (1983-85) and Zambia (1983-91). In 1987, President Kaunda, who lost the IMF "seal of approval" by restricting debt servicing to 10 percent of export earnings in the face of Zambia's 70-percent obligation, asked the multilateral agencies, "Which is a better partner for you in the long run, a nation which devotes all of its resources to paying the debt and, therefore, grinds to an economic and political halt, or a stable nation capable of sustaining the repaying of its entire debt?" (Seshamani 1990, 120).

Low-income sub-Saharan countries that face substantial debt overhangs might be better off defaulting on a portion of its debt than undertaking austere domestic adjustment or timely debt servicing. About 20 LDCs undertook such unilateral action in the 1980s. There may be no Fund/Bank adjustment program for full debt servicing that makes the low-income country better off than forgoing the program by partially suspending debt payments (Sachs 1989a).

Indeed the Bank/Fund needs to adopt a medium- to long-term perspective on economic restructuring. While the IMF's 1983 structural adjustment program (SAP) in Ghana facilitated relatively quick adjustment because of its immediate improvement in the terms of trade (with increased world prices for cocoa), the SAP in Zambia at the same time resulted in no movement toward internal or external adjustment because Zambia's major export, copper, was continuing to experience declining relative world prices. The Bank/Fund could have used structural adjustment for helping Zambia diversify its export and import-substitution sectors, so in the long run a more diversified Zambia would have been less vulnerable to fluctuating world prices.

Economic adjustment and falling foreign capital flows hurt the disadvantaged most. While Africa's political elites incurred debt partly to expand patronage, they responded to pressures from debt crises by slashing spending for the poor and working classes. The international community and the Sub-Sahara can probably reduce the distress of the poorest groups by increasing the adjustment time horizon to, say, 10 to 15 years, so that political elites have time to plan more stable structural changes. Spurring African leaders to undertake political and economic reform requires DCs writing down debt, liberalizing trade, and increasing aid, at least to countries such as Nigeria, Côte d'Ivoire, Tanzania, Senegal, Namibia, Ghana, Cameroon, Uganda, Benin, Gabon, Guinea, Togo, Malawi, and Burkina, if not to Sudan, Somalia, and Zaïre, where political conflict or blatant corruption precludes even minimally effective capital utilization.

What if the DC policy and lending cartel (governments, commercial banks, and the Bank/Fund) should refuse to provide funds to low-income sub-

Saharan African countries without their undergoing IMF-type conditionality? Then, the Sub-Sahara, while recognizing the immense short-run cost, may have no choice but to default on debt payments and undertake adjustment programs by itself, while joining with other LDCs to undermine the cartel's policy and funding stranglehold.

But I am hopeful that DC governments will contribute leadership in assisting the Sub-Sahara while favoring Africans' directing their own planning. To be sure, DC help provides no guarantees, but inaction probably means continued growing poverty and malnutrition in Africa. While the immediate cost of response by rich countries is negligible, this breathing space might enable some sub-Saharan political leaders to focus on long-range planning and investment to improve the welfare of its masses.

# Part III.

Entrepreneurship and Economic Development

# Chapter VII

# Class, Caste, and Community
# of Indian Industrialists

Unto every one which hath shall be given; and from him that hath not, even that he
hath shall be taken away from him (Luke 19, 26).

Although several empirical studies have investigated the socioeconomic
origins of entrepreneurs in parts of India, these studies lack the data essential
for comparing the origins of entrepreneurs with that of the population as a
whole, and for relating socioeconomic characteristics of the entrepreneurs to
their success. In this chapter, I compare data on the distribution of
entrepreneurs by class (paternal economic status) and caste in a south Indian
city with information on the population generally, and relate these data to the
education, entrepreneurial and managerial experience, initial capital, access to
government assistance, and business success of the entrepreneurs. The gross
value added of the firm (value of output minus purchases from other firms)
and the income class of the entrepreneur are the major indicators used for
business success. This evidence provides a test of the prevailing view in the
literature that industrial entrepreneurship is a vehicle for upward mobility to
success in business. The questions I ask in south India about socioeconomic
origins and mobility of entrepreneurs and determinants of their quantity and
success will be focal points for the crossnational analysis of society and the
entrepreneur in chapter 8.

A period of rapid industrial growth and economic modernization, as in
India's independence era, does not remove the advantages of ascribed status,
even in entrepreneurial activity in manufacturing. The traditional Indian upper
classes—local rulers and administrators, landlords, and Brahmins—whose
strength is a legacy of the feudal and colonial periods, have allied, and in some
cases overlapped, with the capitalist, political, and bureaucratic elites, most
of whom originated from high-income families, to control much of the access
to key business positions. Families and communities with wealth and position
use the monopoly advantage resulting from ready access to capital, greater

information and mobility, superior education and training, privileged access to licenses and concessions from government, and a low discount of future income, to become industrial entrepreneurs in disproportionate numbers.

## CONCEPTS, METHODS, PROCEDURES, AND OBJECTIVES OF THE STUDY

Fifty-four industrial entrepreneurs in the southeastern port of Visakhapatnam (Vizag), Andhra Pradesh, a rapidly growing city of 335,000, were interviewed in 1971.[1] Vizag, which experienced an industrial boom after Indian independence, is located about halfway between Calcutta and Madras by rail.

To cope with the problem of identifying the quantities of entrepreneurship, it is assumed there is one unit-the entrepreneur-in each firm. He is identified as the person with the largest capital share in the enterprise (see Knight 1921, 296-98). Even though there are a large number of family enterprises in Vizag, one can readily distinguish the principal of the firm, usually the father or elder brother.

## THE CONCEPT OF CASTE

Socio-cultural variables affect the position and elasticity of supply of entrepreneurship and the success of entrepreneurs by influencing the responsiveness of people to economic incentives and their experience, resources, and connections useful for business activity. I use caste, together with regional and linguistic community, to analyze entrepreneurial activity in this study. Caste refers to the ancient four-rank *varna* system for Hindus— Brahmin (priest), Kshatriya (ruler and warrior), Vaishya (trader), and Sudra (artisan, peasant, and laborer), in addition to the "untouchables" (or Harijans); and religion in the case of the non-Hindu population: Sikhs, Muslims, Jains, Parsis, Christians, and a few others. The first three Hindu *varna* are twice-born castes (that is, higher castes which have gone through a special ceremony in youth indicating a second or spiritual birth). More specific than the *varna* is the *jati*, which is still the basic kinship and social particle in a system of hierarchically arranged, locally integrated, occupationally and ritually specialized, endogamous social strata. Yet the concept of *varna*, recognized by the courts during the colonial period and supported by the leading castes to legitimize their status, has helped to shape social reality and is accepted by ordinary Indians as a conceptual device to understand the caste system (Gould 1963, 427-38; Srinivas 1962, 63, 69; Rudolph and Rudolph 1967, 119).

Caste is *not* an immutable system where the position of each *jati* is fixed throughout time. In the middle regions of the *varna* hierarchy, caste standing is at times vague and flexible. In fact, the Sudra categories range from powerful and rich *jatis* with a relatively high ritual status to those whose assimilation into Hinduism is only marginal. Some former Sudra *jatis* have been able to rise to a higher position in the *varna* hierarchy in a generation or two through Sanskritization (the adoption of the rituals of twice-born castes, Brahmins, Kshatriyas, and Vaishyas) (Srinivas 1962, 7-8, 42, 65).

As in most other studies of Indian business people, caste is used rather than *jati*. First, the sample is too small to make generalizations about *jatis*. Second, the ritual status of a caste aids in defining and identifying a person socially. Although caste may include a number of *jatis*, it is highly correlated with paternal economic status and class in Vizag (Ramana 1971, 132-34, 139-40), as well as India in general, and can, with other indicators of these ranking, help in analyzing social mobility. Despite the diversity of the Sudras, in the aggregate they correspond to the middle socioeconomic group between twice-born castes and Harijans.

## CASTE, FAMILY, AND SOCIAL COMMUNITY

Data on the caste composition of the sample and city indicate that high Hindu castes, Muslims, and Sikhs were overrepresented among the entrepreneurs. Fifty-two percent of the entrepreneurs (in contrast to only 11 percent of blue-collar workers) were from twice-born Hindu castes which comprise only 26 percent of the population of Vizag city. The Sudras (middle castes), who comprise 57 percent of the population of the city account for only 28 percent of the entrepreneurs.[2] None of the entrepreneurs, but a disproportionate share of blue-collar workers, was from low-caste backgrounds (that is, Harijans and Protestant or Roman Catholic Christians) (Table VII.1).[3] There was a significant positive relationship between the caste ranking of the Hindu population and representation in entrepreneurial activity (Table VII.2). The relationship is still significant even if the dominant business community, the Vaishyas, are eliminated (Table VII.3), and even if the analysis is confined to entrepreneurs born in Andhra Pradesh (Table VII.4).

If the Hindu population in Vizag is divided into high (twice-born) castes, middle castes, and low castes, there is a significant positive relationship between caste ranking, on the one hand, and education, income, occupational status, and perceived class and status, on the other (Ramana 1971, 130-31). Thus, as expected, the paternal economic status of entrepreneurs from twice-born castes was significantly higher than those of Sudras (Table VII.5). Entrepreneurs were asked: "Was your father's economic status high, medium, or low?" Eleven high-caste entrepreneurs indicated a high paternal economic status, 15 a medium status, and none a low status; two Sudras indicated a high status, eight a medium status, and four a low status (Table VII.6).[4]

*Table VII.1.* Caste Origin and Birthplace of Entrepreneurs

| | Number of Entrepreneurs born in A.P.[a] | Number of Entrepreneurs born outside A.P.[a] | Number of Entrepreneurs (Total) | Percentage of Entrepreneurs (Total) | Percentage of Blue-Collar Workers in Vizag[b] | Percentage of Population of Vizag[c] |
|---|---|---|---|---|---|---|
| Brahmin | 9 | 2 | 11 | 20.36 | 2.22 | 21.45 |
| Kshatriya | 5 | 0 | 5 | 9.26 | 8.89 | 2.35 |
| Vaishya | 4 | 8 | 12 | 22.2 | 0.00 | 2.15 |
| Sudra | 14 | 1 | 15 | 27.78 | 57.78 | 56.86 |
| Harijan | 0 | 0 | 0 | 0.00 | 15.56 | 11.25 |
| Muslim | 4 | 3 | 7 | 12.96 | 6.67 | 1.30 |
| Christian (Protestant, Caltholic) | 0 | 0 | 0 | 0.00 | 8.89 | 4.55 |
| Christian (Syrian) | 0 | 1 | 1 | 1.85 | 0.00 | 0.00[d] |
| Sikh | 0 | 2 | 2 | 3.70 | 0.00 | 0.00[d] |
| Parsi | 0 | 1 | 1 | 1.85 | 0.00 | 0.00[d] |
| Unknown | 0 | 0 | 0 | 0.00 | 0.00 | 0.10 |
| Total | 36 | 18 | 54 | 99.98[e] | 100.01[e] | 100.00 |

*Notes:* [a] Andhra Pradesh.
[b] Ramana 1971: 137.
[c] Ibid., p. 29.
[d] None of the three groups is represented in the Ramana sample. Sikhs make up 0.09 percent and Parsis 0.01 of the population of Vizag City, according to the 1961 census. Syrian Christians are not separated from Protestant and Roman Catholic Christians in the census, but Ramana suggests that less then 1 percent of the Christians (i.e., less then 0.05 percent of the total population) are Syrian.
[e] May not add up to 100.00 because of rounding.

## *Table VII.2*  Frequency Distribution of Hindu Entrepreneurs by Caste Ranking

| Caste Ranking | Observed Frequency[a] | Expected Frequency[b] |
|---|---|---|
| Twice-born castes | 28 | 11.9 |
| Middle and low castes | 15 | 31.1 |

*Notes:*  Sudras and Harijans comprise the middle and low castes.

Calculated value of $\chi^2 = 30.11$, $\chi^2$ at the .01 level of significance with 1 d.f. = 6.64.

[a] Based on the third column in table 5.

[b] Based on the share of each caste grouping in the Hindu population of Vizag, as computed from the last column in table.

## *Table VII.3*  Frequency Distribution of Non-Vaishya Hindu Entrepreneurs by Caste Ranking

| Caste Ranking | Observed Frequency[a] | Expected Frequency[b] |
|---|---|---|
| Twice-born castes | 16 | 8.0 |
| Middle and low castes | 15 | 23.0 |

*Notes:*  Brahmins amd Kshatriyas comprise the twice-born castes. The middle and low castes consist of Sudras and Harijans.

Calculated value of $\chi^2 = 10.78$, $\chi^2$ at the .01 level of significance with 1 d.f. = 6.64.

[a] Based on the third column in table 5.

[b] Based on the share of each caste grouping in the Vizag, as computed from the last column in table 5.

## *Table VII.4*  Frequency Distribution of Non-Vaishya Hindu Entrepreneurs Born in Andhra Pradesh by Caste Ranking

| Caste Ranking | Observed Frequency[a] | Expected Frequency[b] |
|---|---|---|
| Twice-born castes | 14 | 7.3 |
| Middle and low castes | 14 | 20.7 |

*Notes:*  Calculated value of $\chi^2 = 8.32$, $\chi^2$ at the .05 level of significance with 1 d.f. = 3.84.

[a] Based on the first column in table 5.

[b] Based on the share of each caste grouping in the non-Vaishya Hindu Population of Vizag, as computed from the last column in table 5.

*Table VII.5* Frequency Distribution
of Hindu Entrepreneurs by
Paternal Economic Status

| | Paternal Economic Status[a] | |
|---|---|---|
| Caste Ranking | High | Middle or Low |
| Twice-born castes | 11 | 15 |
| Middle and low castes | 2 | 12 |

*Notes:* Calculated value of $\chi^2 = 9.39$, $\chi^2$ at the .01 level of significance with 1 d.f. = 6.64.
[a] Based on columns entitled "Economic Status of Father," table VII.6.

There were a number of differences between entrepreneurs from twice-born and middle castes that may result, in part, from the higher family economic status of the higher castes. The median initial equity capital of the firms of high-caste entrepreneurs was Rs. 60,000 (or about $8,000 at the official exchange rate), and 14 of 28 of them received the bulk of their initial capital from their families (ancestors, siblings, spouses, and descendants). In contrast, the median initial capital of the Sudras was only Rs. 37,500,[5] and only 5 of 15 of them acquired initial funds from their families. The median and modal educational class for entrepreneurs from twice-born castes was a bachelor's degree, compared to a secondary certificate for Sudras. Only 20 percent of the Sudras had bachelor's degrees and 73 percent secondary certificates, compared to 57 and 89 percent respectively for the high-caste entrepreneurs.[6] High-caste families, with a disproportionate number of enterprises and connections with business friends, could more readily arrange management experience for their sons. Accordingly, the median prior management experience (defined in Table VII.6, note d) of twice-born entrepreneurs was higher than for Sudras. Prior to the involvement of their present firms, the major previous occupation of 20 of the 28 high-caste businessmen and only 5 of the 15 Sudras involved entrepreneurial or managerial responsibility.[7] The lesser socioeconomic status, access to capital, educational achievement, entrepreneurial and management experience, and access to government of Sudra businessmen (Nafziger 1978, 76) was associated with a lower level of entrepreneurial success and a smaller size firm than for businessmen from twice-born castes. The median gross value added of firms (value of output minus purchases from other firms) directed by high-caste entrepreneurs was Rs. 50,000 compared to Rs. 28,000 for Sudras.[8] In addition, high-caste entrepreneurs were in a higher income bracket than middle-caste entrepreneurs. Although the differences diminish when comparisons are confined to those born within the state of Andhra Pradesh, high-caste businessmen still have more education, more management experience, more access to capital, a higher

**Table VII.6.** Firms and Entrepreneurs

| Caste Birth-Place | Number | Median Income Class[a] | Economic Status of Father | | | Major Occupation of Father[b] | | Median Initial Capital | Median Education | Median Years Prior Management Experience[d] | Firms | |
|---|---|---|---|---|---|---|---|---|---|---|---|---|
| | | | High | Medium | Low | Business[c] | Nonbusiness | | | | Median Value Added[e] | Median Employment Level[f] |
| *Brahmin* | | | | | | | | | | | | |
| A.P.[g] | 9 | 2,501-5,000 | 3 | 5 | 0 | 2 | 6 | 35,000 | Batchelor's | 6.0 | 62,300 | 12.0 |
| Other | 2 | 2,501-5,000 | 0 | 2 | 0 | 2 | 0 | 12,500 | Batchelor's, master's | 7.0 | 30,000 | 23.5 |
| Total | 11 | 2,501-5,000 | 3 | 7 | 0 | 4 | 6 | 30,000 | Batchelor's | 6.0 | 41,000 | 12.0 |
| *Kshatriya* | | | | | | | | | | | | |
| A.P.[g] (Total) | 5 | 0-2,500 | 1 | 3 | 0 | 1 | 3 | 80,000 | Secondary | 16.0 | 37,500 | 15.0 |
| *Vaishya* | | | | | | | | | | | | |
| A.P.[g] | 4 | 5,001-10,000 | 0 | 4 | 0 | 2 | 2 | 35,000 | Secondary | 3.0 | 37,500 | 11.0 |
| Other | 8 | 50,001 & above | 7 | 1 | 0 | 8 | 0 | 425,000 | Batchelor's | 18.5 | 325,000 | 20.5 |
| Total | 12 | 50,001 & above | 7 | 5 | 0 | 10 | 2 | 125,000 | Some univ., Batchelor's | 13.0 | 105,000 | 12.0 |
| *Sudra* | | | | | | | | | | | | |
| A.P.[g] | 14 | 5,001-10,000 | 2 | 7 | 4 | 7 | 7 | 30,000 | Secondary | 3.0 | 21,000 | 9.0 |
| Other | 1 | 10,001-25,000 | 0 | 1 | 0 | 0 | 1 | 70,000 | Some secondary | 0.0 | 230,000 | 16.0 |
| Total | 15 | 5,001-10,000 | 2 | 8 | 4 | 7 | 8 | 37,500 | Secondary | 2.0 | 28,000 | 10.0 |
| *Muslim* | | | | | | | | | | | | |
| A.P.[g] | 4 | 5,001-10,000 | 1 | 2 | 0 | 2 | 1 | 21,000 | Secondary | 2.5 | 8,350 | 5.0 |
| Other | 3 | 5,001-10,000 | 2 | 1 | 0 | 1 | 2 | 20,000 | Secondary | 7.0 | 21,000 | 10.0 |
| Total | 7 | 5,001-10,000 | 3 | 3 | 0 | 3 | 3 | 20,000 | Secondary | 5.0 | 19,000 | 7.0 |

(continued)

## Table VII.6. Continued

| Caste Birth-Place | Number | Median Income Class | Economic Status of Father — High | Medium | Low | Major Occupation of Father[b] — Business[c] | Nonbusiness | Median Initial Capital | Median Education | Median Years Prior Management Experience[d] | Firms — Median Value Added[e] | Median Employment Level[f] |
|---|---|---|---|---|---|---|---|---|---|---|---|---|
| *Other*[h] Outside A.P.[g] (Total) | 4 | 10,001-50,000 | 1 | 3 | 0 | 2 | 2 | 100,000 | Batchelor's | 10.0 | 94,000 | 40.0 |
| *Entire Sample* A.P.[g] | 36 | 5,001-10,000 | 7 | 21 | 4 | 14 | 19 | 35,000 | Secondary, Some univ. | 5.5 | 37.500 | 12.0 |
| Other | 18 | 25,001-50,000 | 10 | 8 | 0 | 13 | 5 | 100,000 | Batchelor's | 10.0 | 122,500 | 18.0 |
| Total | 54 | 5,001-10,000 | 17 | 29 | 4 | 27 | 24 | 45,000 | Some univ. | 6.5 | 40,500 | 12.0 |
| *Total Twice-Born* A.P.[g] | 18 | 2,501-5,000 | 4 | 12 | 0 | 5 | 11 | 40,000 | Secondary, Some univ. | 6.0 | 41,000 | 12.0 |
| Other | 10 | 50,001 & above | 7 | 3 | 0 | 10 | 0 | 425,000 | Bachelor's | 13.0 | 160,000 | 20.5 |
| Total | 28 | 10,001-25,000 | 11 | 15 | 0 | 15 | 11 | 60,000 | Bachelor's | 9.0 | 50,000 | 13.0 |
| *Schumpetserian Entrepreneurs* A.P.[g] | 8 | 5,001-25,000 | 3 | 4 | 0 | 4 | 4 | 43,000 | Some univ. | 8.0 | 40,250 | 16.5 |
| Other | 9 | 50,001 & above | 7 | 2 | 0 | 6 | 3 | 560,000 | Bachelor's | 23.0 | 450,000 | 56.0 |
| Total | 17 | 25,001-50,000 | 10 | 6 | 0 | 10 | 7 | 320,000 | Bachelor's | 13.0 | 62,500 | 21.0 |

Notes: [a] Measured in rupees per annum (in fiscal year 1969/70).
[b] The toal number of responses may be less than the number opf entrepreneurs because of cases where there is a lack of response or where the answer is unknown.
[c] Business as a major occupation refers to the management and/or ownership of any business unless it is agricultural or professional.
[d] Refers to the median experience in entrepreneurial and/or management positions (outside agriculture and the professions) prior to the establishment of the firm.
[e] Refers to gross value added (in rupees, in the fiscal year 1969/70), which equals the value of output of a firm minus purchases from other firms.
[f] Measured in terms of average number of full-time wage earners in the firm in fiscal year 1969/70.
[g] Andhra Pradesh.
[h] Includes Kikhs, Syrian Christians, Parsis.

104

parental economic status, and larger firms, but not higher incomes (Table VII.6).

Despite the lack of low-caste entrepreneurs, there were three Protestants, one Roman Catholic, and one Harijan who were the top day-to-day managers of enterprises (usually on the technical rather than on the sales and personnel side). This is consistent with a pattern of a relatively high predisposition by members of low-caste communities in Vizag for salaried positions with a secure tenure and of a low propensity for self-employment. The risk of business activity was not attractive to Harijans, whose designation as "backward" castes entitled them to a portion of the quota of university seats and civil service positions (even though usually at the lower echelons). In addition, Harijans and Christians measured low in family income, access to capital, business experience, training, and education (Ramana 1971, 131-41, 198, 200) (despite scheduled caste legislation). Furthermore, they lacked connections in high government positions, a network of relationships within the business community, and (analogous to the black supervisor of white American workers) a secure psycho-cultural acceptance of their positions of authority.

Among twice-born castes, the Vaishya (mercantile) community, with about 22 percent of the entrepreneurs in comparison to about 2 percent of the population of Vizag, was especially well represented. Most Vaishyas were born out of state. In turn, eight of the 11 Hindu entrepreneurs born outside the state were from traditional business communities. The fathers of out-of-state Vaishyas had the highest economic status and the highest percentage (100 percent) engaged in management or ownership of nonagricultural business. This family background, in part, enabled the Vaishyas from the outside to rank the highest in median education, median prior management experience, median initial capital, and in the percentage who had received the major share of their initial capital from other family members. Not surprisingly, if entrepreneurs were classified according the birthplace (whether in-state or out-of-state) and caste, out-of-state Vaishyas had the highest median value added of the firm and highest median income (Table VII.6).

Each of these eight Vaishya entrepreneurs, together with other members of their families, had at least five to 10 business units scattered throughout India, while four of the families had more than 20 firms. Three entrepreneurs were Khatri, Sindhi (both men were refugees from West Pakistan in 1947), and Bhatia (a Gujarati trading caste initially from Kutch), major trading and financial communities with origins in the eighteenth century. Five in the sample were Marwaris, primarily from rural trading *jatis* in agriculture-poor Rajasthan. Although few Marwaris entered major urban manufacturing before World War I, several decades after the earliest indigenous industrial venture (see Timberg 1969, 17-18; Rungta 1970, 165-67; Nafziger 1986, 39-78), today they are the leading Indian business community. Under the umbrella of British military power during the colonial period, all four of these communities conducted entrepreneurial activity in alien linguistic or religious communities (the Khatri and Sindhi Hindus in Islamic northwestern undivided India, the Marwaris primarily in Calcutta, and the Bhatias in Bombay) (Morris 1967, 604).

Outsiders from specialized business communities were not expected to participate in the network of traditional obligations or to become local community members. Before independence, these communities, including the eight business families, entered sectors of trade and finance (and in a few cases after World War I even manufacturing) that, by and large, did not compete with British industrial interests. Several of the large industrial families in the sample used their control of banks to fund their own enterprises. The families in banking and commerce amassed capital and business experience. They used these to make substantial moves into manufacturing (in some cases buying existing enterprises from the British) after independence in 1947, when conditions—increased protection of industry, the accompanying decline of trade, and the more favorable government policy toward indigenous enterprise—were propitious for doing so. For example, A. R. Balchandani (a pseudonym), a radio importer in the 1940s and 1950s, switched to the manufacture of electronic components and other radio parts in Madras and Vizag in the 1960s after increased protection restricted imported radios. Although the Indian political elite was less favorably inclined toward private capitalism than the British and less accessible to outsiders, at the state level the economic power of the major business communities and families was sufficiently well-established and the economic resources sufficiently abundant that the entrepreneurs could pull the political levers essential to insure the security and expansion of their business interests.

Gradually they moved beyond major industrial cities such as Calcutta and Bombay to establish manufacturing firms in many other cities in India, including Visakhapatnam in the 1960s. These leading families continued control of the far-flung empire despite the abolition of the managing agency system (where two or more legally separate companies are controlled by a single managing firm) in 1970 and the legislation designed to restrict the expansion of large business houses. The country-wide network of firms maintained a "community of interest" through the ties between family members who held management and ownership interest in the various enterprises. In fact, the companies frequently were controlled by one or two principals in the family who for tax purposes dispersed the ownership of enterprises in the names of other family members. Large business families, because of their accumulation of resources, knowledge, organizational skill, and influence, were most likely to receive licenses for establishing a new enterprise or acquiring materials, and were in a better position to take advantage of government schemes to encourage small industry and geographical diversification. Frequently large industrial houses owned a series of "small-scale" industrial enterprises, which under other institutional arrangements would be described as branches of a large-scale enterprise based in a large manufacturing city. In two instances in the sample a large industrial house prevented from establishing new enterprises without an explicit industrial license was able to purchase an establishment that had already been granted a license.

Generally, the leading member of a major business family remained in Calcutta, Bombay, or Delhi, except for occasional visits to firms elsewhere. Other family members were posted in other cities to oversee the construction of the plant and establishment of the enterprise. When production became routine, the day-to-day management of the firm was left to professional managers. Family members would make periodic visits, especially when crises arose or decisions about expansion needed to be made.

The large business family, because of its wealth and financial security, has the latitude to provide for the training, education, travel, and business experience of its sons, and can afford the purchase of the plant and equipment that is most appropriate for the young businessman's entrepreneurial development. As youngsters, the sons learn the nature of the enterprises and are exposed to a business milieu. During school vacations and after graduation each son is moved from job to job within the family firms, gradually having his responsibility increased so that in his early twenties he may be in charge of the day-to-day operations at one of the plants, and a few years later he may be entrusted to make major decisions in a plant in a minor industrial city (such as Vizag) away from the family's headquarters. Marriage may be arranged in part to further an economic alliance with another large business family.

Manufacturing units in Visakhapatnam had only a peripheral role in determining the overall business success of these families. Despite the fact that seven of the eight entrepreneurs had a 1969/70 annual personal income exceeding Rs. 50,000, four of the eight entrepreneurs were incurring business losses from their manufacturing units in Vizag. Although the size of the firms was substantial when compared to others in the sample, the firms were small when compared to other enterprises of the entrepreneur in other parts of India. Among the firms where information was available and which had existed for more than five years, the rates of growth in employment and production for out-of-state Vaishya firms were substantially less than for the rest of the sample. Three out of four of these firms declined in output and employment in the five years previous to 1969/70, while one had an increase in both categories. In contrast, among other firms, 14 grew in output, two remained the same, and three declined; in employment, 11 increased, six stayed constant, and two declined.

In India, the licensing of capacity and materials to specific firms was done by the state government. The evidence concerning growth, profits, and capacity utilization is consistent with the contention that most large business houses acquired licenses to establish factories in Vizag (one of the cities in less-industrialized states favored by government policy) not so much for purposes of expansion, but to obtain licensed imports and materials, undertake transfers of these to sister firms, and protect a market position by foreclosing the growth of licensed capacity by other competitors in the industry.

From early in the Christian era, local trading communities have been active in Andhra, especially near the political centers and temple towns. There is evidence that the merchant castes attained their high ritual and social status as a result of the vital service they rendered to the ruling dynasties and the priestly class. Komatis (the local name for Vaishya) comprise more than one-half of the traders in Vizag city (Rao 1971, 30-31). However, unlike Vaishyas in many other parts of India, Komatis have virtually no experience in manufacturing. Coastal Andhra, because of its comparative advantage in agriculture, its deficiency in power resources and raw materials, its lack of social overhead services, and the relative neglect of its economic development when part of Madras state until 1953, was long industrially backward, and thus never developed an indigenous industrial community. Although Vaishyas are disproportionately represented among in-state entrepreneurs, their income class and firm value added were not even above the median of entrepreneurs born in Andhra. Their low ranking in business success may be related the their relatively low family economic success, which is associated with low educational attainment, business experience, and initial capital (Table VII.6). Two of the four entrepreneurs had fathers involved in business, but the business of only one, a manufacturer of iron hardware whose father had traded the commodity, was related to that of his father or was assisted by him.

For the Brahmin, merchant and industrial entrepreneurship is far removed from the traditional caste occupations of priesthood, teaching, the professions, and government service. Relatively few fathers of Brahmin entrepreneurs were involved in business and none were engaged in the same business as the son (Table VII.6). Yet it is not surprising that the major previous occupation of five of 11 was trade and sales, or that 50 percent of the businessmen with an entrepreneurial background in commerce were Brahmins. For prospective industrialists with a lack of personal or familial expertise and capital, investment and experience in petty trade is a natural stepping stone to a larger, more fixed, and more complex manufacturing enterprise. Nor is it surprising that a disproportionate number of these entrepreneurs acquired their initial capital from themselves (that is, seven of 11 compared to only 20 of 43 from the rest of the sample) and that their median initial capital was below the sample median. Since none could obtain their start in a relative's business, they obtained prior experience and (in some cases) capital as merchants (four), engineers or technicians (three), or sales managers (one) in the same industries they established, or as professionals (two). Nevertheless, the median value added of their firms was as large as that of the sample. Perhaps this is partially associated with their high level of education, as 72.7 percent of them had at least a bachelor's degree, compared to only 46.3 percent of the sample. Their median income is below the median. This may be related to the fact that as many as seven Brahmins were involved in only one business.

The fact that Brahmin participation in industrial entrepreneurial activity in Vizag was about as high as their percentage in the population may result from several "push" and "pull" factors. Major "push" factors have been the administrative orders after World War I which limited the number of Brahmins in government departments, and the scheduled caste legislation after independence which discriminated against high castes. The increase in the status of industrial entrepreneurship accompanying the inducements to indigenous small-scale industry in the independence period and the wealth and influence available to facilitate investment in training and new enterprises are "pull" factors (Hoselitz 1963, 36-40; Berna 1960, 42-44, 83-86, 212-13; Nafziger 1986, 39-78).

Table VII.1 indicates Brahmins are substantially underrepresented among blue-collar workers in Vizag. Owens (1973, 147), in his study of industrialists in Howrah, West Bengal, even suggests Brahmin entrepreneurs are unwilling to do onerous manual labor. I found no evidence that Brahmin entrepreneurs in Vizag are any less inclined than other entrepreneurs to do dirty manual work when that is required in their unit. Brahmins, with a high ritual status, long tradition of literacy, and a background of relative privilege, have an aversion to low-status, demeaning, and ritually polluting work, but not to physical labor in relatively high-status activity, such as industrial entrepreneurship.

The proportionate representation of Muslims in entrepreneurial activity in Vizag was almost as high as for the Vaishyas. Perhaps Muslim participation can be explained partly because of limited alternatives in the civil service, and the absence of traditional barriers to occupations that are polluting to Hindus, such as shoemaking and rope manufacturing. For M. C. Ahmad, who was an administrative head in a coastal Andhran district in old Madras state, and whose father was police superintendent in the former Muslim-led princely state of Mysore, past wealth and influence stemmed a decline in options in government service in the 1950s and 1960s by facilitating two industrial ventures in Vizag. However, none of the other six Muslim entrepreneurs, four of whom were born within the state, had ties with the old Muslim ruling class of the princely states. Local Muslim entrepreneurs, like local Muslims in general, did not enjoy a high parental economic status or high educational status. In Vizag, the caste status of Muslims was relatively low, although not well defined nor as low as for Harijans and Christians (Ramana 1971, 120, 134). This socioeconomic background may have been partially responsible for the low level of initial capital, value added, and income associated with Muslim business endeavors.

# BIRTHPLACE

The birthplace of entrepreneurs were divided equally between Vizag District, the state of Andhra Pradesh outside Vizag District, and South Asia outside Andhra Pradesh. The percentage born outside the state was over five times their share of the population of Vizag city by place of birth, and others born outside Vizag district were also disproportionately represented. This is not surprising, since there is less regional segmentation in the market for high-level personnel, such as entrepreneurs, than for ordinary labor.

Those born outside Andhra Pradesh were most successful and those born within Vizag District generally least successful as entrepreneurs. The four entrepreneurs born outside India's present borders—three who were refugees from West Pakistan in 1947 and one who left Burma (Myanmar) as a result of business nationalization in 1965—were among 13 entrepreneurs in the top two income classes and their firms were all the top 10 in value added.

Why were entrepreneurs from outside the state more successful than entrepreneurs from within the state? Those with little wealth and education tended to be thwarted by financial, psychological, and linguistic barriers to interstate migration. Entrepreneurs usually only immigrated if they had some wealth and education and the prospect for substantial economic advantage. Thus, outside entrepreneurs who migrated to Vizag, a city which lacked local industrial skills and experience, were from a select portion of the population, as the sample totals on caste, class, education, initial capital, and business experience show (Table VII.6). In addition, the challenge of a new environment to immigrants may have had a beneficial educational and psychological effect in breaking tradition and enhancing innovation and success. A related factor was that the geographical dispersion of friends, relatives, and neighbors of the migrants may have spurred the rejection of local values, obligations, and sanctions, like caste propriety, which impeded rational business practice. (Sombart 1928 stresses the same point in his analysis of Jewish entrepreneurs in the Middle Ages.)

In Vizag, the percentage of industrial entrepreneurs from outside the state is 33.3 percent compared to 29 percent of the trading entrepreneurs in Rac's sample, despite the fact industrial activity involves a longer gestation period of investment and a greater extent of fixed capital than trade. Perhaps the percentage of immigrant industrialists in high-income brackets were more likely to have access to the resources to migrate and comprise a higher percentage of industrialists than traders, and because of the fact that greater economies of agglomeration in manufacturing mean that opportunities in industry are more centralized in urban centers such as Vizag.

# PATERNAL ECONOMIC STATUS

The 1969/70 median income of the entrepreneur divided by the median number of dependents (5) was Rs. 1,000-2,000, substantially above Rs. 589.3, the 1969/70 all-India income per capita (which exceeds the all-India median income) (India 1971, 78). Responses by entrepreneurs indicated the economic status of their fathers was high in the aggregate (Table VII.6). This is despite the fact respondents judged the status of unskilled factory workers as low, even though it is at least medium when one considers that 70 percent of India's working population is in the low-income agricultural sector. Table VII.7 reinforces this view of the economic status of fathers, since 20 percent were in cultivation, 2 percent in agricultural labor, and 78 percent in nonagricultural pursuits compared to 50 percent, 20 percent, and 30 percent respectively in India's working population in 1951.[9] In addition, the major occupation of 27 of 51 of the fathers was some form of nonagricultural business (Table VII.6).

The economic status of the father was closely related to the entrepreneurial success of the son.[10] A high paternal economic status of the father assists the prospective entrepreneur in acquiring resources for investment in education,[11] training, and plant and equipment, and in obtaining business experience and government assistance. The median education of the entrepreneurs, who were all male, was some university, which is extremely high when compared to the male population of Vizag District urban areas, 63 percent of which had not completed primary school. Among entrepreneurs, there was a positive relationship between educational attainment and business success.[12] In addition, businessmen with a greater paternal economic status, because of more education and erudition, a more extensive network of influential

*V11.7.* Distribution of Fathers of Entrepreneurs in Economic Sector

| Sector | Major Activities of Fathers of Entrepreneurs (%) | Working Population of India. 1951 (%) |
|---|---|---|
| Cultivation | 20 | 50 |
| Agricultural labor | 2 | 20 |
| Mining, manufacturing household industries, etc. | 29 | 12 |
| Construction | 14 | 1 |
| Trade and commerce | 14 | 5 |
| Transport and communications | 0 | 2 |
| Other services | 22 | 10 |
| Total | 101[a] | 99[a] |

*Sources:* The author's sample, and Tata Economic Consultancy Services, *Statistical Outline of India 1970* (Bombay: Popular Prakashan, 1970), p. 16.
[a] Column may not add up to 100 percent because of rounding.

acquaintances, and more resources available to acquire information, were more likely to be successful in receiving government assistance (Nafziger: 1978, 81-106).

## ENTREPRENEURIAL AND MANAGEMENT EXPERIENCE

For the entrepreneur, the lack of technical, managerial, and marketing experience and training in business is perhaps one of the major barriers to success. The small-scale entrepreneur usually needs to have a minimum level of skills in production, engineering, marketing, financing, purchasing, organization, labor relations, and relationships with government, as the unit cost of acquiring high-level personnel for such a size firm may be prohibitive. Most entrepreneurs who did not belong to the large out-of-state business families did not have the relationships with business-oriented friends and relatives to obtain access to trustworthy managers or even to acquire a reliable evaluation of the ability and integrity of prospective managers. In addition, those with greater experience in business had more time to acquire retained earnings to increase the capital available for their initial venture in manufacturing (Ibid., pp. 86-97, 104-06). Thus, there was a significant positive relationship between the experience of the respondent in entrepreneurial and managerial positions (outside agriculture) and the success of the entrepreneur.

## SOURCES OF INITIAL CAPITAL

Entrepreneurs in single small-scale enterprises have not usually had access to funds from organized financial institutions, at least before bank nationalization. In addition, in Indian society a prospective lender or partner usually did not feel that the social sanctions and networks of relationships were available to feel secure in advancing funds to a person who was not a close relative, of the same caste, or linked in a customary patron-client relationship. Thus, raising the initial capital of the firm was a major barrier to entry. Even the smallest enterprise required Rs. 5,000-10,000, equivalent to a few years earnings for prospective entrepreneurs with a median income.[13]

The extended family, because of its age composition and size, may be able to mobilize funds that the prospective entrepreneur, whose median age of entry into the sample firm was 35 years, would not have been available. Sixty-one percent (33 of 54) of the entrepreneurs indicated a part of the initial capital for the firm was raised from other family members. Forty-four percent received most or all of their initial capital from the family. The figure for at least partial assistance from the family is greater (74 percent), if you consider capital raised for the entrepreneur's initial business venture (that is, not necessarily the sample firm) (Ibid., pp. 104-06).

The family economic status of the entrepreneur was a crucial factor affecting the availability of capital for new industrial enterprises, and thus the supply and success of industrial entrepreneurs. Entrepreneurs with high paternal economic status has a median initial capital of Rs. 167,000, compared to Rs. 35,000 for those with a low and medium economic status. It is reasonable to assume this relationship between parental economic status and initial capital is the tip of the iceberg whose surface depicts a positive relationship between parental economic status and entry into industrial entrepreneurship.

Those with high parental economic status received more initial financial support from their family. Ten of the 17 (59 percent) with a high father's economic status received most of their funds from their family, while four additional ones received some support from this source. In comparison, only 14 of 33 (42 percent) with low or medium economic status received most of their initial financial support from their family, with eight more receiving some support from it. Those who received most of their initial financial support from their families had a higher median capital, Rs. 70,000, than those who provided their own support, Rs. 45,000. Finally, major industrial families used their control of banks before bank nationalization in July 1969 to fund the enterprises of their families and business communities.

## FIRM SURVIVAL

In 1993, I reinterviewed the entrepreneurs of the 22 industrial firms surviving from the initial population of firms. The data collected indicate that firms founded by high-caste entrepreneurs were most likely to survive. Furthermore, older entrepreneurs, with more human capital and less opportunities to change careers, had higher survival rates than younger entrepreneurs. However, higher levels of education of the founding entrepreneur decreased the probability of firm survival, because of the increased opportunity cost of busines activity and the premium put on abilities enhanced by education, such as connections with and persuasion of government bureaucrats, under a controlled regime. Before liberalization in the 1980s and 1990s, well-educated entrepreneurs used human capital to extract rents from materials quotas alloted by government. The management experience of the entrepreneur, whose opportunity cost rose while human capital was being accumulated, was negatively correlated with firm survival. The study also found that firms with higher initial capital and whose entrepreneurs were born out-of-state and had a higher paternal economic status, variables highly correlated with the caste ranking of the entrepreneur, were more likely to succeed. Finally, government assistance to non-survivors exceeded that for surviving firms, as the district government's concessional aid in leasing land or buildings and the state government's loan funds exphasized small firms.[14]

# CONCLUSION

This study of south Indian industrialists offers one perspective on vertical socioeconomic mobility, and the differences in economic opportunities between the privileged and underprivileged portions of the population. A highly disproportionate number of the entrepreneurs (especially successful ones) are from high castes and from families with a high economic status. Members of the dominant castes, leading classes, and large business houses can avert the threat of democratization, industrialization, and modernization to the positions of their families by using the advantages of the past—property, influence, status, and so forth—to obtain the concessions, experience, education, training, and industrial capital usually essential for successful industrial undertakings. Chapter 8 will examine whether the findings in south India apply to other societies.

# NOTES

1.  The universe consisted of the entrepreneurs of the 55 private industrial establishments, with at least 50 percent indigenous ownership, registered with the Industries Department of Vizag District from 1958 through 1970, listed as having five or more employees, and operating at the time of interview (January-April 1971). Nafziger 1978, 131-51.

2.  Statistics of Vizag are based on the universe of 2,000 households from eight representative areas within the city as indicated in Ramana 1971, 21-29, a source consistent with census data on the distribution of the population of Vizag city by religion.

3.  The one Christian in the sample is not an exception to this generalization. He belongs to the Syrian Christians from Kerala, considered, because of the early origins of their religion in India (the first to fourth century A.D.), their emphasis on ritual purification, their endogamy, and their reputation as traders and technicians, to approximate closely the caste standing of the Kerala Kshatriya Atiya 1968, 377.

4.  Calculated value $\chi^2 = 9.70$, $\chi^2$ .01 with 1 d.f. = 6.64.

5.  The *average* initial equity capital is Rs. 191,000 for twice-born castes compared to Rs. 64,000 for Sudras. Calculated value of $\chi^2 = 6.49$, $\chi^2$ .02 with 1 d.f. = 6.64.

6.  The percentage of businessmen from high castes with prior managerial responsibility was significantly higher then the percentage of Sudras. Calculated value of $\chi^2 = 5.76$, $\chi^2$ .02 with 1 d.f. = 5.41.

7.  The percentage of businessmen from high castes with prior managerial responsibility was significicatly higher than the percentage of Sudras. Caluclated value of $\chi^2 = 5.76$, $\chi^2$ .02 with 1 d.f. = 5.41.

8.  I discuss separate Sudra *jatis* in Nafziger 1986: 70-72, 169-70.

9.  Calculated value of $\chi^2 = 379.56$, $\chi^2$ 0.1 with 2 d.f. = 9.21.

10.  Where Y is net income class (1 for less then 0, 2 for 0-2,500, 3 for 2,501-5,000, 4 for 5,001-10,000, 5 for 10,001-25,000, 6 for 25,001-50,000, and 7 for 50,001 or more), $X_1$ is father's economic status (1 for low, 2 for medium, and 3 for high) and $X_2$ is the entrepreneur's age (in years); Y = $1.1353 + 1.353 + 1.389X_1 + 0.0071X_2$, $t_1 = 2.3082$, and the multiple regression coefficient on $X_1$ is significant at the 5 percent level. Net income is measured in rupees annually (in fiscal years 1969/70).

11. There is a positive correlation between the economic status of the fathers and the education of the entrepreneurs. Where Y is educational attainment (0 for none, 1 for some primary, 2 for primary, 3 for some secondary, 4 for secondary, 5 for some university, 6 for a bachelor's degree, 7 for a master's degree, and 8 for above a master's degree) and X is the economic status of the father (see previous note), $Y = 3.13083 + 0.72100X$, $t = 2.15510$, and the regression coefficient is significant at the 5 percent level.

12. Where Y is 1969/70 gross valued added (in rupees per annum), $X_1$ is the entrepreneur's education (as indicated in the previous note), $X_2$ the entrepreneur's age, $Y = 36,7982 + 0.1938X_1 + 0.0754X_2$, $t = 2.2238$, and the multiple regression on $X_1$ is significant at the 5 percent level. Nafziger 1978: 103-04, shows a positive relationships between the education and the net income class of the entrepreneur.

13. Where Y is net income class (as indicated above) and X is the number of years of management and entrepreneurial experience of the entrepreneur, $Y = 2.88302 + 0.089694X$, $t = 2.48273$, and the regression coefficient is significant at the 2 percent level. Where Y is 1969/70 gross value added and X is the number of years of expeirence of the entrepreneur, $Y = -53670.37500 + 15114.0078X$, $t = 2.14681$, and the regression coefficient is significant at the 5 percent level.

14. These findings are based on colllaborative work with Dek terrell and R. Sundarsana Rao.

# Chapter VIII

# *Society and the Entrepreneur*

As indicated earlier, the entrepreneur is a major contributor to the rate of economic growth. What are the determinants of entrepreneurship, especially its supply and success? The first section of this chapter demonstrates the importance of social (as well as economic) factors in explaining entrepreneurship. Subsequent sections analyze questions concerning the effect of social structure on entrepreneurship. How valid are the major socio-psychological approaches of McClelland and Hagen in explaining activity? Are marginal individuals more likely to be innovative entrepreneurs? Does the extended family inhibit or facilitate business activity? What effect does education have on entrepreneurship? Are women well-represented among entrepreneurs? These include several of the most frequently discussed questions concerning the influence of social structure on entrepreneurial activity.

## THE RELATIVE IMPORTANCE OF SOCIAL AND ECONOMIC VARIABLES

Scholars have long disputed which factors—social or economic—are the more important determinants of entrepreneurship. Papanek studied 250 industrialists in Pakistan whose industrial growth was rapid between 1947 and 1959. With Indian-Pakistani partition in 1947, opportunities opened up for the Muslim business community, because of separation from Indian industry and the exodus of the dominant Hindu businessmen. The government protected domestic production, undervalued foreign exchange, and provided industrial incentive programs (such as generous depreciation allowances) to increase manufacturing's rate of return relative to trade and stimulate industrial entrepreneurship. Forty-three percent of Muslim industrialists were from ethnic groups that accounted for less than 0.5 percent of the Pakistani population. Trade was the primary occupation for 45 percent of those who became industrialists. Papanek (1962, 46-58) argues entrepreneurship in manufacturing arises in response to powerful economic incentives rather than

117

significant changes in socio-psychological variables. Yet Papanek did not systematically investigate whether Pakistan's social structure changed. Indeed Hagen's evidence (1962a, 59-61) concerning the small trading communities from which the entrepreneurs originated suggests substantial socio-psychological changes.

Berna (1960) argues in his study of manufacturing entrepreneurs in the light-engineering industry of Tamil Nadu, India, that social variables do not explain entrepreneurial activity and success. His 52 entrepreneurs are members of 10 different social communities. Only four sample entrepreneurs are in the traditional caste-assigned family occupation. This break with tradition indicates to Berna that "sociological factors, such as caste, attachment to traditional activities, and approval or disapproval of the social group to which a potential entrepreneur belongs are less important than economic factors such as access to capital and possession of business experience and technical knowledge."

Hoselitz (1963, 36-39) contends, however, that Tamil Nadu's social structure must be undergoing a profound change. One important indication is the decline in occupational choices assigned by caste, which needs sociological explanations. Brahmins, for example, have been more inclined to become entrepreneurs than previously for a number of reasons: discrimination in universities and government because of the Brahmins' favored position during colonialism, the decline in caste-determined occupations, an increase in the status of business occupations resulting from the emphasis on economic growth, and the wealth and influence available for investment in training and new enterprises. In short, economic development led to the erosion of the Brahmins' traditional position, so they saw entrepreneurship as increasingly attractive. A parallel exists in Nigeria, where numerous Yoruba and Hausa traditional political rulers thwarted possible economic decline accompanying modernization by using their wealth and influence to establish sizeable trade and manufacturing firms (Nafziger 1977, 126-48).

The Papanek-Hagen and Berna-Hoselitz controversies indicate the limitations of the approach of a single discipline in discussing factors affecting entrepreneurship. Reality is an unbroken totality, a seamless robe, and is not compartmentalized into social and economic spheres. Thus, for Brahmins, impelled by a declining socio-economic position and advantages accruing from their wealth and influence (accesses to capital, good educational background), entrepreneurial activity resulted from the interaction of both social and economic factors.

# ACHIEVEMENT MOTIVATION AND ENTREPRENEURSHIP

Since the 1960s, industrial extension centers, spurred by McClelland and Winter (1971), have introduced achievement motivation training to develop entrepreneurs. Psychological evidence indicates that a person learns unconsciously in earliest childhood behavior what is safest and most rewarding, and that this learning substantially influences adult behavior. For example, the individual who is encouraged to be curious, creative, and independent as a child is more likely to engage in innovative and entrepreneurial activity as an adult. Although a society might consciously attempt to nurture imagination, self-reliance, and achievement orientation in child rearing and schooling, scholars had assumed that it would take at least a generation before deliberate efforts affected entrepreneurship and economic growth.

McClelland, in *The Achieving Society*, contends a society with a generally high need for achievement or "urge to improve" (*n* Ach) produces more energetic entrepreneurs who bring about more rapid economic development. As a first step, he established a significant positive relationship between *n* Ach scores (in children's readers) and subsequent rates of growth in electrical output (a proxy for economic growth) in a crossnational sample from the twentieth-century. McClelland's laboratory work found that those persons with a high *n* Ach are more likely to behave like an entrepreneur—namely (1) to take personal responsibility for decisions, (2) to prefer decisions involving a moderate degree of risk, and (3) to evince interest in concrete knowledge of the results of decisions. Furthermore, his empirical evidence suggests that persons with high *n* Ach tend to be attracted to entrepreneurial positions (when society accords these occupations high prestige) (McClelland 1961, reviewed by Schatz 1965, 234-41; Higgins 1968, 241-49).

*The Achieving Society* is pessimistic about policy measures to increase *n* Ach as this depends on child-rearing techniques and parental attitudes. But even if these changed, entrepreneurial activity and economic growth would not be affected until the children grew up. A next step for McClelland (and Winter) was to restate the theory to test whether *n* Ach might be increased among adults.

The laboratory for their "intervention effort" was businessmen taking a 10-day course in 1964 and 1965 at the Hyderabad, South India's Small Industries Extension Training Institute, a government institution that collaborated in the undertaking. The purpose of the experiment was to investigate whether achievement motivation could be inculcated in businessmen through motivational training courses in small groups, and whether the training would result in heightened business activity. In the course, participants were to acquire a higher need to achieve through (1) learning to recognize and produce achievement-related fantasies, (2) self-study to ascertain how the achievement syndrome relates to their lives, careers, goals, and values, (3) defining more precisely their basic goals, the blocks to these, methods to overcome blocks, and ways to measure progress toward these goals, and (4) new interpersonal supports and reference groups to reinforce values associated with the urge to improve (McClelland and Winter 1971).

I argue that a program of $n$ Ach acquisition for entrepreneurs, while it may be suitable to Western societies, is less appropriate in India and other LDCs. First, in a society with substantial limitations on resource availability, high $n$ Ach, associated with a competitive spirit, "becomes a sin against one's fellows." When available resources are scarce, persons with a high need for cooperation will produce more than those with high $n$ Ach (Sinha 1969, 233-46). Second, high $n$ Ach may be appropriate where an individual can control his activity, but not where he faces substantial restraints on decision making. Persons with a high n Ach may be frustrated and counter-productive in sectors of a society that places an emphasis on "a socialist pattern of society" with public economic decision-making. Third, a "course [which] is basically one of self-development" and emphasizes "a personal decision" regarding life goals may have merit in the United States, which emphasizes independence and self-reliance, but not in India, where the communal and family nexus are important. In India, where the extended family is the basic unit for identification and frequently for business ventures, $n$ Ach, a measure of individual achievement motivation, does not explain entrepreneurial behavior (Javillonar and Peters 1973, 314-28).

McClelland and Winter seem not to be seriously aware of the moral ambiguities that arise when "change agents" and behavior modification are introduced in a society which, by their own admission, they understand little. Nandy (1972, 578) puts it this way:

> One must...recognize that something more than mere achievement training was involved. What these quasi-therapeutic interventions tried to do could be crudely summed up as an attempt to generate personality vectors functional to modern economic behaviour and help individuals to integrate these vectors in their personality system by altering, among other things, self-image, significant others, access to the relevant aspects of their own fantasy life, and sense of efficacy vis-é-vis the external world. The inputs package represented, in this sense, more nearly a program of total personality change. Such a program of intervention demands some awareness of the cultural forces which shape a person's behaviour and with which he has to cope at so many levels as well as sectors of social living.

One problem in interpreting the authors' finding is the lack of a genuine control group to compare with those entrepreneurs given the achievement motivation course. Given the claims of the course, the prestige of Harvard sponsorship, and the support of the District Collector, Chamber of Commerce, and leading local officials, it is not surprising if the course attracted a select group of entrepreneurs especially interested in personal and business development. Among other things, the high level of personal capital and subsequent business activity of participants in the first courses, in comparison to the last two courses, suggests the attempt, especially in early courses, to attract leading businessmen with a substantial interest in self-improvement, was successful. The group of businessmen who did not participate in the course is not, contrary to what McClelland and Winter maintain, really a control group, because they could have taken the course but did not. To obtain a bona fide control group—that is to control for the variable of desire to seek self and business improvement—it would have been essential to prevent some who sought to enroll in the course (perhaps a systematically paired control group) from taking the course.

There is no information presented on the relationship between $n$ Ach and entrepreneurial activity before training. Naturally, $n$ Ach scores for participants increased after training, since they were guided in practice sessions to obtain higher scores than they did at first.[1] Otherwise, the only data available on $n$ Ach scores is a comparison between participants who were active in expanding their business and those who were inactive: "For all practical purposes the $n$ Ach acquisition and retention [scores for those active and those inactive] are identical." On the other hand, other variable measures—the number of mutual friendship bonds with other participants, scores with regard to efficacy of thinking, and observations by the chief architect of the course regarding the probability of change by various participants—proved to be more powerful in predicting business than did $n$ Ach (McClelland and Winter 1971, 32, 258, 268, 271-72, 324-27).

The authors contend the courses, as intended, had a number of benefits besides raising the participants' $n$ Ach. Yet they present no hypothesis on the relationship between $n$ Ach, economic opportunities and social structure, and between these variables and entrepreneurial activity. Nandy (1972, 578) contends the authors' approach "still is not a comprehensive theory of personality which considers personality as an open system and individual motive structure as an interface between personal and community pasts."

How does the performance of the course participants compare to what the authors considered a control group? Given the fact that the data on firm performance—employment, investment, sales, and so forth—over a first-year period were oral, and "given the continuous and apparently successful attempts to generate a 'Hawthorne effect' (which also tends to obscure any personality change), there is a strong presumptive bias favouring positive results from the training" (Kilby 1971, 21). Toward the end of the course, the faculty, through its help in preparing businessmen for future contacts and surveys by the sponsors, may have inadvertently reinforced a positive bias. Course participants were told that the staff of the host institute "would keep in touch with them not only informally over [the two-year] time period but would be back every six months to find out how they were doing in terms of their personal and group plan and in terms of such general business criteria as gross income, capital invested, profit, and so forth. They practiced filling out the forms they would be asked to return in six months' time so that they would be guided in their actions by the thoughts of how they would be evaluated later." (Pabaney, Danzig, Nadkarni, Pareek, and McClelland 1964). Reports from visitors who evaluated the entrepreneurs after the course suggest embarrassment by some respondents as a result of the lack of business progress, and "an occasional guilt feeling." In view of this, it would not be surprising if the entrepreneurs overstated their progress, or understated their setbacks.

Yet despite the predilection for favorable reports on performance, there are no significant differential percentage increases in the gross incomes of the course participants, although there are significant differential percentage increases in the entrepreneur's time input, attempts to start new businesses, labor employed, and capital invested when compared to those considered controls (McClelland and Winter 1971). Thus, as Kilby (1971, 21) notes: "If the test were to be treated as valid, it would indicate that motivational training engenders a willingness to increase inputs while at the same time it reduces entrepreneurial efficiency and, thereby, the returns to entrepreneurial effort."[2]

There is an alternative hypothesis to explain the association between *n* Ach and entrepreneurship. McClelland's data (1961, 362, based on Rosen 1959, 51-52) indicate in the United States there is a positive correlation between social class and *n* Ach (p < .001). African-Americans, especially those from the lower classes, score low in *n* Ach. LeVine's study (1966, 48, 56-57) of achievement motivation in Nigeria indicates a significant positive correlation between *n* Ach, on the one hand, and paternal class and education, on the other. However, because the conceptual matrix of McClelland and LeVine is not oriented toward dealing with class, they do not pursue the implications of these findings. Upper-class individuals, who encounter fewer blocks (that is, deficiencies in education, training, experience, and skills, and lack of capital and contacts), are more likely to be achievement-oriented and to be able to take advantage of economic opportunities. On the other hand, for those members of underprivileged classes who live in a "subculture of poverty," low *n* Ach and low aspirations are an adaptation to the low probability of economic success resulting from blocks to economic advancement in society, educational institutions, and the family milieu (see Lewis 1968, xlii-liii; Grier and Cobbs 1968). McClelland and Winter (1971, 9) are correct when they contend that "energetic striving to improve one's lot may seem rational enough to a man with high *n* Achievement, but not to a man with low *n* Achievement." But whereas in McClelland's and Winter's scheme the lack of striving by those with low *n* Ach is a result of a lack of sensitivity to changes in economic opportunities and incentives, in the alternative scheme it is seen as a result of blocks to class mobility.

My hypothesis is that *n* Ach is not a primary variable but merely a correlate of socio-economic class, which is significantly related to entrepreneurial activity through differential provision of economic opportunity. The basis for this hypothesis is not only the positive correlation between class and *n* Ach discussed in the preceding paragraph, but also the positive relationships I find between socioeconomic class and entrepreneurship in my study of South India and my interpretation of other studies in chapter 7. To be more specific, a highly disproportionate number of the industrial entrepreneurs (especially successful ones) in my sample are from high castes and from families with a high economic status. Furthermore, other empirical studies in India, Pakistan, the Philippines, Nigeria, Greece, and the United States discussed below indicate that the socioeconomic class of entrepreneurs is high.

Unfortunately, McClelland and Winter have no data on the relationship between caste or class, on the one hand, and $n$ Ach, on the other.[3] Thus, one can only suggest by inference that all cross-relationships between $n$ Ach, socioeconomic class, and entrepreneurial activity are positive. In the future, scholars might wish to investigate more explicitly the relationship between $n$ Ach and socioeconomic class in samples of entrepreneurs.

Whatever the difference between the McClelland approach and my approach in terms of explanatory variables, there is an equally important implication in terms of the legitimacy of the position of the dominant elites in society. For example, McClelland and Winter indicate that in Pennsylvania, unemployed workers with high $n$ Ach were more likely to seek and find jobs than those with a low $n$ Ach, although a critic might suggest that those most unemployable adapt to this state by keeping their achievement expectations low. The McClelland paradigm, with its premise that $n$ Ach can be changed, suggests that the individual bears responsibility for unemployment or for lack of entrepreneurial activity. The alternative approach implies that the fault may lie, in part, with the impediments that society and its dominant classes place in the road to upward mobility to high-level jobs and business activity. A key issue is the extent to which the economically weak are responsible for their poverty, unemployment, and lack of entrepreneurial activity, and the extent to which their class mobility is impeded by the cumulative advantages of the prevailing economic elite.

Yet achievement motivation training programs run entirely by indigenous personnel might be more effective than those conducted by the McClelland group. Indeed a preliminary study by Buchele (1972) indicated several motivation programs established since 1971 in North India were successful as components in entrepreneurial development programs. Although not fully evaluated, we might expect these programs, initiated, planned, and directed by indigenous people, to be less objectionable than those conducted by the McClelland group. First, it is possible that indigenous "change agents," in contrast to foreigners, can more readily adapt the training to the needs and aspirations of prospective local entrepreneurs, while avoiding some of the unnecessary violations of local social mores. One obvious advantage of indigenization is the wider choice of language; usually, the use of the regional language instead of English increases the number of candidates who can potentially benefit from the course. In the second place, it is easier for indigenous personnel to establish programs to attract entrepreneurs from underprivileged groups. For example, the Maharashtra Small Scale Industries Development Corporation charged concessional entrance fees to candidates from underprivileged classes, that is, "scheduled castes, scheduled tribes, and other backward communities." Third, it may be that achievement motivation training is effective only as a part of an integrated package of training that includes management, finance, and marketing—parts of the programs of the National Institute of Motivational and Institutional Development and two North Indian industrial corporations—perhaps accentuating the fact that achievement motivation will be eventually frustrating unless there is some concomitant business training to help entrepreneurs with new or expanded business activity. However, the sparsity of evidence makes further research essential (Oza 1988).

# A THEORY OF TECHNOLOGICAL CREATIVITY

This theory, like McClelland's, a comprehensive explanation of entrepreneurship, utilizes psychology, sociology, and anthropology to explain how a "traditional" agricultural society (with a hierarchical and authoritarian social structure, where status is inherited) becomes one in which continuing technical progress occurs. Since the industrial and cultural complex of low-income societies is unique, they cannot merely imitate Western techniques. Thus, economic growth requires widespread adaptation, creativity, and problem-solving, in addition to positive attitudes toward manual labor.

The childhood environment and training in traditional societies tend to produce an authoritarian personality with low $n$ Ach, high need for dependence and submission, and a view of the world as consisting of arbitrary forces. Where parents perceive children as fragile organisms without the capacity to understand or manage the world, they are treated oversolicitously and prevented from taking initiative. The child, while repressing anger, avoids anxiety by obeying the commands of powerful persons.

Events that cause peasants, workers, or lower elites to feel they are no longer respected and valued may be the catalysts for economic development. The adults get angry and anxious, while their sons retreat and reject their parents' unsatisfying values. After several generations, the women, reacting to the ineffectiveness of their husbands, respond with delight to their sons' achievements. Such maternal attitudes combined with paternal weakness provide an almost ideal environment for the formation of an anxious driving type of creativity. If the sons are blocked from alternative careers, they will become entrepreneurs and spearhead the drive for economic growth (Hagen 1962a).

One problem with Hagen's theory is that withdrawal of status respect is defined so broadly that it may occur once or twice a decade in most societies.

Nor does the theory explain groups, such as the seventeenth-century English Catholics, who lost status respect but did not become entrepreneurs. Even identifying the creative personality is imprecise. Furthermore, the interval between status withdrawal and the emergence of creativity varies so much that McClelland suggests that almost any case can be made to fit Hagen's hypothesis (McClelland 1964, 320-24). The time from the derogation of the samurai (warriors), merchants, and wealthy peasants to the modernization of Japan following the Meiji Restoration (1868), and from the contempt expressed toward Basque immigrants to Antioquia to the beginning of modern Columbian industry in 1901-1906, was about 25 years. On the other hand, the lag between the Norman conquest of England (1066-1087) and her Industrial Revolution was close to 700 years. Hagen indicates that all currently underdeveloped countries will achieve economic growth, although whether the transition will take 30 or 70 years cannot be forecast.

Although Hagen charges economists with ethnocentrism, he applies a personality theory based on modern American material to very different societies and historical epochs. In addition, his country case studies provide no evidence of changes in parent-child relationships and child-training methods during the early historical periods of status withdrawal. Moreover, economic historian Gerschenkron (1965, 90-94) argues that the position, training, and severe discipline of the child in modern Austria, Sweden, and Germany resemble those described in Hagen's traditional society. Finally, Hagen slights the effect of changes in economic opportunities, such as improved transportation, wider markets, and the availability of foreign capital and technology, on entrepreneurial activity. Yet, despite the inadequacies, Hagen's insights have made economists more aware of the importance of noneconomic variables in entrepreneurial development.

# RELIGIOUS AND ETHNIC ORIGIN

## *Weber's Thesis: The Protestant Ethic*

Capitalism is an economic system where private owners of impersonal means of production and their agents, making decisions based on private profit, hire free but capital-less workers. In 1904-1905, Weber, in *The Protestant Ethic and the Spirit of Capitalism* (1930), tried to explain why the continuous and rational development of the capitalist system originated in Western Europe around the sixteenth-century. Although pockets of capitalism existed in the ancient and medieval periods, capitalist civilization is a modern phenomenon.

Weber noted that European businessmen and skilled laborers were overwhelmingly Protestant, and that capitalism was most advanced in Protestant countries such as England and Holland. Protestantism, like medieval Roman Catholicism, was ascetic, manifesting itself in the planned and systematic regulation of the whole conduct of the Christian. This "inner-worldly" asceticism was expressed by vigorous activity in a secular vocation or "calling," in contrast to the "other-worldly" asceticism of the Catholic monastery.

Although ascetic Protestants opposed materialism as much as the Catholic Church did, they did not disapprove of the accumulation of wealth. They did, however, restrict extravagance, conspicuous consumption, and indolence. This resulted in a high rate of savings and continued hard work—both favorable to economic progress.

Calvinists, together with Pietists, Methodists, Baptists, Quakers, and Mennonites, were the major ascetic Protestants. Elected by God, the Calvinist was to be diligent, thrifty, honest, and prudent—virtues coinciding with the spirit essential for capitalist development.

Although Tawney (1926) supports Weber's contention there was a relationship between the Protestant Reformation and the rise of capitalism, he makes two modifications. First, he emphasizes the Protestant movement as a whole, together with general political, social, intellectual, and economic conditions of the sixteenth and seventeenth-centuries, as being responsible for the rise of capitalism. Second, his analysis includes the effect of socioeconomic change on Protestantism, as well as Weber's stress on its impact on capitalism. Robertson (1959) pushes Tawney's second point further, arguing that the Puritan ethic changed to accommodate the needs of the rising capitalist class. Samuelsson (1957, 66-67, 152) even argues that Protestantism was used to legitimize what businessmen were doing.

Correlation between two variables, such as the Protestant Reformation and the rise of capitalism, need not indicate causation. Some scholars argue that a third and independent factor, such as the disruption of the Roman Catholic social system and civil power (Cunningham 1913) or the ease with which new ideas spread among trading nations (Robertson 1959), was responsible for both the Protestant ethic and the rise of capitalism. Another explanation is that the secularization, ethical relativism, and social realism of Protestantism is as important as its "this-worldly" asceticism in explaining its contribution to economic development (Nafziger 1965, 187-204, reprinted in Nafziger 1986, 261-82). Even so, many critics (for example, Samuelsson) fail to understand that Weber's argument for the affinity of Puritanism and the capitalist spirit is not based so much on the reformers' teachings about work and economic activity as on the concept of a "calling" to a life of strict discipline in a secular sphere.

For McClelland, who reinterprets Weber's thesis as a special case of his findings, the emphasis on self-reliance by ascetic Protestants resulted in stronger internalized achievement drives among their sons, which in turn led to the rise of capitalism. However, McClelland's evidence is from modern capitalist societies which, according to Weber, no longer need the support of religious asceticism, by then moribund in the west.

The study of Protestantism by Weber is part of an ambitious series, which includes studies indicating religion in India and China inhibited their modernization. He contended the caste system, the concept of ritual purity, and the doctrines of fate (*kharma*), duty (*dharma*), and rebirth associated with Hinduism are not conducive to the economic development of India (Weber 1958) According to Singer (1972, 272-78), Weber's error in examining Indian religion was to rely on scriptural texts to construct the ideal-typical Hindu, a mistake Weber did not make in his investigation of ascetic Protestantism in the west.[4] Singer finds caste affiliation and religious beliefs to be less decisive than such factors as individual and family experience, previous occupation, education, and capital as determinants of recruitment to and success in positions of industrial leadership. Paralleling critiques of Weber's linking the Protestant ethic with the spirit of capitalism, Singer places more emphasis on the rational adaptability of Hinduism to innovation, modernization, and industrialization, and less on the intrinsic affinity of the Hindu value system to industrial capitalism. Ironically, his evidence indicates Hindu industrialists, like Weber's Puritan entrepreneurs, exhibited "worldly" asceticism in economic activity, sensed a "calling" to responsibility in a secular vocation and believed that prosperity was a sign of divine blessing.

Scholars have looked for analogies to the Protestant ethic in non-western societies. Jacobs' study of Japan discovers no analogies but finds no dominant ideology opposed to capitalism (Jacobs 1958, 211-17). Bellah (1957), however, who searches outside the Japanese capitalist sector, finds a correlation between religion of the Tokugawa era (1600-1867) and bureaucratic values conducive to economic growth, especially among the samurai class of aristocratic officers (see chapter XI). Other scholars have noted puritanical sobriety, discipline, and frugality among India's Jain and Parsi entrepreneurs, Java's Muslim *santris*, and even the Chinese masses. While many were not Protestant dissenters, Hagen (1962a, 279) contends innovators were all protestant dissenters, a statement difficult to accept in light of the widespread participation of established communities in entrepreneurship noted in the section below. Bellah argues that a search for parallels to Protestantism in Asia should not focus on similar motivation and institutions but on a reformation ideology that transforms social structure and values. This approach is essential to making Weber's framework useful in examining the many paths to economic modernization taken in the last century or so.

## Marginal Individuals as Entrepreneurs

Weber's work has stimulated scholars to ask questions about differences in participation in entrepreneurial activity by religious, ethnic, and linguistic communities. Even Schumpeter's innovative entrepreneur (1961, 84-89), who carries out new combinations by introducing new products or production functions, opening new markets, exploiting new material sources, or reorganizes an industry, is a deviant, breaking tradition and facing opposition from his social community. Accordingly, one question concerns marginal ethnic and social groups—those whose values differ greatly from the majority of the population. To what extent do marginal individuals, because of their ambiguous position, tend to be innovative?[5]

In a confirmation of Weber's study, Hagen (1962a, 294-97) finds Nonconformists (Quakers, Methodists, Congregationalists, Baptists, Anabaptists, and Unitarians), with only 7 percent of the population, contributed 41 percent of the leading entrepreneurs during the English Industrial Revolution (1760-1830). Other marginal communities disproportionately represented in entrepreneurial activity include Jews in medieval Europe, Huguenots in seventeenth- and eighteenth-century France, Old Believers in nineteenth-century Russia, Indians in East Africa before the 1970s, Chinese in Southeast Asia, Lebanese in West Africa, Marwaris in Calcutta, and Gujaratis in Bombay. Refugees from the 1947 partition between India and Pakistan and the exchange of minorities between Turkey and Greece in the 1920s were overrepresented among industrialists in the four countries. Displaced Armenians, Jews, Europeans, Palestinians, and Arab expatriates, escaping persecution, political hostility, and economic depression, were responsible for the rise in entrepreneurial activity in the Middle East between 1930 and 1955. For migrants, the challenge of a new environment may have a beneficial educational and psychological effect and the geographical dispersion of friends and relatives may allow the rejection of local values and obligations that impede rational business behavior (Meyer 1959; Brenner and Kiefer, 517-34; chapter 7).

If Schumpeter's concept of deviance is to have meaning, it cannot be merely interpreted as new behavior but must imply innovation opposed to existing approved behavior. Thus in Italy in the fifth through ninth centuries, when Christian doctrine regarded taking interest as sinful, moneylenders—Syrians, Byzantines, and Jews—were deviants (Hoselitz 1960, 62-63). On the other hand, the enmity of Hausa-Fulanis toward Ibo and Yoruba traders in northern Nigeria is less a result of a conflict of values than of resentment from being in the competition for the benefits of modernization.

In the contemporary world, most dominant indigenous communities value economic achievement. Thus leading business communities include Protestants of Northern and Western European origin in the United States, and Hindu high castes in India (chapter 7). In Lebanon in 1959, the politically dominant Maronites and other Christian communities comprised 80 percent of the innovative entrepreneurs but only 50 percent of the population (Sayigh 1962, 69-70). The Yorubas and Ibos, the largest ethnic communities in the more industrialized region of southern Nigeria, are also the leading entrepreneurs.

Aliens have not been innovative in industry, which requires a fixed investment that is easier to confiscate. Furthermore, technical changes introduced by aliens usually are not imitated by other groups. The English Nonconformists, Huguenots, Old Believers, Marwaris, Gujaratis, and the South Asian and Mediterranean refugees mentioned above are not aliens, since their roots are in their country's culture (Hagen 1962a, 247-50). Even though some aliens have made important contributions to technical change, there is no evidence they are generally more innovative than natives.

Are marginal men especially innovative? Many scholars question whether culturally marginal individuals are especially creative, since they are more likely to experience social disorganization. Theoretical concepts and empirical findings about marginal individuals have not advanced enough to provide sufficient evidence concerning their relative participation as entrepreneurs. Examples abound of innovations among both marginal and non-marginal men, but no one has provided a world-wide test of whether one of these groups is overrepresented.

## CLASS AND CASTE ORIGIN

Economists have been preoccupied with increasing the size of the GNP pie while slighting its distribution. Empirical data on the distribution of income, business opportunity, and economic power are in short supply. My study of the socioeconomic origins of industrial entrepreneurs in south India serves as a basis for comparing the class and caste of entrepreneurs (chapter 7; Nafziger 1978).

Many studies on entrepreneurship and economic development either rationalize ruthless capitalist exploitation or glorify the capitalist entrepreneur without examining class origins and monopoly advantage (Baran 1957, 254-57). To Schumpeter (1961, 78-79, 93-94), entrepreneurs, with varied class origins and the dream and will to found a private kingdom, to conquer adversity, to achieve success for its own sake, and to experience the joy of creation are heroic figures. In a scheme labeled moral theory by one critic (Bernstein 1971, 148), McClelland views the entrepreneur (in both capitalist and socialist economies) as largely responsible for the global association between a high need for achievement (a psychological measure of the urge to improve) and rapid economic growth. The entrepreneurial role is assumed to be characterized by moderate risk-taking as a function of skill rather than chance, energetic or novel instrumental activity, individual responsibility, inner satisfaction from money earned as a measure of achievement, and long-range planning and organizational abilities. For Papanek (1967, 2, 25-36, 199), the frugal, hard-working, farsighted, remarkably able private entrepreneur willing to take political risks is in large part responsible for the "success" of Pakistan in achieving rapid industrialization.

Three separate empirical studies, drawn from the United States, Nigeria, and Greece, and focusing on the socioeconomic mobility of the entrepreneur, have reinforced this heroic conception. Collins, Moore, and Unwalla (1964, 238) found most entrepreneurs in medium manufacturing firms in Michigan "clearly moved a long way from the somewhat impoverished economic level of their childhoods." Both Nigerian and Greek industrialists were considered highly upwardly mobile in status by Harris (1971, 336-37) and Alexander (1964, 80-95), respectively. I call these views of upward mobility to success in business the "Horatio Alger model," although obviously these empirical works are far more systematic and less simplistic than the heroic fictional biographies by the nineteenth-century U.S. author. This view is consistent with the orthodox economic paradigm, which tends to disregard questions of class origin, to abstract from considerations of conflict and political power (Higgins 1968, 227), and to assume relatively open competition in a polity characterized by the balancing of independent interests. However, the appearance of substantial upward socioeconomic mobility in these three empirical studies results from the peculiar way in which the question is posed, and I find that the data can be interpreted as corroborating the low degree of vertical class mobility I find in the south Indian case.

My study, summarized in chapter VII, shows a highly disproportionate number of Vizag (India) entrepreneurs (especially successful ones) are from high castes and families with a high socioeconomic status, and that members of the large business houses use their wealth and influence to acquire experience, training, and capital for successful industrial activity.

## THE STATUS OF SCHUMPETERIAN ENTREPRENEURS

Does the high caste and paternal economic status of the Vizag entrepreneur result from his designation as one who commits ownership capital? Schumpeter (1961, 1939) contends innovators, who embody some new idea or invention in commercial practice, arise from all economic classes. Might the Schumpeterian entrepreneur be more likely to originate from a lower class and caste than entrepreneurs generally?

No. The socioeconomic background of persons from sample firms who carried out "new combinations" in the coastal Andhran economy was even higher than that of sample entrepreneurs. Innovators had a higher paternal economic status than that of entrepreneurs as a whole, as 10 of 16 innovators indicated their status as high and none indicated it was low (Table VII.6). The overrepresentation of twice-born Hindu castes (59 percent of the innovators),

Muslims (18 percent), and Sikhs (12 percent) was more, and the under-representation of other Hindu castes (6 percent) was less among Schumpeterian entrepreneurs than among the sample. The median management experience, education, and initial capital of the entrepreneur, and the percentage of the fathers of the entrepreneurs in business among Schumpeterian entrepreneurs, are higher than for sample entrepreneurs as a whole, whether the figures refer to in-state, out-of-state, or all entrepreneurs. Finally, Schumpeterian entrepreneurs ranked higher than the sample in median income, and in the firm's median value added and employment (Table VII.6).

Schumpeterian entrepreneurs can be expected to originate from a class and caste background as high as other entrepreneurs, as ideas, techniques, or inventions need to be put into business practice before they become an innovation. The opportunities to arrive at new business ideas are not distributed randomly within a population, but are partly dependent on the availability of training, education, information, facilities, access to creative associates, and other advantages, all expedited by wealth and position.[6] The carrying out of ideas and inventions also depends on access to funds and influence. Their availability to the innovator is especially vital in a country such as India, with a poorly developed capital market, and a low propensity to provide capital for projects initiated outside the family, clan, or *jati*.

The findings concerning the higher socioeconomic status of Schumpeterian entrepreneurs in the Indian sample can, however, only be suggestive. First, the sample of innovators is small. Second, all the Schumpeterian entrepreneurs (and their families) had to take the responsibility for providing the initial capital for the firm which embodied the innovation. In large firms, such as joint stock companies, where innovation is more institutionalized, or in economies more advanced than India where legal, social, and economic sanctions, and the nexus of relationships foster a wider market for loans and investment, innovation may not be as dependent on the availability of capital from the entrepreneur's family. More research is needed on the socioeconomic origins of Schumpeterian entrepreneurs in various types of enterprises, sectors, and economies.

## COMPARATIVE DATA ON SOCIOECONOMIC MOBILITY

Other studies of Indian industrialists point to a concentration of entrepreneurial activity among the sons of the members of the large business houses, who represent a small fraction of the population. Although Berna (1960) remarks on the extremely varied backgrounds of sample industrialists in the state of Tamil Nadu, 41 of the 46 Hindu entrepreneurs with some caste designation were from twice-born castes, and the rest were Sudras. A highly disproportionate number of the fathers of manufacturing entrepreneurs in Pakistan, which had a common history with India before 1947, were from traditional business communities, while a low percentage of fathers were in wage employment or agriculture. Contrary to Papanek's interpretation (1962, 46-58), this pattern would suggest that the socioeconomic class status of entrepreneurs was high when compared to the population. Indigenous managers of large public, foreign, and private enterprises in India also originate from a highly select portion of the population, as none of the fathers were laborers, only 10 percent were farmers (all of whom were small farm operators or large farm owners), and the rest were white-collar workers, government officials, business executives, professional men, and business owners (Prasad and Negandhi 1968, 27). Adding a perspective to the social origin of businessmen is a study of factory laborers in Poona indicating no significant difference between caste and social community of the workers and the city population (Lambert 1963, 33-38).

Contrary to a widely-held viewpoint, this low degree of socioeconomic class mobility is found not only in India but also in most of the rest of the nonsocialist world, at least if evidence is based on empirical studies of entrepreneurs. The proportion of fathers of Filipino manufacturing entrepreneurs from an upper socioeconomic position was 36 times that of the population. Opportunities for industrial enterprise were available chiefly to those who were already well established financially (Carroll 1965, 100-26). Similarly, in Harris's sample (1971, 35) of Nigerian entrepreneurs, 56 percent of the 262 fathers were in the nonagricultural sector, compared to 21 percent of the Nigerian male population (Nigeria 1963, 3). Furthermore, in Alexander's study of Greek industrialists, 54 percent of the 522 fathers were big merchants, industrialists, professional men or business executives, compared to 2 percent of the total working population (Alexander 1964, 45, 97). These figures support the contention that the socioeconomic class of the entrepreneurs was far above that of the population at large.

Many development scholars identify a "rigid" social structure with LDCs and a fluid social structure with developed economies in the United States and Western Europe (Smelser and Lipset 1966, 9, 44; Rostow 1961; Alexander 1964, 80; Harris 1971, 337, cf. chapter 1). However, innovators during the English Industrial Revolution were primarily "the sons of men in comfortable circumstances" (Hagen 1962a, 301).

Likewise, entrepreneurs in the United States have a substantially higher socioeconomic background than the population as a whole, despite United States folk heroes who go from rags to riches through business success. The most celebrated was the steel magnate, Andrew Carnegie (1835-1919), a poor immigrant with little education, the son of a working man who was forced to seek employment at a young age. Through cleverness and hard work, he rose from bobbin boy to messenger to assistant railroad superintendent and industrial leader. For him, "the millionaires who are in active control started as poor boys and were trained in the sternest but most efficient of all schools— poverty." (Carnegie 1902, 109)

Even so, his story is atypical. The Horatio Alger stories of the nineteenth-century are largely legend. Scholarship since World War II shows the successful industrial leader in the late nineteenth century and early twentieth century was usually "American by birth,... English in national origin,... urban in early environment,... born and bred in an atmosphere in which business and a relatively high social standing were intimately associate with his family life," and educated through high school. Both entrepreneurs and business bureaucrats in the first two decades of the twentieth century were from similar backgrounds. None of the business elite studied by Miller et al. (1962) in either period were female or nonwhite.

In 1952, the U.S. business elite was comprised of "the sons of men of relatively high occupational status, the sons of business and professional men." Among the fathers of this elite, the number of executives or owners of larger businesses was eight times its proportion within the general population, while the number of unskilled or semiskilled laborers was one-sixth its percentage in the population (Warner and Abegglen 1955, 41-42).

It is true that two-thirds of the sample entrepreneurs in Michigan studied by Collins, Moore, and Unwalla (1964, 238) described their early family life as "poor" or "underprivileged." But the only other choices were "affluent" or "well-off." Given the lack of any choice of a middle-level category, respondents may have avoided designations implying higher incomes. Furthermore, entrepreneurs may have evaluated parental family income from a contemporary perspective (the 1960s), in comparison with their own high level of economic well-being. The vast underrepresentation of Michigan sample fathers in unskilled, semiskilled, clerical, sales, and kindred work (24 percent from the sample and 61 percent from the general labor force), together with the disproportionate representation of fathers in business, executive, managerial, and professional work, and who owned or managed farms (57 percent compared to 26 percent), points to median incomes substantially above the corresponding population of the period (U.S. Bureau of the Census 1943, 87; Nafziger 1978, 123-26).

Entrepreneurs in Nigeria, Greece, and Michigan underwent, in the aggregate, an intergenerational upward movement (that is, from father to son) in occupational status and material level of living. The socioeconomic status of entrepreneurs was higher than the status of their fathers, which was substantially higher than that of the general population.

The foregoing discussion should make clear that the Horatio Alger model of the entrepreneur presented by empirical studies resulted from the types of questions posed to informants. Although the data indicating the upward socioeconomic mobility of industrialists are useful, this focus detracts from the considerable contrast between the socioeconomic class background of entrepreneurs and that of the general population.

# INNOVATORS AND MANAGERS IN SOCIALIST ECONOMIES

In the Soviet Union in 1936, the latest data for reliable information on parental occupational origins, sons of white-collar employees, professionals, or business-owners had six times the representation in industrial, executive positions that the sons of manual workers and farmers had. The situation existed despite the 1917 revolution, which had ostensibly overturned the existing class structure (Granick 1961). Even in China, capitalists, supporting the 1949 revolution who had not been allied to foreign interests, continued (except for the Cultural Revolution, 1966-1976), to receive interest on their investments and to be paid fairly high salaries for managing joint public-private enterprises. Members and children of the prerevolutionary Chinese bourgeoisie still hold a large number of positions in industry, administration, and education, despite attacks on their privileges from 1966 through 1978 (Deleyne 1971, Lyons 1987).

Motivating innovative activity in centrally planned economies is usually difficult. In 1959, Soviet Premier Nikita Khrushchev complained about an unsatisfactory rate of technological change.

> In our country some bureaucrats are so used to the old nag that they do not want to change over to a good race horse, for he might tear away on the turn and even spill them out of the sleigh! Therefore, such people will hold on to the old nag's tail with both hands and teeth (Berliner 1971, 586-58, citing Pravda, 2 July 1959).

Under central management, Soviet managers resisted innovation, since effort and resources diverted to it might threaten plan fulfillment. While kinks in the new technology were being ironed out, managers might have lost part of their take-home pay, which was often tied to plan targets, or they may have been demoted. When evaluating managers for bonuses and promotions, party officials gave little weight to their innovative abilities. Also the tightly planned system had little latitude for servicing and spare parts for new equipment or for acquiring new resources and suppliers. Furthermore the prices of new products usually counted for less in computing plan fulfillment than older, standard goods. Finally introducing new models required extensive testing and negotiations with research institutes as well as approval from official agencies before production was authorized (Berliner 1971, 569-97). The bureaucratic maze hampers innovation. However, Mikhail Gorbachev's form of perestroika, 1985-1991, to spur innovation, collapsed from its own contradictions.

From 1966 to 1970, the early years of the Cultural Revolution, China's leaders took control of industrial innovation and management from the professional managerial elite. Management changed from one person to a "three-in-one" revolutionary committee, consisting of government officials, technicians, and workers. Campaigns urged workers to invent or improve machines, tools, and processes—a policy that began after Soviet technicians took their blueprints and withdrew from unfinished factories in 1960.

According to the Chinese press in the late 1960s, numerous technical activists among the workers, previously unrecognized, introduced new techniques, persevered when criticized by bureaucrats and peers, and received support from the Communist party. Through its help, they acquired more sophisticated technical advice and frequently received further training and education leading to promotion (Suttmeir 1974). Since the 1978 industrial reforms, professional managers and technicians reasserted their authority and quelled the innovation of technical activists.

## THE FAMILY

The family enterprise, widespread in developing countries, is usually small and managed primarily by the father or eldest brother. As the dominant form of organization in nineteenth-century France, the family firm was conceived as a fief to maintain and enhance the position of the family, and not as a mechanism for wealth and power (Landes 1949, 45-61). However, some of the leading industrial conglomerates in developing countries are family-owned. For example, India's largest private manufacturers are usually members of old trading families who exercise control of several companies. Frequently, there is specialization by family members according to industry, location, or management function. The advantages of family entrepreneurship are its ability to mobilize large amounts of resources, its quick unified decision making, its access to trustworthy personnel to oversee operations and its constraints against irresponsibility. Among Nigerian Ibos, families guarantee that debts are paid, and their solidarity provides strong sanctions against default, since individual failure reflects on family reputations. The extended family frequently facilitates entrepreneurship by providing funds for apprentice training and initial capital, even though it may hinder the expansion of the firm by diverting resources to current consumption (Nafziger 1969, 25-33). Other disadvantages of family entrepreneurship may be conservatism about risk, innovation, and delegation of authority; paternalism in employer-employee relationships; and reluctance to hire professional managers. This reluctance, however, may be less the problem in developing countries than the critical shortage of professionals and managers, especially those who can occupy positions of authority without ownership. In addition, most family firms are too small to afford outside managers. Finally, paternalism and overcentralization are feudal legacies characteristic of many LDC enterprises and not unique to family business.

# EDUCATION

Most studies indicate a higher level of education among entrepreneurs than for the population as a whole, and a direct relationship between the education and success of the entrepreneur. Persons with more education have more knowledge with which to make decisions. In addition, the verbal skills of the better educated person assist him in acquiring new ideas and methods, corresponding and conversing in business relationships, and understanding instruction manuals and other routine written information. Finally, the quantitative ability of the educated entrepreneur facilitates computation and record-keeping.

There are exceptions to this pattern, including Ibadan and Aba market women in Nigeria, Chinese business people in Singapore, and Mahisyas (a cultivator caste) in Howrah, India, many of whom are illiterate. Moreover, in rare instances—for example, among artisans in such crafts as weaving, blacksmithing, goldsmithing, shoemaking, and leathermaking, where success virtually requires a lengthy apprenticeship with a master—the education of the entrepreneur may be negatively related to success. The foregone cost of effort and funds to acquire education are training and experience more closely related to entrepreneurial activity (Nafziger 1970, 349-60).

Education may limit entrepreneurship by giving people other occupational choices. Thus, in the early 1960s, when Nigerians were replacing the remaining British in the civil service, Nigeria's few university graduates turned to those jobs, with their high salary, security, prestige, and other perquisites, rather than to entrepreneurial activity with its relatively low earnings and high risk. On the other hand, where university graduates are in excess supply, as in South India, some choose entrepreneurship to avoid unemployment or blue-collar jobs.

# GENDER

In the United States, there are relatively few women in business—not merely because of sex discrimination but because of the whole female socialization pattern. Some feminists charge that girls are brought up toaspire to be secretaries, nurses, dancers, and kindergarten teachers, rather than to start a business.

In many Afro-Asian LDCs, the percentage of women in business is lower than in the United States. Despite certain exceptions, such as the concentrations of female traders in some large open-air marketplaces in West Africa, only a small proportion of the large-scale entrepreneurs in developing countries are women.

Most LDCs have cultural norms about how males and females should behave at work. Frequently, a woman's physical mobility and social contact are restricted. Lessinger (1980) states that in India women are not allowed to deal directly with strange men, since it is assumed that all unmonitored contact between unrelated men and women must be sexual. Furthermore, according to Lessinger, women are viewed as naturally weaker, more emotional, less socially adept, less rational and inferior to men. These views have been used not only to limit competition between women and men in business, but also, in some instances, to justify a woman's restriction to the household.

Moreover, the culture may view the characteristics of the successful entrepreneur—shrewdness, quick judgement, gregariousness, and force of personality—as inconsistent with those of a good and proper woman. Even where a woman is determined to be an entrepreneur, she is reminded of social conventions daily by sexual harassment if she steps beyond the bounds of accepted behavior. While a woman can get around these restrictions by surrounding herself with relatives, neighbors, and other women who can vouch for her good behavior, this strategy is cumbersome for the entrepreneur, who must be mobile. In addition to these restrictions on contacts with men, the businesswoman in a developing country may be refused credit by bankers and suppliers.

In general, despite some possible variations among developing countries, the types of expectations, restrictions, and discriminatory practices analyzed above help to explain why there are so few female entrepreneurs in LDCs.

# SUMMARY

It is fruitless to argue whether economic or social factors are the most important in determining the quantity and success of entrepreneurs. Using economics to analyze entrepreneurship does not preclude the possibility that it might also be explained by sociological variables.

McClelland contends that a society with a generally high need for achievement produces more energetic entrepreneurs who bring about more rapid economic growth. While some training institutions have used achievement motivation training as a part of programs at centers to develop entrepreneurship, there is little evidence that this training contributes to business success.

Hagen argues that societies where children are raised democratically so that they are encouraged to take initiative and be self-reliant, are more likely to produce entrepreneurs. However, critics are skeptical about Hagen's claim that this creativity is linked to a prior period of withdrawal of status respect.

According to Weber, the spirit of the modern capitalist entrepreneur in Western Europe in the sixteenth-century was found disproportionately among Puritans, whose asceticism was manifested in worldly activity. Despite criticism of Weber's thesis, his work has stimulated scholars to ask questions about religious and ethnic differences among entrepreneurs.

Empirical studies indicate that the class and caste status of business people is substantially higher than the status of the general population in mixed and capitalist economies. Industrial business activity, rather than being a path for substantial upward socio-economic mobility, is a way of maintaining or defending privileged status, and enhancing or consolidating the high economic position of the family.

While the family enterprise has the advantage of quick unified decision making, its disadvantages include conservatism about risks, reluctance to hire professional managers and paternalism in labor relationships.

Although education can increase the supply of entrepreneurs by providing people with more skills suitable for business, it can also decrease the supply of entrepreneurs by increasing options in other occupations.

Industrial entrepreneurs in developing countries come from a wide variety of occupational backgrounds, including trade, sales, and crafts. Few manufacturing entrepreneurs, however, originate in farming, government employment, or factory work.

Many of the cultural norms in both industrialized countries and developing countries about how women should behave at work limit their entrepreneurial activity.

## NOTES

1. The participants "first take a form of the Thematic Apperception Test in which they write imaginative stories about a series of pictures. They then learn how to code what they have written according to the standard system for identifying n Achievement.... They then rewrite the stories at various times, trying to maximize the number of scoring categories they can introduce.... Few can [obtain a maximum score] without considerable practice, but most are able after a few lessons to get much higher scores than they did at first."

"The idea behind this training is very simple. It is to form the associative network, which in a certain sense could be considered the motive itself." McClelland and Winter 1971, 46-47.

2. Although the working report by Pabaney, Danzig, Nadkarni, Pareek, and McClelland 1964 suggests the entrepreneurs were to report profits, McClelland and Winter 1971 provide no information on these data. The decrease in entrepreneurial efficiency and returns suggests the possibility that profits increased less among course participants than in the control group.

3. Ironically, the only references to a measure of n Ach among Indian entrepreneurs who were trained are in the context of a comparison of the precourse scores of entrepreneurs who were active and those inactive after the course, and the aggregate trend in n Ach of participants from before the training to two to three years later. McClelland and Winter 1971, 270, 324-30.

4. Samuelsson 1957, 151-52, who lacks Weber's understanding of how religious values change historically, makes a similar error when he tries to refute Weber's thesis by pointing out the inconsistencies between the New Testament and the spirit of capitalism.

5.   Weber 1930, 39-40 noted ethnic and religious minorities excluded from political influence, such as the Huguenots in France, the Nonconformists and Quakers in England, and the Jews in ancient and medieval Europe, tend to be driven into economic activities. Park 1950, 345-76 argued "marginal men" tended to be especially innovative.

6.   Fifty-nine percent of Schumpeterian entrepreneurs received most or all of their initial capital from the family, and 88 percent received at least partial assistance from the family, indicating the Schumpeterian entrepreneurs were at least as dependent on the family for initial funds as other entrepreneurs. Nafziger 1978, 81-84, 104-06, 171.

Beveridge and Oberschall 1979 reconfirm my findings on the socioeconomic status of Schumpeterian entrepreneurs.

# Part IV.

## Comparative Development

# Chapter IX

# *Bangladesh and Biafra: The Political Economy of Secessionist Conflict*

Communal and interregional conflict is a persistent feature of political life in the modern nation-state. An extreme form of interregional antagonism and national disintegration is the secessionist political conflict, associated with such historical examples as the U.S. Confederate South and the Republic of Ireland, and more recently, Quebec, Scotland, Northern Ireland, the Basque provinces, Sarawak, Eritrea, Cabinda, Katanga, Biafra, and Bangladesh. In the analysis of internal war and violence, scholars have emphasized ethnic and regional enmities, with much less stress on elite economic competition, economic deprivation and class interests. Moreover, the nation-state has often been regarded as an autonomous social and political system, without consideration of transnational linkages to the international system. Additionally, the tendency of investigators has been to focus on the short-term "precipitants" of internal war, which "are almost always unique and ephemeral in character" (Eckstein 1965, 140).

As Gurr (1970, 6) notes, there have been few case studies of political violence in the non-western world, and even fewer systematic comparative studies. This chapter attempts a comparative analysis of two prominent Afro-Asian cases of secessionist civil war: Nigeria (1967-1970), in which the Eastern Region unsuccessfully attempted to gain independence as the Republic of Biafra, and Pakistan (March-December 1971), in which East Pakistan succeeded in its bid for independence as the Republic of Bangladesh.

Emphasis is on longer-range conditions underlying secessionist conflict rather than on questions of how either war was precipitated or ultimately resolved.[1] A comparative case study may help to distinguish the idiosyncratic and historically unique characteristics of major political phenomena from their general underlying conditions. It may also suggest hypotheses to be tested by use of crossnational aggregate or survey data or identify relevant variables which might need to be added to existing data banks (e.g., Taylor, Hudson, and others 1972; and Morrison, Mitchell, Paden, Stevenson, and others 1972).

This study focuses on economic factors which contribute directly or indirectly to secessionist conflict. These are treated within the following broad categories: the colonial legacy, the post-colonial international economic system, elite economic interests, class structure and conflict, regional and sectoral economic relationships, and several aspects of economic policy.

Colonial and global factors are perceived as having more of an *indirect* effect on the incidence of secessionist conflict. Where there has not been a protracted violent struggle for independence, the structure of the polity and economy, the nature of rules and institutions, and the shape of class relationships and elite structure existing at the time of independence are very much a product of policies and relations of the colonial era. In the post-colonial international system, the metropolitan nations, with their means of coercion (military, economic, and political power) and superior resources (resulting in aid, investment, and a dominant trade position), are able to structure their relationships with the peripheral nations so that, even though there is a conflict of interest between the rich and poor nations in general, there is a harmony of interest between the elites of these nations. The center nation develops a bridgehead in the peripheral nation, which enables the former to maintain political and economic hegemony in the latter, and in the process to support and assist those in the periphery willing to cooperate, that is, those whose interest comes to be in harmony with that of the center. The commonality of interest between elites in the center and peripheral nations corresponds to a disharmony of interest between the elites and masses in the peripheral country (Galtung 1971, 83-84), which becomes the basis for political discontent and the potential for political violence. Internal economic factors—regional economic rivalries, contradictions among elite groups, class conflict, and domestic economic policy—which are partially dependent on international variables—influence the probability of secessionist conflict.

Consideration of economic factors, including examining the international economic context, implies the inadequacy of the "ethnic model" of secessionist conflict and other forms of political violence (Rabushka and Shepsle 1972; Glazer and Moynihan 1975). Far from being primordial "givens" in the explanation of various forms of conflict, ethnic factors need to be viewed as subject to a wide range of economic conditions, including economic competition for the benefits of employment and business activity, the accentuation of communal identification by ruling elites to transfer potential hostilities away from class discrepancies, and the rise of communalism in response to a lack of participation in the benefits of nationalism or modernization.

# THE COLONIAL LEGACY

In the century or so before World War I, Britain occupied the central position in the international capitalist system as the major banker, trader, investor, and industrialist. Colonies, such as India (which before 1947 included present-day Pakistan and Bangladesh) and Nigeria, became integrated into the system as economic satellites specializing in primary products instrumental to the industrial development of the leading capitalist countries. Integration of subject countries within world capitalism, by interfering with the internal logic of their political and economic development, and especially by affecting their national boundaries and political structures, helped contribute to postcolonial instability. By providing the overriding economic and political opportunity structure within which individual and collective competition was to operate, colonial rule conditioned the growth of nationalism, communalism, and regionalism.

## The Differential Impact of Colonialism

The impact of British rule differed substantially from region to region within Nigeria and India. The coastal areas of Southern Nigeria and East Bengal, where British intrusion was of longer and more intense duration, had more experience in parliamentary government, a greater political consciousness, higher literacy, and more developed industrial capitalist institutions, than inland regions.

Bengal, most of which became East Pakistan in 1947, had become an important administrative and trading center after the British East Indian Company gained a foothold there in the late seventeenth-century. Bengal was given legislative institutions in 1861, and Punjab, the largest West Pakistani province, in 1897. In Nigeria, British administration was not formally established until 1900, but coastal groups, particularly in the Niger Delta region, had already experienced economic contact with the west for more than two centuries.[2] Africans were represented in the Legislative Council in Southern Nigeria after 1923, but in the North not until 1946.

British suzerainty was exercised in Northern Nigeria and in parts of West Pakistan under "indirect rule," an arrangement mutually advantageous to the colonial power and to the native princes and emirs. Britain economized on officers and utilized indigenous systems of tax collection and maintenance of order, while the traditional rulers, under British hegemony, obtained security through the elimination of important sources of both external and internal opposition. The maintenance of these indigenous chiefs hampered the development of nationalism and a strong native bourgeoisie, and strengthened the concentration of land holdings among overlords and zamindars. Princely states which joined Pakistan maintained a semi-independent status long after independence.

## Communal and Regional Conflict

The British, by use of the classic techniques of divide and rule, helped create or exacerbate differences of class, caste, region, and community among the people they ruled. In part, this was accomplished by bringing diverse ethnic groups, with separate historical identities, under a common administrative and economic system, and also by perceiving alien societies in racial categories.

In Nigeria, especially before World War II, the British supported the development of separate institutions and identities for different ethnic and religious communities, and a system of "native administration" to foster communal loyalty. In the early 1920s, Governor Hugh Clifford clearly emphasized that the idea of a Nigerian nation was both inconceivable and dangerous. Even the nationalist leaders before 1934 tended to think of nationalism in terms of regional or ethnic community (Coleman 1958, 192-210).

In India, where conflict and competition between Hindu and Muslim led ultimately to partition and the creation of Pakistan, the British encouraged the development of separate legal, political, and social institutions for different religious, caste, and ethnic communities, especially when these demonstrated loyalty to the colonial rulers. The army was recruited among (usually dependable) ethnic groups regarded as "martial races," which included the Pathans and Punjabi Muslims from (then) northwestern India, but excluded Bengalis. The consequence of this policy after independence was a Pakistani military with a very disproportionate representation of Westerners, who felt a disdain for their Bengali countrymen.

By providing protection to loyal communities, such as the Muslims in India, and regional elites, such as the Northern traditional aristocracy in Nigeria, the colonial power impeded assimilation and integration. The British support of Northern resistance to a Nigerian self-government dominated by Southerners led to agreements in 1953-54 and 1958 to leave the North intact with a majority of representatives in the Federal legislature. In both India and Nigeria, the creation of new administrative units led to the evolution of new communal identities, and the strengthening and politicization of old ones. Migration under colonial aegis brought groups into closer contact under competitive conditions. Thus, Punjabis reacted adversely to Bengali officials of the colonial government, as did Northern Nigerians to the influx of Ibo workers.

## Nationalism

Nationalist movements are generally spearheaded by those whose personal and collective destinies are tied to the removal of alien rule and economic domination. Communalism or ethnic nationalism grows stronger as other groups perceive their own lack of participation in the benefits of modernization and self-government and join the struggle. In Nigeria, the heightening of Yoruba nationalism in the West beginning around 1948 was partly in response to the disproportionate weight of Ibos in the leadership of the Nigerian national movement. Hausa-Fulani nationalism was aroused later in response to the threat of southern economic and political supremacy. In Pakistan, the overriding salience of Hindu-Muslim conflict overshadowed and even precluded the development of other ethnic cleavages until after independence. The dominant cultural group in Pakistan—the Urdu-speaking immigrant from North India—displayed little respect for the language or culture of the majority Bengalis until compelled by political pressure to do so after nearly half a decade of independence.

## Patterns and Processes of Decolonization

Former ruling powers may affect the polities and economies of their colonial possessions long after departure, by the manner in which they leave. Partition and federalism were two devices by which the British retained their influence in former colonies.

Partition left Pakistan, created from the economic backwashes of India, without a major industrial or urban economic center. Traditional commercial patterns between the jute-growing areas of East Bengal and the major jute-processing center of Calcutta were broken. Trade with India dropped from more than 65 percent of Pakistan's total foreign trade in 1948-49 to about 3 percent in 1951, not rising above 6 percent for any year in the 1950s (MacEwan 1971, 42-52). A large portion of the class which had been associated with commerce and the embryonic beginnings of manufacturing was lost by their exodus to India. The vacuum was filled by a new class of Muslim industrial capitalists, whose power and influence grew during succeeding years.

Federalism, both in Pakistan and Nigeria, was designed to prevent national domination by a popular majority, but in practice facilitated regionalization of political support, and ultimately the domination by an elite from communities which represented a minority of the population. The fragility of the federal structure given to both countries is demonstrated by the changes made in both in subsequent years.[3] The political organizations which served as the prime vehicles for the nationalist movements in the 1940s, the Muslim League in Pakistan, and the National Council of Nigeria and the Cameroons (NCNC), increasingly lost ground to more regionally-oriented political parties with the rising subnational consciousness of the 1950s. The League, which had secured the independence of Pakistan, lost heavily in the 1954 provincial elections in the East to the newly formed Awami League. During 1951-60, each of the three major Nigerian political parties, which played leading roles in unifying and mobilizing the regional socioeconomic elite, achieved security and hegemony in one region only. The contradictions which arose when the security of one regional elite interfered with that of another were important factors contributing to the coups and civil war in Nigeria (Olorunsola 1972a, 23-26; and Nafziger 1973, 508-16).

Another legacy of British rule enhanced by the methods of decolonization adopted in Nigeria and Pakistan was an efficient and professional military establishment, generally isolated from and antagonistic toward popular political movements. British commanding officers were retained well after independence, thereby increasing the military's political isolation. In both countries the military was drawn into political intervention shortly after the departure of the British commanding officer.

In Pakistan, the military intervened in 1958 to forestall a threatened loss of power by the West to the East in the upcoming elections, and in 1969 to restore order after riots occurring in both wings of Pakistan. The 1958 establishment of martial law thus consolidated the domination of the predominantly West Pakistani industrial and commercial capitalists, civil servants, army officers, and technocrats (Wright 1973, 13-15).[4]

In Nigeria, the efforts of the mutineers in the coup d'etat of January 1966 and the succeeding Ironsi government can be interpreted, in part, as an attempt to insure the security of the southern and, more specifically, the Ibo elite, by the removal of the firm hold of Northern emirs and administrators on the federal government. The countercoup in the following July, directed against Ibo domination of the military government, was led by representatives of the smaller ethnic minorities, especially from the lower North.

Though the evidence presented thus far does not support the theory that states as diverse as Pakistan and Nigeria were doomed from their inception, it does reveal that British colonial rule has had an extensive and varied impact on regional identities and interests, class structure, political parties, and successive governmental structures in independent Pakistan and Nigeria.[5]

## TRANSNATIONAL ECONOMIC LINKAGES AFTER INDEPENDENCE

Colonial policy which discouraged industrial growth, increased economic dependency, integrated the peripheral economies into the world capitalist system, and helped create and support a native elite oriented toward cooperating with the metropolitan nation, facilitated Pakistan's and Nigeria's satellite economic relationships after independence. Although Pakistan extricated itself from the British colonial economic nexus to a greater extent than Nigeria, it did not cut its dependency on the rich capitalist countries, but largely replaced British with American domination. The Pakistani political leadership negotiated a long-term military and economic aid pact with the United States in 1954. The continuing political, military, and economic assistance from the United States, which provided the resources and support for a perpetuation of the West Pakistani ruling group, kept the country open to foreign investment and trade, and allied to the western capitalist world. These ties, however, were costly to the Pakistani population at large, influencing the balance of internal political forces, affecting the shape of the class structure, making available additional means of repression against dissidents and ultimately contributing to increased political instability. In Nigeria, British private capital, together with aid programs, cemented the pro-British sympathy of the Northern-dominated civilian government. The Northern ruling aristocracy, highly sympathetic to British economic and military interests in Nigeria, and opposed to the influence of communist countries, could reasonably expect the British to resist any threat to Northern hegemony and regional security, including the danger of a high concentration of southern manpower in the North, and threats from radical socialists or from potential southern dominated ruling coalitions. However, the supremacy of the Northern traditional rulers exacerbated the unrest of the southern proletariat and bourgeoisie.

By the period after World War II, the international division of labor had shifted so that some LDCs were specializing in light manufacturing goods, in addition to primary products. In 1969/70 in Pakistan, 55.7 percent of exports and 55.0 percent of imports were secondary goods (chemicals, machinery, transport, equipment, and manufactured goods), compared to 2.7 percent of exports and 86.9 percent of imports in 1954/55. Yet most of Pakistan's (1971-72) secondary exports in 1969-70 involved the processing of raw materials, or light manufactures; for examples, 40.4 percent of exports were jute, cotton, or leather goods. On the other hand, Nigeria (1968, 20) still maintained a colonial-type trade pattern in 1965, with 7.8 percent of exports and 80.9 percent of imports secondary goods.

After World War II, in both countries trade with the United States. expanded at the expense of the colonial power, Britain. Despite this, in 1965 the United Kingdom was still by far the major trading partner of Nigeria, accounting for 38.5 percent of the exports, and 30.9 percent of its imports. In the 1960s, the largest share of Pakistan's imports (for example, 38.6 percent in 1964-65) was from the United States (Pakistan 1972: appendices 71-77).

Both Pakistan and Nigeria were highly dependent on patron nations for external financing. However, the chief form of this in Pakistan was loans, investment, and aid, from the U.S. government, in contrast to private capital flows from the United Kingdom to Nigeria. The United States provided 64.3 percent of the grants, and 42.7 percent of total assistance (grants and loans) to Pakistan from 1951 through 1971. The aid consortium, representing the rich capitalist countries, contributed 93 percent of total assistance to Pakistan from 1951-1957. In 1969/70, Pakistan received Rs. 3.100 billion in foreign grants and loans, to compare with a balance of trade deficit of Rs. 2.690 billion (from exports of goods and services of Rs. 4.350 billion). Debt service obligations (virtually all of which were owed to the Consortium of western countries, the International Monetary Fund, and the World Bank) as a percentage of foreign exchange earnings increased from 3.6 percent in 1960/61, to 9.9 percent in 1964/65, to 25.3 percent in 1970/71 (Pakistan 1972, 79-81).

Development plans and strategies, dependent on foreign aid for a large percentage of projects, were submitted to the Consortium, which frequently insisted on changes before committing funds (Hamid 1970, 132-33, 146). The U. S., for example, with a contribution of 18.6 percent of the total amount of Pakistani development projects in 1966, could control most of these, as technical and financial assistance was distributed over a large number of government projects (Alavi and Khusro 1970, 64-66).

The overriding influence of the United States in the economy of Pakistan distorted the inner logic of its economic development, and took away potential gains in government policy and technical project development that the indigenes could have received from experience, and learning by doing. Foreign aid gave a major impetus to the emerging industrial capitalist elite (disproportionately migrants from India at the time of partition), allied with and overlapping with large landowners, top civil servant, and army officers in the Punjab. The severance of Pakistan from the more industrialized parts of India and the flight of the previously dominant Hindu mercantile community at the time of partition gave further impetus to the new manufacturing and commercial entrepreneurs of Pakistan. The maintenance of a coalition of the business classes with the older elite was only possible with the large injection of military, economic, and technical aid in the 1950s and early 1960s, and the concomitant rapid economic growth, especially industrial growth (MacEwan 1971, 48). This support was needed so that enough patronage, perquisites, and resources were available to satisfy the various economic interests within the coalition, and to have sufficient access to a range of sanctions and rewards to consolidate control and to prevent restiveness among the lower elites.

Foreign assistance, primarily from the United States, then, helped in the creation of a new capitalist elite, who in coalition with other conservative forces, placed little emphasis on improving the level of living of the masses. As indicated below, Pakistan's rapid growth in the first two decades of independence was accompanied by a decline in real wages, and in foodgrains per capita. Assistance allowed the United States to have a role in the shaping of forces contributing to the rising Pakistani elite—an elite whose interest would be in harmony with U.S. economic and political hegemony in Asia. However, military support, accounting for approximately one-fourth of U.S. aid to Pakistan since its independence, allowed the ruling elite to maintain power despite this neglect of the population at large (Alavi and Khusro 1970, 64-66).

Yet the existence of this coalition depended on continued military and economic support from the United States This support plummeted sharply after the Indo-Pakistan War of 1965, while Pakistan's debt servicing ratio was increasing. Total assistance by the U.S. declined from $964.280 million in the Second Five-Year Plan (1960-65) to $668.799 million in the Third Five-Year Plan (1965-70), while grants decreased even more drastically (Pakistan 1972, appendix p. 89). The decline in foreign help for the coalition of elites meant that some elements in the alliance would have to be suppressed. The withdrawal of the support of the landed elite threatened the power of the capitalist class, who lacked the power to overcome this elite and its military allies (MacEwan 1971, 48).

In Nigeria in 1964, foreign interests—primarily British—owned three-fourths of the book value of industrial assets from firms in Nigeria with a value of £N25,000 (about $70,000) or more. At the same time, 90 percent of total demand deposits were held in banks where foreign capital was at least a majority. Concessions granted by government to business, such as income-tax holidays, favored the large corporate foreign sector. Debt servicing became a major problem just before the civil war, as in 1966 the net international outflow of private direct investment income was greater than the net inflow of private direct investment, by £N73.4 million to £N55.0 million, a reversal from 1960-64 when its annual average was less than the net inflow by £N33.0 million to £N12.3 million. Furthermore, a major argument for overseas investment, which centers around the necessity to transfer techniques of modern production, has been of little validity in Nigeria where foreign firms have remained technological enclaves which contributed little to the indigenous sector.

Foreign investors during the civilian regime formed partnerships with members of the governing elite or their business constituents, or with parastatal corporations, which widened the patronage base; or rendered other favors or provided concessions for the business interests of the leading politicians. Business interests by foreigners in Nigeria were generally supplemented by overseas political, military, and economic assistance, designed to help support those who wished to keep the country open to foreign investment and trade, and closed to communist influences. British trade, investment, and assistance cemented the pro-western sympathy of the Northern-dominated civilian government, which could reasonably expect the British to resist any threat to Northern supremacy.[6]

British foreign policy throughout the Nigerian crises, the two coups in 1966 and from the beginning of the civil war, was consistent with support for an economically integrated area that would leave the Federation open to international trade and investment. After the July 1966 coup, British and (in some cases) American diplomats were influential in dissuading Head of State Yakubu Gowon from announcing the disintegration of the Federation, and in discouraging those who attended the September constitutional conference and the January 1967 Aburi conference from agreeing on confederation. The insistence on a strong Federation helped foreclose a possible compromise between the East and the rest of Nigeria based on a looser confederation.

In June 1967, the British government, a majority shareholder in Shell-BP, countermanded its offer of a token payment of £UK250,000 on the oil royalties demanded by Biafra. Doubtless, in the wake of a disruption of oil supplied from West Asia. Britain did not wish to risk severing her increasing share of oil originating outside Biafra, in the Mid-West and offshore oil wells. After the first months of the war, the United Kingdom prodded by Soviet support to Nigeria, increased its military sales and diplomatic support to the Federation, assistance which contributed to the eventual Nigerian victory.

British foreign policy in favor of a united Nigeria, and U.S. military and economic support of the dominant coalition of West Pakistanis, helped preclude the possibility of a relatively peaceful breakup of the countries, and exacerbated the level of political violence.

## CLASS FORMATION AND CONFLICT

The strength and position of broad socioeconomic groupings in society, conditioned by colonial and neocolonial political and economic factors, constitute important background considerations in explaining secessionist conflict (see Moore 1966). The relative position and regional distribution of such "social forces" and their representation in the ruling elites of Nigeria and Pakistan served to intensify regional identities and competition and to lay the ground for secessionist civil war. The dynamics of elite formation and class composition in both countries led to the subordination and transformation of intraregional class and ethnic differences to interregional cleavages. At the same time, the decline in economic opportunities relative to economic aspirations intensified the feelings of discontent which helped to fuel the civil war in both countries.

In Pakistan, landlords, zamindars, traders, lawyers, and other professionals were formed as a part of the elite in the West in the one-half century before independence, as a result of their leadership role in the movement of Muslim nationalism in India (through the vehicle of the Muslim League, in opposition to the larger nationalist movement, led by the Indian National Congress). These were joined after independence by an emerging class of Muslim industrial and merchant capitalists, the essentially newly created civil service, army officers, and white-collar workers. The competition between elements of the landed, industrial, and bureaucratic elite for state power and for economic benefits, in a period of decelerating economic growth in the late 1960s, and the higher aspirations of those not yet a part of the elite, helped contribute to the subsequent disintegration of the Pakistan nation-state.

In West Pakistan, where the top 0.1 percent and bottom 64.5 percent of the landowners each owned 15.0 percent of the agricultural land in 1960 (Gini index of inequality = 0.64), large landlords have been the dominant social group since the early British period. At least 200 of the 310 members of the interim West Pakistan assembly set up in 1955 "came from the landed interests." In the East, by contrast, land owners were limited to a ceiling of 15 hectares per head, as a result of land reform legislation passed in the 1950s, which took land from Hindu rajas, who held 75 percent of the land just before partition (Maniruzzaman 1966, 84-86. Huntington 1968, 382, indicates the Gini index for the West was substantially higher than for East Pakistan).

At independence, when more than one-half of the manufacturing sector was controlled by Hindus, the government, or foreigners, the percentage of national income originating in manufacturing was barely one percent. By 1959, this percentage rose to over six percent. Muslims indigenous to the Indo-Pakistani sub-continent controlled two-thirds of the sector (Papanek, 1962: 49). The industrial elites, with their allies in the bureaucracy, used the levers of state economic policy and planning to give their enterprises privileged protection from foreign competition; ready access to licenses for foreign exchange and domestic inputs at less than a market price; and subsidies or tax concessions. In the East, the petty bourgeoisie, who constituted the top of the class hierarchy, directed their discontent against the dominant feudal and business elite in the West. This elite feared that if a major bourgeoisie class were allowed to be established in East Pakistan, with a majority of the country's population, its politico-economic strength would make it the dominant force in national politics. In 1950-57, with Prime Minister H.S. Suhrawardy, founder of the Awami League, based in the East, the government awarded more import licenses to newcomers in import trade (particularly from the East), distributed U.S. aid for modernizing industry disproportionately to the East, gave the East parity with the West in the allocation of foreign exchange, and proposed to establish a public shipping corporation for coastal trade between the wings to compete with private shippers in the West. The vehement reaction by the coalition of landed and business interests in the West encouraged President Iskander Mirza to compel Suhrawardy's resignation, after which most of the measures which benefited aspiring business groups in the East were cancelled (Ibid., 46-58; Ali 1970, 61). The class struggle, from the viewpoint of major Bengali interests, became increasingly identified as a regional struggle against the supremacy of the Western wing.

In Nigeria, the traditional Northern ruling aristocracy and the nationalist leaders were joined by far-sighted chiefs, senior civil servants and government administrators, leading businessmen, and professionals in the 1950s to form the political elite. Once this elite mustered a majority at the center, it was able to control the dispensation of a wide range of political favors and economic sanctions to retain its position and power, and keep the underprivileged classes subordinate.[7]

A major restive element, especially in Nigeria, has been the relatively deprived and politically discontented members of the educated classes. Just after 1947 in Pakistan, and in the 1950s and 1960s in Nigeria, a large number of elite positions in the civil service, armed forces, police, government corporations, and universities were opened in a short period of time. However, by the late 1950s in Pakistan, and the middle 1960s in Nigeria, there were only a few vacancies, since the process of indigenization was virtually complete and those who had been only recently recruited were still relatively young.

Younger men, especially in southern Nigeria (with a high educational rate, and virtually complete indigenization) and East Pakistan, became frustrated with the abrupt decline in openings. The substantial unrest by students, who perceived themselves as a part of a future elite and, at times, an alternative present elite, stemmed, in part, from frustration over the sharp decline in high-level employment. Parallel frustrations were to be found among the military in both countries. One of the roots of the aborted Rawalpindi conspiracy to overthrow the Pakistan civilian government in 1951 was the considerable unrest among officers caused by high expectations created with the swift promotions from junior to senior ranks. A drop in the rate of openings and promotions was a major factor explaining the low morale in the army before the revolt by the Nigerian majors in January 1966. By the 1960s, the scramble for the few remaining posts in both countries was very intense, and regional competition for these contributed to the enmity and bitterness which set the spark for the civil wars.

Labor has been relatively weak and unorganized in both Nigeria and Pakistan in most of the period since 1950, with the overwhelming majority of the population "self-employed" in agriculture, petty trade, or crafts. Thus, in Nigeria, wage-paid employment comprised only about 5 percent of the economically active population of 17.6 million in 1965. In Pakistan, the nonagricultural labor force constituted 8 percent of the economically active population in 1961. Furthermore, in the 1950s and 1960s the labor movement in both countries was fragmented into hundreds of trade unions, and into several feuding, ideologically divided labor federations (Maniruzzaman 1966, 94).

Labor discontent in both countries resulted from a growing sense of injustice at the wide gap between the incomes of entrepreneurs and white-collar workers, on the one hand, and blue-collar workers, on the other. After Nigerian independence in 1960, with the British no longer the whipping-boy, many workers gradually began to feel that the political elite was making no effort to erase the inequities of the colonial wage structure. This consciousness, together with the awareness of frequent exposes of corruption among African leaders, resulted in the erosion of the sense of legitimacy attached to the wide income gap, especially among urban workers.

In the fiscal year 1963/64, supervisors in the public service were paid 33 times as much as daily-paid and semi-skilled workers, compared to a multiple of 5 to 10 in the United States and about 5 in the USSR. Indirect taxes were high, and personal income tax rates were low (that is, a 3.2-6.0 percent average rate for single persons in the 99th percentile income class—an annual income of £N700), and regressive in all regions except the East. To exacerbate the frustration, the government, which helped set the pattern for wages and working conditions in the private sector also, had not increased wages since 1959, despite an increase in overall prices by 2.5 percent annually, and an annual real growth in GDP per capita of about 4 percent from the fiscal year 1959 to 1963 (Aluko 1969, 16; Adedeji 1969, 188). Furthermore, the high rate of unemployment and the communal competition for jobs contributed to labor unrest.

In response to worker dissatisfaction, the major labor federations joined together to from the Joint Action Committee, which mobilized 800,000 supporters to stop work for 13 days in June 1964, to pressure the government to raise wages and salaries. The strike disrupted the vital economic and administrative services of the country, posed a challenge to the legitimacy and authority of the civilian government, demonstrated its ineptness and powerlessness, raised questions about the future use of the army and police for the repression of popular demands, and increased the likelihood of further attempts by dissident forces to use political violence to effect political change (Cohen 1974, 166-68). Much of organized labor supported the progressive opposition to the Northern-dominated coalition in the 1964-65 election boycott and constitutional crisis, and at the end of 1965 workers helped to foment the mass violence directed against a Northern-supported Western regional government with little popular support. These events, especially the near-anarchy in the West, were precipitants for the military mutiny of January 1966 which set the stage for the countercoup and civil war.

One distinct feature of the strategy of Pakistan's Planning Commission, supported by official and foreign economists, was a conscious promotion of income inequality to achieve a high rate of domestic savings and economic growth. The concentration of income and wealth in the hands of high-income groups was a key ingredient in a strategy which used government policies with regard to taxes, subsidies, licenses, and foreign exchange to redistribute resources from agriculture to industry, and from East to West Pakistan. In the 15 years before 1967, when this strategy was promoted, real wages in industry declined by at least 25 percent, while the real per capita gross income of the country increased by 21 percent (Griffin and Khan 1972, 199-206; Pakistan, 1972, appendices pp. 2-3).

In Pakistan, where political parties and independent trade unions were suppressed during the late 1950s and early 1960s, the most politically mobilized segment of the population was the students. They formed the vanguard of the revolts, subsequently joined by workers, against the rule of General Ayub Khan in the 1960s (Ali 1970). After 1966, however, Pakistani labor was mobilized in both wings as discrepancies between their static or declining real wages, and the increasing elites became more obvious. Through tactics of direct action, the workers won wage increases, and participated in toppling the Ayub regime.

The demands of labor in West Pakistan, directed against the Ayub government, remained essentially based on class. In East Pakistan, however, labor discontent was also channeled into support for regional autonomy. In turn, the entry of workers into the fray further radicalized the student activity and increased the level of violence in the East.

# DEVELOPMENT PLANNING
# AND INDUSTRIAL POLICY

In both countries, the central government pursued projects and policies primarily oriented toward benefits for a "modernizing" elite—the capitalist and bureaucratic classes in Pakistan, and the politico-bureaucratic elite and their business constituents in Nigeria—and their allies among the landed and feudal upper classes. Planning and implementation were hamstrung by the desire of the ruling elites to keep control of the bounties distributed by government.

In Pakistan, after the Six Year Development Programme initiated in 1951 was not completed because of the lack of planning machinery, the planning commissions of the next three plans (1955-70) relied heavily on foreign advisors (Waterston 1963, 13-129). In Nigeria, the earliest national plans, between 1946 and independence, were framed by colonial administrators. Even the First National Development Plan after independence (1962-68), was drawn up primarily by foreign economists.

Planners in both countries, assisted heavily by U.S. agencies, favored an emphasis on decision-making by private units, a stress on marginal governmental adjustment rather than fundamental structural change, the eschewal of increased tax rates at high-income levels (to encourage private incentives), an accent on a high economic payoff from directly productive investment (as opposed to an indirect return from social overhead capital), a conservative monetary and fiscal policy with an emphasis on relatively few expenditures for social welfare measures, an economy open to foreign trade and investment, and a substantial reliance on overseas assistance. There was little coordination between the planning units, dominated by foreigners, and the government officials in the formulation of the plan. This deficiency was one reason for the lack of implementation of plan projects (Stolper 1962, 85-91; Ghouse 1969b, 177; Jiliani 1968, 362; Allan 1968, 219-21).

Waterston (1963) and Lewis (1967, 37-39) suggest some major weaknesses of planning in both countries between independence and civil war were: incomplete feasibility studies and inadequate evaluation of projects; meager public participation, especially at the regional and local levels; excessive political intervention in the making of economic decisions; lack of authority of the planning units relative to the Ministries; insufficient attention to the small indigenous sector; inadequate emphasis on the agricultural sector; and unsatisfactory machinery for the implementation of projects in a public sector. If a strong program had been designed to foster economic development among the masses, the power and privileges of the ruling elite would clearly have been threatened—especially in West Pakistan and Northern Nigeria. A dispersion of economic power to the multiplicity of small businessmen without a quid pro quo would have threatened the economic interests of the political leaders— the viability and monopoly return of the large business interests influential in government (especially in Pakistan) and the public corporations which served as a basis for the disposal of patronage (particularly in Nigeria). The 1962- 68 Nigerian and 1955-70 Pakistan plans encountered major shortfalls in expenditures as a result of the lack of clear identification of feasible projects, and a lack of details concerning supporting government policies. The lack of preparatory work by specialized professionals resulted from the ineffective coordination, a shortage of high-level personnel, and the introduction of political criteria for determining projects. Ruling elites in both countries lacked goals and priorities that could be articulated to the masses, and—preoccupied with the preservation of their power and access to patronage—did not encourage government decision making from below.

The dominant class in both instances had no desire to establish adequate machinery to implement and independently evaluate the plan. If such an apparatus had been controlled by professionals and bureaucrats not oriented toward the interests of the political leaders, this would have undermined a system by which they stood to profit. The lack of department reports, the secrecy of official information, and the paucity of program evaluation, together with political intervention, allowed the political elite to keep control of the instruments vital for the maintenance of their influence. An emphasis on socioeconomic development for the low-income classes was no priority to ruling regimes preoccupied with the struggle to retain their power and perquisites.

One widely-held prescription for increasing the rate of economic development and modernization, but at the same time enhancing the profits or patronage of the political leaders of the country, has been the transfer of resources from the agricultural to the industrial sector. In Pakistan, the process of redistributing resources from agriculture to industry coincided with, and was an integral part of, a redistribution of income from the poor to the rich, and from East to West Pakistan. Because of the financially weak position of the emerging capitalists at independence, rapid industrialization could not be attained in a free, competitive market environment without massive assistance from government. Direct controls were needed to indigenize and modernize the country through industrialization, and ensure that the industrialists took the leadership positions of the economy. Foreign exchange policy, together with the compulsory government procurement of foodgrains at low prices for urban areas, the generous tax concessions to industry, and the lack of these to peasant agriculture, had the effect of compelling the transfer of savings from agriculture to industry, especially in the first decade after independence. Conservative estimates, based on world prices, indicate that over 24 percent of gross product originating in the agricultural sector—or about 70 percent of its savings—was transferred to the nonagricultural sector in 1964-65. Perhaps as much as 75 percent of this transfer was used to increase urban consumption. The transfer of resources from farming occurred throughout the 15 years before 1964/65, when real rural income per capita was declining (Griffin and Khan 1972, 26, 30, 134-36; Griffin 1965, 637, 644-45; Chowdhury 1968-69, 75-76).

In Nigeria, high tariffs on inputs for the production of domestic commodities, together with tariff rebates and tax incentives for pioneering companies and other favored applicants, had the effect of benefiting selected manufacturing enterprises. Import taxes on a number of industrial materials were so high that many unsuccessful applicants for tariff relief on vital inputs could not afford to stay in business, while favored enterprises made sizeable gains, especially as a result of a lack of competition by other firms within the industry. Parastatal corporations dominated by leading politicians, or foreign or indigenous producers allied with them, were more likely to receive tariff rebates.

In contrast to Pakistan, in Nigeria the greatest pressure for increased protection for manufacturing was not from domestic producers, but from foreign capitalists and their local collaborators, including substantial numbers of the political elite. A primary motive for establishing foreign industry was to transform a highly competitive market in international trade to one where competition was virtually eliminated behind a protective wall (Nafziger 1973, 518).

A policy of transferring resources from agriculture to industry through Marketing Board surpluses, agricultural export duties, and limited government expenditures in rural areas benefited the political elite in Nigeria, even though they were less involved in the private industrial sector than Pakistan political elite. Those controlling federal economic policy were involved in government industrial firms, collaboration with foreign enterprise, "rakeoffs" on the contracts of foreigners, intermediary roles in land deals, sales of inputs and services, and positions on the boards of directors, in addition to private industrial entrepreneurial activity.

In Nigeria and Pakistan, as workers and peasants became increasingly conscious of the way in which much of economic policy was being used on behalf of the indigenous ruling elite, discontent with the political leadership intensified.

# REGIONAL ECONOMIC COMPETITION AND CONFLICT

Regional and communal economic competition crosscuts class conflict.[8] The dominant class accentuated the precolonial and colonial identification with traditional political and cultural entities, and utilized—in furtherance of their own special interest—these sentiments, which became the "political formula" used to transfer potential hostility from class discrepancies (within their own communities) to the rulers and subjects of others.

Muslim nationalism and the creation of Pakistan helped divert attention away from the way the upper classes were using the state at the expense of the population as a whole. Punjab identification with rapid economic growth and modernization in the region tended to detract from the deteriorating economic position of the Punjabi workers and small farmers.

Although the NCNC, the base for the nationalist movement in Nigeria in the 1940s, started as a pan-regional organization with some radical and trade union support, when the first elections were held in 1951 its strength remained only in the East and Lagos. The Action Group, which in the early 1960s became the first major party to try to mobilize its support on a pan-regional and class basis, was undercut by the ruling regionally oriented parties. From time to time labor parties were formed, but they won virtually no seats because of the small size of the wage-earning class and the cross-pressures between communal and class-oriented parties. Furthermore, in the North, consciousness and political mobilization on a class basis was minimal partly because of the dominance of a political and religious ideology which legitimized authority and inequality (Diamond 1966, 34).

Though the number of key ethnic communities and the relative distribution of political and economic advantages differed in Nigeria and Pakistan, in both cases competition for economic and political power became increasingly regional in character. Competition in Nigeria was primarily among the three major communal groups, the Hausa-Fulani (North), Yoruba (West), and Ibo (East), who eclipsed the smaller ethnic groups within these three major regions. The southerners (Yorubas and Ibos) were aggressive, better educated, and more experienced in the modern sector than northerners. But in the competition for jobs and business activity, the latter compensated for some disadvantages by wielding political power at the federal level. The resentment of Eastern Nigerian arose from this competition for jobs and their substantial loss of relative standing around 1966, as well as the exodus of Eastern refugees from the North and other regions.

In Pakistan, competition was increasingly viewed as being between the Eastern and Western wings, especially with the consolidation of the West into a single province in 1955. While the "problem of parity" was ostensibly one of balancing the power of two wings, in practice it meant that the majority in the East (with 55 percent of the population) was effectively neutralized so as to give dominant Western interests unbridled sway in both political and economic spheres. It was an exploitative, colonial-type relationship, with some of the Bengali elite cooperating with the West Pakistanis in order to gain position and affluence. The resentment of East Pakistan arose in part from the lack of its sharing in the economic fruits of independence and modernization. The hopes of Bengalis, stirred by the fall of Ayub in 1969 and the 1970 elections, were thwarted by the maneuvers of Western political leaders and the military. While the grievances of the East Pakistanis arose from heightened aspirations to alleviate their low economic position within the country, the discontent of the Eastern Nigerians resulted from attempts to maintain a relatively high economic status within the Nigerian Federation.[9]

In Pakistan, the average material level of living was probably higher in the West than in the East at independence, and these disparities increased over time. In 1949-50 GDP per capita, based on official sources was 10 percent higher in the West than in the East. This difference increased to 30-36 percent in 1959-60, and to 60 percent in 1969-70. For the West, this represented a real growth in GDP per head of 1.1 percent annually in the decade, 1949/50-1959/60, at the same time this measure was declining in the East by at least one percent yearly. In the next decade, 1959/60-1969/70, real GDP per capita grew in the East at 1.5 percent yearly, and in the West by 3.6 percent annually (Khan and Bergan 1966, 187; Griffin and Khan 1972, 5, 29).

The dominant structural change in the Nigerian economy before the civil war was the rapid growth in the value of the output of crude oil, 78 percent per annum between 1958 and 1966. By then Nigeria, with an output of £N100 million, or 415,000 barrels daily, about two-thirds of which was in the East, ranked fifteenth in the world on the basis of crude oil production in that region alone (Nafziger 1983, 104-07, 147-50).[10] In the fiscal year 1966, the oil sector made a net positive contribution of £N43.4 million to the balance on current and capital account, to counter a deficit balance of £N54.2 million in other sectors. This is significant in an economy where merchandise exports were £N279.0 million in the same year.

When viewed in 1967, the oil sector promised to be even more important in the future. Pearson's low projections (1970, 137-52) indicated that the positive balance-of-payments impact of oil in 1973 would be £N111 million in an independent Biafra whose output would not be disrupted by war, and £N160 million in Nigeria, each more than double the figure for the entire Federation in 1966. No doubt the political and military elites in the East and the Federation during the early and middle 1960s foresaw the potentially rapid growth in petroleum production. In the East, this perception of the future reinforced the case for autonomy. Biafran separation became inevitable with the creation of 12 states in May 1967, which undercut the regional hegemony of the ruling Ibos, who would have been left with control of the landlocked

East-Central State, with merely 6 percent of Nigeria's oil output in April 1967, and without the East's major industrial city and Nigeria's only oil refinery. Since, by and large, Biafra's potential gain constituted a loss for the Federation, the latter took measures to quash to rebels.

East Pakistan, like Eastern Nigeria and Katanga, resented the low proportion of foreign exchange it could use in relation to that which it generated. The East Pakistani demand for decentralization increased because of its strong prospective international balance-of-payments position, and the fact it could shed the burden of having foreign exchange diverted to the West.

Between 1949/50 and 1969/70, Bengal generated the bulk of Pakistan's foreign exchange earnings (with exports primarily of raw jute, jute goods, and tea) while the West used about 70 percent of Pakistan's foreign exchange. This policy effected resource transfer from East to West, as the rupee was overvalued in international exchange. The East, as a price taker on its exports, received less local currency than at an equilibrium exchange rate, and still bought manufactured goods at inflated prices because of high tariffs. On the other hand, the artificially-induced low price of foreign exchange encouraged an increase in the West's dollar imports of capital goods and industrial inputs, which exacerbated Pakistan's balance-of-payments problems.

In 1959/60, 58.6 percent of Pakistan's exports were from the East, compared to only 26.6 percent of the imports; in 1964/65, the corresponding figures were 52.7 and 31.7 percents; and even in 1969/70, 50.0 and 35.6 percents respectively. This is despite the fact that exports of raw jute declined and imports of foodgrains increased in the East, while manufacturing exports increased and foodgrain imports decreased in the West during the 1960s (Pakistan 1971, 90-91), as a result partly of economic policy favoring industry and large-scale agriculture, which were concentrated disproportionately in the West.

The West was favored when it came to development plan expenditures, receiving an expenditure per head 4.9 times as much as the East in 1950/51-1954/55, and even 2.2 times as much in 1965/66-1969/70. During the last part of the 1960s, Eastern agriculture remained stagnant whiie Western agriculture encountered breakthroughs, especially in wheat. In the West, large subsidies were given for farm inputs such as water, fertilizers, seeds, plant protection service, and pesticides, while the East lacked government assistance in drainage, irrigation, flood control, extension service, and credit. One of the most striking instances of exacerbation of regional (and class) differences was that the high-yielding grain varieties associated with the Green Revolution were adapted to cropland under controlled irrigation—land owned primarily by rich commercial farmers in the West (Griffin and Khan 1972, 29; Bose 1972, 69-93; Cleaver 1972, 181).

A major source of interregional contention in Nigeria was the determination of a formula for the allocation of oil revenue. The East was especially dissatisfied that, after 1959, only a fraction of the revenue from crude petroleum (that is, none of the profits tax and only one-half of the rents and royalties) was received by the region of production in contrast to all the revenue from agricultural exports. Before 1959, all the revenues from mineral and agricultural products (that is, export duties) had been retained by the producing region. If all the government revenue from the crude-oil industry in the East in the war-affected year of 1967 had been retained by the region, it would have been equal to 59 percent of its approved estimates for current revenue. The discontent of the East reached a peak in early 1967 when its Ministry of Information charged that the region had been contributing more to the central treasury than it was receiving, and had benefited least from the siting of Federal investment projects in the previous decades (Nafziger 1973, 532-33).

One of the major grievances of East Pakistan was its substantial underrepresentation among the political elite, the bureaucracy, and the large bourgeoisie, even as late as the 1960s. In 1968, the representation of the East in the Civil Service of Pakistan was only 36 percent, comparable to her representation in other government services. Only in the last part of the 1960s were a few Bengalis appointed to posts as high as Secretary in the Central Government. None, however, was Secretary or Minister in the crucial Ministries of Defense, Home, and (except for a four-day portfolio) Finance. In the army, East Pakistanis constituted no more than five percent of the officers in 1963, a figure that did not change in a major way during the 1960s. While west Indian business communities, Memons, Khojas, and Bohras, which comprised only 0.5 percent of the Muslim population in Pakistan, accounted for 43 percent of industrial investment by Muslims, Bengalis, consisting of 50 percent of the Muslim population of the country, accounted for only 4 percent of industrial investment in Pakistan between 1947 and 1958 (Ayoob 1971, 202; Papanek 1962, 54).

The rise of political discontent was dampened in the 1950s in Pakistan, while a facade of democracy was maintained, and the East's representation in the legislature was at least on a par with the West. But after the coup of 1958, with the legislature dissolved, the Bengali upper and middle classes felt politically impotent, with only limited representation in the army and civil service, and none in higher political circles. This feeling of political ineffectiveness, together with the growing economic disparity between the Western and Eastern wings, was a factor contributing to the increased political violence directed against the military government of Ayub Khan by Bengalis in the 1960s.

In Nigeria, communal identity received its staying power because it was the major framework used by the political elite for distributing jobs to clients. Apart from the persistent clashes between the dominant and minority ethnic groups in the various regions, the Ibos, later dominant in Biafra, were at the center of the communal competition for employment and business activity. Ibos competed with Yorubas for key positions in the federal civil service, and for other jobs in the modern sector in Lagos and the West, and with them and Northerners for positions in business and employment in government and foreign firms in the North.[11]

In short, regional economic factors played a major role in fanning discontent in Eastern Nigeria and East Pakistan. East Pakistan, poorer than West Pakistan at independence, became more disadvantaged over time relative to the West. Additionally, the East was making little progress in terms of obtaining high-level positions in the economy and polity. As Easterners grew more conscious of the role of the coalition of Western landlords, industrialists, and army officers in using the levers of the state to increase regional income disparities, they became more restive. Their increasing aspirations and politicization, together with subsequent frustration with Western tactics to nullify any advantages of the electoral majority of their dominant political party, exacerbated their bitterness and discontent. Eastern Nigeria was by no means a disadvantaged region, and was more comparable to Punjab in terms of relative economic position. Discontent in the East was partially linked to the possible decline in its relatively high economic status and the benefits from oil that formed a basis for its affluence. Additionally, policies instituted because of the dominance of the North, such as Northernization of the government and private sectors in the North, and quotas for the recruitment of armed forces personnel to bring Northern representation up to its percentage of the population, added to the anticipated loss of position as a result of the exodus of Ibos from other regions due to the violence of 1966, and led to fear of a relative decline in the Ibo and Eastern standing in positions of high-level personnel in the country.

## SUMMARY

Class, regional, and communal conflicts which influence the probability of secessionist war are affected substantially by the nature of the colonial economic system and the post-colonial international economic nexus. In Nigeria and India, British colonial rule brought about imbalances in the mobilization of populations, reinforced or created ethnic identities, and provided a framework for competition between classes and regional groups.

The post-independence political and economic ties of Nigeria and Pakistan to Britain and the United States further intensified these imbalances by strengthening the dominant elite with each less developed country. Military and economic assistance and private capital from the United Kingdom and the United States served also to shield this elite from peripheral groups within its own nation-state.

The dominant classes utilized sentiments associated with subnational identities to transfer potential hostilities from class disparities within their own communities to differences with and antagonisms toward other ethnic groups and regions. Major political elites pursued and implemented economic policies which served their economic advantage. These policies had the effect of increasing interregional discrepancies in Pakistan, and threatening established regional economic interests in Nigeria. Though patterns of perceived deprivation thus differed in the two cases, both Bangladesh and Biafra came to view their membership within a federal union as one entailing persistent economic costs. The precipitants of the two political conflicts—the reorganization of the Nigerian federation and the postponement of the Pakistan constituent assembly—were only final steps on the long road to secessionist civil war.

# NOTES

1. The scope of this study precludes a detailed consideration of the factors contributing to the success of the secession of Bangladesh, almost entirely without indigenous military forces when the conflict broke out on 25 March 1971, and the failure of Biafra, whose army officers possessed the experience and skills which led Odumegwu Ojukwu to boast, with some basis, at the beginning of the war, that Biafra had the best army in black Africa. In short, however, we might suggest that the difference in success can be explained by the assistance to Bangladesh by a relatively powerful neighboring country, India; the substantial excess in foreign military and diplomatic assitance from major powers to Nigeria over Biafra; the logistical problems encountered by Pakistan in transporting supplies sixteen hundred kilometers across hostile territory; the lack of international assitance to Biafra to insure its continued production of oil; the international recognition of the blockade of biafran ports by Nigeria's small naval unit.

2. Trade in the upper North, which had been substantial with Mediterranean cities since the Middle Ages, dropped markedly during the colonial period.

3. In 1955, Punjabi control was solidified by the merging of the several provinces of West Pakistan into a single unit, which was given equal representation with the more populous East. In 1970, popular discontent in both East Pakistan and the non-Punjabi regions of the West forced a return to four West Pakistani provinces, and representation based on population. In Nigeria, in 1966, the military government of General J.T. Aguiyi-Ironsi, brought to power following a coup the preceding January, decreed that a unitary state and unified civil service was to replace the four-region federation, previously dominated by the Northern Region. The new military regime, which resulted form a countercoup of July, reverted to a federal structure on 27 May 1967, composed, however, of 12 states. As indicated below, this new structure was the precipitant for Biafran secession on 30 May 1967.

4. Wright notes these groups' replacement of the earlier, predominantly immigrant, elite of lawyers, professionals, and landlords.

5. Suchs findings suggest the need for additional comparative studies—in former French, Portuguese, Belgian, and other non-British colonial territories, in countries where independence was achieved throught protracted violent struggle, or in countries which somehow avoided colonial dependence. It would also be valuable to speculate on what the potential for political violence would have been in Nigeria, Pakistan, or other countries in the absence of colonialism, that is economic isolation, economic independence, or imperialism without colonialism. See Manning 1974, 17-22.

6. The counterpart to a high degree of integration within the world capitalist system is a low degree of interregional economic intergration (for example, trade flows and migration), a

partial determinant of the extent of political cohesion. The 1,450 kilometer corridor between East and West Pakistan, together with the location of a hostile country in between and the long distance by ship, precluded an integrated national economy. Interzonal trade flows as a percentage of GDP in 1969/70 was only 3.68 percent, higher than the figure one would get if we calculated the GDP originating in the exporting zone of the goods entering into interzonal trade. Pakistan 1971, 100-01; and Pakistan 1972, appendices pp. 4-5. For a discussion of the low degree of interregional trade flows in prewar Nigeria, see Nafziger 1983, 94-98.

7.  For an elaboraltion on class formation and contradictions among the elites, see Sklar 1965, 201-13.

8.  For an elaboration of the criss-cross of ethnicity and social class, see Himmelstrand 1969, 81-103.

9.  To use the terminology of Gurr 1970, 46-52, the East Pakistanis suffered aspirational deprivation while the Eastern Nigerians underwent decremental deprivation.

10.  Although Nigerian income and population data are subject to a sizeable margin of error, the figures available indicate that the East ranked between the West and North in GDP per capita, 1963/64. Time series data indicate that the rate of growth in per capita product between 1962/63 and the coups was fastest in the East (Adedeji 1969, 291).

11.  The contribution of communal competiion, economic regionalization, and interregional migration to the disintegration of the Federation, and the relationship between problems of employment and pressures for new states and secession are explored more at length in Nafziger 1973, 525-30.

# Chapter X

# *India vs. China: Economic Development Performance*

During the height of the Cold War in the 1950s, the west's foreign policy community stressed the importance of the comparative long-term economic performance of China and India, the world's two most-populated countries, regarded as showcases for two opposing systems (Bowles 1956). Although moderates and radicals in China vied for control of economic policy-making, both "lines" pursued centralized socialism from liberation in 1949 through the late 1970s. In India, with the exception of 1977-79, the Congress Party provided leadership from independence in 1947 through 1985. The major figures were Prime Ministers Jawaharlal Nehru (1947-64) and his daughter Indira Gandhi (1965-77 and 1979-84). They directed a mixed economy, with state ownership of strategic and much of heavy industry, but most other sectors open to private enterprise, though subject to central government planning and regulation.

This chapter primarily focuses on comparative growth indicators for the period between the early 1950s and late 1970s, and indicators of *levels* of development from the late 1970s to early 1980s, thus generally reflecting policies before China's post-1978 liberalization reforms (chapter 2) and India's late 1970s trend of reduced government regulation. A brief coda between the main body and conclusion indicates how this reform period modifies Sino-Indian comparisons.

## CHINA'S POLICIES

Following war rehabilitation, China's Communist Party, under Chairman Mao Zedong's leadership, centralized planning during the first five-year plan, 1953-57, expanding heavy industry and capital-goods production, raising the rate of investment, and developing agricultural cooperatives culminating in communes by 1958. China's slogan during the 1950s, "Learn from the Soviet Union," was also indicative of heavy dependence on it for financial and technical aid. The conflict from Chinese objections to Khrushchev's revisionism resulted in Soviet advisors pulling out in mid-1960, leaving projects partially finished and taking blueprints. Of necessity, the Chinese stressed the importance of national and regional self-reliance.

Severely declining output in 1959-61 followed in the wake of poor planning of water conservation projects, growth of communes, and decentralized making of tools, as well as drought and flood, during the Great Leap Forward, 1958-60. In reaction to the crisis, Liu Shao-ch'i, a moderate critical of Mao's policies, instituted the New Economic Policy (NEP), 1961-64, with private farm plots, financial incentives, and a stress on expertise, not ideology for managers. Liu's policies were supported by academics, administrators, managers, technicians, party officials, civil servants, and state enterprise directors. This liberalization contributed to rapid economic growth in 1961-66.

Mao, whose ideas were criticized by the pragmatists, undertook a counterattack, 1960-64, to prevent revisionist market socialism from taking over Chinese culture. He stressed learning from the radical, cohesive, non-professional People's Liberation Army (PLA), an integral part of economic construction.

The Cultural Revolution began in mid-1966 during a power struggle within the Beijing party committee, *Beijing Review*, and Beijing University. Students who could not reconcile socialism with their education dismissed the university's president, and led a revolt of Red Guards which spread to other schools. Mao used the revolt to undermine pragmatists opposed to a continuing class struggle against the encrusted bureaucracy and upper classes. The Cultural Revolution disrupted production during the first two years. It lasted through 1976, radically changing political leadership, education, and factory management.

Soon after Mao's death in 1976, the new leadership purged the radical "Gang of Four" and its followers, restoring pragmatist Deng Xiaopeng to leadership. Reforms after 1978 relied more on individual initiative, price decontrol, decentralized decisions, revenue sharing with provinces, financial incentives, Chinese-foreign joint ventures, and higher urban wages (Prybyla 1970; Wheelwright and McFarland 1970; Zhong 1984, 15-24; World Bank 1983, vol. 1, 14-20, 151-57).

# INDIA'S POLICIES

Intellectuals and nationalist leaders, especially in the Indian National Congress, believed laissez-faire capitalism during the colonial period was responsible for India's stagnation. Decades before he took office, Nehru had been attracted by English democratic socialism as well as Soviet industrial planning. He and other leaders supported state economic planning at independence to remove deep-seated obstacles.

India's policy fluctuations during the Nehru-Indira Gandhi period were less abrupt than China's. The Indian constitution directs the state to promote social justice and improve income and wealth distribution. Accordingly, the Congress party in 1955, though envisioning a mixed economy, set a goal of a "socialist pattern of society." The Nehru-Indira Gandhi model also included state direction through indicative planning, self-sufficiency in consumer goods and basic commodities, minimal reliance on foreign aid and investment, policy intervention to reduce poverty gradually, and (beginning in the 1960s) new seed-fertilizer technology in agriculture.

Yet planning emphases did change. The first five-year plan, 1951/52-1955/56, was only a collection of projects, rather than an integrated plan.

The Mahalanobis model, used for the second plan, 1956/57-1960/61, aimed at rapid industrialization by modifying the Fel'dman model used by the Soviets in the mid-1920s. The driving force was increasing investment in "machines to make machines," through raising the fraction of investment in steel and other capital goods. But the model left investment choice virtually unaffected, since Indian planning does not represent a binding commitment by a public department to spend funds. Moreover, it was difficult to identify capital-and consumer-goods sectors at any reasonable level of disaggregation. Finally, there were not enough investors ready to buy the capital goods produced. In contrast, in the Soviet Union, comprehensive government planning provided the market for capital goods from other industries producing capital goods and armaments.

The third plan, 1961/62-1965/66, tried to continue expanding industry, increase savings, promote exports, and achieve agricultural self-sufficiency, but failed partly because of India's conflicts with China and Pakistan. Annual real per capita GDP growth, less than 1/2 percent, was even slower than the roughly 2 percent annual growth for the first two plans. India abandoned the Mahalanobis approach by the late 1960s, because of slow agricultural and capital-goods growth, and balance-of-payments crises from growing food and capital imports, during the second and third plans.

Despite two bad harvests, the plan holiday, 1966-69 increased economic growth to slightly higher rates than the first two plans. During the fourth plan, 1969/70-1973/74, which stressed reducing poverty and inequality, and greater food self-sufficiency, growth slowed to third-plan rates. Despite the impact of high-yielding varieties of wheat after the late 1960s green revolution, agricultural output per capita grew less than 1 percent annually. Income inequality and poverty rates, which most studies indicated increased during the 1960s, continued to rise through the mid-1970s.

While the fifth plan, 1974/75-78/79, continued the goals of the previous plan, with more emphasis on reducing unemployment, there were few employment programs. The oil price rise, worldwide inflation, and increased food imports in 1972-74 hampered growth (no faster than in the fourth plan) and self-reliance gains. The plan, terminated in 1978 with Indira Gandhi's party's election defeat, was followed by a sixth plan, 1978-83. The policies of the opposition Janata Party government, 1977-79, were not greatly different from the Congress's. Janata continued the trend of reduced government industrial regulation begun in the mid-1970s and maintained by Indira Gandhi (1979-84) and by her son, Prime Minister Rajiv Gandhi, from 1984, after she was assassinated, to 1989 (Datt and Sundharam 1983). Per capita annual growth during the sixth plan, extended to 1985 by Indira Gandhi, was more rapid than for any other plan period.

Vishwanathan Pratap Singh and Charan Singh from the National Front were prime ministers in 1989-91. After Rajiv Gandhi was assassinated during the May 1991 election, his successor as leader of the Congress Party, Prime Minister P. V. Narasimha Rao, liberalized the economy further, opening it to foreign investment and Bank/Fund adjustment programs.

## DEVELOPMENT INDICATORS

To assess India's mixed democratic socialism vis-á-vis China's centralized authoritarian socialism, I use GNP per capita and its growth; income equality, poverty alleviation, and their trends; hunger alleviation and per capita food output growth; literacy and education; life expectancy; and infant survival.

## GNP PER CAPITA

GNP is an economy's total output of goods and services. The World Bank focuses on comparisons among India, China, and other LDCs, rather than a wider range of comparison; adjusts for purchasing power; and discusses its methods in detail.

Table X.1 indicates China has a 1979 nominal GNP per capita of $256, higher than India's $190. Both countries are classified as low-income countries, a category including some South and Southeast Asian and sub-Saharan African countries.

## REAL GNP PER CAPITA

Using market prices valued at official exchange rates to measure GNP distorts international comparisons of GNP per capita (Nafziger 1990, 22-25). The UN International Comparison Project (ICP) calculates the physical volume of goods and services in 150 categories of final products at average world prices to obtain GNP in international adjusted dollars (I$). GNP (I$) divided by nominal GNP (US$) converted at exchange rates equals the exchange rate

*Table X.1.*  Real Gross National Products Per Capital, 1979
(adjusted for purchasing power)

| | GNP per capita based on official exchange rate. 1979 (US$)[a] | Exchange rate deviation Index 1973[3b] | Real GNP per capita (I$) 1979[c] |
|---|---|---|---|
| India | 190 | 3.06 | 581 |
| China | 256 | 3.06 | 783 |
| Kenya | 380 | 2.06 | 783 |
| Philippines | 600 | 2.91 | 1,746 |
| Malaysia | 1,320 | 1.86 | 2,455 |
| Colombia | 1,010 | 2,51 | 2,535 |
| South Korea | 1,500 | 2.47 | 3,705 |
| Japan | 8,800 | 1.06 | 9,328 |
| France | 9,940 | 0.99 | 9,840 |
| United States | 10,820 | 1.00 | 10,820 |

*Notes:*  [a] World Bank, 1980a; and World Bank, vol. 1, 1983: 77.
[b] World Bank, vol. 1, 1983: 89. Exchange rate deviation index is from the UN Internatinal Comparision Project.
[c] Column 1 multiplied by column 2.

deviation index (ERD), reflecting the deviation of purchasing power of goods and services from the actual exchange rates. The ICP figures ERDs for 1967, 1970, 1973, 1975, and 1980. The last two ICP phases includes 34 benchmark countries, for which detailed price and output comparisons were made for numerous goods and services, and 90 non-benchmark countries, for which purchasing-power adjustments were based on a short-cut equation (Kravis, Heston, and Summers 1983).

India's 1979 nominal GNP per capita, $190, when multiplied by its ERD of 3.06, equals I$581 (Table X.1). For the United States, the base country, both nominal and real 1979 GNPs per capita were $10,820. U.S. GNP per capita as a multiple of India's was 57 in nominal terms, but only 19 in real terms. United States per capita expenditure on food was almost 11 times what it is in India, but only 6 times as much with adjustments in purchasing power. For staples like bread, rice, and cereals, US per capita consumption was twice India's, but only 1 1/2 times as much with the adjustment (Kravis, Heston, and Summers 1978, 204-05).

The ICP's 1967-1975 purchasing power adjustment did not include China, and the 1980 estimate for China was flawed.[1] Thus, I rely on the World Bank's comparison (vol. 1, 1983, 78, 263-300) of ERDs for India and China. Since internal price data are short for China, the World Bank valued GNP originating in each sector in China at prices for that output in India. The sum of the prices times quantities for sectors in China was compared to the same sum for India (using Indian prices).

China's GNP vis-á-vis India's is overstated if India's prices are used; and India's GNP overstated with China's prices. Valuation by own prices results in lower GNP because the set of own quantities adapts to these prices (Usher 1968, 3-12, 24-36). Assume that spices are relatively abundant in India, and pork in China. Then, spices will be valued at relatively low prices and pork at relatively high prices in India, and vice versa in China. India's abundant spices weigh little in GNP at own prices, but heavily at Chinese prices. Thus, the World Bank adjusts India's GNP upward vis-á-vis China to compensate for biases from using Indian internal prices. The Bank calculates that China's ERD was about the same as India's. Hence, China's 1979 GNP per capita in internationally adjusted dollars ($783) relative to India ($581) was about the same as the relative per capita GNPs based on official exchange rates. China's real GNP per capita was 35 percent higher than India's (20-50 percent with the margin of error) (Table X.1).

## GROWTH OF REAL GNP PER CAPITA, 1950-80

My Sino-Indian growth comparisons begin in 1950, the year of India's partial recovery from the disruption of the 1947 Indian-Pakistani partition. The source, Malenbaum (1982, 49-50, 81), relies on the Government of India's GNP series, and the National Foreign Assessment Center, the research arm of the US Central Intelligence Agency (CIA), for China's GNP, since both sources adhere to the UN Statistical Office's concepts. China's official data are inadequate, as it has only published summary measures of net material product (excluding depreciation and services production) for plan years in the early 1950s.

For both countries, GNP figures, measured in national currencies, are in constant prices of a base year used extensively in each country: 1970-71, India, and 1957, China. We can compare growth, but not level, of real GNP per capita without using a common currency.

A sector's value of output depends on the price weights of the base year selected. But, to illustrate, China's 1957 prices would not overstate the crude-oil sector in 1969 GNP as much as 1974 prices, while India's 1970 prices would not exaggerate the importance of the machine-tool industry as much as 1950 prices.

Table X.2 indicates India's annual real GNP growth, 1950-80, was 3.6 percent compared to China's 6.7 percent. Annual population growth rates of 2.1 percent over the same period for both countries result in an annual real GNP per capita growth of 1.5 percent for India and 4.5 percent for China, faster than average among LDCs. Among LDCs with a population of at least 5 million, only Taiwan, South Korea, and (then) capital-surplus oil exporters Iraq and Iran had a 1950-1975 real annual GNP growth rate in excess of China's 4.2 percent (Morawetz 1977, 15).

***Table X.2.*** Average Annual Rates of Real
Growth of GNP and GNP per Capita by Decade

|          | GNP(%) | | GNP per capita (%) | |
|----------|--------|-------|--------|-------|
|          | *India* | *China* | *India* | *China* |
| 1950-60  | 3.8    | 7.9   | 1.8    | 5.6   |
| 1960-70  | 3.7    | 5.6   | 1.3    | 3.3   |
| 1970-80  | 3.3    | 6.7   | 1.3    | 4.6   |
| 1950-80  | 3.6    | 6.7   | 1.5    | 4.5   |

*Source:*  Malenbaum 1982: 197.

The major sector contributing to China's rapid GNP growth was industry. China's annual growth in industry value-added, 1952-75, was 10.2 percent (11.0 percent, 1952-80) in 1957 constant yuan prices, compared to India's 5.3 percent yearly growth the same period (5.5 percent, 1952-80) in 1970-71 constant rupee prices. However, China's services output growth advantage over India was small and its agricultural growth about the same as India's.

China's fast growth, especially in industry, rapidly transformed a predominantly agricultural economy to one whose largest sector was industry. Industry's output share increased from 20 percent of China's net domestic product in 1952 to 48 percent in 1975 (55 percent in 1980), while agriculture's share declined from 48 percent in 1952 to 21 percent in 1975 (19 percent in 1980). India's industrial share only increased from 14 percent in 1952 to 21 percent in 1975 (24 percent in 1980), while its agricultural share declined slowly from 61 percent in 1952 to 47 percent in 1975 (42 percent in 1980). However, because of China's policies of high agricultural labor absorption and restricted rural-urban migration, its shift from agriculture to industry in labor force shares was only slightly faster than India's (Malenbaum 1982, 56-62).

If we use table X.2's long-term rates to project China's 1979 nominal GNP per capita, $256, and India's $190 backwards, China's 1950 GNP per capita ($71) is 42 percent lower than India's ($123). Even though China was recovering from two decades of war (internal and with the Japanese), its average GNP could not have been that much lower than India's, only a little above subsistence.

Malenbaum's figures, based on 1957 constant prices, overstate China's annual real growth rate, 1950-80. Unusually high relative industrial prices for the base year, 1957, if applied to later years of greater industrialization, exaggerate industrial and total output for 1980.

When the World Bank (vol 1, 1983, 77). uses 1979 internal prices instead, China's long-term growth rate decreases by 23 percent, from 4.5 percent annually (Table X.2) to 3.5 percent. If this growth is applied backward, China's 1950 GNP per capita is $94, 24 percent less than India's. This difference is consistent with Swamy's (1973) and Eckstein's (1975, 214) estimates. Since

China had been through two decades of war, this figure is plausible, and does not contradict the widely held view that China's average material welfare in the 1920s and 1930s, when economic damage was less, was higher than India's.

But China's 1950-1980 annual growth rate, even if assumed only 3.5 percent, is faster than other LDCs' rate, 3.0 percent. In fact, China's rate, if maintained, would multiply income 31 times a century, an increase almost as fast as the fastest DC growth rate, Japan's, 3.6 percent yearly, between the 1860s and 1975 (Morawetz 1982, 11, 80; Nafziger 1990, 43-61; World Bank 1985, 146-175) (Table II.1).

# INCOME INEQUALITY

Economic growth probably cannot solve the problem of widespread poverty, unless attention is given to how income is distributed. The Gini coefficient, measuring 1979 regional inequality in income per capita, was slightly lower in India (0.168) than in China (0.181). However, since the 1950s, China's regional discrepancies narrowed with deliberate policies to restrain growth in the northeastern industrial centers, while India's differences have increased because of disproportionate investment in the wealthier states (Datt and Sundharam 1983, 362-62; World Bank, vol. 1, 1983, 84).

Because of the marked interprovincial differences in Chinese agricultural incomes, rural-urban inequality varied widely from province to province. Overall China's urban-rural income ratio was comparable to that of India's—higher on a per capita basis—2.2 to 1.9, but lower on a household basis—1.7 to 1.8 (Table X.3).

But China's urban-rural discrepancy increased while India's decreased from the 1950s to the 1970s. China's urban per capita real income growth, 1957-79, was 2.9 percent yearly compared to rural growth of 1.6 percent. In contrast, India's per capita real consumption growth (which moves parallel to income growth), 1950/51-1954/55 through 1975/76-1979/80 was only 0.0 percent annually in urban areas compared to 1.4 percent in rural areas (World Bank, vol. 1, 1983, 85-87, 276, 309; Rao 1983, 82-83).

China's allocation, pricing, and tax policies have been characterized by urban bias, and India's, despite Lipton's (1977) opposing contention, by rural bias. Since 1947, India's democratic government, under pressure from landed elites and an agrarian majority, has levied no income tax on agriculture, virtually abandoned land taxation, spent much on irrigation and other agricultural projects, and provided substantial farm credit, the major contributor to a net resource inflow to agriculture since independence (Mody, Mundle, and Raj 1985, 266-93).

India did not restrict migration to the cities, while China directly controlled it, sending many wartime urban emigrants back to the countryside during the

**Table X.3.** International
Comparison of Rural-Urban Inequality

| | Ratio of average urban income to average rural income | |
|---|---|---|
| | Per capita | Per household |
| India, 1975/76 | 1.9 | 1.8 |
| China, 1979 | 2.2 | 1.7 |
| Bangladesh, 1966/67 | n.a. | 1.5 |
| Sri Lanka | n.a. | 1.7 |
| Indonesia, 1976 | n.a. | 2.1 |
| Malaysia (Pen.) 1970 | 2.2 | 2.1 |
| Philippines, 1971 | n.a. | 2.3 |
| Thailand, 1975/76 | 2.2. | n.a. |
| Brazil, 1976 | 2.3 | n.a. |

*Source:* World lBank, vol. 1, 1983: 86.

1950s, and city youth to "learn from the peasants" during the Cultural Revolution. Despite China's low urban wage increases, India was more successful in narrowing urban-rural wage differences, because it allowed migration from low-wage rural to higher-wage urban areas. Partly because of restricted rural-urban migration, Chinese agricultural output per worker rose very little over the period. Moreover, urban labor force participation rates increased rapidly (from 33 percent in 1957 to 55 percent in 1979). Other factors contributing to China's increasing income gap were high income supports, higher-quality educational and health facilities, and low rents in urban areas, and low agricultural procurement prices, which kept the urban price of necessities low (World Bank, vol. 1, 1983, 85-87).

China's faster overall growth meant that its income per capita increased more rapidly in both urban and rural areas, even though the urban-rural gap widened. Despite China's urban-rural differential in health facilities and school opportunities, these were so much more widely available in China than in India (see below) that China's rural areas were better served than India's.

Chinese urban inequality, 1980, was extraordinarily low (Gini = 0.16), while India's (1975/76) was moderate (0.42). The poorest 40 percent of the urban population received 30.0 percent of the income in China, compared to only 16.9 percent in India, while China's richest 10 percent received only 15.8 percent to India's 34.5 percent (Table X.4). China's low urban inequality resulted from no private property income, no income from self-employment (until 1979), and the comparatively equal distribution of wages and salaries, with managerial, professional, and technical salaries much lower than in India. But wage differences among manual workers were not much different from India, even though she had a higher proportion of rural emigrants (Ibid., vol. 1, 88-89).

*Table X.4.* International Comparison of Urban Income Inequality

| | Income share of recipient groups | | | |
| --- | --- | --- | --- | --- |
| | *Poorest 40%* | *Richest 20%* | *Richest 10%* | *Gini coefficient* |
| India | 16.9 | 48.8 | 34. | 0.42 |
| China, 1980 | 30.0 | 28.2 | 15.8 | 0.16 |
| Bangladesh, 1966/67* | 17.1 | 47.2 | 31.5 | 0.40 |
| Pakistan, 1970/71* | 19.1 | 44.4 | 29.7 | 0.36 |
| Sri Lanka, 1969/70* | 16.3 | 47.5 | 31.7 | 0.41 |
| Indonesia, 1976* | 16.0 | 49.4 | 34.5 | 0.43 |
| Malaysia (Pen), 1970 | 11.2 | 56.5 | 40.3 | 0.52 |
| Philippines, 1971* | 13.7 | 54.1 | 35.3 | 0.47 |
| Thailand, 1975/76* | 17.5 | 46.6 | 32.2 | 0.40 |

*Note:* * Distribution by households ranked by total household income, not of people ranked by household per capital income.
*Source:* World Bank, vol. 1, 1983: 89.

Because of China's rationing, and low price of necessities relative to luxuries, its real consumption distribution was more equal than its income distribution, and contrasts with India's, with less extensive programs to improve consumer distribution (Ibid., vol. 1, 89).

China's rural income inequality (Gini 0.31) was lower than India's (0.34) (Table X.5).

After China's revolution, land reform and collectivization reduced rural inequality substantially. No one owned land and capital, and their returns have been distributed among production team members. But sources of inequality include differences between teams in quantity and quality of land per person, variations in labor participation rates per household, and restrictions on urban migration to reduce rural poverty and inequality.

India's land reform was not effective, because of the absence of up-to-date land records, the difficulty of verifying ownership rights, and conflict with powerful landed interests in the legislatures and bureaucracies. Federal and state laws frequently had deliberate exemptions or loopholes inducing fictitious land transfer to relatives or concealing ownership through reclassifying lands under exempted categories. Thus, land concentration remained high. By 1970, only 0.3 percent of the total cultivated land had been distributed under legislation. Moreover, large moneylenders, farmers, and traders often controlled village cooperatives, and utilized most of the credit and services provided by community development programs (Bardhan 1974, 255-62).

Chinese data undervalue income in kind, household earnings variations within production teams, and private farm and handicraft activity. But even if we adjusted for these, Chinese rural inequality was still no higher than India's (Table X.5) (World Bank, vol. 1, 1983, 90-92).

*Table X.5.* International Comparison of Rural Income Inequality

| | Income shares of recipient groups | | | |
|---|---|---|---|---|
| | Poorest 40% | Richest 20% | Richest 10% | Gini coefficient |
| China, 1979 | 20.1 | 39.4 | 22.8 | 0.31 |
| India, 1975/76 | 20.2 | 42.4 | 27.6 | 0.34 |
| Bangladesh, 1966/67* | 19.9 | 41.7 | 26.1 | 0.33 |
| Pakistan, 1970/71* | 21.,9 | 38.8 | 24.0 | 0.30 |
| Sri Lanka, 1969/70* | 18.6 | 42.5 | 26.4 | 0.35 |
| Indonesia, 1976* | 16.4 | 46.0 | 32.0 | 0.40 |
| Malaysia (Pen), 1970 | 12.2 | 54.8 | 39.3 | 0.50 |
| Philippines, 1971* | 17.3 | 46.7 | 31.7 | 0.39 |
| Thailand, 1975/76* | 17.8 | 46.5 | 31.1 | 0.39 |

*Note:* * Distribution by households ranked by total household income, not of people ranked by household per capita income, as where no asterisk.
*Source:* World Bank, vol. 1, 1983: 94.

Although China's urban and rural inequalities were low, its overall inequality was not much lower than India's, because of China's relatively large urban-rural gap. In China, urban people were only 13 percent of the population, but constituted less than half of the country's richest 20 percent of the population. The poorest half of China's population was virtually all rural. The 22 percent of India's urban population constituted less than half of the country's richest 20 percent of the population, although the rural share of the poorest half probably did not vary much from China.

Overall income distribution in China (Gini = 0.33) was more equal than India (0.38), which has less equality than Bangladesh (0.34), but greater equality than Thailand, Indonesia, the Philippines, and Malaysia (see Table X.6). China's equality was about the same as Sri Lanka's, but probably less than Taiwan's or South Korea's. Jain indicates Taiwan's and South Korea's ratio of incomes of the richest fifth to the poorest fifth was 5:1, India's 11:1, the Philippines' 14:1, Mexico's 15:1, and Brazil's and South Africa's 25:1, but he has no figure for China (Jain 1975). Eberstadt (1979b) estimates a 9:1 ratio for China as comparable to Jain's other figures. This ratio relative to India's was the same as the relative ratios for the richest 20 percent to the poorest 40 percent between China and India in Table X.6.

Since Chinese government policy before 1979 insured that food, clothing, housing, medical care, and schooling were distributed in a relatively egalitarian way, income distribution figures may understate equality. On the other hand, there are inadequacies in rural income distribution stated above that overstate equality. If we adjusted incomes for these distortions, China's rankings vis-á-vis India and other LDCs would probably not be changed.

*Table X.6.*  International Comparison of Overall Income Inequality

| | Income shares of recipient groups | | | |
| --- | --- | --- | --- | --- |
| | Poorest 40% | Richest 20% | Richest 10% | Gini coefficient |
| China, 1979 | 18.4 | 39.3 | 22.5 | 0.33 |
| India, 1975 | 18.5 | 46.5 | 31.4 | 0.38 |
| Bangladesh, 1966/67* | 19.6 | 42.3 | 26.7 | 0.34 |
| Pakistan, 1970/71* | 20.6 | 41.5 | 26.8 | 0.33 |
| Sri Lanka, 1969/70* | 20.8 | 41.8 | 27.4 | 0.33 |
| Indonesia, 1976* | 14.4 | 49.4 | 34.0 | 0.44 |
| Malaysia (Pen), 1970 | 12.5 | 55.1 | 39.8 | 0.50 |
| Philippines, 1971* | 14.2 | 54.0 | 38.5 | 0.47 |
| Thailand, 1975/76* | 15.8 | 49.3 | 33.4 | 0.42 |
| Yugoslavia, 1973* | 18.4 | 40.0 | 22.5 | 0.32 |

Note:   * Distribution by households ranked by total household income, not of people ranked by household
           per capita income, where there is no asterisk.
Source:   World Bank, vol. 1, 1983: 84.

## POVERTY

Absolute poverty is below the income that secures the bare essentials of food, clothing, and shelter. Determining this level is a matter of judgment, so that it is difficult to make comparisons between countries. Moreover, what is considered poverty varies according to the living standards of the time and region. Using widely-discussed Indian methods, Ahluwalia, Carter, and Chenery define the international poverty line as the income needed to attain 2,250 calories per capita daily, a figure of I$200 per capita in 1975. Data on 1975 income distribution indicate 46 percent of the Indian population was below the poverty line (or potentially undernourished). Given information on income distribution, poverty in other countries, Ahluwalia, et al. determine poverty in other countries by finding the percentage of the population from households with a 1975 income of less than I$200 per capita (Ahluwalia, Carter, and Chenery 1979, 299-341). World Bank figures since Ahluwalia et al.'s computations provide a basis for comparable poverty rates on China. I use 1975 World Bank figures on Chinese per capita GNP and yuan-U.S. dollar exchange rates, a Chinese ERD from Table X.1, and the World Bank's overall Chinese income distribution from 1979 to calculate the percentage of the 1975 Chinese population from households with an income less than I$200 per capita (World Bank, vol. 1, 1983, 92-95, 267-269, 314). The poverty rate was 41 percent at official exchange rates, but 27 percent if adjusted for exchange rate deviation (see Table X.7). Given China's higher real GNP per capita and lower income inequality, it is not surprising that China's poverty rate was much lower than India's.

*Table X.7.* Per Capita Income, Population, and Poverty, 1975

| Country[a] | GNP per capita[b] | | Papulaton 1975 (Millions) | Percentage of Population in Poverty in 1975 | |
|---|---|---|---|---|---|
| | At Official Exchange Rates | Using Adjustment for Purchasing Power | | Using Adjustment for Purchasing Power | Using Official Exchange Rates |
| Bangladesh | 72 | 200 | 80.7 | 64 | 60 |
| Burma | 88 | 237 | 30.9 | 65 | 56 |
| Indonesia | 90 | 280 | 130.0 | 59 | 62 |
| **India** | **102** | **300** | **599.4** | **46** | **46** |
| Pakistan | 121 | 299 | 73.0 | 43 | 34 |
| **China** | **137** | **419** | **950.0** | **27** | **41** |
| Low-income[c] | 117 | 373 | 1956.3 | 39 | 45 |
| Nigeria | 176 | 433 | 75.3 | 35 | 27 |
| Philippine | 182 | 469 | 42.5 | 33 | 29 |
| Sri Lanka | 185 | 471 | 14.1 | 14 | 10 |
| Thailand | 237 | 584 | 41.6 | 32 | 23 |
| Lower-middle[d] | 206 | 507 | 255.5 | 31 | 24 |
| South Korea | 325 | 797 | 34.1 | 8 | 6 |
| Malaysia | 471 | 1006 | 12.2 | 12 | 8 |
| Taiwan | 499 | 1075 | 16.1 | 5 | 4 |
| Brazil | 509 | 1136 | 106.8 | 15 | 8 |
| Mexico | 758 | 1429 | 59.6 | 14 | 10 |
| Upper-middle[e] | 574 | 1213 | 433.5 | 13 | 8 |
| Total | 218 | 548 | 2445.3 | 37 | 40 |

*Notes:* [a] Countries are ranked in ascending order by 1975 GNP per capita. Some countries ommitted in the table are used to calculate the subtotals for low-income, lower-middle, and upper-middle countries, and the LDC total.

[b] In 1970 U.S. dollars.

[c] Low-income countries are those with GNP per capita under $150.

[d] Lower-middle income countries are those with GNP per capita from $150 to $300.

[e] Upper-middle income countries are those with GNP per capita greater than $300.

*Sources:* Ahluwalia, Carter, and Chenery, 1979, pp. 302-303; and World Bank, vol. 1, 1983: 92, 314.

# TRENDS IN POVERTY AND INCOME INEQUALITY

India's and China's income inequality both increased from the 1950s to the 1970s.

In India, the poor's income share dropped from the 1950s through the early 1970s, while no appreciable dent was made on absolute poverty. Poverty rates in both rural and urban areas appear to have increased throughout the 1960s and early 1970s, decreasing in the 1970s, and holding steadily in the late 1970s (Bardhan 1974, 255-62). In China, despite the rapid economic growth from the late 1950s through 1977, poverty (and malnutrition) rates did not decline, suggesting that income inequality increased (Lardy 1983, 175-76).

## HUNGER AND FOOD OUTPUT

Mao claimed China had succeeded in feeding a people ravished by hunger for centuries. Western scholars widely accept this view. Imfeld (1976, 157) maintains that "in contrast to India, China has eliminated hunger." Here we look at how China's food output, growth, and distribution, and nutritional levels compare to India's.

Lardy (1983, 148) indicates China's daily per capita calorie consumption in the early 1930s was 2,125-2,225, substantially in excess of India's. China's average calorie consumption declined during the 1940s' war years, while India's was probably increasing at a moderate rate. Yet China's agricultural techniques, as well as average food output (and consumption) were substantially in excess of India's in the early 1950s.

The vagaries of weather make farm production volatile. Yet the literature abounds with growth rates based on one-year comparisons (Malenbaum 1982, 68-72). A country's record depends partly on the beginning and ending years selected. China's annual growth in foodgrain output per capita relative to India's appears favorable for 1953-1958, 1970-1972, and 1977-1980, but unfavorable for 1957-1958, 1965-1970, and 1974-1975 (see Table X.8, columns 3 and 7).

To avoid distortions due to weather fluctuations, I use a five-year moving average, in which foodgrain output per person in the year 1954, for instance, is computed as an average of the outputs of 1952 through 1956 (Table X.8, columns 4 and 8).

Table X.8's foodgrain output data are comparable for either country over time, but not between countries the same year, without adjustment. Unlike India, China measures foodgrain on an unhusked basis, and includes potatoes, tubers, soybeans, peas, and beans among grains, so that Chinese output figures need to be multiplied by roughly 82 percent to find their Indian output equivalents (Ibid., pp. 70-71; Lardy 1983: 147-50). Thus, India's 1954 foodgrain output per person, 0.171 tons, was 28.4 percent below China's, 0.239 tons, 0.291 times 0.82.

China's food output per person increased much during rehabilitation from war, 1950-52, and rose more slowly from 1952, a year when civil order was restored and land reform completed, to 1957, when average per capita calorie intake was 2,020 calories, still below the early 1930s level. India's growth per capita, 1950-57, was slower.

## *Table X.8.* Foodgrain Output

| | India | | | | China | | | |
|---|---|---|---|---|---|---|---|---|
| | (1) | (2) | (3) | (4) | (5) | (6) | (7) | (8) |
| | | | | (3)-5 yr. | | | | (7)-5 yr. |
| | Output | Population | Output | moving | Output | Population | Output | Moving |
| Year | mvt[a] | (ms) | per person | average | mmt | (ms) | per person | average |
| 1950 | 52.4 | 359 | 0.146 | | | 552 | | |
| 1951 | 52.8 | 365 | 0.145 | | | 563 | | |
| 1952 | 58.6 | 372 | 0.158 | 0.161 | 164 | 575 | 0.285 | |
| 1953 | 69.0 | 379 | 0.182 | 0.165 | 167 | 588 | 0.284 | |
| 1954 | 66.6 | 386 | 0.173 | 0.171 | 170 | 602 | 0.282 | 0.291 |
| 1955 | 66.8 | 393 | 0.170 | 0.171 | 184 | 615 | 0.299 | 0.295 |
| 1956 | 70.0 | 401 | 0.175 | 0.171 | 193 | 628 | 0.307 | 0.298 |
| 1957 | 63.3 | 409 | 0.155 | 0.171 | 195 | 647 | 0.301 | 0.292 |
| 1958 | 75.7 | 418 | 0.181 | 0.173 | 200 | 661.5 | 0.302 | 0.276 |
| 1959 | 74.1 | 426 | 0.174 | 0.175 | 170 | 672.5 | 0.253 | 0.260 |
| 1960 | 79.4 | 434 | 0.183 | 0.177 | 143.5 | 665.5 | 0.215 | 0.248 |
| 1961 | 81.3 | 444 | 0.183 | 0.175 | 147.5 | 650.5 | 0.227 | |
| 1962 | 75.5 | 454 | 0.166 | 0.171 | 160 | 661.5 | 0.242 | |
| 1963 | 78.7 | 464 | 0.170 | 0.164 | 170 | | | |
| 1964 | 72.9 | 474 | 0.154 | 0.158 | 187.5 | | | |
| 1965 | 72.3 | 485 | 0.149 | 0.162 | 194.5 | 725 | 0.268 | |
| 1966 | 74.2 | 495 | 0.150 | 0.165 | 214 | | | |
| 1967 | 96.0 | 506 | 0.190 | 0.172 | 218 | | | |
| 1868 | 94.9 | 518 | 0.183 | 0.182 | 209 | | | |
| 1969 | 99.5 | 529 | 0.188 | 0.191 | 211 | | | |
| 1970 | 108.4 | 541 | 0.200 | 0.188 | 240 | 826 | 0.291 | |
| 1971 | 106.9 | 554 | 0.193 | 0.187 | 250 | 848 | 0.295 | |
| 1972 | 98.2 | 566 | 0.173 | 0.183 | 240 | 867 | 0.277 | 0.293 |
| 1973 | 104.7 | 579 | 0.181 | 0.183 | 265 | 887 | 0.299 | 0.297 |
| 1974 | 99.8 | 591 | 0.169 | 0.180 | 275 | 904 | 0.304 | 0.299 |
| 1975 | 121.0 | 606 | 0.200 | 0.186 | 284.5 | 920 | 0.309 | 0.299 |
| 1976 | 111.2 | 620 | 0.179 | 0.190 | 286 | 933 | 0.307 | 0.307 |
| 1977 | 126.4 | 634 | 0.199 | 0.189 | 283 | 945 | 0.299 | 0.315 |
| 1978 | 131.9 | 648 | 0.204 | 0.188 | 305 | 958 | 0.318 | 0.318 |
| 1979 | 109.7 | 663 | 0.165 | 0.190 | 332 | 971 | 0.342 | 0.322 |
| 1980 | 129.6 | 678 | 0.191 | 0.187 | 320.6 | 983 | 0.326 | 0.332 |
| 1981 | 133.3 | 693 | 0.192 | 0.187 | 325 | 996 | 0.326 | 0.345 |
| 1982 | 130 | 717 | 0.181 | 0.193 | 353 | 1,008 | 0.350 | 0.356 |
| 1983 | 152 | 733 | 0.207 | 0.194 | 387 | 1,019 | 0.380 | 0.363 |
| 1984 | 146 | 749 | 0.195 | 0.193 | 407 | 1,029 | 0.396 | 0.372 |
| 1985 | 151 | 765 | 0.197 | 0.191 | 379 | 1,040 | 0.364 | 0.377 |
| 1986 | 144 | 781 | 0.184 | 0.190 | 391 | 1,054 | 0.371 | 0.374 |
| 1987 | 138 | 798 | 0,173 | | 402 | 1,068 | 0.376 | |
| 1988 | 164 | 816 | 0.200 | | 394 | 1,088 | 0.362 | |

*Notes:* Indian data are for 1 April of given year through 31 March of the following year.
*Sources:* China, State Statistical Bureau, *Statistical Yearbook of China* (Beijing) (annual); and India, Central Statistical Office, Department of Statistics, Ministry of Planning, *Indian Economic Survey* (New Delhi) (annual).

China's food production, as well as calorie consumption, per capita barely increased between 1957 and 1975, a time when India's per capita growth accelerated some (Table X.9), partly due to gains from the late 1960s' high-yielding varieties of wheat. But China's surge in grain imports (to 4 percent of 1978-79 production) and agricultural output increased per capita calorie intake between 1977 and 1979 by 19 percent (Lardy 1983, 157-66; World Bank, vol. 1, 1983, 101, 178).

Thus, as table X.10 indicates, the average food consumption in China was much higher than in India. China's 1979 food energy consumption, 103 percent of estimated requirements, was above India's (91 percent), though below middle-income countries (108 percent). Protein availability per person (163 percent of requirements) is also above that for India (135 percent), but below Pakistan, Mexico, and South Korea.

Using a five-year moving average, India's annual growth in foodgrain output per capita from the mid 1950s to late 1970s was slightly faster than China's. India's per capita growth, 1956-77, was 0.48 percent to China's 0.36 percent (Table X.9). (India's growth margin over China's was even narrower, 1954-79 and 1956-79, the five-year average for 1979 being much influenced by China's strong performance, 1979-81.) India's 1979 per capita foodgrain output, 0.190 tons (column 4, Table X.8) was 28.0 percent below China's, 0.264 (0.322 times 0.82), only a slight narrowing of the 1954 relative gap.

China's slow foodgrain output growth resulted partly from a lack of emphasis on agricultural research and technology. Since the 1950s, Chinese agricultural institutes were isolated from international institutes, and did little basic agricultural research. During the height of the Cultural Revolution, 1966-1970, some leading agricultural scientists were sent to rural areas to learn from the peasants. At about the same time, the matriculation of agricultural students was disrupted because the educational system was shut down (Howe 1978, 26-27, 81). During the late 1970s and early 1980s, Deng argued that lagging research and low-quality education in agriculture constituted the "greatest crisis" in contemporary China.

*Table X.9.* Annual Growth Rates in Foodgrain Output per Person
(in percentage)

|        | 1954-79 | 1956-77 | 1956-79 | 1954-77 | 1957-75 | 1954-72 | 1954-60 |
|--------|---------|---------|---------|---------|---------|---------|---------|
| India  | 0.42    | 0.48    | 0.46    | 0.44    | 0.47    | 0.38    | 0.58    |
| China  | 0.40    | 0.36    | 0.44    | 0.34    | 0.13    | 0.04    | -2.63   |

Source:Calculated from five-year moving averages in columns (4) and (8), table X.8.

***Table X.10.*** Food Availability, 1977

| | Per capita daily availability of | | | | |
| | Energy | | | Protein | |
| | Calories | Percent of requirement | Total (grams) | Percent of requirement | Percent animal and pulse |
|---|---|---|---|---|---|
| India | 2,021 | 91 | 50.0 | 136 | 26 |
| China[a] | 2,441 | 103 | 62.6 | 163 | 26 |
| **Low-income countries** | | | | | |
| Bangladesh | 1,812 | 78 | 36.0 | 100 | 18 |
| Indonesia | 2,272 | 105 | 47.0 | 130 | 13 |
| Pakistan | 2,281 | 99 | 63.0 | 165 | 32 |
| Sri Lanka | 2,126 | 96 | 43.0 | 121 | 16 |
| Average[b] | 2,052 | 91 | n.a. | n.a. | n.a. |
| **Middle-income countries** | | | | | |
| Brazil | 2,562 | 107 | 62.7 | 161 | 56 |
| South Korea | 2,785 | 119 | 73.0 | 183 | 21 |
| Mexico | 2,654 | 114 | 66.0 | 173 | 41 |
| Thailand | 1,929 | 105 | 49.0 | 136 | n.a. |
| Average[b] | 2,590 | 108 | n.a. | n.a. | n.a. |

*Notes:* [a] 1979.
  [b] Average includes some countries not listed.
*Source:* World Bank, vol. 1, 1983: 101; vol. 3, 1983: 33.

While India's record was only marginally better, its fast growth, 1965-1969, 4.2 percent annually, began during the breakthrough by the Rockefeller Foundation and the Ministry of Food and Agriculture in developing shorter and much higher-yielding varieties of wheat. These hybrids of Mexican wheat and Japanese dwarf strains, capable of absorbing much higher doses of chemical fertilizer without falling over, required greater price incentives, as well as improvements in irrigation, tubewells, credit, seed distribution, fertilizer, transport, extension, and storage, especially in the Punjab (Frankel 1978, 275-78). Because of the powerful link between individual investment and effort to income, India's commercial farmers responded more quickly to innovations than China's communes.

Yet foodgrain figures understate India's relative food consumption. Despite some members of high Hindu castes who do not eat meat for religious reasons, the Indian diet included a larger share of meat and dairy products than China's, and a smaller share of bread and cereals than China's. But China still had higher average food consumption levels than India, especially among the poorest 25 percent of the population. India's average food consumption was higher than China's, however, among the richest 25 percent of the population (Malenbaum 1982, 70-72; World Bank, vol. 1, 1983).

But a country's malnutrition was less related to average food consumption, than to how food was distributed, including the relative consumption levels of the lowest income groups. Although Brazil, a country with high food inequality, had a 1979 GNP per capita ($1,770) seven times as high as China's and average nutrient availability higher than China's (Table X.10), it had a larger proportion of its population severely malnourished than China (World Bank 1982a: 22; and Eberstadt 1979a).

Yet China, contrary to Imfeld, did not eliminate malnutrition. Table X.7's figure of 27 percent for a nutritionally-based poverty rate suggests the error of Imfeld's view. Moreover, in 1979, Beijing leaders admitted that in 1977 about 100 million people, or more than one-tenth of China's population, did not have enough to eat (Barnett 1981, 305, citing China 1979, 1-18). Though this does not define malnutrition precisely, it indicates that China's hunger rates are within the range of other LDC rates rather than close to zero, as Imfeld contends.

Gurley (1976, 234) indicates "the Chinese have what is in effect an insurance policy against pestilence, famine, and other disasters." But though China normally has a lower malnutrition rate and distributes food more equally than India, it was more subject to famine than India was. As Sen (1983, 757-60) points out, one-third of the Indian population went to bed hungry every night and led a life ravaged by regular deprivation. India's social system took non-acute endemic hunger in stride; there were no headlines or riots. In China, the situation was almost the opposite. Its political commitment ensured lower regular malnutrition through more equal access to means of livelihood, and through state-provided entitlement to basic needs of food, clothing, and shelter. In a normal year, China's poor were much better fed than India's. China's life expectancy was 67 to India's 55 years. Yet if there was a political and economic crisis that confused the regime so it pursued disastrous policies with confident dogmatism, then it could not be forced to change its policies by crusading newspapers or effective political opposition pressure, as in India.

While China's per capita food production and calorie consumption were not much higher in 1977 than in 1957, they dropped sharply during the 1959-61 famine. Foodgrain output per person in 1960 dropped 25 percent below its 1952 level, resulting in widespread malnutrition. The cause of this decline was not only bad weather, floods, and drought, but also poor quality work during the Great Leap Forward (GLF), 1958-60. Reservoir construction work destroyed soil, river functioning, and existing irrigation systems. Reservoir and water conservation work raised underground water levels, alkalized, salinized, and waterlogged soil, halted stream and river flow, left irrigation channels unfinished, and lacked drainage. Moreover, GLF water projects took land from cultivation (Ibid., p. 101; Prybyla 1970, 264-69; Barnett 1981, 271, 302). Yet the GLF political pressure for agricultural success made local officials unwilling to report food shortages (Lardy 1983, 152-53).

Sen (1983, 757-60), using Beijing University figures, calculates an extra mortality of 14-16 million people from famine in China in 1959-61, greater in absolute or relative terms than the 3 million extra mortality in India's largest twentieth-century famine, the Great Bengal Famine of 1943. So although China was more successful than India in eliminating regular malnutrition, China had more famines than India.

# LIFE EXPECTANCY

Life expectancy and infant mortality are indicators that represent the effects of nutrition, public health, income, and the general environment. China's life expectancy at birth (64 years) was more than middle-income countries' (61), and much higher than India's (51) in the late 1970s. China's high position relative to India continued from the early 1950s (Table X.11).

The first reason for China's higher life expectancy was its higher average consumption of food, housing, fuel, soap, and clean water, especially among the poorest 50 percent of the population. A second reason was greater understanding by the Chinese people of nutrition, health, and hygiene, partly from greater literacy and education (discussed below). A third reason was medical care, public sanitation, and avoidance of communicable diseases. In the 1970s, China's four-tiered rural health system included one or two auxiliary health workers for each production team (usually a village of 100-400 people), a medical station staffed by two to three "barefoot doctors" for the production brigade (7-12 teams), the health center for a commune (often 4-15 brigades), and a county general hospital. Cities had even more adequate health and medical care.

Although the Chinese health policy emphasized preventive measures and improving the health environment, it also diffused widely basic curative care by western and traditional Chinese medicine. In 1982, China had 2,500 people per fully qualified non-traditional doctor, compared to 9,900 in other low-income countries and 4,300 in middle-income countries. The ratio of population to other medical personnel is even more favorable when compared to other LDCs (World Bank, vol. 1, 1983, 64-65, 97-99).

In contrast to China, most of India's medical doctors practiced in large cities, so that medical care was rarely available in the villages. Although state government set up primary health units or small medical centers in some of the larger rural towns or district headquarters, the vast majority of mortal illnesses in rural areas (and many in urban areas) went undiagnosed (Lamb 1975, 171-72).

Although China's 1979 medical personnel cost was under $7 per capita, compared to $2 in India and $1 in Indonesia, China's health-care coverage was more accessible to the population, especially to the rural poor.

*Table X.11.* Life Expectancy at Birth (years)

|  | 1935-1939 | 1950-1955 | 1965-1970 | 1975-1980 |
|---|---|---|---|---|
| China | n.a. | 48 | 60 | 64 |
| India | n.a. | 41 | 48 | 51 |
| Indonesia | n.a. | 39 | 46 | 48 |
| Sri Lanka | n.a. | 60 | 67 | 69 |
| South Asia | 30 | 41 | 46 | 49 |
| East Asia | 30 | 45 | 55 | 61 |
| Africa | 30 | 36 | 43 | 47 |
| Latin America | 40 | 52 | 60 | 64 |
| Low-income countries | n.a. | 35 | 44 | 50 |
| Middle-income countries | n.a. | 52 | 56 | 61 |
| All developing countries | 32 | 42 | 49 | 54 |
| Developed countries | 56 | 65 | 70 | 73 |

*Sources:* Morawetz, 11977, p. 48; World Bank, 1980c, 442-47; World Bank, vol. 1, 1983; 98.

# INFANT MORTALITY

China's 1980 infant mortality rate, 45 per 1000 live births, was less than India's 123, and middle-income countries' 80, and more than high-income countries' 20 (Lewis and Kallab 1983, 210-11). China's low rate reflects soap and water availability, health and hygiene understanding, preventive health care and education, and clinics for maternal and child health care.

# LITERACY AND EDUCATION

Literacy is a measure of well-being as well as a requirement for a country's economic development. China, like the Soviet Union and Cuba after their communist revolutions, emphasized spending on basic education to diffuse literacy and numeracy. Since 1949, China expanded primary and junior secondary schooling, and established an extensive network of adult and informal education.

Because of this effort, the proportion of primary school age children enrolled rose from about 25 percent in 1949 to 93 percent in 1979, while secondary ratios increased from 2 to 51. If you include the large number of overage children and adults in primary schools, the 1979 ratio of pupils to children in the primary age group was 158 percent. During the same period, the adult (15 years and older) literacy rate increased from 20 to 66 percent (see Table X.12).

***Table X.12.*** Basic Education in the 1970s (%)[a]

|  | Primary Schoool net enrollment ratio[b] | Secondary School gross enrollment ratio[c] | Adult literacy rate |
|---|---|---|---|
| China | 93 | 51 | 66 |
| India | 64 | 28 | 36 |
| Indonesia | 66 | 21 | 62 |
| Sri Lanka | 62 | 47 | 78 |
| Low-income countries | 56 | 25 | 38 |
| Middle-income countries | 75 | 28 | 71 |
| All developing countries | 62 | 26 | 51 |
| Developed countries | 94 | 68 | 99 |

*Notes:* [a] Data for China refer to 1979, for other countries to 1975 or 1977.
[b] Proportion of primary school age group enrolled.
[c] Secondary school enrollment as ratio of secondary school age group.
*Source:* World Bank, Vol. 1, 1983: 96.

But the Cultural Revolution severely disrupted education. Many primary and secondary schools remained closed for two or three years in the late 1960s, while some universities, post-secondary institutions, postgraduate schools, and vocational and technical secondary schools were closed through the early 1970s. The Cultural Revolution cost China two million middle-level technicians and one million university graduates, while reducing the quality of those educated. Yet overall, China's educational development after 1949 was generally impressive (World Bank, vol. 1, 1983, 136).

India's schools did not expand as rapidly as China's. The proportion of India's primary school age children enrolled increased from about 40 percent in 1949 to 64 percent in the 1970s, and its secondary proportion from about 10 percent in 1949 to 28 percent in the 1970s. During the same period, its adult literacy rate increased from 15 to 36 percent (India 1982, 46-47).

India was ahead of other low-income countries in the 1970s, while China was way ahead of both low- and middle-income countries and almost at the same level as DCs in primary school ratios. India's secondary ratios were slightly more than other low-income countries, while China was substantially ahead of both low- and middle-income countries, although much behind the DCs (Table X.12). But India surpassed China in higher educational enrollment as a percentage of the age group—with a 1.1 percent compared to 0.7 percent in China (World Bank, vol. 3, 1983, 135).

China's adult literacy rate, similar to other low-income countries and way behind middle-income countries in 1949, was well ahead of the low-income countries, and not far behind middle-income countries, in the late 1970s. India's literacy rate, slightly behind China's in 1949, was way behind China in the 1970s, and even below average for low-income countries.

China's high average primary and secondary school enrollment rates, emphasis on adult education, and low higher educational rates, reflect more equal distribution of education opportunities by age, gender, income, and rural-urban area. The proportion of rural primary school age children enrolled in the late 1970s was 92 percent, compared to less than 100 percent in urban areas. Additionally, 84 percent of primary school age girls in China were enrolled, compared to 50 percent in India (Ibid., vol. 1, 96).

The quality of China's basic education has been high by LDC standards. In the late 1970s, about 72 percent of those entering China's primary schools completed 4 years education, compared to 41 percent in India, 68 percent in Indonesia, and 38 percent in Brazil. Although the quality of school buildings varied widely, China has had an ample supply of textbooks. Mathematics achievements have probably been ahead of most LDCs. The World Bank estimates that, despite China's low pupil-teacher ratio, 1979 basic education cost only $20 per pupil yearly, less than half the average for other LDCs. Major reasons were low teacher salaries and low spending on physical facilities.

# THE REFORM PERIOD AFTER 1978

This section discusses how development patterns and performances changed after China's market reforms and India's modest liberalization after 1978. Despite World Bank figures suggesting India's nominal GNP per capita (1988) in excess of China's (Table II.2), a purchasing power adjustment meant China's real GNP per capita was more than India's, Indeed, China's faster growth than India's since the late 1970s meant average GNP (in I$) in China relative to India in 1988 even exceeded that ratio in the late 1970s in Table X.1.

According to Swamy, both China and India moved to higher growth rates in the 1980s. Swamy's (1989: 114) series (not comparable to Table X.2) points out the average real GDP growth per capita (adjusted for purchasing power parity) in China, 1978-86, a "spectacular" 7.5 percent annually compared to India's 2.9 percent annually.

Although India reduced the relative gap of its average foodgrain output vis-á-vis that of China from the early 1950s to the late 1970s, the gap widened from the late 1970s to the mid 1980s. Using a five-year moving average to reduce distortions from weather fluctuations indicates China's annual growth in foodgrain output per persons, 1979-86, 2.16 percent, compared to India's stagnation (0.00 percent) (Table X.13). China's gains through 1986 are understated, since oilseed, livestock, and cotton output gains were even more rapid than progress in foodgrain. Yet China's foodgrain gains require observation through the twenty-first century to determine whether the slower growth since 1986 reflects a delayed response to the reduced attention to soil conservation and infrastructure under the individualization of the reform (see chapter 2).

***Table X.13.*** Annual Growth Rates in Foodgrain Output
per Person (late 1970s-mid 1980s) (in percentages)

|  | 1977-1986 | 1979-1986 | 1977-1984 | 1979-1984 |
|---|---|---|---|---|
| *India* | 0.06 | 0.00 | 0.30 | 0.31 |
| *China* | 1.93 | 2.16 | 2.40 | 2.93 |

*Source:* Calculated from five-year moving averages in columns (4) and (8), Table 19.

Swamy's data (1989, 110-16) show in China both agricultural and industrial annual growths since 1978 accelerated relative to their 1952-1978 growths, while in India growth accelerated in industry but decelerated in agriculture since 1978. Since 1978, both China and India continued increasing production and employment shares in industry relative to agriculture, but China's structural changes (in output and labor) were faster than India's.

World Bank (1990c, 29) data indicate China's 1985 poverty rate (20 percent) still lower than India's (55 percent) rates, not comparable to Table X.7. However, growth acceleration reduced poverty rates in both countries from 1978 through the late 1980s (Singh 1990, 334).

Income distribution trend data for India after 1978 are lacking. Ironically, in China, despite Deng's repudiation of Mao's egalitarian slogans and increasing moral (not material) incentives, Whyte (1986, 103-23) thinks decollectivization and price decontrol under reform diminished income inequality. While Mao attacked privilege among encrusted bureaucrats and intellectuals, his opposition to financial incentives decreased income, especially among peasants. Mao's urban bias policies widened the urban-rural gap from the mid-1950s to the mid-1970s. While post-1978 agricultural reforms encouraged enterprising peasants "to get rich" and widen interrural income differentials, the rapid growth of agricultural income vis-á-vis industrial income narrowed the urban-rural income differences from 4.6:1 in 1978 to 3.1:1 in 1987 while widening regional differences, yet probably reducing overall income inequality. Additionally relaxing restrictions on urban emigration permitted rural families from depressed areas to reduce populations and benefit from nonfarm remittances (Lee 1990, 73-102). As implied in chapter 3, agricultural price reforms may reduce inequalitieꜱ fostered by the state's town-biased policies.

China ranked better than India on social indicators and (as chapter 2 indicated) the human development index, although both countries improved substantially from the late 1970s to 1985-90. Post-1978 social indicators include: life expectancy—China (70 years) and India (59) (1990), infant mortality—China (35 per 1,000) and India (89) (1985), and adult literacy—China (68 percent) and India (44 percent) (Table 2 and Sewell, Tucker, and contributors 1988, 248). But India may have slightly narrowed its gap with China on social indicators; moreover, medium-ranking India ranked significantly better than low-ranking China on the human freedom index (HFI) (chapter 2).

# CONCLUSION

China outperformed India in most indicators of welfare for the late 1970s to early 1980s and of growth from the early 1950s to the late 1970s. China's real GNP per capita was 20-50 percent higher and its real growth was about three times higher than India's. Rural, urban, and overall income inequalities in China were lower than in India. China's poverty and malnutrition rates were significantly lower than India's, while its per capita levels of foodgrain output, and calorie and protein consumption were significantly higher. China had a higher literacy rate, basic educational rate, and life expectancy, and a lower infant mortality than India.

But India's urban-rural income ratio was comparable to China's, and this ratio declined while China's was increasing. Moreover, India's growth in foodgrain output per capita was slightly better than China's. And, while India has been less successful than China in eliminating regular malnutrition, it has had fewer famines than China.

Despite India's narrowing urban-rural income differentials, China's average rural income levels were higher and growth faster than India's. And even though India's growth in average foodgrain output was faster, its 1979 figure was 28 percent below China's.

How have differences in government planning contributed to China's superior performance? China used Soviet-type planning, centralizing resource allocation, and communicating decisions by commands. The planners' controlling calculation was a national table of material balances, which, unlike the Indian approach, specified industry and consumer demand to correspond to the supply of controlled commodities. The Chinese government channeled capital resources to industry, using the Fel'dman approach of investment priorities in capital-goods, especially in the first plan, 1953-57. China repressed non-essential consumption more than India, contributing to gross investment rates of gross product more than 20 percent compared to India's less than 15 percent in the late 1950s, 23 percent to India's 17 percent in 1960, 25 percent to India's 18 percent in 1965, and 26-30 percent to India's 17-24 percent in the 1970s. Moreover, China, with a more educated labor force, and central and regional government allocating investment to high-priority industries and planning high capital utilization, had a higher capital productivity than India (Malenbaum 1982, 63-66; World Bank, vol. 1, 1983, 78-82; World Bank 1984, 226; World Bank 1985, 182; Howe 1978, 53-54).

Indian planning suffered from the paradox of inadequate attention to programs in the public sector, and too much control over the private sector.

Indian planners frequently chose public-sector investments on the basis of rough, sketchy, and incomplete accounts, with little or no cost-benefit calculations for alternative project locations. And the ministries, having selected the project, often failed to do the necessary, detailed technical preparation and work scheduling related to the project. The bureaucracy was slow and rigid, creating input bottlenecks, and stifling quick and imaginative action by industrial managers. (Even public firms had to apply for materials and capital import licenses a year or so in advance.) Poorly stated criteria for awarding input licenses and production quotas led to charges of bribery, influence peddling, and communal or political prejudice. Key public-sector products were often priced lower than scarcity prices, increasing waste and reducing savings. Furthermore, political involvement in public enterprises meant unskilled labor overstaffed many projects (Nafziger 1990, 422-24).

Planning problems led to profit rates for public enterprises lower than for indigenous, private operations, even when adjusted for commercial and social profit discrepancies. This inefficiency explains why the Indian public sector, despite its domination of large industry, contributed only 18 percent of India's total capital formation, 1950-1975 (Uppal 1977, 58).

Despite limited planning resources and control, the Indian government, on the other hand, tried to influence private investment and production through licensing and other controls. The effect of these controls, intended to regulate production according to plan targets, encourage small industry, prevent concentrated ownership, and promote balanced regional economic development, was to curtail private output and investment substantially, while increasing private industrial concentration (Nafziger 1978, 108-22).

China, with its vast size, skill shortages, and unreliable statistics, suffered from policy overextension. Its planners, like India's, tried to plan and control economic relations beyond their capabilities. Furthermore, Chinese planning stressed physical output targets instead of quality, costs, or efficiency, often resulting in waste. Moreover, Deng complained about bribery, overstaffing, and lack of technical innovation during the 1960s and 1970s (World Bank, vol. 1, 1983, 146-50). But these planning problems were not as acute as India's. In general, China used centralized planning to get the high investment and capacity utilization rates to transform its economy rapidly, while meeting the basic needs of food, shelter, health, and education for the overwhelming majority of its population.

India's policy approach has had some limited successes. Its democracy prevented disasters similar to China's Great Leap Forward, 1958-60, when ill-conceived drainage and water conservation projects, and immunity to effective political pressure, worsened the subsequent famine. India's free labor migration has helped to narrow urban-rural differentials. Its open scientific community, cooperating with foreign scholars, made a Green Revolution, absent in China, possible. Yet overall India has not been successful in combining democracy, government planning, and a sizeable private sector to achieve her goals of major poverty reduction and rapid growth.

## NOTES

1. Nicholas Lardy and Thomas Rawski argue in Kravis 1981, 60-78 that the ICP China estimates are flawed.

2. Problems with their poverty line include a single caloric norm, much caloric variation at a given level of expenditure, variations for even the same individual, different age and sex compositions of populations, and neglect of other nutrients.

## Chapter XI

# *Learning from the Japanese: Japan's Development Model and Afro-Asia*

This chapter focuses on the extreme poles of the world's economic development performance: the slowest growing countries since the mid- to late nineteenth-century, 45 countries of Africa and Asia, and the fastest growing economy, Japan. Japan, whose 1868 level of economic development was only slightly more than other Afro-Asian countries, has had the world's fastest growth in real GNP per capita since then (Table X.1), or second fastest to Sweden if computed through the early 1950s. Developing Asia is "looking East" to learn development lessons from the major non-western industrialized country, Japan. Capitalist Japan is a favorite of "modernization" theorists, disillusioned with slow U.S. growth and interpreting USSR perestroika (economic restructuring) and breakup as an admission of the failure of centralized socialism.

Though the Tokugawa shoguns isolated Japan from foreign influence from 1638 to the 1860s, they provided a more favorable legacy for modernization than many present LDCs. Mid-nineteenth century feudal Japan had a literacy rate about as high as England, a well-integrated transport system, a well-developed tax system, a highly commercialized agriculture whose productivity per hectare exceeded Southeast Asia today, and guild and clan-monopoly workshops producing silk textiles, *sake*, rapeseed oil, cotton cloth, candles, and other processed products for a national market, especially the large urban populations of Edo (Tokyo), Osaka, and Kyoto (Nakamura 1983; Lockwood 1954, 4).

## THE FOCUS OF THE STUDY

The Japanese development model (JDM) from 1868, following the restoration of the Meiji emperor, through the late 1930s, is different from the JDM after the 1945-47 U.S. occupational land, educational, labor union, antitrust, and political reforms. Doubtless South Korea, Taiwan, and Hong Kong, newly-industrialized countries that account for more than one-third of total LDC manufactured exports, have learned from post-World War II Japanese development. But I limit the JDM's application to low-income and lower-middle income countries from sub-Saharan Africa and East, South, and Southeast Asia with less than $900 GNP per capita (1989). These countries are in earlier stages of industrialization, account for 75 percent of the LDCs' 1989 population, and have an average real income perhaps comparable to 1868 Japan.[1] Thus, the appropriate period for testing the JDM's application to these countries is from 1868 through the late 1930s, rather than the period after 1945.[2]

This chapter concentrates on major ways in which the pre-1940 JDM differs from other non-western development approaches, and how this JDM applies to Afro-Asia today. The major focus—the third through second to last sections—is capital formation and technology policies that contributed to Japan's rapid industrial capitalist growth: technological borrowing, education, business assistance, financial institutions, transfer of agricultural savings to industry, and wages. These policies even benefited the traditional sector of the dual economy; most contemporary Afro-Asian countries are also dualistic. Growth in productivity per person was increased substantially by Japan's policy of participating in the growing international specialization in the decades following the 1868 Meiji Restoration. But a key to the ability of Japan to pursue these favorable policies was that, unlike most non-western countries of the time, she was not dominated by western imperialism (see next section).

## SELF-DIRECTED DEVELOPMENT

Despite unequal treaties with the west, from 1858 to 1899, Japan had substantial autonomy in economic affairs compared to other Afro-Asian countries, either colonized or subject to informal imperial economic controls. Although the west limited Japanese import tariffs to 5 percent, Japan partially circumvented these protective limits through tax rebates, subsidies, government purchase contracts, and state industrial enterprises. Furthermore, the 1868-1912 Meiji government was committed to economic and military development. It promulgated laws encouraging joint-stock organization and freedom of enterprise. The Act of 1872 established a national system of education stressing scientific and technological education, rather than skills for the junior civil service like schools in the European colonies. Unlike colonial India, Japan discouraged foreign investment between 1868 and 1899 (with minor exceptions like coal mining and shipbuilding in 1870-72), hiring thousands of foreigners to adapt and improve technology under ministry (or local business) direction. The Meiji government invested large amounts in infrastructure—telegraphs, postal service, water supply, coastal shipping, ports, harbors, bridges, lighthouses, river improvements, railways, electricity, gas, and technical research. In the last quarter of the nineteenth century, Japan organized a banking system (with the Bank of Japan, semi-official development banks, and locally-run private banks), expanded bank credit for government infrastructure and private investment, regulated banks, and stabilized the currency. In contrast, even after 1935, the Indian colonial government interfered little in private foreign-dominated banks, whose power was only gradually eroded even after independence in 1947. Nor did a colonial government and foreign trading houses thwart industrial exports and import substitution, as in early twentieth-century Nigeria. The post-1868 Japanese government, in contrast, helped domestic business find export opportunities, exhibit products and borrow abroad, establish trading companies, and set marketing standards.

The experience of Japan indicates the clear advantages of domestic political and economic control, which contrasts to the experience of Afro-Asia, subject to informal imperial domination and colonial rule from the late nineteenth century through the middle to late twentieth century, and neocolonialism since then. Since 1979-80, OECD countries, the major shareholders of the World Bank and the International Monetary Fund, have set in motion a new way to retain its economic suzerainty in Africa. Commercial banks, OECD governments, and the World Bank rely on the IMF agreeing to stabilization programs (usually contingent on the borrower's reducing demand) before arranging adjustment loans and debt writeoffs for African countries. Requiring this approval creates a monopoly position leaving Africa's debt-ridden stagnant economies little room to maneuver. In reality international policy enforcement is cartelized, with OECD governments, especially the United States, the EC, and Japan, largely determining policy through their control of the Bank and Fund and their regulation of commercial banks.

Furthermore, the JDM does have lessons indicated below for how technological borrowing can be more self-directed.

## BORROWING AND MODIFYING FOREIGN TECHNOLOGY

To maintain independence, the Meiji rulers tried to "enrich the nation and strengthen the army," goals requiring adopting western technology. But since Japan could not rely on foreign aid then, the central government and private firms had to pay the full cost of foreign technical expertise. This cost, together with introducing universal primary education and compulsory adult male military service, caused a serious financial strain. Between 1868 and 1892, the central government spent 1.5 percent of its total expenditures for foreign employees, and an additional 0.4 percent for expenses to send more than 4,000 students and government officials for training and education abroad. The

Ministry of Industry, which invested in heavy and chemical industries, mining, and infrastructure, employed almost 1,000 foreign advisors and teachers from 1870 to 1885. The Ministry of Home Affairs hired almost 250 foreigners from 1873 through 1895 to establish agricultural experiment stations to introduce western farming methods and products, and model factories to transfer technology to light industry. During the same period, the Ministry of Finance drew on about 125 foreign experts to help set up a modern monetary system and introduce corporate business organization. Other ministries and public enterprises hired almost 5,000, and the private sector about 12,500, foreigners during 1870-99 (Inukai 1981, 79-85).

Japan learned a lesson in the 1870s that many contemporary Afro-Asian countries learned only recently or not at all: that importing replicas of western institutions and capital-intensive technology may exacerbate unemployment and balance-of-payments problems if the local country lacks the capital and skills needed. Foreign techniques were modified—substituting hand-powered machines in silk reeling factories and wood for iron in Jacquard weaving machines—to save capital. Japan's Ten-year Plan of 1884, the Kogyo Iken, advocated projects conforming to local conditions and capital, urging improvement engineering, that is, upgrading indigenous (including artisan) production, rather than importing western replicas (Ibid., 85-95; Nakamura 1983, 70). For Meiji Japan, foreigners were teachers, transferring technology and other knowledge, not, as in much of twentieth-century Afro-Asia, more or less permanent advisers.

In agriculture, two German experts at the Komaba School of Agriculture in the early 1880s, advised that Japanese farms, with a small average size, should rely on biological and chemical, not western mechanical, innovations. Beginning in 1885, the Ministry of Agriculture and Commerce used foreign farm scientists to develop technology to suit small farms and local soil, and sent veteran farmers and new Japanese agricultural school graduates to diffuse the best seed varieties then used on Japanese farms. For most of Afro-Asia, with high worker-land ratios, the Japanese biochemical emphasis is more sensible than the capital-intensive approaches of the United States and Canada.

Many Japanese agricultural innovations, like better seed varieties (a green revolution in rice beginning around 1911), improved irrigation, improved seedling beds, and deeper plowing increased labor used per hectare. Filipino innovations of high-yielding rice varieties and chemical fertilizers, following the JDM, almost doubled labor requirements per acre between 1966 and 1975 (Inukai 1981, 86-87; Hayami 1975; Ishikawa 1981, 18, 32).

In industry, both in government training schools and private firms, foreign experts were often unsuitable, importing techniques they were acquainted with, regardless of their relevance. In the raw silk industry, imported machines and equipment were too costly and mechanically sophisticated, and their capacity inconsistent with the inadequate storage facilities for the perishable cocoon.

In flood control, Dutch experts introduced a system identical to that in Holland, where flood water rises from sea level, overlooking the fact that Japan had to handle flood water coming down the mountains! Repeated failures of Dutch technology to control floods finally convinced the Japanese government to change control measures completely. By the last two decades of the nineteenth century, the Japanese realized the necessity of questioning foreign industrial and flood control experts in light of differing local conditions (Inukai 1981, 85-88).

The Meiji government hired foreign experts directly and restricted foreign direct investment. While the immediate financial cost of limiting investment was substantial, Japan avoided the foreign restrictions placed on the transfer of technical knowledge, and continuing technological dependence on foreign sources and associated foreign technical concentration that many contemporary Afro-Asian economies face. Regarding foreign experts, the Japanese learned by the 1880s the necessity of insuring that technology introduced by foreigners be modified to fit local conditions and factor proportions.

During the Meiji period, labor was relatively more abundant in Japan than in the most advanced economies of Western Europe and the United States. Accordingly, Japan frequently substituted more appropriate labor-intensive technology for the "best-practice" techniques available from capital-abundant western countries.

Following are some major patterns of Japan's appropriate technology, 1868-1939:

1.   Emphasizing the production and export of more labor-intensive goods like raw silk, and silk and cotton textiles.

2.   Labor-intensive adaptation where the production process is simplified. Silk-reeling equipment appearing in 1875 consisted of a blacksmith-made steam boiler, ceramic cocoon boiling and silk-reeling kettles, and a frame built by a village carpenter. Additionally, many Japanese manufacturing firms purchased second-hand machinery in good condition from western countries. The cotton textile industry used two shifts, and substituted labor in ancillary and peripheral processes. Furthermore, much of the ancillary activities, like transport and machine repair, for large manufacturing units, were done cheaply by small firms using simple equipment and labor-intensive processes.

3.   Using manual labor instead of western-type ancillary equipment in coal and mineral mines.

4.   Adoption of technology used in an earlier stage in the west.

5.   Adaptation of foreign technology to industries catering to tastes unique to the indigenous market, including traditional soybean sauce, and indigenous dyeing houses. As these enterprises learned through experience, many made the transition to technology needed for export markets.

6. Substituting labor-intensive techniques to produce goods of lower quality and performance than imported goods, like bicycles (beginning in 1890), machine tools, three-wheel trucks, and small-sized cars (Datsuns in the 1930s). (Ishikawa 1981, 355-87; Nafziger 1990, 229-34, discuss possible LDC strategies for more appropriate technology.)

Meiji Japan imitated, borrowed from, and modified techniques and approaches from the advanced western economies. A question today is: Can Afro-Asian LDCs be as successful emulating, borrowing, and adapting innovations and procedures from the west and Japan?

If anything, contemporary Afro-Asian countries have to be even more cautious than Meiji Japan in importing foreign capital and technology. Since present-day Afro-Asia is even more technologically backward relative to the most technologically advanced economies than Japan was relative to the west in the late nineteenth century, it is probably more difficult to adapt technology to local conditions and indigenous production. For example, most internationally available yield-increasing farm inputs for early developing Japan were labor-using while most yield-increasing inputs for today's latecoming LDCs are labor-saving.

Today's Afro-Asian countries are also less likely to control directly experts transferring technology than the Japanese did. Finally, contemporary Afro-Asia is more likely to face unalterable capital-labor ratios in production processes and to pursue policies creating factor-price distortions (subsidized capital and foreign exchange prices, and above-market wage costs) than the Japanese a century ago (Nafziger 1990, 226-29).

A major contributor to these distortions is the multinational corporation (MNC), frequently established jointly with public enterprises in Afro-Asia, but virtually absent in Meiji Japan. Foreign capital usually enters Afro-Asia only if political leaders, civil servants, or private middlemen or -women are rewarded for facilitating the venture. These MNC-associated enterprises tend to use technology designed for the headquarter country, which has high wages and relatively abundant capital. Estimates based on capital resources available indicate that the appropriate capital stock per person in the United States is at least 20 times that of African countries (Stewart 1974, 86-88.)

Technical change requires a prolonged learning process embodied in indigenes improving capital and controlling experts transferring technology and improving capital. Under colonialism and neocolonialism, Afro-Asians have had little experience directing their own economic plans and technical adaptation and progress. Even today, Afro-Asia faces externally-imposed conditions by the World Bank, IMF, and DC governments on technology use and other policies. Each successive piece of capital equipment is more productive since learning advances are embodied in new capital goods (Arrow, 1962, 154-94; Nafziger, 1990, 259-60).

Afro-Asian finance and planning officers want to rely more on government ministries and local research institutions and chambers of commerce and industry for technological policy analysis. National authorities, rather than foreign advisers from bilateral donors and international agencies, need to prepare adjustment and technological programs. Afro-Asians must direct, as the Meiji Japanese did, their planning and development for them to capture technological learning gains.

## PRODUCT CYCLE

Comparative advantage may be based on a technological advantage, as in nineteenth-century Britain, the United States, and Germany and as in today's Japan, the United States, and Germany, perhaps a Schumpeterian innovation like a new product or production process that gives the country a temporary monopoly in the world market until other countries are able to imitate (Schumpeter 1961; Schumpeter 1939). The product cycle model indicates that while a product requires highly skilled labor in the beginning, later as markets grow and techniques become common knowledge, a good becomes standardized, so that less-sophisticated countries can mass produce the item with less skilled labor. Advanced economies, such as Britain and the United States, 1868-1939, had a comparative advantage in non-standardized goods, while less-advanced economies, like Meiji Japan, had a comparative advantage in standardized goods (Vernon 1966, 190-207).

Product cycle is illustrated by cotton textiles. England specialized in cotton textiles from the mid-eighteenth to late-nineteenth centuries. In the 1880s and 1890s, Japan substituted indigenous production of cotton textiles, manufactured with British machines, for imports from Britain. By 1921-39, Japan's cotton goods invaded English and other western markets. Japan's comparative advantage in textiles was suggested by the fact that 41.0 percent of all factory labor in Japan was engaged in textiles compared with only 20.5 percent in Britain and 13.4 percent in the United States in 1934. In the 1960s, Japan imported cotton textiles from South Korea, Taiwan, Hong Kong, Singapore, and China, many of which used Japanese investment and technology to compete in Japan or third countries (the boomerang effect discussed in chapter XII).

However, contemporary Afro-Asia cannot compete as readily as nineteenth-century Japan did at the bottom range of the product cycle, imitation and low-level innovation. Contemporary LDCs, unlike Meiji Japan, are competing in an integrated global economy against multinational corporations (MNCs). The markets MNCs operate in today are often international oligopolies with competition among few sellers whose pricing decisions are interdependent. Large corporations invest overseas because of international imperfections in the market for goods, resources, or technology. The MNCs benefit from monopoly advantages, such as patents, technical knowledge, superior managerial and marketing skills, better access to capital markets, economies of large-scale production, and cost savings from vertical integration (Hymer 1970, 441-53). MNCs can compete in a large range of industries with today's indigenous Afro-Asian firm in the use of imitation or innovative technology, and unskilled or highly skilled labor.

# EDUCATION

The 1985 literacy rate for lower and lower-middle income countries was 58 percent, a level reached in Japan about the first decade of the twentieth century. Japan's primary enrollment rate, 28.1 percent in 1873, reached virtually 100 percent by 1911. Furthermore, the state made serious efforts to expand primary and vocational education, and stress western scientific and technical education in the last three decades of the nineteenth century, when Asian countries like Siam were only educating elites for government service (Sewell, Tucker, and contributors 1988, 245-57; Yasuba and Dhiravegin 1985, 26-27). Starting with a common language, the Meiji government developed a relatively uniform primary education that fostered national unity as well as speeding up acquiring western ideas and technologies.

Education in the colonies in Afro-Asia provided the intellectual skills necessary for clerks, administrative assistants, noncommissioned officers, and operatives for the colonial government, army, or European firms but not for engineers, scientists, farm and industrial managers, entrepreneurs, and government executives and technicians. With political independence in Afro-Asia in the quarter century after World War II, the primary enrollment rate (as a percentage of children aged 6-11) and secondary enrollment rate (denominator 12-17 years old) increased (World Bank, 1981: 181, World Bank, 1989a, 274-75; World Bank, 1992, 274-75.) A UNICEF study indicates that falling government spending from an external debt crisis and Bank/Fund adjustment programs of last resort in the 1980s was accompanied by declining real educational spending (Commander, 1989a, 231-34). Nigeria, after a 1986 structural adjustment loan from the World Bank in 1986, cut spending, especially on education substantially; during the subsequent protest in the late 1980s, the military government closed universities, detained and dismissed university critics, and killed tens and arrested hundreds of students and academics while squashing strikes, demonstrations, and political opposition (Africa Watch, 1991, 41-52).

Low literacy and primary enrollment rates have impeded labor enskillment and economic growth in Africa. Moreover, the setbacks to literacy and education during the adjustment programs of the 1980s contributed to the negative economic growth of that decade.

The emphasis on "Japanese spirit and western technology" meant education from 1868 through 1945 stressed subserviency to superiors and the state, superiority to other Asian countries, and acquiring western technological expertise, but not human dignity, or learning the method for developing science in Japan (Munakata 1965, 540-59). However, starting with a common language, the Meiji government developed a relatively uniform primary education that fostered national unity as well as speeding up acquiring Western ideas and technologies. While the Meiji Japanese experience reinforces studies indicating a high rate of return to Afro-Asian investment in primary, science, and vocational education, it provides no model for countries using the educational system to promote democracy, human rights, and female equality.

## AN INDIGENOUS CAPITALIST CLASS

Political revolutions in Western Europe (England, France, and the Netherlands) in the seventeenth and eighteenth centuries reduced the power of the church and landed aristocracy, and eventually the industrial and commercial capitalist classes took over much of this power. Since most Afro-Asian countries, like nineteenth-century Japan, do not have the strong middle- and capitalist-class leadership for capital accumulation and technical progress, can they look to Japan's "guided capitalism" as an alternative model to centrally-managed state capitalism?

Following the fall of the Tokugawa shogun, 1860 to 1868, the Meiji government was controlled primarily by lower-ranking samurai, not merchants and industrial capitalists. From 1870 to 1885, this government owned and operated factories and mines, many expropriated from the shogunate and feudal lords (Shishido 1983, 259). Throughout the late nineteenth century, the Meiji regime accounted for about half the investment outside agriculture, including not only infrastructure, but also shipbuilding, iron and steel; other heavy industries, and arms factories to strengthen the military, as well as mines and construction, engineering, cement, soap, and chemical industries (though not textiles, the leading export sector). After private-sector skills improved, government profits proved meager, and the state needed funds for armament, it sold most industrial properties, often at bargain prices, to private businessmen, many of whom were samurai. Additionally, in 1876, the state strained its public credit to commute the pensions of 400,000 feudal lords and samurai to cash and bonds, and to pay off debts owed to relatively privileged merchants and moneylenders (like the House of Mitsui) who had financed the 1867-1868 coup restoring the emperor. The more enterprising recipients used these funds to invest in new industrial enterprise. Moreover, the state aided private industry through a laissez-faire labor policy (low wages and child labor), low taxes on business enterprise and high incomes, a favorable legal climate, destruction of economic barriers between fiefs, lucrative purchase contracts, tax rebates, loans, and subsidies. (For example, the government imported spindle spinning machines, 1878-79, to sell on lenient credit terms to private enterprise in the textile industry, Japan's leading export sector.)[3] From these state-assisted entrepreneurs came the financial cliques or combines (zaibatsu) that dominated industry and banking through World War II. The zaibatsu's concentration of wealth helped perpetuate high income inequalities at least 75 years after the Meiji restoration. To be sure, the zaibatsu reaped large-scale economies, managed ably, were generally frugal, invested productively, provided assistance to small industry (see below), and were partners in building national power (Lockwood 1954).

Both late nineteenth-century Japan and contemporary Afro-Asia have favored existing elites in their privatization schemes. The World Bank, IMF, and bilateral donors insisted on abrupt privatization, which created a highly concentrated business elite from newly privatized firms falling into a few hands, similar to early Japan. However, in other ways, Meiji Japan's stress on private entrepreneurs differed substantially from that of contemporary privatization. Meiji Japan provided more assistance to small industrialists. Moreover, Japan's privatization was initiated by the state whereas privatization in many parts of Afro-Asia was thrust on it by adjustment programs initiated by the IMF, World Bank, and OECD creditors. Thus emerging private enterprise in Japan was virtually all indigenous, while the World Bank insisted that Africa open investment to foreign private enterprise. For example, Nigeria, under two World Bank structural adjustment programs (SALs), 1986-88 and 1989-91, not only sold equity in public enterprises to private investors but allowed foreign investors in most manufacturing, large trade, and petroleum sectors. Foreign investors are major contributors to high industrial concentration and (as pointed out above) factor-price distortions.

Perhaps as many as one-fourth to one-fifth the farmers in the late Tokugawa and early Meiji periods managed second businesses such as small bars, rapeseed oil selling, lumber vending, eating house management, bean curd making, confection making, tobacco selling, sundry shopkeeping, carpentry, and plastering. Landlords were fertilizer merchants, pawnbrokers, moneylenders, doctors, dry goods merchants, and brewers of sake, soy sauce, and bean paste. The landed class especially increased investment during the inflation of 1876-81, when rapidly increasing rice prices provided windfall gains when land taxes were fixed and rents received in kind. Furthermore, many merchants became landlords (Nakamura 1983, 51).

Yet empirical studies on entrepreneurship indicate landowners and wealthy farmers in Afro-Asia today rarely invest in industry. Afro-Asian landlords tend to value highly consumption and real estate expenditure, and lack experience in managing and coordinating a production process with specialized work tasks and machinery and in overseeing secondary labor relations.

Many economists, noting the disproportionate samurai representation among early Meiji industrialists and bankers, stress the spirit of the community-centered samurai entrepreneur, sacrificing for national economic progress (Hirschmeier 1964); Ranis 1955, 80-98). But Yamamura's evidence (1968, 148-58) indicates samurai status in the early Meiji period was blurred, as many from peasant and merchant families purchased this status during the late Tokugawa period. The major force to establish banks and factories came from merchants and landlords motivated by profit, not longstanding samurai motivated by nationalism.

Meiji Japan's policies illustrate an alternative to the Soviet approach for accumulating capital where there is no strong bourgeois class. And selling government-owned industrial properties to private firms reduces public financial loss since their bankruptcies eliminate inefficient enterprises. Yet this selling may, as in Japan, contribute to high industrial concentration, high income inequalities, and slow growth of a politically independent middle class. Moreover, today populist pressures prevent most Afro-Asian political elites from pursuing the low-wage policies, unrestricted labor rules, low welfare spending, and large subsidies that nineteenth-century Japan used to foster indigenous capitalist development. Furthermore, few Afro-Asian societies have the Japanese nexus of community reciprocal obligation that reduces the destructive power of capitalist rivalries.

Yet Meiji Japan's bourgeoisie, though weaker than that in Western Europe and the United States, were more experienced in large commercial ventures, and were not as far behind the most technologically advanced economies as Afro-Asia today. The Japanese capitalist class was capable of responding to government policies to encourage private industrial ventures. Furthermore, Meiji's government bureaucracy had the vision and skills to plan programs to abet private entrepreneurs. The irony is that while the weakness of the contemporary Afro-Asian bourgeoisie indicates the need for stronger government intervention and more skilled government planning to spur entrepreneurial activity, technical progress, and capital accumulation in industry, few Afro-Asian government bureaucracies have the capabilities to facilitate these in the private sector, or manage these in the public sector.

## FINANCIAL INSTITUTIONS

Goldsmith (1983, 4-5) thinks a knowledgeable 1870 economist would have indicated India as more likely to be economically developed by 1970 than Japan. India, a British colony, possessed a unified currency, rudiments of a western-type banking system, access to the British capital market, and British financial technology, while Japan, just emerging from feudalism, had a negligible modern sector, a chaotic currency, and no modern financial institutions.

But Britain constructed India's modern financial system, while the Meiji government created Japan's system through conscious selective adaptation of features of the American, British, French, and German systems. British civil servants, entrepreneurs, and investors operated, owned, and organized India's modern financial institutions, while foreign ownership or management of Japan's institutions was practically nonexistent. Furthermore, the British colonial government in India intervened little in regulating bank and financial institutions, had little contact with the small number of indigenous bankers, and in the half century before World War II created few new financial institutions. In contrast, the Meiji government organized most of the modern financial institutions during the first two to three decades after the 1868 restoration, and cooperated with and supported local private bankers and financiers.

In contrast to India, Meiji Japan's development of currency and credit institutions through the mid-1890s was "supply-leading," created in advance of demands for industrial loans and financial services, and private saver deposits. In 1872, the government set up national banks, and in 1876 permitted private commercial banks. Other major financial reforms were the conversion of the rights of feudal lords to negotiable government bonds, and the land tax, which provided the revenue for the government's Reserve Fund (RF), 1873-81, and the Industrial Promotion Fund (IPF) beginning 1878, for loans to industry. Other special banks established included the Yokohama Specie Bank (1880) for foreign exchange for importers, the Hypothec Banks (1896) at the prefectural level to make long-term loans to industry and agriculture, and the Industrial Bank (1900) to make medium- to long-term loans to industry (Patrick 1967, 239-89).

The national and private banks' high ratio of currency issues to specie, as well as the RF and IPF liberal lending policies, contributed to rapid inflation, 1876-81, reducing peasant and former military real incomes, and increasing capitalist speculative profits, thus forming substantial initial capital accumulation for industrialists.

Finance Minister Matsukata Masoyoshi created a central Bank of Japan in 1882 (54 years before the Reserve Bank of India) to limit paper currency, levied new consumption taxes, restrained RF lending except to export industries accumulating specie, and balanced the government budget, bringing about more stable expectations among capitalist investors (Takeda 1965, 432-36).

All in all, the new financial institutions standardized the currency, integrated the national market, and channeled savings into industry. By 1897, Japan's credit standing had improved so she could borrow in foreign capital markets. With few exceptions, the money supply grew rapidly from 1880 to 1940, enabling rapid though fluctuating growth rates, but virtually avoiding recessions with negative growth (Nakamura 1983).

The symbiotic relationship between government and private finance strengthened zaibatsu bank concentration, contributing to the 1920s' sharp decline in small banks. While banks collected private savings for affiliated zaibatsu enterprises and helped determine which firms survived, these large financial concentrations, under Japanese state guidance, still supported traditional small-scale industry and trade. Bank concentration was not reduced until the post-World War II occupational antitrust reforms.

The rapid growth of Japan's banking and credit institutions in advance of industrial and saver demands indicates the advantage of more than a century of self-directed financial development. However, the Japanese government, in its drive for national economic and military power, tolerated growing financial concentration, a pathology of growth that contemporary Afro-Asia may want to avoid.

## TRANSFER OF AGRICULTURAL SURPLUS

Economic historians differ on the relationships between agriculture and industry in the development process, and the timing of initial sustained growth in both sectors. As in England, where an agricultural revolution preceded the industrial revolution, in Japan late Tokugawa agricultural growth (despite the substantial output share cultivators paid to the shogun) preceded the beginning of the early industrialization spurt of the 1880s. Agricultural growth accelerated through the Meiji period before slowing down beginning in the 1910s. During Meiji, agriculture contributed to rapid industrialization. The next two sections look at how capital, labor, and food from agriculture helped industry.

A major concern for newly industrializing countries is the source of early investment capital for industry. Many economists advocate relying heavily on agricultural surplus for industrial capital, since agriculture is usually an Afro- Asian country's largest sector; for example, before 1915 it contributed more to Japan's NDP than any other sector. Agricultural surplus refers to an excess of savings over investment in agriculture, an amount transferred (through taxes and private savings) to nonagriculture (or industry). This transfer includes both private savings and taxes.

Meiji centralized government replaced the feudal landed gentry (daimyo) who politically controlled large fiefs with smaller, capitalist village landlords who had purchased their land. These gentry remained wealthy, but lost their land and political power. The village landlords, who were often themselves farmers during the early Meiji period, frequently improved productive methods (Dore 1965, 487-93).

The Meiji bureaucrats controlling policy had no personal interest in protecting agricultural incomes at the cost of slowing industrial growth. They imposed a land tax in 1873 to squeeze investment capital from agriculture, partly through a moderate inflationary policy redistributing resources to finance state and private industrial ventures. In that year, the land tax accounted for 94 percent of central government revenue, appropriating one-third of the total crop, nearly as much as the share appropriated by the feudal lord under the pre-1868 Tokugawa shogun (Lockwood 1954). The land tax continued to provide more than 80 percent of total government revenue through 1882, and contributed to continuing, though reduced, net resource outflows from agriculture to government through 1922 (Ohkawa, Shimizu, and Takamatsu 1982, 10). Government investment in agriculture was only a small fraction of agricultural tax revenue used for nonagricultural investment (Mody, Mundle, and Raj 1985, 272-73).

From 1888 to 1937, the significant surplus flows of private savings from agriculture to industry are concentrated during the period 1903-22, when cultivator-landlords were being replaced by "parasitic" landlords using tenant rents to accumulate capital for industries like brewing, pawnbroking, retail shops, and village moneylending (Ohkawa, Shimizu, and Takamatsu 1982, 11-12). But the amount of net capital private flows from agriculture to industry is not certain, since price indices to estimate the effect of changing terms of trade on net resource flows from agriculture, and figures on private inflows to agriculture are not reliable (Ishikawa 1982, 264).

Part of this intersectoral resource transfer was from colonies Korea and Taiwan, 1911-40. During this period, Taiwan's net resource outflow from agriculture equalled its balance of trade surplus (with exports predominantly agricultural) with metropolitan Japan (Lee 1971). Japanese investors in the colonies acquired prime agricultural land for producing food exports to Japan. These cheap rice imports from Taiwan and Korea kept Japanese food prices low, keeping industrial wages low and increasing industrial profits (see below).

Meiji Japan, like the Soviet Union subsequently in the 1930s, accumulated industrial capital by squeezing it from agriculture. With the possible exception of the Soviet Union, where the collectivization of 1929-33 involved forcible collection of grain, confiscation of farm property, destruction of tools and livestock, class warfare between peasants and prosperous kulaks, administrative disorder, disruption of sowing and harvest, and an accompanying famine that led to the deaths of about five million people, Japan has probably relied more on a strategy of using agricultural savings for initial industrial capital formation than any other presently industrialized country.

The land tax had little or no effect on farm output. The owner, unable to shift the tax forward to farm-good middlemen or consumers, could only shift the tax incidence to a tenant, who rarely had alternative employment. The high and regressive land taxes, required in cash, the growing burden of other taxes (1890-1910), and high rents reduced farm disposable income and consumption, especially among tenants and peasants, the last of whom faced heavy debts, frequent bankruptcies, and abject poverty.

Dore (1959, 115-25) argues that the agrarian poverty and distress from taxes and tenancy contributed to the rise of Japanese totalitarian and military expansion abroad in the following ways: (1) tenant distress and farm population pressures provided a powerful motive for securing emigration opportunities through expansion, (2) rural poverty and the interrelated low industrial wages (see below) limited domestic market size, spurring Japan to use force to acquire external markets for its industry, (3) ruling elites used overseas expansion to divert attention from agrarian distress and foster national unity, and (4) landlord paternalism and agrarian pressures for social conformity facilitated susceptibility to authoritarianism.

Other countries may find it difficult politically to extract agricultural surplus through land taxes. In England, unlike Japan, the landed aristocracy maintained political influence until a relatively advanced stage of industrial development. Likewise, landlords in many contemporary Latin American countries are too powerful for the state to capture an agricultural surplus. Few low-income Afro-Asian countries have enough agrarian surplus and political tolerance to allow the squeezing of agriculture in excess of the substantial agriculture-industry transfers already being made.

Japan's agricultural growth relied heavily on research by local scientists (assisted by foreign experts hired by the Ministry of Agriculture), biochemical (not Western mechanical) innovations, and extension by veteran farmers and new Japanese agricultural school graduates to diffuse the best seed varieties then used on Japanese farms to a highly literate farm population. Despite the land tax, agricultural technological progress was fast, contributing to the rapid annual percentage growths of 1.8 in agricultural gross value added and 2.0 in farm productivity per worker, 1880-1920, that facilitated substantial surplus transfer to industry.[5] The agricultural surplus in many African countries is too small and growing too slowly and the material levels of living of peasants too low for industry to exploit without severe human costs.

Additionally, Japan's agricultural technological progress was fast, contributing to the rapid annual percentages growths of 1.8 in agricultural gross value-added and 2.0 in farm productivity per worker, 1880-1920, that facilitated substantial surplus transfer to industry (calculated from a five-year moving average from Ohkawa and Shinohara 1979, 86; Hayami 1975, 228). The agricultural surplus in many low-income Afro-Asian countries is too small and growing too slowly for industry to exploit without severe political costs.

Afro-Asia needs a thriving agriculture to produce adequate food and raw materials for other sectors. Should we not discourage the following policies African and Asian LDCs frequently use today to transfer a large share of the agricultural surplus to industry: (1) food price ceilings and industrial price floors to raise industrial prices relative to the prices of farm goods, (2) concentration of government investment in industry, (3) tax incentives and subsidies to pioneering firms in industry, but not in agriculture, (4) setting below-market prices for foreign currency, reducing domestic currency receipts from agricultural exports, but lowering the price of capital goods and other foreign inputs to large industrial establishments, (5) tariff and quota protection for industry, raising its prices to farmers, and (6) spending more for education, training, housing, plumbing, nutrition, medical care, and transport in urban areas than in rural areas. These policies of urban bias have contributed to farm production disincentives and high rates of rural poverty and undernourishment in low-income countries (Nafziger 1990, 131-62).

These disincentives in much of contemporary Afro-Asia are perhaps as great as those that threatened widespread rural rebellion in Meiji Japan. Rural poverty and undernourishment rates are probably no less than those in Meiji Japan. Additionally, rural populist pressures in many contemporary LDCs are greater and more politically destabilizing than peasant pressures in the 1870s' Meiji Japan.

In Pakistan a below-market foreign exchange price coupled with industrial price guarantees resulted in the transfer of about 70 percent of savings in agriculture and over 24 percent of its gross product to the nonagricultural sector in 1964 and 1965—a transfer largely from poor to rich, and from East to West Pakistan. This transfer exacerbated the East Bengali peasant discontent that contributed to Bangladesh secession (chapter 9). Few low-income Afro-Asian countries have the rural political stability sufficient to squeeze agriculture in excess of surplus transfers already being made.

In fact, some like democratic India, faced with fast population growth, low agricultural incomes and savings, and potential farmer discontent, have no income tax on agriculture, and a net resource inflow to agriculture since independence in 1947 (Mody, Mundle, and Raj 1985, 283-291).

While this analysis, similar to that of the IMF, indicates that price controls and exchange-rate misalignments have contributed to stagnation and external crisis in sub-Saharan Africa and least developed countries such as Bangladesh, I reject the IMF policy prescription of immediately freeing markets and contracting spending to resolve the disequilibrium. After 1981, the IMF emphasized shock treatment for demand restraint in low-income countries, rarely provided financing for external adjustments, and cut programs from three years to one year, applying Reaganomics internationlly. One year is not enough for adjustment. Demand restrictions, inflation deceleration, and currency depreciation do not switch expenditures to exports and import substitutes or expand primary production quickly enough to have the desired effect on prices and trade balance. Studies indicate, even in DCs (for example, the United States, 1985-88), the current-account improvement from devaluation usually takes about two to five years, usually beginning with a worsening trade balance in the first year. The time for adjustment is due to the lags between changes in relative international prices (from exchange-rate changes) and responses in quantities traded. Lags include time for recognition, decision (assessing the change), delivery, replacement (waiting to use up inventories and wear out machines), and production (Grubel, 1981, 349-88). Even after 1988, despite increased emphasis of SAPs on productive capacity and long-term sectoral change, in practice African and least developed countries still face unrealistically short adjustment times, resulting in severe economic disruption and excessive hardship for the poor.

The IMF has stressed devaluation and foreign-exchange decontrols to improve the balance of trade, increase domestic prices and terms of trade for agriculture, and reduce shortages of foreign inputs, along with market interest rates to improve capital allocation. Green (1989, 36) supports African states' complaints that World Bank or IMF adjustment programs fail to consider African market imperfections. However, government frequently creates market imperfections through policies of financial repression, encouraging interest-rate ceilings, foreign exchange controls, high reserve requirements, and restrictions on private capital markets to increase the flow of domestic resources to the public sector without higher taxes, inflation, or interest rates. Yet even though it helped to create these market imperfections, government cannot immediately decontrol all prices and liberalize foreign exchange and capital markets. Although devaluation raises import prices, the demand for foreign exchange may not be restrained, as relaxing foreign-exchange licenses and import restrictions spurs the use of foreign inputs and probably increases capital flight in the short run. Indeed, substantial devaluation may generate hyperinflation, as the domestic currency experiences a free fall which expectations make irreversible (Zambia in 1985-87 and Sierra Leone in 1986-87).

The effect of devaluation (say, from C90 = \$1 to C228 = \$1) on the trade balance depends on demand and supply elasticities, considered by critics to be low in African and other LDC agriculture, especially over a one- to two-year period. The elasticity of demand for African primary products like tea, coffee, sugar, and cocoa is so low that increasing the output of agricultural exports to undertake Bank/Fund-sponsored adjustment might result in reduced revenues from increased output. On the supply side, African farmers have little short-run (one year or less) but substantial long-run elasticity (0.3-0.9) for cash crops, as farmers respond to allocate labor and land variously to commercial output, subsistence commodities, black-market activity, nonfarm work, or leisure. Supply response would be at least a year or two for cotton and tobacco and between five and six years for tree crops such as coffee, tea, cashews, and sisal in Tanzania. Cost-induced inflationary pressures due to devaluation (from economic interests fighting to maintain income and consumption shares) should reduce output expansion. Inadequate infrastructure, such as poor transport for Ghanaian cocoa, limits supply increases, slowing export response to higher cedi prices for a given dollar price of cocoa. Indeed, African countries remove balance-of-payments deficits quickly not from exchange-rate changes (and expenditure switching) but from reduced import demand due to a fall in real income (or a depressed economy). Still, most African countries no longer oppose devaluation, but want more control on its size, timing, structure (such as single versus multiple exchange rates), and accompanying policy measures (Ibid.; Godfrey 1985, 32; Chhibber 1989, 56; Loxley 1989, 13-36; Campbell and Stein 1992, 20-22).

# LOW INDUSTRIAL WAGES

From 1868 to 1915, agricultural unskilled *real* wages remained at a subsistence level. Unlike the Lewis-Fei-Ranis models (LFR), the marginal productivity of labor (MPL) was positive, though less than the wage (Minami 1973, 200), since the village supplied subsistence to those with a $MP_L$ below it. As in LFR, employers in the formal (or organized) industrial sector paid a premium (say 30 percent more than the agricultural wage) to compensate for migration costs, psychological costs of city life, and so forth. This premium remained low partly because much of industry's wage labor—female, second and third sons, or off-farm part-time—merely supplemented household income (Shinohara 1970, 342-44). But subsistence levels rose over time as the minimum maintenance level expected by society increased. The relatively stable agricultural (and thus industrial) real wages can be attributed partly to technical progress and increased productivity in agriculture (and cheap food from colonies after 1911) which enabled the industrial sector to buy food without declining terms of trade. These low real industrial wages increased industrial profits, business savings, and labor-intensive manufactured export competitiveness.

Over a normal range, where product and labor demand increase gradually, labor supply elasticities were high (though not infinite as in LFR), benefiting from vast reserves in the rural and informal industrial sectors (Minami 1973). But the 1915-1919 increase in demand for industrial products and labor resulting from World War I was too substantial to be satisfied by labor from the elastic portion of the supply curve. Wage equilibrium could only be attained at the inelastic portion of the labor supply curve, thus increasing industrial wages, and subsequently through greater food demand by new workers, increased agricultural product (especially rice) and labor prices. In the 1920s and 1930s, industrial wages, sticky downward with emerging unions, remained high, while agricultural (and informal industrial sector) wages declined from their war peak. Following war and recovery years, 1935-55, the labor surplus ended and industrial formal sector labor supply turned inelastic permanently, as innovation-led demand for industrial products and labor increased rapidly, while labor supply growth from agriculture and population growth was drying up (Hayami 1975).

Developing Japan's labor supply grew slower than contemporary Afro-Asia. Late nineteenth-century Japan's birth rate, 22 per 1,000, kept down by farmland shortages, extended-family dissolution, and high literacy levels, was lower than Afro-Asia's 32 per 1,000 (1990), while Japanese death rates, 18 per 1,000, were higher than Afro-Asia's rates of 11 per 1,000, lowered by access to the nutritional, medical, health, and production techniques of the past century. Japan's annual labor growth, which never exceeded 1 percent during the nineteenth century, rose to 1.3 percent per annum, in 1930-1931, slowing to less than 1 percent by 1955.[34] In contrast, Afro-Asian yearly labor force growth was 1.7 percent in the 1960s, 2.0 percent in the 1970s, and 2.3 percent in the early 1980s (each figure slightly less than population growth). Yet Meiji Japan's density of farm population per cultivated hectare of land (higher than India, Taiwan, and most other Asian LDCs today) put pressure on the nonagricultural sector. But Japan's annual industrial employment growth rate, 1878-1914, was 3.9 percent of the total labor force, compared to the Afro-Asian figure in the early 1980s of about 0.4 to 0.7 percent. While Afro-Asian industry in the early 1980s absorbed only 17 to 30 percent of the increased labor force, Japanese industry at the turn of the twentieth century absorbed 4.5-5.0 times the labor increase. Crucial in Japan's successful absorption was slower population growth, together with highly labor-intensive industrialization, spurred by government's low-wage and appropriate technology policies, but *not* a faster annual industrial growth rate than Afro-Asia from 1960 to 1985 (Tachi and Okazaki 1965, 497-515; Nafziger 1990, 215-17).

While Africa and South Asia face labor surpluses today from rapid population growth and slow industrial employment demand, these surpluses are more likely to be reflected in urban unemployment instead of low wages, due to political pressures for minimum wages, labor union strength, factor-price distortions (low capital and foreign-exchange costs), unsuitable capital-intensive technologies, unrealistic job aspirations by school graduates, bias toward urban amenities, and wage pressures from food price rises.

Japan had faster food output growth and more stable food prices than contemporary Afro-Asia, because of rapid technical progress in agriculture during the Meiji period, and cheap food from colonies during the early twentieth century. Afro-Asian food supply problems often result from urban bias in investment and amenities, agricultural price disincentives, and bureaucratic mismanagement in supplying farm inputs. But Afro-Asian food demand has risen relatively fast, because of high income elasticities of demand for food resulting from rapid population growth.

In the midst of a large urban wage premium, the flood of urban immigrants is restrained only by high open urban unemployment rates, which keep down expected urban wages (wages times the probability of employment as in Harris-Todaro 1970, 126-42), but not actual urban wages. The LFR model's unlimited long-run supply of labor to the industrial sector, roughly valid in Japan from 1868 to 1915, is replaced by relatively high wages in Afro-Asia today, reducing industrial profits and savings.

# INDUSTRIAL DUALISM

Meiji Japan had a dual economy consisting of: (1) a traditional, peasant, agricultural sector, producing primarily for family or village subsistence, with little reproducible capital, using old or intermediate technology, and a marginal productivity of labor lower than the wage (together with semi-subsistence agriculture, petty trade, and cottage industry), and (2) capital-intensive modern manufacturing and processing operations, mineral extraction, and commercial agriculture, producing for the market, using reproducible capital and new technology, experiencing high and growing labor productivity, and hiring labor commercially. This dualism was exacerbated by Japan's continuing rapid growth, especially in technology.

As implied above, the modern-sector wage was more than the traditional-sector wage for identical labor skills from 1868 to 1915. After World War I, these wage differentials widened, as demand increased especially for skilled labor, which large firms tried to keep through rationalization, lifetime employment policies, seniority preference, and fringe benefits. The large firms' price-controlling power in product markets and credit rationing in the capital market made higher wages possible. Additionally, large firms economized on unskilled labor by hiring temporary workers, contributing to greater labor market dualism (Nakamura 1983). By 1955, in the midst of the labor shortage of the postwar economic boom, the dual market for similar labor disappeared (although there were still wage differentials for different levels of skills and experience).

In this section I go beyond industrial-agricultural dualism to discuss dualism within the industrial sector, including regional dualism. Due to geographical labor immobility, a labor market usually consisted of a village, or no more than a few districts. Moreover, poor transport provided natural protection for regions with high wage costs.

Japan has not stressed large leaps to the most advanced state of industrial technology available, but step by step improvements in technology and capital as ministries, regions, industries, firms, and work units learn by doing. In the early Meiji period, this meant technical and management assistance and credit facilities to improve and increase the scale of small workshops, handicraft producers, and cottage industry left from before 1868, causing less social disruption, as small industry's environment was not alien. The 1884 plan emphasized improving traditional technology through applied science and favored postponing massive foreign large-scale factory transplantation until traditional enterprises could utilize new techniques (Inukai 1979, 5). Factory enterprises in Japan developed faster than in India, but were less destructive of cottage and workshop industry than in India.

Large industry evolved, after state assistance and two wars (1894-1895 and 1904-1905), into zaibatsu concentration by 1910, but small industry, encouraged by government to take cooperative action, was retained, even in the leading manufacturing industry, textiles. Large-scale enterprises created external economies in the supply of raw materials, working capital, and markets. Additionally, these enterprises could not manufacture every item needed, and found it cheaper to buy parts and components from independently-run small workshops, to which the large firms provided technical advice, scarce inputs, credit, and, where needed, access to a large international trading company (*sogo shosha*), which economized on the scarce language skills of both Japanese and foreigners. Small industry (establishments with less than 50 workers) increased its real output (though not output share) from 1884 to 1930, contributing 65 to 75 percent of Japan's employment and 45 to 50 percent of her gross manufacturing output in 1934. But many small firms were not independent, being dominated by major banks, industrial companies, and trading corporations (Lockwood 1954).

Many African and Asian LDCs use training, extension, credit, and industrial estate programs to encourage small-scale manufacturing establishments. From 1958 to 1978, China had a policy of "walking on two legs," with large urban manufacturing augmented by a "second leg," small- and medium-size industry on the rural communes. Since the 1950s, India has limited the expansion of large firms, and provided subsidies for the establishment of small-scale industry, especially in non-metropolitan areas.

But few contemporary Afro-Asian countries have had as well-developed a small-scale manufacturing sector as post-1868 Japan. Many LDCs, trying to modernize industry, have emphasized capital-intensive technology representing the most advanced state of arts in rich countries, allowing small industry to decline (see Nafziger 1990, 264-65, on appropriate technology). These countries have not stressed gradual technical improvement and learning from experience among existing ministries and industries, together with dissemination of technology consistent with local factor endowment and culture. Creating small industry from scratch is not as effective as maintaining and upgrading workshop, handicraft, and cottage industry left from an earlier stage of development. Once small industry has been disrupted or destroyed, it is difficult to reconstruct.

To be sure, the technological gap between DCs and Afro-Asia is greater today than during the Meiji period. But contemporary third-world countries still have many alternatives to best-practice capital-intensive techniques.

# EXPORT EXPANSION AND IMPORT SUBSTITUTION

From 1868 to World War II, the Japanese had a policy (first forced and later chosen) of multilateral, nondiscriminatory foreign trade outside their empire (1904-1945). This trade policy contributed to rapid growth, although it would be a mistake to regard Japan's drive for foreign markets as the motor force of her industrialization.

Although nineteenth-century Meiji Japan partially circumvented western tariff limitations by providing protection through subsidies and state undertakings, it was more open to international trade than most contemporary Afro-Asian countries. While foreign trade was modest by western standards during the Meiji government's first 25 years, its influences stimulated technological learning. The large domestic market usually absorbed most of the products of this new technology. Subsequently, as the Japanese mastered and modified innovations, they often began exporting, as with textiles, the leading export, 1874 to 1940; other light manufactures like consumer goods and simple machines that replaced primary-product exports in second place at the turn of the twentieth century; and the leading sector after World War II, heavy and chemical manufactures (especially electronics, vehicles, and sophisticated consumer goods in the 1970s, 1980s, and early 1990s).

Unlike contemporary Afro-Asia, Japan did not discriminate against exports. Increased tariff protection in the first quarter of the twentieth-century reduced the price of foreign exchange, but government export promotion through a bank to finance trade, exhibiting Japanese products overseas, sales bureaus abroad, chambers of commerce and commodity guilds for cooperative export activity, merchant-marine subsidies, and business privilege in the new empire (Lockwood 1954, 531) brought export inducements near that of the equilibrium exchange rate through 1937 (except for the 1920s). Japan's annual real average growth rates in exports were 8.4 percent between 1880 and 1913 (compared to 3.2 percent for the world as a whole, 2.6 percent for Britain, and 4.2 percent for the United States), and 5.2 percent between 1913 and 1937 (compared to 1.4 percent for the world, 0.4 percent for Britain, and 1.4 percent for the United States). Today many Afro-Asian LDCs overvalue their domestic currency relative to foreign currency, discouraging domestic producers from exporting and substituting imports unless protected by massive subsidies (Power 1979, 44-55).

A study by the National Bureau of Economic Research of 10 LDCs indicates the Japanese approach—an emphasis on foreign-exchange rate equilibrium and export promotion—is generally more effective than import substitution in expanding output and employment in contemporary LDCs (Krueger, Lary, Monson, and Akrasenee 1981). As an example, Chile, in the 1960s and 1970s, provided outlandish incentives for import substitutes, and implicitly discouraged export development. During the same period, South Korea, on the other hand, generally pursued a policy consistent with the Japanese model, providing few incentives for import substitution, while heavily encouraging export activity through capital subsidies, depreciation allowances, import duty exemptions, and exchange rates near equilibrium. From 1960 to 1980, Chile's real annual growth rates were 2.5 percent in industry and 1.6 percent overall, compared to Korea's 16.3 and 7.0 percents—spurred by scale economies, international competition, price flexibility, and no agricultural and foreign exchange shortages associated with export promotion.

Meiji Japan's exports also benefited from favorable international economic conditions. In 1868-97, the yen chronically depreciated vis-á-vis the U.S. dollar. In 1882-1897 the yen was on a de facto silver standard, as silver declined relative to gold. While Chinese indemnities after 1897 (which strengthened the yen) and the military expenses of the 1904-1905 Russo-Japanese War strained the international balance of trade, World War I's export demand spurred a large trade surplus. Although the immediate postwar and early Great Depression trade balance was in deficit due to slow growth of exports, they grew well after 1931, when Japan went off the gold standard (Nakamura 1983).

Today's international economic conditions are not as favorable to Afro-Asian export expansion. The most rapidly expanding Afro-Asian manufactured exports during the 1970s and early 1980s were textiles, clothing, footwear, and simple consumer goods requiring labor-intensive technology widely available. But the competition from other aspiring newly industrial exporting countries is more severe than it was for Meiji Japan.

A *single country*, such as Meiji Japan, exporting agricultural and light manufacturing goods, would often be a price take with substantial scope in expanding export receipts alongside a long-run elastic supply curve. However, today a single-country analysis suffers from a fallacy of composition: What is true for one country is not necessarily true of numerous LDCs under pressure from Bank/Fund adjustment programs to expand primary-product exports. Afro-Asia is caught in an export trap, since as these LDCs expand export supply, relative prices fall substantially. Primary-product export growth reduced terms of trade, thus reducing export purchasing power, 1977-83, and only increasing this power slightly, 1983-90. The high DC effective rate of protection also blocks technologically feasible primary-product processing and light industry, tightening the export noose blocking export expansion as an engine of growth for Africa and many other low-income countries. Widespread currency devaluations under Bank/Fund adjustment programs also spur export expansion in primary products, suggesting that the export trap, rather than anti-farm bias, may be the impulse supporting LDC resistance to devaluations (Nafziger, 1993, xxii, 111-12).

# CONCLUSION

Since 1979-80 the World Bank, OECD or DC governments, and DC commercial banks—whose funding for LDCs depends on the IMF "seal of approval—together with the IMF, form a policy cartel. The IMF-World Bank-OECD (Bank/Fund for short) model prefers that LDCs be democracies.

However, since lenders and aid-givers depend on IMF approval, the OECD and World Bank rarely provide concessional funds to compensate for the additional inflationary and external payments pressures faced by countries making the transition to democracy. In practice, the Bank/Fund provides funds to LDCs on the basis of its economic liberalization and other economic criterion, while paying little attention to achieving political democracy. Thus the Bank/Fund model closely resembles the development model of pre-World War II Japan, economic liberalism with state action but without political democracy and widespread indigenous economic decisionmaking. For the Japanese model, similar to the contemporary Bank/Fund approach, emphasizes acquiring foreign technology, encouraging and subsidizing local entrepreneurs, strengthening indigenous financial institutions, reducing industrial wages to market rates, increasing profits, achieving market-clearing exchange rates, expanding exports, and eschewing import substitution.

How applicable is the Japanese development model (1868-1939) to present-day Afro-Asia?

First, Meiji Japan received a high return from its investment priority on primary, vocational, and scientific education. Basic literacy facilitates technological adaptation and learning. Afro-Asia would benefit from a similar investment emphasis. While the Bank/Fund model matches Meiji Japan's emphases, Bank/Fund policies toward Afro-Asia adjustment programs contributed to low investment rates in education and literacy, especially in the highly indebted countries of low-income Africa. Many low-income countries, having endured years of austerity and stagnation, cannot afford to reduce consumption to effect an external transfer, and thus they shift the burden to investment (Nafziger 1993). Moreover, African needs to be selective in using pre-World War II Japanese schools as models, as they emphasized rote memory and subservience to authority and were antithetical to creativity, democracy, human rights, and female equality.

Second, high labor supply elasticities resulting from vast reserves from the agricultural and informal industrial sectors, together with low industrial wage premiums, kept Japanese unskilled industrial wage rates relatively low before World War I, increasing business profits and reducing urban unemployment. Before the Bank/Fund adjustment programs of the 1980s, minimum wage legislation, strong trade union movements, and unadaptive capital-intensive technologies in Afro-Asia contributed to wages much higher than in Meiji Japan, reducing Afro-Asian profits and savings. Most Afro-Asian elites were afraid of losing political support from revising labor codes, curtailing wages, eliminating capital subsidies, adjusting foreign exchange rates, or making pay scales more flexible. Today, with austere policies essential to obtaining loans of last resort from the IMF, World Bank, or OECD, Afro-Asian political leaders have frequently resorted to repression to retain power (Ibid.).

Third, Japanese-type "guided capitalism" is limited in Afro-Asia today, because of inadequate government capability to spur private business, and political elite and populist opposition to large business subsidies, high industrial concentration, high income inequality between business people and others, and favorable legal and labor policies for business.

Fourth, Japanese economic history demonstrates the importance of a government role in creating and regulating financial institutions, without tolerating growing concentration of private financial institutions. However, similar to Meiji Japan, most contemporary Afro-Asian countries lack the ability and will to prevent indigenous concentration.

Fifth, many Afro-Asian countries, like Meiji Japan, have tried to transfer large amounts of agricultural income to industry for investment capital but, like Japan, some have sacrificed rural incomes and nutritional levels, and spurred agrarian rural discontent.

Sixth, Meiji Japan exemplifies the importance of improving capital and technology step by step, utilizing existing small industry, rather than making substantial leaps to the most advanced technologies available.

Seventh, given a product cycle, as goods become standardized, less advanced countries, such as those in Africa and Asia, similar to Meiji Japan, can mass produce items with less skilled labor. However, today's Afro-Asian countries are at a disadvantage compared to nineteenth-century Japan, as their firms compete against oligopolistic multinational corporations. Still although today's international economic conditions are less favorable to Afro-Asia than those of the late nineteenth century were to Japan, Afro-Asia could still benefit from the Japanese approach of using international competition and market-clearing exchange rates to spur rapid export expansion.

Finally, the 1868-1939 Japanese experience indicates the advantages of self-directed development. However, the Bank/Fund model for Afro-Asia neglects self direction, emphasizing a close monitor of lending and policy by the IMF and Bank. To be sure, many small Afro-Asian countries are limited in their options of reducing dependence on DC trade and capital movements.

The Japanese development model underlines the importance of Afro-Asian governments controlling DC capital flows and the employment of DC personnel introducing technology. This is especially important since the technological distance between today's DCs and Afro-Asia is large, making it less likely that foreign experts will adapt technology to local conditions and indigenous production without Afro-Asian administrative direction.

Many components of the Japanese model associated with industrial growth also engendered emperor-system authoritarianism. The nationalism and militarism that provided a motive force for rapid technological change and substantial government investment also contributed to imperial expansion and fascism. The universal primary educational system of the late nineteenth century that improved Japanese productivity also proclaimed the virtues of the emperor and state worship.

Japan's government of the 1930s used foreign aggression and war as tools for forging macroeconomic expansion and domestic integration. After the Great Depression, low tariffs, a legacy of the late nineteenth century, gave way to increased protection (and cartelization and military expansion), programs to expand spending and employment. However, during the 1930s, the state intervened to freeze workers' pay and dissolve unions, reducing the low real wages even further. This policy, consistent with mass repression and rising inequality, contributed to high profits and savings. Indeed, the military and bureaucracy's alliance with the zaibatsu enabled its share of industry and banking and its monopoly profits to skyrocket during the total mobilization of war (Bix 1982, 2-19).

While a contemporary Afro-Asian LDC can learn useful lessons from the Japanese development model, these lessons are limited because of Meiji Japan's historically specific conditions, and because some aspects of the Japanese approach also contributed to pathologies of growth, such as zaibatsu concentration, income inequality, labor union repression, militarism, and imperialism. In the seven decades before World War II, the indenturing of young workers by parents, the increased tenancy rates and greater tenure insecurity, the slums in major cities, the serious environmental noise and pollution problems, the cost of soldiers and civilians killed, crippled, and disabled under imperialism, the torture and imprisonment of opponents to the regime, the suffering of colonial peoples in Taiwan and Korea, the suffering of adversaries (especially in Asia) during World War II, the independence of the military command from cabinet control, the rampant militarism in the 1930s, and authoritarianism were connected to an economic strategy emphasizing low wages, a stronger military, samurai subsidies, zaibatsu facilitation, capital transfer from agriculture, little spending on social welfare, and the neglect of human rights (Halliday 1975; Dower 1975). These pathologies were not reduced until military defeat was followed by the democratic reforms of an occupational government, a series of events not to be recommended, nor likely to improve income equality, accelerate economic growth, and democratize the political economy in developing countries as it did in Japan (Halliday 1975; Dower 1975; Kunio 1986). Today's Afro-Asian countries cannot wholly adopt the Japanese model but must select components piecemeal, such as self-directed development planning, technological adaptation, scientific and practical education, state role in infrastructure and human capital investment, labor-intensive industrial export expansion, improvement capital and engineering step by step, and learning by doing.

# NOTES

1.  Computations from the World Bank 1991b, 204-05, indicate 45 of the 50 countries in this income category were from sub-Saharan Africa and East, South, and Southeast Asia.

I had initially intended to concentrate on mixed and capitalist but not socialist (centrally directed) LDCs like China and Vietmam. But economic reform in these two countries suggest the Japanese model may apply to them. Moreover, the interest Chinese scholars indicated when I lectured on the Japanese development model to the International Technology and Economy Institute, Research Center of Economical, Technical, and Social Development of the State Council, Beijing, and the China-U.S. Economic and Trade Exchanges Symposium, 14-19 May 1987 suggested I expand the application's scope to China, from whose civilization Japan borrowed law, government, economic ideas, philosophy, religion, culture, art, sciences, learning, and part of its writing script *kanji* for much of the last two millennia.

2.  Scholars have usually rejected concepts of abrupt historical thresholds like Rostow's takeoff (1961) or Engels' industrial revolution. Even Kuznets' modern economic growth (1966), a rapid, sustained increase in real per capita GNP associated with capital accumulation and rapid technical change under private or state capitalism, begins so gradually that its start cannot be dated by a given year or decade. In Japan, we cannot pinpoint the beginnings of modern (or capitalist) growth more precisely than the Meiji reform era of the late nineteenth-century period.

3.  In contrast, independent Siam, which in 1868 faced initial conditions somewhat comparable to Japan, did not establish government factories or provide assistance to private industrial entrepreneurs in the latter part of the nineteenth century.

4.  I use the figure for East, South, and Southeast Asia and sub-Saharan African (except China); including China reduces the birth rate to 29 per 1000 and the death rate to 10 per 1000. Population Reference Bureau 1991.

5.  Calculations are from five-year moving averages from Ohkawa and Shinohara, 1979, 86; Hayami, 1975, 220.

# Chapter XII

# *Why has Japan Succeeded?*

## COMPARING JAPAN'S AND THE UNITED STATES'S ECONOMIC PERFORMANCES

Vogel (1979) argued that, considering the sparse natural resources of Japan, its economic performance is number one in the world. Futurologist Herman Kahn labeled the twenty-first century the Japanese century, just as Henry Luce, the founder of *Time* magazine, named the twentieth century the American century.

Annual GNP per person, 1990, which uses a 1988-90 three-year average yen-dollar exchange rate, indicates Japan (with $25,430) second to Switzerland ($32,680), and ahead of eighth-ranking United States (with $21,790) (World Bank 1992, 219). However, the UN International Comparison Project converts a country's gross product in local currency into international dollars (I$) by measuring the purchasing power relative to all other countries rather than using the exchange rate. Adjusting for the relative domestic purchasing power of currencies, the United States, with I$21,449 leads Japan, with I$17,616 in GDP per person, 1990 (UN 1993, 135).

Comparative income figures understate, for example, the safety (a murder rate one-sixth of that in the United States) and convenience of Japanese intercity and intracity transport, but overstate Japanese welfare in several other ways. The congestion in swimming pools, tennis courts, expressways, and subways in Japan is generally worse than in the United States. (Tokyo hires pushers to pack people into subway cars during rush hour.) Middle-income people typically can afford no better than a two-bedroom apartment one to two hours away from Tokyo's central city. A study by the Organization for Economic Cooperation and Development (OECD, which represents the capitalist DCs) shows the worker in Japan spends more time commuting to work than in any western country.

For the last 125 years or so, Japan's annual 3.6 percent real growth in GNP per person is first in the world and substantially in excess of the U.S.'s annual growth (Table II.1). Japan is also the top DC grower after 1960 or even if limited to the 1980s. However, Japan, wracked by the recession as the yen strengthened, had a slower growth rate than the United States during 1992-93. While I expect Japan's growth rate to decelerate during the last few years of the twentieth century and the early years of the twenty-first century, when compared to the 1970s or 1980s, I still expect Japan to have among the fastest growth rate of OECD countries.

As of 1990, Japan is more productive than the United States in motor vehicles (producing 14 million, including Japanese plants overseas, to the U.S.'s 8 million annually), auto parts, electrical machinery, metal working, consumer electronics, steel, and transport equipment, but less productive in computers, professional and scientific instruments, paper and pulp, fibers, soap and detergent, processed food, and tobacco (Franko 1983, 5-16, with author's adjustment for subsequent changes, and Lewis 1993, A11.). Indeed an increasing portion of General Motors's, Ford's, and Chrysler's components are made in Japan, other parts of Asia, or Europe. Overall Japan's *level* of manufacturing productivity (adjusted for exchange rates) is slightly lower than the U.S.'s, (Japan's inefficient industries do not export and are invisible to American eyes), although Japan's productivity growth is much faster than the U.S.'s.

Chapter 2 mentioned Olson's theory of encrusted special interests and Kennedy's theory of military overcommitment as explanations of American decline relative to Japan's. To be sure, leader economies, as the United States in recent decades, almost invariably grow slower than follower economies. The laggards in innovation can learn more from the frontrunners than vice versa. The fruits of a successful productivity-enhancing policy are ultimately shared by others. Yet Thurow (1985, 149) in examining industrial sectors, detects a disturbing trend: even when other countries surpass the United States, its productivity growth rates lag behind the others.

Japan's 1990 life expectancy (79 years) was the highest and its 1990 infant mortality rate (5 per 1000) the lowest in the world. The United States's life expectancy was 76 years (thirteenth to fourteenth internationally) years and its infant mortality 9 per 1000 (eighteenth to nineteenth), falling, despite no improved prenatal care, because of better medical technology (World Bank 1992, 219, 273; UN Development Programme 1991, 119). These indicators are the best measures of nutrition, public health, and the general environment.

Japan's income distribution during the 1980s was among the lowest two of 19 OECD countries, with much less income inequality than the United States. During this period, the income shares of the bottom 20 percent of the population in Japan was 8.7 percent of the total compared to 5.3 percent in the United States, while the top quintile in Japan received only 37.5 percent of the total compared to 39.9 percent in the United States. The Gini coefficient, a measure of income concentration, was 0.26 in Japan and 0.33 in the United States (World Bank 1991: 263).

Japan has the highest savings rate among OECD countries, 34 percent of GNP, compared to the U.S.'s 15 percent, the lowest OECD rate in 1989 (World Bank 1992, 235), linked to the U.S.'s huge bilateral deficit with Japan. Japan's exports excess capital, while the U.S. imports capital to augment its meager domestic capital formation.

## THE JAPANESE POLITICAL ECONOMY: FROM MILITARY-INDUSTRIAL OLIGARCHY TO LIBERAL DEMOCRACY

Japan, just before World War II, was ruled by a fascist oligarchy that was imperialist (with Korea, Taiwan, Manchuria, and a subservient China providing privileged markets and raw-material sources) and highly militarized. Financial cliques or combines (zaibatsu), like Mitsui, Mitsubishi, Sumitomo, and Yasuda, had dominated industry and banking from the late nineteenth-century through the eve of the war. Land ownership was concentrated and tenancy rates high. Government repressed labor unions. Lockwood estimates Japan's income inequality in the mid to late 1930s was higher than any industrialized country (Lockwood 1968: 271-74).

Soon after Japan's unconditional surrender in August 1945, the Allied occupational forces disarmed the country. With the prewar leadership discredited, the local population supported the Allied Powers' democratization of the Japanese political economy. By 1951, the occupational government carried out land reform, labor reform, educational reform, constitutional liberalization, financial stabilization, demilitarization, and zaibatsu dissolution, making postwar Japan more egalitarian, competitive, and peaceful (Kunio 1986, 15-22). The occupation contributed institutions supporting political and economic freedom.

The 1951 peace treaty with the United States limited Japan's military spending to self-defense forces, which has not exceeded (an elastic) 1 percent of GNP since. In May 1987, a vice minister, the Director of the International Technology and Economy Institute of the State Council, Beijing, expressed to me his concern about the threat of revived Japanese militarism to China, as 1 percent of rich Japan's GNP is consistent with the eighth largest armed forces in the world!

Although the zaibatsu's successor companies increasingly cooperated over time, the zaibatsu never came close to attaining prewar concentration. The relationships between constituent units (such as the Mitsubishi companies) were looser and vaguer. But Japanese government officials, viewing the international (not domestic) economy as the appropriate market, are less likely than U.S. policy makers to break up oligopolies. Ironically, most postwar Japanese challengers to the west have been entrepreneurial mavericks such as

Sony, Matsushita, Honda, Toyota, and Sharp rather than the old zaibatsu groups.

The owner-farmer law of 1946 abolished non-working landlords, limited owners to only about one cultivated hectare, and banned resale for 30 years. Labor-union membership increased from virtually zero in 1945 to 7 million members in 1949 to about one-third of the employed labor force today. Japan enjoyed a relatively egalitarian income distribution throughout the postwar period (Allen 1981, 23-72; Patrick 1984, 5).

Japan had reached a high level of technological sophistication by the end of the war, and there was pent-up demand for consumption goods, a spur to rapid early postwar economic growth. The United States at first showed little interest in rebuilding Japan's economy until the outbreak of the Cold War, when the United States was concerned about a counterweight to the Soviet Union in Asia. At the beginning of the Korean War in June 1950, the U.S. began to encourage Japanese economic recovery, especially in light of the need for reliable suppliers for the U.S. military (Allen 1981, 19-21; Kunio 1986, 21-22).

## GUIDED CAPITALISM: SMALL GOVERNMENT AND INDUSTRIAL TARGETING

### Industrial Policy and Targeting

Since the 1868 Meiji Reformation, the state has had a strong role in building Japan's private capitalism, as chapter 12 indicates. Is the charge of "Japan Incorporated" accurate? Lockwood (1954, 649) says

> The hand of Government is everywhere in existence [engaged] in an extraordinary amount of consultation, advice, persuasion and threat. The Industrial Bureaus of the Ministry of International Trade and Industry (MITI) proliferate sectoral targets and plans; they confer, they tinker, they exhort. This is economics by administration to an extent inconceivable in Washington or London. Business makes few major decisions without consulting the appropriate government authority; the same is true in reverse.

Yet while government had a strong influence in the reconstruction period of the 1950s and 1960s, and has substantial informal, extrastatutory powers today, government does not dictate policy to the private sector. Policy-making results from widespread consultation between government and business, which seek consensus through negotiation.

MITI's contribution to Japan's success is overstated. While MITI facilitated memory-chip output for semiconductors, it did not encourage electronics production and tried to consolidate Japan's automobile production, attempting to prevent Soichiro Honda from producing automobiles! Nor did government have much influence on the commercial banks' priorities and their contribution to high saving rates. Although government was accommodating and supportive, private entrepreneurs invested and coordinated the essential resources (Schultze 1983, 3-12). For Thurow (1984, 12), the difference between industrial policies is not magnitude but that the United States has a back-door policy, while Japan's policy is up-front.

## The Size of Government

The ratio of total tax (including social security) revenues to GDP in Japan (33 percent) is about the same as in the United States (33 percent), and lower than Sweden (57 percent), France (45 percent), Italy (43 percent), and Britain (38 percent) ("Tax Revenues," 1991: 123). Social program spending to GNP is: Japan (9 percent), the United States (11 percent), Canada (15 percent), Britain (18 percent), Germany (20 percent), and Sweden (30 percent). Japan has, however, had a national health program for a long time, but its social security system is not so well developed as western countries'. Research and development (R and D) as a percentage of GNP is 3.0 Japan, 2.9 Germany, 2.8 United States, 2.3 France, and 2.3 United Kingdom (1989). But since Japan places more emphasis on encouraging R and D through tax inducements and since half of U.S. spending is in the military sector, Japan spends much more per person on civilian R and D. Indeed defense expenditures per capita are the U.S. $759, Britain $512, France $483, Germany $405, Italy $155, and Japan $98 (Keizai Koho Center 1982, 16, 70-72; Patrick 1984, 5-16; Shigehara 1992: 22).

## Planning

Saburo Okita, member of the Club of Rome, acquired his international reputation as planning minister who overfulfilled his 10-year plan for doubling national income during the 1960s. Yet few economists doubt Japan would have doubled national income with no plan at all. For in Japan plans are neither prescriptive for private firms nor even targets, but expectations or intentions. Indeed in 1985, Prime Minister Yashu Nakasone abandoned pretensions by abolishing ministry planning altogether.

# CAPITAL FORMATION: BUSINESS AND PRIVATE SAVING

Franko (1983, 13) argues that Japanese fast productivity growth is as expected, given its high savings rate, calling into question "managerial" or "labor relations" explanations for Japan's performance.

Japan, unlike Asian countries under colonialism, developed credit and savings institutions, set up government development banks (especially for foreign exchange for importers), and established a central bank (to regulate the money supply) in the last two decades of the nineteenth century. Additionally, the Meiji rulers of the last quarter of the nineteenth-century accumulated investment capital by squeezing it from the peasants through moderate inflation and a land tax comprising the lion's share of government revenue (chapter 11).

After the early 1950s, the commercial banking system channeled Japan's household savings to business, overloaning deposits (with Bank of Japan support) to fuel (almost) non-inflationary postwar expansion. High investment rates aided Japan's high-technology, capital-intensive industries, while providing auxiliary and subcontracting opportunities for small- and medium-sized firm with abundant labor. Japan virtually eschewed investment in "prestige" projects and the military. By the 1960s, Japanese firms invested substantial funds in improving product reliability (quality control) through automation and robotization, reversing their early postwar reputation for shoddy products (Allen 1981, 24-60; Franko 1983; Saxonhouse 1981, 252; Peck and Tamura 1976, 525-85).

While high postwar rates of reinvested business profits (with growth begetting growth) were crucial, high household savings rates were another key factor. Individual families needed to make more provisions than in the west against illness, unemployment, and old age. Also, Japan's high cost of housing and poor mortgage credit markets (including high down-payment requirements) delays housing purchases. Moreover, savings for children's education are important, as parents pay high fees for coaching their children for university entrance examinations and sending them to expensive private colleges and universities when they fail to obtain admission to the cheaper eminent state universities. Furthermore, since a large share of workers' annual earnings are from biannual bonuses, workers relate current consumption to the monthly wage and apply bonuses to savings (Allen 1981, 97-99; Patrick 1984, 16).

To increase U.S. savings rates relative to Japan's, Thurow would abolish consumer credit for consumer durables, require higher down payments for houses, withhold deductibility for residential interest or property tax payments, rely more on bonus incentives, abolish private pensions, make savings accounts tax-free, and emphasize value-added taxes (not income taxes) in the United States, just like the Japanese. Yet all except credit and house payment policies would increase disposable (post-tax) income inequality in the United States, already in the OECD's highest one-third.

# EDUCATION, SCIENCE, AND TECHNOLOGY: THE WORLD CHAMPION BORROWERS

Chapter 11 lists technology policies the late nineteenth-century Meiji ruler used to "enrich the nation." The sequence of a century of Japan's technological borrowing has been: (1) imported product, (2) the copy, usually inferior in quality, and (3) slow improvement, even finer grades and specialties, with learning by doing (Lockwood 1954, 331-32). Latecomer Japan grew faster than technological leaders—the United States, Britain, and Germany—by exploiting technology developed by the advanced countries.

## Civilian Technology

The Japanese are without doubt the world's champion importers of other people's technology. Unlike other industrial nations which may have forgot how much technological development was based on seeking out, stumbling on, or helping themselves to foreign discoveries and innovations, Japan has continuously sent its sons to travel, live, or be educated abroad to find ways of catching up with the west (Franko 1983, 23).

In the 1950s, the Japanese Productivity Center and general trading companies sent people to learn and (sometimes) buy technology overseas. At the same time, MITI worked with Japanese firms to limit the costs, restrictions, and length of technology agreements with foreigners, especially in chemicals, iron, and steel where Japan tried to increase its self-sufficiency. From 1960 to 1965, technology sales were more competitive, making technology cheaper. But foreign technological sales in joint ventures and direct investment were still controlled by government. From 1966 to 1972, technology imports were more oriented toward improving, modifying, and adapting technology previously imported.

Japan paid for most foreign technology. And when Japan paid little for technology, it was due to western short-sightedness not Japanese perfidy (Peck and Tamura 1976, 525-85; Franko 1983, 23). Japan and Germany, high-performing countries, have been among the largest net importers of technology during the postwar period, while low-performing U.S. and Britain are net exporters, suggesting that technological advance may be related to an awareness of what others have invented and developed.

Japanese research is more in industry, less concentrated among larger firms, less in new research-oriented companies, and less from government funds than in the United States. In dispersing technology to small firms, Japan relies more on subcontractors, small business associations, and government research institutions than the United States does.

Most of Japan's investment is not substituting capital for labor but conserving energy and raw materials, or saving space (through miniaturization of existing technology such as precision machine tools, tubes and components, optics, and ceramic packaging for micro-circuits) (Franko 1983, 15-39; Peck and Tamura 1976, 559-66).

## Education

In the last quarter of the nineteenth century, Japan established universal education for all classes. Its high homogeneous standards, still characteristic today, did much to foster Japanese national unity and cultural homogeneity.

Japan's primary enrollment rate reached virtually 100 percent in 1911. Today I think Japan has the highest uniform primary and secondary school standards, while the U.S. has one of the lowest standards, among OECD countries. Japan's public schools may be the strongest in the world in mathematics and science. Additionally, the Japanese Ministry of Education estimates Japan's functional illiteracy rate at 1 percent compared to the U.S. Department of Education estimates of 20 percent in the United States (Tharp 1987, 1). Japanese elementary and secondary students attend classes 240 days (U.S. 180 days) per year, do more homework, and are more highly motivated to achieve than their American counterparts. Moreover, Japan has emphasized technical education and (because of longer employment commitments in government and large firms) systematic training within the work unit.

With high standards, Japanese firms can rely more on decentralized worker decisions on computers, robots, and other sophisticated equipment. Thus Japanese firms can unlock numerically controlled machine tools since blue-collar workers can be taught to do the necessary programming, while American companies lock their machine tools partly because of inadequate U.S. work skills (Allen 1981, 93; Thurow 1985, 186).

In the early postwar period, secondary and university education in Japan was almost as widespread as in Western Europe. While 40 percent of Japanese males in their late twenties have finished a four-year college compared to about 30 percent of American males today, the U.S. has a higher combined rate of completions than Japan (or any western country) for *both* males and females of that age. Once a student is admitted to an outstanding university like Tokyo University and earns a degree, he is virtually guaranteed an elite job. Which university you go to, not what your grades are, is the key to getting an excellent job with the government bureaucracy, a large company, or some other highly desired employer. Many Japanese educators, however, feel their students fall behind Americans in college, and are further behind in graduate school, which only a small fraction of Japanese university graduates attend.

The government strove to increase science and engineering graduates beginning in the 1950s. Today Japan has more engineers and scientists per 1,000 population than any western country. Two-thirds of the members of the boards of directors of leading companies and most administrative civil servants are professional engineers or applied scientists. Thurow indicates two-thirds of American chief executive officers are trained as lawyers, accountants, or advertising executives, while only 9 percent train as engineers. He recommends U.S. companies pay engineers more than managers (as Digital Equipment Corporation), and return to the days when everyone who wanted promotions would spend time on-line in production management (Peck and Tamura 1976, 575-80; Allen 1981, 95; Thurow 1985, 169).

## Science and Technology

Yet Japan is not first in science, and receives few Nobel prizes. Japanese scientists explain they receive few international science prizes because of their language isolation, their greater emphasis on rote learning and applied research, and their lack of stress on creativity among a small elite of scientists and intellectuals. Indeed the United States's role as the world's leader in pure science has little correlation to economic success. If it did, the U.S. would not have reached economic parity with Britain at the turn of the twentieth century almost half a century before becoming the world's scientific leader. In the first half of the twentieth century, American mass education beat Europe's elite education economically but lost the race for scientific stardom. Since the United States achieved its economic success without simultaneously dominating pure science, it should not be surprising the Japanese can do the same today. Japanese firms have been able to put their huge savings to work at moderate risk at high returns by upgrading their investment with known technologies (Thurow 1985, 51; Schultze 1983, 6). To be sure, Japan will need to reorient its educational system toward more originality at the technical frontier as it shifts from being a technological follower to a leader. But Japan's educational emphases on innovation, developing ideas, improvement engineering, and commercial payoff are still more oriented to rapid economic growth than the U.S.'s stress on science, original work, and invention (Patrick 1984, 5).

# LABOR-MANAGEMENT RELATIONS: DECENTRALIZED DECISIONS, LONGTERM EMPLOYMENT, AND UNIONS

## Longterm Employment

In Japan a substantial portion of government and large-firm employees, which comprise about one-third of the total labor force, have "lifetime employment." Virtually all employees are hired directly from school: blue-collar workers from junior and senior high school, clerical workers from senior high school, and managerial personnel from college. Japanese firms stress general ability. character, and team orientation when hiring management, while

U.S. enterprises emphasize the work to be done and job specification. After a probationary period, often as long as a year, the employee acquires tenure, continuing until 55 or 60, when for most retirement is compulsory (Galenson and Odaka 1976, 614; Allen 1981,95-96). However, with slower growth in the two decades after 1990, some major employers may have to abolish lifetime employment guarantees for new workers and even go back on guarantees to existing employees.

In the best-run large enterprises, employees regard themselves as members of a group or family. Japanese worker identity is usually with the company (Toyota or National) instead of the job (tool maker or accounts manager) as in the U.S. In return for firm loyalty, the young recruit, even if not promoted, can expect his income to rise at a steeper rate than in the west. Where jobs become obsolete, the company is expected to retrain (for example, from mechanic to salesman). Additionally, firms invest far more than U.S. enterprises in education and improved skills. Human investment by the company also reduces worker resistance to technical innovation. Japanese blue-collar workers generally dine in the same hall and enjoy the same amenities as white-collar workers. Moreover, while in 1991, major U.S. corporations paid top executives 53 times their employees' average wage, the same multiple for major Japanese corporations was only 17. A large portion of income is directly related to profitability through biannual bonuses, reinforcing identification with the firm. High company orientation, in turn, means the hierarchy is more vague (Allen 1981, 95-146; "Wage Gap in Japan Narrows," *Wall Street Journal,* 3 May 1993, p. A10).

Some males, especially those that are young, relinquish employment security. Most leave voluntarily, although Japanese managers are skillful in making unacceptable transfers or otherwise easing out undesirable workers without firing them. In some companies, 10-20 percent of the young workers may leave each year, even though their chances for attractive re-employment elsewhere are not good. But older employees are not likely to move because of substantial wage increases with seniority and enterprise policies against hiring employees from competitors (although labor shortages in the early 1990s have been diminishing the premium for seniority). Most new employees needed are hired from recent graduates or smaller firms (Galenson and Odaka 1976, 616-17).

## Management

Japanese managers are usually highly committed to the firm, with which they remain until they retire. There is a strong financial inducement to stay with the company, as salary and promotion are determined largely by seniority within the enterprise. While managers can be shifted to affiliated companies without penalty, shifting to another firm usually means starting over again (ibid., pp. 95-96).

The Japanese manager has a vested interest in the success of the company and plans for the long run. In contrast, the American manager's time horizon of 2-3 years is shorter. U.S. chief executive officers and middle managers get paid, promoted, and demoted relative to current profits—sometimes quarterly. For Thurow, the best advice for a newly hired M.B.A. is to "get on the fast track" by some brilliant piece of short-run profit maximizing that brings him to the attention of top management. Once there, he avoids risks leading to mistakes that might derail him. According to Thurow, a successful U.S. manager does not plant or harvest but is a Viking raider (Thurow 1985, 149-51; Franko 1983, 125).

## Turnover and Layoffs

U.S. male turnover rates, 1965-66, were twice that of the Japanese (four times higher among 20-24 year olds). Among women, the turnover rates were about the same. Yet we should not overstate Japanese company success and stability, even among large firms. Japanese large firms have about as many failures as American ones. And employee stability with the company in Japan is no greater than in Western Europe.

Yet slow growth and economic recession (generally absent in Japan, 1953-72) pose a challenge to permanent employment commitment. During 1973-74, with the "Nixon shock" of U.S. dollar devaluation, the oil crisis, and the recession, some large firms laid workers off, but guaranteed 65 to 100 percent of pay, usually for short duration. Komatsu Manufacturing Co., a global competitor of Caterpillar Tractor Co. (which has produced jointly with Mitsubishi in Japan since 1963), laid off 1,125 workers for ten months at 65 percent of earnings in 1971. When the workers were called back, 168 were informed their layoff was to be extended four months. Komatsu, taken to court, agreed to reinstate all 168 with back pay before final adjudication.

In 1974, Toshiba Electric, Hitachi, Sanyo, Nissan Motors, and others furloughed workers at 90 percent pay. Toyobo reached agreement to reduce the labor force by 10 percent through early retirement. The chairman of the enterprise union at a major camera company attempted suicide after a company decision to dismiss 900 employees following a plant closure (Franko 1983, 53-58; Galenson and Odaka 1976, 617-18).

In the two decades after 1990, as growth slows down compared to earlier decades, some major employers may have to abolish lifetime employment guarantees for new workers and even go back on guarantees to existing employees. Indeed in late 1993, the Ministry of Labor indicated that 60 percent of of the companies in Japan had begun cutbacks ("Recession Takes Toll on Japan Companies," *Kansas Ciy Star*, 10 October 1993, p. A8).

*Employment Flexibility*

However, even in 1993, companies dismissed few workers with lifetime employment understandings. For large Japanese firms still had substantial flexibility through: (1) cutting overtime, bonuses, and allowances, (2) reducing subcontracting, (3) shifting employees to sister plants or firms, and (4) relieving temporary workers (including those recruited for short periods, most women, seasonal workers, and retired 55-year old employees retained at low wages). Temporary workers have accounted for about 12 percent of large-firm employees on the average and about two-thirds at the extreme. These workers have been generally excluded from union membership but may receive some benefits from union wage negotiations.

A woman, usually hired by employers for routine monotonous jobs, loses her tenure at about 25 years, even if she does not marry. She may receive a permanent commitment when she returns to work later on (perhaps after being an "educational mama" to children spaced more widely apart than North American children), but she is usually treated as a second-class employee (retiring at 50 years compared to a man's 55) (Galenson and Odaka 1976, 615-22; Allen 1981, 147-48). While women made employment gains in the late 1980s, this was reversed during the slump of the early 1990s. Still, even in 1991, women comprised 38 percent of the people employed.

A few firms, like Matsushita Electric Company (maker of Panasonic products), are giving women who marry after three or more years of service the right to return within 10 years with reinstatement to the same kind of job they left and with credit for previous service in determining retirement allowances. In the long run, this trend could continue, especially if labor gets more tight and women more insistent on equal rights (Galenson and Odaka 1976, 615-16).

Employees of small and medium firms (roughly less than 300 employed), who comprise two-thirds of the private labor force, are weakly organized and lack the large firms' employment security. Between small and medium firms and temporary large-firm workers, overall only about 20 percent of Japanese employees have a lifetime employment commitment.

*Management Organization and Ringi-sei Decision Making*

The best-run large Japanese corporations lack U.S.-style bosses, although a dominating personality may become the nucleus for a clique, comprised of people at various levels. Japan's traditional *ringi-sei* decision making involves a two-way flow of information. Major companies do not decide by fiat from the top nor by majority rule, but by consensus. When someone low in an organization's hierarchy originates a proposal, he and his colleagues draft a recommendation circulated throughout the company, and ultimately bring it to the company president for approval. Success in top management is measured less by personal achievement than by the ability to forge a consensus. Ringi-sei, while sometimes time-consuming and contributing to avoiding responsibility, often works well because knowledge of policies is widely diffused. But Americans, when negotiating with Japanese chief officers, frequently become frustrated, since they, unlike American top officials, rarely make decisions on behalf of the company without wide consultation.

Management is not just quality control circles, lifetime employment, and enterprise unions, which, while characteristic of the Japanese, are probably not keys to Japanese management success. At its best, Japanese management is about maintaining clarity of organizational mission, keeping continuity of investment, developing products, processes, and people through R and D, bearing and managing risk, coping with highly competitive environments, and thinking longterm. (Allen 1981, 50-53, 96-97).

Still, in 1993, the strong yen's adverse effect on Japanese companies' profits exposed some weaknesses in Japanese management. Increasingly, Japanese business leaders have been concerned about the slow decision making and lack of precise responsibility within Japan's corporations, blaming these faults on a tradition of consensus management and shared responsibility.

### Worker Attitudes and Productivity

Throughout most of the 1980s, the average Japanese wage was higher than in the United States and many Western European countries, so that the epithet of "cheap foreign labor" hardly explains U.S. industrial competition with Japan. Japanese workers have been willing to form voluntary circles to reduce waste, raise productivity, and ensure high standards of quality (ibid., p. 146). Do work attitudes contribute to Japan's faster growth in productivity than the United States's? Thurow's evidence (1985) indicates American workers with Japanese managers outperform American workers with American managers— hardly a commendation for American management or a condemnation of American workers. The fact that Americans want to make work self-fulfilling, less dangerous, cleaner, and more pleasant is not evidence of poorer work attitudes. Franko (1983, 11) finds no evidence the Japanese work longer hours than Americans or other westerners. Japan's rapid increases in productivity result from superior management, better education, higher savings rates, and more investment in quality control, not harder working employees.

For Thurow, America's productivity problem lies less with indolent factory workers and featherbedding unions than non-union white-collar workers. Private bureaucracy is being added to the American economy at a rate which can only sink it. Japanese companies can operate in the United States under its rules with far fewer white-collar workers than their American counterparts. Two-thirds of Japan's labor-cost advantage in the automobile industry comes from factors under the sole control of management—low white-collar worker cost per unit.

Thurow (1985, 145-49) argues the United States's major handicap is its inability to spur labor to take a direct interest in raising productivity. Putting together high-quality, well-motivated employees interested in working as a team, a direct management responsibility, is a major source of productivity growth.

### Labor Unions

In 1945 labor unions had ceased to exist and worker legislation was of little importance. The occupational government, in its attempt to democratize Japan, passed a number of laws to encourage worker organization, bargain collectively, strike, set up industrial mediation and arbitration machinery and government wage regulation machinery, and establish standards on hours of work, working conditions, overtime pay, dismissal procedure, unemployment benefits, and accident compensation. Between August 1945 and December 1948 union membership rose from zero to 6.75 million.

The Japanese union tends to be an enterprise union (separate unions for each plant), not an industrial or occupational union. Enterprise unions are usually affiliated with several regional or national associations representative of workers in the same trade.

Enterprise unions are not "company unions" anathema to American unionists. While enterprise union headquarters and offices are often at the plants and companies recruit personnel officers from union organizers, Japanese unions have substantial influence on management and are usually independent and effective in bargaining.

Usually the enterprise unions, not the national or regional ones, do the bargaining, although during the annual Spring Offensive (*Shunto*) in April, all unions put forth new wage claims simultaneously. The central organizations usually choose which unions should initially take the offensive. These are often unions in steel, engineering, or chemical industries, which strengthens weaker unions. The Spring Offensive negotiations focus on basic wages, while overtime allowances, bonuses, and other items are negotiated the rest of the year.

Since wages are negotiated firm by firm, they are not standard for the same job between firms. But workers rarely move to a higher wage-scale firm, as this would entail giving up substantial increments from seniority (Allen 1981, 136-42).

### Unemployment

In the 1980s, the official unemployment rate in the United States has tended to be more than twice the Japanese rate. In September 1993, Japan's unemployment was 2.5 percent of the labor force compared to 6.7 percent in the United States [*Economist* (23 November 1993), p. 131]. Even if we adjust for Japan's unemployment rate being understated because first-time applicants and women are not counted as unemployed, the U.S. unemployment rate is still higher (even during U.S. high levels of business activity). However, during the global employment crunch in the early 1990s, Japanese university graduates faced declining job opportunities or even unemployment.

## FOREIGN TRADE AND INVESTMENT: THE NEW FEEDBACK

Since 1868, Japan adhered to the principle of multilateral, nondiscriminatory trade in foreign, non-empire trade. Japanese firms learned multinational management first at home from their western joint venture and suppliers of technology.

The foremost factor responsible for Japan's extraordinary success in international marketing was business's ability to adapt to changing international demand. Japan's silk industry quickly adapted to the exacting demand of American female consumers. In the late 1920s, Japan switched to investment in rayon, becoming the second largest producer to the United States in 1935.

The Japanese government was active in giving assistance to businessmen searching trading opportunities by export promotion schemes, including the study and development of foreign trade techniques, exhibiting Japanese products abroad at expositions, establishing sales bureaus in major overseas cities, and forming chambers of commerce and commodity guilds for cooperative activity in exports. Additionally, the state pressured the great trading companies, like Mitsui Bassan, Mitsubishi, Okura, Sumitomo, and Yasuda, to make loans to small producers and become their agents to sell their products overseas. Because of the trading company and its international network, a far larger proportion of Japanese exports and foreign direct industrial investment has involved small- and medium-sized firms than has been the case in Europe and the United States (Mahajan 1976, 35-60; Lockwood 1954, 210-11, 531; Franko 1983, 62).

### The Importance of Japan's Foreign Trade

Even though Japan is, next to the United States, the world's largest leading international trader, many people overestimate Japan's trade dependence. To be sure, Japan is dependent on foreign trade in a purely physical sense, for she has to buy a large part of her food and almost all her raw materials and fuel from abroad. But the proportion of raw materials in Japan's import trade has fallen steeply in the last 20 years due to synthetic substitutes and the rapid growth in output shares of metals, machinery, and chemicals that require relatively small import content by value. Japanese exports or imports as a share of their GNP are 13 percent compared to the United States's 9 percent, Britain's 22 percent, France's 19 percent, Germany's 23 percent, and the Netherlands's 47 percent. Unlike the exceptional Sony, most successful Japanese companies dominate the domestic market (124 million people with more than a trillion dollars GNP) before penetrating world markets. Japanese companies, unlike their U.S. counterparts, design products to meet the specific needs of foreign consumers. The president of Nippon Telegraph and Telephone Co. complained major American suppliers tried to sell him equipment incompatible with the existing Japanese telephone system, implying the Japanese should shift to the American system (Patrick 1984, 3; Allen 1981, 105). Moreover, American auto manufacturers continued until 1993 to put steering columns on the left side of vehicles, even though the Japanese drive on the left side of the road. Chrysler Chairman Lee Iacocca, who accused Japanese auto makers of "predatory trade," called for a "reversal of Japan's mercantilistic trade policies" and using our most effective political weapon, "good old-fashioned American impatience." ("Iacocca Blasts Japan," 1992, A1, A15; Iacocca 1991, D16; Chipello and Chandler 1992, A2).

### Japan's Bilateral Trade Surplus with the United States

From 1980 to 1985, the United States changed from the largest international creditor to the largest international creditor. During the late 1980s and 1990-92, the U.S. dollar was overvalued vis-á-vis the Japanese yen (¥ 125=$1 in mid 1992) and the United States's bilateral trade deficit with Japan ranged from 40-50 percent of the U.S. deficit, while Japan's surplus with the United States comprised roughly 70 percent of its surplus. In 1992, the U.S. merchandise trade deficit was $89 billion and in 1993 $94 billion (projected), while Japan's trade surplus was $136 billion and in 1993 $135 billion (projected).

During 1993, the dollar depreciated against the yen, so that the exchange rate hovered near a parity between the American penny and the Japanese yen. Roughly maintaining this parity and price stability in the two countries should contribute to a vastly improved U.S. trade balance with Japan by the mid 1990s (as the trade balance lags exchange rates changes by two to five years). Indeed exchange-rate changes already had a visible effect in improving American industrial and electronic competitiveness and reducing the competitiveness and profits of Japan's global companies (Nissan and Minolta suffered losses) in 1993. Patience in waiting for the effect of these lags is a better policy than the Clinton Administration's effort in 1993 to negotiate statistical benchmarks for U.S. firms in specific sectors, an approach that encourages collusive price increases at the expense of buyers. Americans should, however, be prepared for the adverse effect of currency depreciation, a reduced bilateral deficit, the servicing of past borrowing, and the foreign repatriation of investment income in the United States on the standard of living during the mid to late 1990s.

## Japan's Protection against Trade and Capital Movements

House majority leader Richard A. Gephardt from Missouri, speaking in early 1992, regarded the Japanese economy as "essentially different from ours, fundamentally different than... ours in the way it's structured," and not as an opportunity to make gains from increased specialization and trade. Instead "the almost complete uncompatibility [of Japan] makes a normal trading relationship that we have with other countries virtually impossible." A major reason for our large bilateral deficit is "our inability to have fair access to [Japan's] markets" (Crumpley 1992, A9.)

Laura D'Andrea Tyson, chair of the Council of Economic Advisors in the Clinton Administration, complains of the U.S.'s lack of access to Japan's market, charging that Japanese institutions are "so obviously different in ways that disadvantage American producers." Indeed, "the distinctive features of Japanese capitalism—vertical integration, keiretsu groups, cooperative business-government relations, and strict, often paternalistic regulatory arrangements—hamper the efforts of foreign producers to sell in Japan" (Tyson 1992, 6, 58). In response, she supports subsidies, duties, market sharing, and other devices to promote U.S. industries in their competition with Japan.

Tyson argues that the United States needs sector-specific negotiations with particular trading partners to secure improved trade and investment opportunities for U.S. producers. She cites as an example the increased U.S. semiconductor exports to a 22 percent global market share in 1992. These shares were just in excess of shares under a 1986 U.S.-Japanese agreement, negotiated under U.S. pressure (Ibid., 111-13, 255).

She contends that the United States needs to focus on technology-intensive exports, which make special contributions to the long-term health of the American economy. She states that the global shares of these exports fell from the late 1980s to the early 1990s.

According to Tyson, three sectors—computers and office equipment, communciations and electronics, and aircraft and parts—contributed a sizeable majority of the U.S.'s high-technology exports. Tyson's data indicate that despite the United States's strong competitive advantage in electronic products, the U.S.'s trade deficit in electronics improved only 3.4 percent from 1986 to -$19.7 billion in 1991 (Ibid., 12, 25-27).

Tyson favors the Super 301 legislation, passed by the U.S. Congress in 1989, which compels the president to increase tariffs and quotas against countries like Japan which have substantial bilateral surpluses with the United States.

For her, Super 301, although unilateral, is defensive—a response to foreign trading practices and structural barriers that harm U.S. economic interests. The alternative, she contends, is not a world of free trade, but one of trade barriers which inflict substantial harm on U.S. economic interests (Ibid, 255-63).

However, the U.S.'s huge bilateral deficit with Japan does not result from Japanese high protection. Saxonhouse (1980, 248) indicated in House hearings that "Looking at (the merchandise trade) imbalance and looking at more comprehensive accounts of Japanese and American transactions with each other and with the rest of the world economy will divert this committee from a proper assessment of U.S.-Japanese relations, and the U.S. competitive situation in the world economy."

Bhagwati (1992, A14) contends the most "plausible explanation of Japanese behavior in trade negotiations seems to be that, since the 1930s, they have not been allowed to trade by the rules. Their export successes have always been met by demands for quantitative restraints" and by an "aggressive unilateralism" (including Super 301) by the United States that imposes on others its views of unfair trade practices.

According to the OECD (1985, 41) and Washington's Institute for International Economics (Bergsten and Cline 1985, 53-119), Japan has the lowest nominal tariff level of any country in the OECD, including the United States. To be sure, tariffs on agricultural products and subsidies to rice growers resulting from substantial farmer influence with the ruling Liberal Democratic Party (1958-93); control of domestic tobacco distribution by the government-owned Japan Tobacco and Salt Public Corporation (JTS) which has limited cigarette imports; and product standards higher for imports than domestic goods have been irritants to U.S. trade negotiators (we probably cannot expect the coalition government that defeated the LDP in 1993 and subsequent governments to change agricultural trade policies radically). Moreover, Japan has levied import quotas, but these are exceeded by U.S. orderly marketing agreements (OMAs) on Japanese automobiles, televisions, consumer electronics, and other items, "voluntarily" agreed to by Tokyo for fear the U.S. Congress will levy even higher trade restrictions. Overall Japan is *not* more protectionist than the United States.

Despite Japan's early postwar protectionism, it encouraged vital internal competition and removed trade protection as the industry became globally competitive. Since Japan's entrance into the General Agreements on Tariffs and Trade (GATT) and the International Monetary Fund in 1964, Japan has greatly liberalized controls over trade, capital, and foreign exchange. Some foreigners still believe the controls exist (Stein and Thurow 1983, 2-7).

University of Michigan economist Saxonhouse (1980, 248) argues "if Congress were to permit the sale of Alaskan oil to Japan, the bilateral trade balance would be substantially reduced." Such a step would benefit the U.S.

Midwest which, unlike Japan, could buy oil more cheaply from the Middle East than from Alaska. Ironically the chief government policy aiding the Japanese automobile industry today is U.S. protection of its steel industry! Moreover, U.S. OMAs on Japanese products are spurring export competition from newly industrialized nations like South Korea (for example, Hyundai).

Furthermore, U.S. goods' per capita share of the Japanese market is about twice Japanese goods' share of the U.S. market (if you add sales by U.S. companies or joint ventures in Japan to U.S. exports) (Drucker 1989, A10).

The purchase of Rockefeller Center and Columbia Pictures notwithstanding, Japan ranks only third to Britain and the Netherlands in foreign investment in the United States. The trend of Japan's growing investment in western industrialized economies (interrupted temporarily during the Japanese recession in the early 1990s) is mainly an attempt to circumvent western efforts to use trade restrictions to limit Japanese world market shares. The United States can hardly afford now to rescind a principle it has strongly supported for decades—the free movement of capital within the capitalist world.

# THE ASIAN BOOMERANG

Kojima (1978, 234-51) argues that whereas U.S. MNCs invest abroad because of oligopolistic advantages from technology, management, and marketing, Japanese multinationals invest overseas not only to avoid falling market shares from increased western trade protection but to take advantages of the home country's comparative advantage in natural resources or labor-intensive commodities, a pattern that promotes trade and specialization.

The product-cycle theory, discussed in chapter XI, indicates specialization may be based on a temporary technological advantage. Thus LDCs have a comparative advantage in standardized goods. Foreign investment and technological transfer by U.S. automobile companies in Japan (for example, General Motors with Isuzu) and Japanese companies in South Korea (Mitsubishi with Hyundai) help shift comparative advantage. Indeed Shinohara (1982, 32-33, 72-75, 127-28) speaks of a boomerang effect, imports in reverse or intensification of competition in third markets arising from western or Japanese enterprise expansion in, and technology exports to, less advanced countries. Thus Japanese joint ventures in Asian LDCs have begun undercutting Japanese companies domestically.

The world trade shares of Asian NICs (newly-industrialized countries Taiwan, South Korea, Hong Kong, and Singapore) and the ASEAN-4 (Indonesia, Malaysia, Thailand, and the Philippines) are increasing rapidly. In 1965, the Asian NICs (2 percent), ASEAN-4 (2 percent), and Japan (4 percent) comprised 8 percent of international trade, while the Uunited States consisted of 16 percent. By 1986, the NICs accounted for 6 percent, the ASEAN countries 2 percent, and Japan 8 percent (a 16 percent total), while the United States had a 15-percent share. Overall the 10 Pacific Rim countries' shares rose from 24 percent of total world trade in 1965 to 31 percent in 1986. From Asian NICs, Japan's imports of manufactured goods as a percentage of total imports increased from 39 percent in 1970 to 66 percent in 1987, an indication of the boomerang. Japan's industrial imports from NICs increased tenfold during this period. The strong yen may stimulate growing Japanese manufacturing imports from the NICs (Tatanabe 1988, 10-13).

After the suppression of pro-democracy demonstrations in Beijing in June 1989, Japan moved quickly to normalize economic relations with the Chinese. By 1992, Japan's trade with China was $30 billion, a figure second in Asia to trade with South Korea.

# JAPAN AND THE EUROPEAN COMMUNITY

The European Community (EC), also with a bilateral deficit with Japan, has resisted Japan's exports and investment to a greater extent than the United States. While Japanese auto makers have captured 25 percent of the U.S. market, they have only 9 percent of the European market, including less than 3 percent of the market in each of France, Italy, and Spain—countries with quotas on Japanese automobile imports. Until 1984, the Japanese could circumvent EC protection through foreign investment.[1]

The French customs policy in the late 1970s to allow free entry for Japanese videocassette recorder (VCRs), but only through a customs office in the hinterland, where officials only had the capability of processing one application per day was well publicized. By the late 1980s, Sony had one VCR plant in each of three European countries: France, Spain, and Germany.

But Europeans resented Japanese "screwdriver" plants, in which Japanese MNCs assembled components from Japan. EC local-content legislation, which requires 40 percent of inputs purchased from within the EC, is primarily directed at Japanese companies. Some auto companies, like Honda (with Britain's Rover), have signed joint venture agreements with a European company to ease market penetration.

In the early 1990s, the European Community (EC) is taking steps toward integration of currencies, outside tariffs, and factor movement. But Fiat Chairman Umberto Agnelli contended that the Japanese should be required to maintain existing automobile restrictions until 1997, when European auto makers should be able to compete. Peugot's Jacques Calvet supported no Japanese auto imports after 1992 unless European exports to Japan rise. However, consistent with present policy in Germany, Mercedes-Benz President Werner Niefer, dependent on exports, advocated no automobile import restrictions.[2]

Indeed in the early 1990s, Paris and Madrid led a possible EC thrust toward benefiting Latin American exporters at the expense of both Japan and the Asian NICs, especially in steel, electronics, and footwear.

## CONCLUSION

The boomerang Japan worries about is its growing international trade in absolute terms, even while trade is shrinking relative to GNP. Since the 1970s, trade by Japan has been sizeable enough for it to consider how its expansion affects the strategic response of its trading partners.

The Japanese are concerned about what they regard as European and American emotional reaction to Japanese investment and exports. Indeed some consider the western focus on the Japanese threat as a renewal of racism. The Japanese are increasingly aware that their political and military influence falls far short of their economic importance. Some economists even warn of a repeat of the 1930s, when Japan perceived western trade policies were severely restraining its economic growth.

Trade and investment relationships between the west and Japan are mutually advantageous. The United States needs to relax economic barriers to Japan's participation in international markets, not only in the interest of world harmony but also in the interest of U.S. and global prosperity.

## NOTES

1. This section relies on issues of the *Nikkei Weekly*.

2. Other EC members worry about the recommendations by Britain's Monopolies and Merger Commission to lift curbs on Japanese automobile imports ("British Call Worries EC," 1992, A10). But General Motors' profitable European subsidiary endorsed a proposal asking Japanese to limit their automobile exports to and investments in Europe until 2000 (Everett 1991, A11).

Since this book went to press, the European Comunity has become the European Union.

My *Learning from the Japanese: Japan's Pre-War Development and the Third World* (Armonk, NY.: M.E. Sharpe, 1994), incorporates insights from Tokunaga Shojiro, ed., *Japan's Foreign Investment and Asian Economic Interdependence*] (Tokyo: University of Tokyo Press, 1992), on the Japanese-led Asian borderless economy.

# Chapter XIII

# *Concluding Remarks*

## SELF-DIRECTED AND DEPENDENT DEVELOPMENT IN AFRO-ASIA

Western colonialism and imperialism of the eighteenth through the early twentieth-centuries diverted most Afro-Asian economies from production, technological borrowing, and mutually beneficial trade to spur widespread economic development. One major exception, Japan, despite its unequal treaties with the west in the late nineteenth-century, had substantial autonomy in economic affairs compared to other Afro-Asian countries, either colonized or subject to informal imperial controls. Japan is also the most prominent Afro-Asian country to have graduated to become a highly industrialized economy.

The experience of Japanese capitalism indicates the importance of domestic political and economic control. Even when foreign aid and joint ventures are well conceived, Afro-Asian LDC officials fail to learn how to do something until they have the power to make their own decisions. The proliferations of donors and collaborators and the constraints they have imposed have weakened Afro-Asian institutions and have reduced management capacity. The correct LDC strategy must be a judicious and careful blend of facilitating foreign entry and licensing and the stimulation of local technological effort (Lall 1985, 76).

Where indigenous people supervise new capital projects (as in India and Zimbabwe but much less often in Bangladesh and Zambia), technical change can be viewed as a prolonged learning process based on experience and problem solving. Each successive piece of capital equipment is more productive, since learning advances are embodied in new machines. Learning not only takes place in research, educational, and training institutions, but also through using capital equipment. Japan, which copied western techniques for producing toys, cameras, and electronics after World War II, has become a leader in these industries through this kind of hands-on learning.

# AFRO-ASIAN CAPITALISM AND THE STATE

Like early Meiji Japan, most contemporary Afro-Asian countries lack the entrepreneurial class to provide the leadership for capitalist economic growth. Can Japan's guided capitalism provide an alternative model to socialism and statism? A limitation to applying the Japanese approach is the inadequate bureaucratic skills to spur private capitalism and plan effective public enterprise.

Nevertheless, in most low-income countries (Bangladesh, Pakistan, and sub-Saharan Africa), indigenous capital depends on collaboration with state officials or foreign capital. Afro-Asian governments may select certain local capitalists to support with monopolies or favors in exchange for concessions or even kickbacks. In other instances, local capital may front for foreign capital, which requires cooperation from local middlemen to initiate the venture. Indigenous business people receive a reward for economically unproductive activity rather than entrepreneurial ventures. Frequently local collaborators are paid for by tariff and quota protection, higher consumer prices, or by subsidies from tax revenue. In these low-income countries, where direct taxes like income taxes are not well-developed, the tax structure is usually regressive, meaning people with lower incomes pay a higher percentage of income in taxes. Any subsidy to inefficiency tends to fall disproportionately on low- to middle-income workers and farmers.

# ADVANTAGES OF PRIVILEGED
# BACKGROUNDS FOR ENTREPRENEURS

Entrepreneurs frequently profit from having some monopoly advantage, usually the result of greater opportunities such as (1) access to more economic information than competitors, (2) superior access to training and education, (3) a lower discount of future earnings, (4) larger firm size, and (5) lucrative agreements to restrict entry or output. All five are facilitated by wealth or position (Dobb 1926).

Accordingly in India, high castes, upper classes, and large business families use such monopoly advantages to become industrial entrepreneurs in disproportionate numbers. In a south Indian city, 52 percent of these entrepreneurs (in contrast to only 11 percent of blue-collar workers) were from high Hindu castes, which comprise only 26 percent of the total population. None of the entrepreneurs, but a disproportionate share of blue-collar workers, was from low-caste backgrounds (that is, Harijans and Protestant or Roman Catholic Christians). This lopsided distribution of business activity—which reflects differences in economic opportunities between the privileged and less-privileged portions of the population—is typical of many countries outside India as well.

Entrepreneurial activity is frequently a means of moving one or two notches up the economic ladder. The evidence indicates the socioeconomic status of entrepreneurs is higher than their parents' status, which is substantially higher than that of the general population.

## INEQUALITY AND ECONOMIC DEVELOPMENT

Studies on entrepreneurship indicate substantial inequality in opportunity reflected in differences in socioeconomic status, initial capital, access to government assistance, training and education, and experience. Papanek, ul Haq and Stolper, like most economists, however, assume a conflict between equality and growth. Evidence from Africa in the 1970s and the 1980s indicates otherwise as the coalitions elites formed to survive politically reduced both equality and growth.

## DC POLICIES FOR LOW-INCOME AFRO-ASIA

Since 1980, most Latin American and low-income Afro-Asian countries have experienced chronic balance-of-payments disequilibrium, requiring adjustment to attain external and internal balances. For the overwhelming majority of these countries, this adjustment required the International Monetary Fund seal of approval on macroeconomic stabilization and borrowing as a last resort from the Fund or World Bank.

The increasing competition by Central Europe, Russia, and Ukraine for loans from the DCs and international agencies reduces the share of funds for low-income countries. Yet the end of the Cold War provides the potential for the OECD increasing resources from 0.33 percent of GNP in 1989 toward the targeted 0.70 percent of GNP, with a rise in concessional funds to IDA-eligible (most low-income) countries. Moreover, a Debt Reduction Consortium (DRC), consisting of the Bank, Fund, Paris (official creditor) Club, London (private creditor) Club, and UN Development Programme can organize a concerted action by commercial creditors to write down the debt of the poorest countries.

# References

Abramovitz, Moses. 1956. "Resources and Output Trends in the United States since 1870." *American Economic Review* 44 (May): 5-23.

Acapulco Summit Meeting of Latin American Presidents. 1987. "Final Communique." 30 November.

Acharya, Shankar N. 1981. "Perspectives and Problems of Development in sub-Saharan Africa." *World Development* 9 (February): 109-47.

Adedeji, Adebayo. 1969. *Nigerian Federal Finance: Its Development, Problems, and Prospects.* New York: Africana Publishing Corporation.

Adedeji, Adebayo, ed. 1981. *Indigenization of African Economies.* London: Hutchinson.

Adelman, Irma. 1974. "On the State of Development Economics." *Journal of Development Economics* 1 (March): 1-5.

Adelman, Irma, and Morris, Cynthia Taft. 1978. "Growth and Impoverishment in the Middle of the Nineteenth Century." *World Development* 6 (March): 245-73.

Africa Leadership Forum, Organisation of African Unity, and Economic Commission for Africa. 1990. *Report on the Brainstorming Meeting for a Conference on Security, Stability, Development and Cooperation in Africa.* Addis Ababa: 17-18 November.

Ahluwalia, Montek S., Carter, Nicholas G., and Chenery, Hollis B. 1979. "Growth and Poverty in Developing Countries." *Journal of Development Economics* 6 (September): 299-341.

Alavi, Hamza, and Khusro, Amir. 1970. "Pakistan: The Burden of U.S. Aid." In Rhodes, pp. 58-71.

Alexander, Alec P. 1964. *Greek Industrialists: An Economic and Social Analysis.* Athens: Center of Planning and Economic Research.

Ali, Tariq. 1970. *Pakistan: Military Rule or People's Power.* New York: William Morrow and Company.

Allan, Pyarali G. 1969. "Tax and Fiscal Policy and its Impact on Private Enterprise." In Ghouse, pp. 211-25.

Allen, G. C. 1981. *The Japanese Economy.* London: Weidenfeld and Nicholson.

Aluko, Samuel A. 1969. "Wages, Costs and Prices." Conference on National Reconstruction and Development in Nigeria, University of Ibadan. 24-29 March.

Amin, Samir. 1972. "Underdevelopment and Dependence in Black Africa." *Journal of Peace Research* 9(2): 97-121.

Amin, Samir. 1973. *Neo-colonialism in West Africa.* Trans. by Francis McDonagh. New York: Monthly Review Press.

247

Amin, Samir. 1976. *Unequal Development: An Essay on the Social Formations of Peripheral Capitalism*. Trans. by Brian Pearce. New York: Monthly Review Press.

Anyang' Nyong'o, Peter. 1987. "The Development of Agrarian Capitalist Classes in the Ivory Coast, 1945-1975." In Lubeck, pp. 185-86.

Atiya, Aziz S. 1968. *The History of Eastern Christianity*. London: Methuen and Co.

Ayoob, Mohammed. 1971. "Pakistan's Political Development, 1947 to 1970: Bird's Eye View." *Economic and Political Weekly* 6(3, 4, and 5) (January): 199-204.

Baran, Paul A. 1952. "On the Political Economy of Backwardness." *Manchester School* 20 (January): 66-84.

Baran, Paul A. 1957. *The Political Economy of Growth*. New York: Monthly Review Press.

Baran, Paul A. 1969. *The Longer View–Essays Toward a Critique of Political Economy*. New York: Monthly Review Press.

Bardhan, Pranab K. 1974. "India." In Chenery, Ahluwalia, Bell, Duloy, and Jolly, pp. 255-62.

Barnett, A. Doak. 1981. *China's Economy in Global Perspective*. Washington, D.C.: Brookings Institution.

Barnett, A. Doak, and Clough, Ralph N., eds. 1986. *Modernizing China: Post-Mao Reform and Development*. Boulder, CO: Westview.

Bates, Robert H. 1981. *Markets and States in Tropical Africa: The Political Basis of Agricultural Policies*. Berkeley: University of California Press.

Bauer, Peter T. 1981. *Equality, the Third World, and Economic Delusion*. London: Weidenfeld and Nicolson.

Baumol, William J., Blackman, Sue Anne Batey, and Wolff, Edward N. 1989. *Productivity and American Leadership: The Long View*. Cambridge, MA: MIT Press.

Bellah, Robert N. 1957. *Tokugawa Religion*. Glencoe, IL: Free Press.

Benjamin, Nancy C., and Devarajan, Shantayanan. 1986. "Oil Revenues and the Cameroonian Economy." In Schatzberg and Zartman, eds., pp. 161-88.

Bergson, Abram, and Kuznets, Simon, eds. 1963. *Economic Trends in the Soviet Union*. Cambridge, MA: Harvard University Press.

Bergsten, C. Fred, and Cline, William R. 1985. *The United States-Japan Economic Problem*. Washington, DC: Institute for International Economics.

Berliner, Joseph S. 1971. "Bureaucratic Conservatism and Creativity in the Soviet Economy." In Riggs, pp. 569-97.

Berna, John J. 1960. *Industrial Entrepreneurship in Madras State*. New York: Asia Publishing House.

Bernstein, Henry. 1971. "Modernization Theory and the Sociological Study of Development." *Journal of Development Studies* 7 (January): 143-162.

Bettelheim, Charles. 1978. *Class Struggles in the USSR*. 2 vols. New York: Monthly Review Press.

Beveridge, Andrew A., and Oberschall, Anthony R. 1979. *African Businessmen and Development in Zambia*. Princeton, NJ: Princeton University Press.

Bhagwati, Jagdish N., ed. 1973. *Economics and World Order from the 1970's to the 1990's*. New York: Macmillan.

Bhagwati, Jagdish N. 1992. "The Fraudulent Case against Japan." *Wall Street Journal* (6 January): p. A14.

Biersteker, Thomas J. 1987. "Indigenization and the Nigerian Bourgeoisie: Dependent Development in an African Context." In Lubeck, pp. 249-79.

Bird, Richard M., and Oldman, Oliver, eds. 1975. *Readings on Taxation in Developing Countries*. Baltimore: Johns Hopkins University Press.

Bix, Herbert P. 1982. "Rethinking 'Emperor-System Fascism': Ruptures and Continuities in Modern Japanese History." *Bulletin of Concerned Asian Scholars* 14 (April-June): 2-19.

Bose, Swadesh R. 1972. "East-West Contrast in Pakistan's Agricultural Development." In Griffin and Khan, pp. 69-93.

Bowles, Chester. 1956. *The New Dimensions of Peace*. London: Bodley Head.

Brenner, Reuven, and Kiefer, Nicholas M. 1981. "The Economics of the Diaspora: Discrimination and Occupational Structure." *Economic Development and Cultural Change* 29 (April): 517-34.

"British Call Worries EC." 1992. *Wall Street Journal* (7 February): p. A10.

Bruton, Henry J. 1965. *Principles of Development Economics*. Englewood Cliffs., NJ: Prentice Hall.

Buchele, Robert B. 1972. "The Development of Small Industrial Entrepreneurs as a Tool of Economic Growth." East-West Technology and Development Institute Working Paper No. 31. Honolulu, October.

Byres, T. J., ed. 1972. *Foreign Resources and Economic Development*. London: Frank Cass.

Cairncross, Alex. 1955. "The Place of Capital in *Economic Progress.*" In Leon H. Dupriez, ed. Economic Progress: Papers and Proceedings of a Round Table Held by the International Economic Association. Louvain, France: Institut de Recherches Economiques et Sociales, pp. 235-48.

Callaway, Archibald. 1964. "Nigeria's Indigenous Education: The Apprentice System." *Odu: University of Ife Journal of African Studies* 1 (July): 1-18.

Callaway, Archibald. 1965. "From Traditional Crafts to Modern Industries." *Odu: University of Ife Journal of African Studies* 2 (July): 35-51.

Camdessus, Michel. 1991. "Managing Director's Address: A Viable Economic System is a Priority for Emerging Democracies." *IMF Survey* (29 July): 227.

Cameron, Rondo, ed. 1967. *Banking in the Early Stages of Industrialization: A Study in Comparative Economic History*. New York, Oxford University Press.

Campbell, Bonnie K., and Loxley, John, eds. 1989. *Structural Adjustment in Africa*. New York: St. Martin's Press.

Campbell, Horace, and Stein, Howard, eds. 1992. *Tanzania and the IMF: The Dynamics of Liberalization*. Boulder, CO: Westview.

Carnegie, Andrew. 1902. *The Empire of Business*. New York: Doubleday, Page and Co.

Carroll, John J. 1965. *The Filipino Manufacturing Entrepreneur: Agent and Product of Change*. Ithaca, NY: Cornell University Press.

Cesaire Aimé. 1970. "On the Nature of Colonialism." In Markovitz.

Chenery, Hollis. 1964. "Objectives and Criteria of Foreign Assistance." In Ranis, ed.

Chenery, Hollis, Ahluwalia, Montek S., Bell, C. L. G., Duloy, John H., and Jolly, Richard. 1974. *Redistribution with Growth*. London: Oxford University Press.

China. Communist Party Central Committee. Foreign Broadcast Information Service. 1979. *Daily Report-People's Republic of China*. 25 October. Supplement 032.

Chipello, Christopher J., and Chandler, Clay. 1992. "U. S. Car Makers Face Many Problems in Efforts to Attract Japanese Buyers." *Wall Street Journal* (8 January): p. A2.

Chowdhury, A.H.M. Nuruddin. 1968-1969. "The Implications of Intermediation by Income Redistribution from Rural to Urban as a Result of the Direct Controls on Pakistan's Foreign Trade." *Pakistan Economic Journal* 21(1): 72-64.

Claessens, Stijn, and Diwan, Ishac. 1989. "Liquidity, Debt Relief, and Conditionality." In Husain and Diwan, pp. 213-25.

Cleaver, Harry M., Jr. 1972. "The Contradictions of the Green Revolution." *American Economic Review* 62 (May): 177-86.

Cohen, Daniel. 1989. "How to Cope with a Debt Overhang: Cut Flows Rather than Stocks." In Husain and Diwan, pp. 229-35.

Cohen, Robin. 1974. *Labour and Politics in Nigeria, 1945-71*. New York: Africana Publishing Co.

Coleman, James S. 1958. *Nigeria: Background to Nationalism*. Berkeley: University of California Press.

Collier, Paul. 1983. "Oil and Inequality in Rural Nigeria." In Ghai and Radwan, pp. 191-217.

Collins, Orvis F., Moore, David G., and Unwalla, Darab B. 1964. *The Enterprising Man*. East Lansing, Mich.: MSU Business Studies.

Committee for Academic Freedom in Africa. 1991. "The World Bank and Education in Africa." *CAFA Newsletter* no. 2 (Fall): pp. 2-12.

Corden, W. Max, and Neary, J. Peter. 1982. "Booming Sector and Deindustrialisation in a Small Open Economy." *Economic Journal* 92 (December): 825-48.

Cornia, Giovanni Andrea, Jolly, Richard, and Stewart, Frances, eds. 1987. *Adjustment with a Human Face*. 2 vols. Oxford: Clarendon Press.

Crumpley, Charles R. T. 1992. "Gephardt Envisions Slow Progress." *Kansas City Star* (5 February): p. A9.

Cuddington, John T. 1986. *Capital Flight: Estimates, Issues, and Explanations*. Princeton Studies in International Finance no. 58, Princeton University.

Cunningham, William. 1913. *An Essay on Western Civilization in Its Economic Aspects*. New York: G. P. Putnam's Sons.

Curtin, Philip, Feierman, Steven, Thompson, Leonard, and Vansina, Jan. 1978. *African History*. Boston: Little, Brown, and Co.

Datt, Ruddar, and Sundharam, K.P.M. 1983. *Indian Economy*. New Delhi: S. Chand.

Deleyne, Jan. 1971. *The Chinese Economy*. New York: Harper & Row.

Devlin, Robert. 1989. *Debt and Crisis in Latin America: The Supply Side of the Story*. Princeton, NJ: Princeton University Press.

Diamond, Larry, Linz, Juan J., and Lipset, Seymour Martin, eds. 1988. *Democracy in Developing Countries*. Vol. 2. *Africa*. Boulder, CO: Lynne Rienner.

Diamond, Stanley. 1966. *Nigeria: Model of a Colonial Failure*. New York: American Committee on Africa.

Dillard, Dudley. 1967. *Economic Development of the North Atlantic Community: Historical Introduction to Modern Economics*. Englewood Cliffs, NJ: Prentice Hall.

Dillard, Dudley. 1979. "Capitalism." In Wilber, pp. 69-76.

Dobb, Maurice. 1926. *Capitalist Enterprise and Social Progress*. London: Routledge.

Dore, Ronald P. 1959. *Land Reform in Japan*. London: Oxford University Press.

Dos Santos, Theodore. 1970. "The Structure of Dependence." *American Economic Review* 60 (May): 231-36.

Dower, John W., ed. 1975. *Origins of the Modern Japanese State: Selected Writings of E.H. Norman*. New York: Pantheon.

Drucker, Peter F. 1989. "U. S.-Japan Trade Needs a Reality Check." *Wall Street Journal* (10 January): A10.

Dube, S. C. 1955. *Indian Village*. London: Routledge and Kegan Paul.

Eatwell, John, Milgate, Murray, and Newman, Peter. 1987. "Pareto." In *The New Palgrave: A Dictionary of Economics*. Vol. 3. New York: Macmillan.

Eberstadt, Nick. 1979a. "Has China Failed?" *New York Review of Books*, 25, no. 5 (5 April): 33-46.

Eberstadt, Nick. 1979b. "China: How Much Success?" *New York Review of Books*, 25, no. 7 (3 May): 38-44.

Eckstein, Alexander. 1975. *China's Economic Development*. Ann Arbor: University of Michigan Press.

Eckstein, Harry. 1965. "On the Etiology of Internal War." *History and Theory* 4(2): 133-63.

Economic Commission for Africa. 1983a. *Commodity Market Structures, Pricing Policies and Their Impact on African Trade*. E/ECA/TRADE/3. Addis Ababa.

Economic Commission for Africa. 1983b. "ECA and Africa's Development, 1958-2008: A Preliminary Perspective Study." Addis Ababa.

Economic Commission for Africa. 1985. *Survey of Economic and Social Conditions in Africa, 1983-1984.* E/ECA/CM.11/16. Addis Ababa, April.

Economic Commission for Africa. 1986. *Survey of Economic and Social Conditions in Africa, 1983-1984.* E/ECA/CM. 11/16. Addis Ababa.

Economic Commission for Africa. 1987. *The Abuja Statement.* Abuja, Nigeria: 15-19 June.

Economic Commission for Africa. 1989. *African Alternative Framework to Structural Adjustment Programmes for Socio-economic Recovery and Transformation [AAF-SAP].* E/ECA/CM.15/6/Rev. 3. Addis Ababa, 10 April.

Economist Intelligence Unit. 1986. *Multinational Business Quarterly,* no. 4: pp. 17-18.

Edwards, Edgar O., ed. 1974. *Employment in Developing Countries.* New York: Columbia University Press.

Eicher, Carl K., and Baker, Doyle C. 1982. *Research on Agricultural Development in Subsaharan Africa: A Critical Survey.* East Lansing, Mich.: Michigan State University International Development Paper No. 1.

Enke, Stephen. 1963. *Economics for Development.* Englewood Cliffs, NJ: Prentice Hall.

Erbe, Susanne. 1985. "The Flight of Capital from Developing Countries." *Intereconomics* 20 (November/December): 268-75.

Evans, David. 1986. "Reverse Dutch Disease and Mineral Exporting Developing Economies." *IDS Bulletin* 17 (October): 10-13.

Everett, David. 1991. "Big Three Show New, United Front against Japan." *Kansas City Star* (9 June): p. A11.

Feinberg, Richard E., Echeverri-Gent, John, Muller, Friedemann, and contributors. 1990. *Economic Reform in Three Giants.* New Brunswick, NJ: Transaction Books.

Findlay, Ronald. 1985. "Primary Exports, Manufacturing and Development." In Lundahl, pp. 218-33.

Firth, R., and Yamey, B. S., eds. 1964. *Capital, Saving, and Credit in Peasant Societies.* Chicago: Aldine.

Fischer, Stanley, and Husain, Ishrat. 1990. "Managing the Debt Crisis in the 1990s." *Finance and Development* 27 (June): 24-27.

Food and Agriculture Organization of the UN. 1991. *The State of Food and Agriculture, 1990.* Rome.

Forrest, Tom. 1987. "State Capital, Capitalist Development, and Class Formation in Nigeria." In Lubeck, pp. 307-42.

Frank, André Gunter. 1969. *Latin America: Underdevelopment or Revolution–Essays on the Development of Underdevelopment and the Immediate Enemy.* New York: Monthly Review Press.

Frankel, Francine R. 1978. *India's Political Economy, 1947-1977.* Princeton, NJ: Princeton University Press.

Franko, Lawrence G. 1983. *The Threat of Japanese Multinationals–How the West Can Respond.* Chichester: Wiley.

Galenson, Walter, and Odaka, Konosuke. 1976. "The Japanese Labor Market." In Patrick and Rosovsky, pp. 609-27.

Galtung, Johan. 1971. "A Structural Theory of Imperialism." *Journal of Peace Research* 9(2): 81-118.

Geiger, Theodore, and Armstrong, Winifred. 1964. *The Development of African Private Enterprise.* Washington, D.C.: National Planning Association.

Gerschenkron, Alexander. 1965. "Review of Hagen, *On the Theory of Social Change.*" *Economica* 32 (February): 90-94.

Ghai, Dharam, ed. 1991. *The IMF and the South: The Social Impact of Crisis and Adjustment.* London: Zed Books.

Ghai, Dharan, and Radwan, Samir, eds. 1983. *Agrarian Policies and Rural Poverty in Africa.* Geneva: International Labour Office.

Ghouse, Agha M., ed. 1968a. *Pakistan in the Development Decade: Problems and Performance.* Lahore: Economic Development Seminar.

Ghouse, Agha M. 1968b. "Profitability in Public Enterprise with Special Reference to WPIDC." In Ghouse, pp. 168-181.

Glazer, Nathan, and Moynihan, Daniel P., eds. 1975. *Ethnicity, Theory and Experience.* Cambridge, MA: Harvard University Press.

Goldman, Merle. 1989. "Vengeance in China." *New York Review of Books* 36 (9 November): 5-9.

Goldsmith, Raymond W. 1983. *The Financial Development of India, Japan, and the United States: A Trilateral Institutional, Statistical, and Analytical Comparison.* New Haven, CT: Yale University Press.

Gordon, L., and Grommers, E. 1962. *United States Manufacturing Investment in Brazil.* Boston: Harvard Business School.

Gould, Harold A. 1963. "The Adaptive Functions of Caste in Contemporary Indian Society." *Asian Survey* 3 (September): 427-38.

Gould, Thomas B. 1985. "China's Private Entrepreneurs." *China Business Review* (November-December), pp. 46-50.

Granick, David. 1961. *The Red Executive: A Study of the Organization Man in Russian Industry.* New York: Anchor Books.

Green, Reginald Herbold. 1989. "Articulating Stabilisation Programmes and Structural Adjustment." In Simon Commander, ed., *Structural Adjustment and Agriculture: Theory and Practice in Africa and Latin America.* London: Overseas Development Institute, pp. 33-51.

Gregory, Paul R., and Stuart, Robert C. 1990. *Soviet Economic Structure and Performance.* New York: Harper & Row.

Grier, William H., and Cobbs, Price M. 1968. *Black Rage.* New York: Bantam Books.

Griffin, Keith B. 1965. "Financing Development Plans in Pakistan." *Pakistan Development Review* 5 (Winter): 601-30.

Griffin, Keith B. 1969. *Underdevelopment in Spanish America–An Interpretation.* Cambridge, MA: MIT Press.

Griffin, Keith B. 1972. "Pearson and the Political Economy of Aid." In Byres, pp. 73-82.

Griffin, Keith B., and Khan, Azizur Rahman, eds. 1972. *Growth and Inequality in Pakistan.* London: Macmillan.

Gurley, John G. 1976. *China's Economy and the Maoist Strategy.* New York: Monthly Review Press.

Gurr, Ted. 1970. *Why Men Rebel.* Princeton, NJ: Princeton University Press.

Gylfason, Thorvaldur. 1987. *Credit Policy and Economic Activity in Developing Countries with IMF Stabilization Programs.* Princeton Studies in International Finance no. 60. Princeton, NJ: Princeton University Press.

Hagen, Everett E. 1962a. *On the Theory of Social Change.* Homewood, IL: Dorsey Press.

Hagen, Everett E. 1962b. "Problems of Economic Development: Discussion." *American Economic Review* 52 (May): 59-61.

Hagen, Everett E. 1968, 1975. *The Economics of Development.* Homewood, Ill.: Irwin.

Haggard, Stephan, and Kaufman, Robert R. 1989. "Economic Adjustment in New Democracies." In Nelson and contributors, pp. 57-77.

Halliday, Jon. 1975. *A Political History of Japanese Capitalism.* New York: Pantheon.

Hamid, Naved. 1970. "A Critical Appraisal of Foreign Aid Strategy." *The Punjab University Economist* 8 (December): 132-46.

Harding, Harry. 1987. *China's Second Revolution: Reform after Mao.* Washington, DC: Brookings Institution.

Harris, John R. 1967. "Industrial Entrepreneurship in Nigeria." Ph.D. dissertation, Northwestern University.

Harris, John R. 1971. "Nigerian Entrepreneurship in Industry." In Kilby, pp. 321-43.

Harris, John R., and Todaro, Michael P. 1970. "Migration, Unemployment, and Development: A Two-sector Analysis." *American Economic Review* 60 (March): 126-42.

Hayami, Yujiro. 1975. *A Century of Agricultural Growth in Japan: Its Relevance to Asian Development.* Tokyo, University of Tokyo Press.

Harsch, Ernest. 1989. "After Adjustment." *Africa Report* 34 (May/June): 47-50.

Heston, Alan, and Summers, Robert. 1968. "Comparative Indian Economic Growth: 1870-1970." *American Economic Review* 70 (May): 96-101.

Higgins, Benjamin. 1968. *Economic Development.* New York: Norton.

Higgins, Benjamin. 1979. "Development Economics in the United States: A Comment." *Journal of Development Studies* 15 (January): 243-46.

Hill, Polly. 1968. "The Myth of the Amorphous Peasantry: A Northern Nigerian Case Study." *Nigerian Journal of Economic and Social Studies* 10(2): 239-60.

Himmelstrand, Ulf. 1969. "Tribalism, Nationalism, Rank-Equilibration, and Social Structure— A Theoretical Interpretation of Some Socio-political Processes in Southern Nigeria." *Journal of Peace Research* 6(2): 81-103.

Hirschman, Albert O. 1986. "The Political Economy of Latin American Development: Seven Exercises in Retrospect." Paper for the 13th International Congress of the Latin American Studies Association. Boston. October.

Hirschmeier, Johannes. 1964. *The Origins of Entrepreneurship in Meiji Japan.* Cambridge, MA: Harvard University Press.

Hôrvat, Branko. 1974. "Welfare of the Common Man in Various Countries." *World Development* 2 (July): 29-39.

Hoselitz, Bert F. 1960. *Sociological Aspects of Economic Growth.* Glencoe, Ill.: Free Press.

Hoselitz, Bert F. 1963. "Entrepreneurship and Traditional Elites." *Exploration in Entrepreneurial History/Second Series,* 1 (Fall): 36-40.

Howe, Christopher. 1978. *China's Economy: A Basic Guide.* New York: Basic Books.

Huizinga, Harry. 1989. "The Commercial Bank Claims on Developing Countries: How Have Banks Been Affected?" In Husain and Diwan, pp. 129-43.

Humphreys, Charles, and Underwood, John. 1989. "The External Debt Difficulties of Low-income Africa." In Husain and Diwan, eds., pp. 45-65.

Huntington, Samuel P. 1968. *Political Order in Changing Societies.* New Haven, CT: Yale University Press.

Husain, Ishrat, and Diwan, Ishac, eds. 1989. *Dealing with the Debt Crisis.* Washington, DC: World Bank.

Husain, Ishrat, and Mitra, Saumya. 1989. "Future Financing Needs of the Highly Indebted Countries." In Husain and Diwan, pp. 199-209.

Hymer, Stephen. 1970. "The Efficiency (Contradictions) of Multinational Corporations." *American Economic Review* 60 (May): 441-53.

"Iacocca Blasts Japan." 1992. *Kansas City Star* (11 January): A1, A15.

Iacocca, Lee. 1991. "U. S. and Japan are Economic Foes this Time." *Kansas City Star* (3 December): D16.

Ignatius, Adi. 1988. "Fast-growing Chinese Electronics Firm Emulates IBM." *Wall Street Journal* (3 June): p. 10.

Ignatius, Adi. 1989. "Computer Whiz Leads China's Opposition." *Wall Street Journal* (22 August):, p. A1.

Imfeld, Al. 1976. *China as a Model of Development*. Trans. Matthew J. O'Connell. New York: Orbis.

Independent Commission on International Development Issues. (Brandt report). 1980. *North-South: A Program for Survival]*. Cambridge, MA: MIT Press.

India. Central Statistical Office. Department of Statistics. 1971. *Indian Economic Survey 1970-71*. New Delhi.

India. Ministry of Information and Broadcasting. 1982. *India: A Reference Annual, 1982*. New Delhi.

International Labour Office. 1972. *Employment, Incomes, and Equality: A Strategy for Increasing Productive Employment in Kenya*. Geneva.

International Labour Office, Jobs and Skills Programme for Africa. 1981. *First Things First: Meeting the Basic Needs of the People of Nigeria*. Addis Ababa.

International Monetary Fund. 1980-1992. *World Economic Outlook*. Washington, D.C.

Inukai, Ichirou. 1979. "The Kogyo Iken: Japan's Ten Year Plan, 1884." *Kyoto Sangyo University Economic and Business Review*. (May), pp. 1-100.

Inukai, Ichirou. 1981. "Experience in Transfer of Technology from the West: Lessons from False Starts." In Nagamine, pp. 79-85.

Ishikawa, Shigeru. 1981. *Essays on Technology, Employment, and Institutions in Economic Development: Comparative Asian Experience*. Tokyo, Kinokuniya.

Ishikawa, Shigeru. 1982. "Relevance of the Experiences of Japan to Contemporary Economic Development." *The Philippine Review of Economics and Business* 19: 255-79.

Jacobs, Norman. 1958. *The Origin of Modern Capitalism in Eastern Asia*. Hong Kong: Hong Kong University Press.

Jain, Shail. 1975. *Size Distribution of Income: A Compilation of Data*. Washington, D.C.: World Bank.

Javillonar, Gloria V., and Peters, George R. 1973. "Sociological and Social Psychological Aspects of Indian Entrepreneurship." *British Journal of Sociology* 24 (September): 314-28.

Jiliani, M. S. 1969. "Social Welfare and Economic Development." In Ghouse, pp. 346-69.

Jimenez, Emmanuel. 1986. "The Public Subsidization of Education and Health in Developing Countries: A Review of Equity and Efficiency." *World Bank Research Observer* 1: 111-29.

Kahler, Miles. "International Financial Institutions and the Politics of Adjustment." In Nelson and contributors, pp. 139-59.

Kaldor, Nicholas. 1975. "Will Underdeveloped Countries Learn to Tax?" In Bird and Oldman, pp. 29-48.

Keizai Koho Center. 1982. *Japan, 1982: An International Comparison*. Tokyo.

Kennedy, Paul. 1988. *African Capitalism: the Struggle for Ascendancy*. Cambridge: Cambridge University Press.

Kennedy, Paul. 1987. *The Rise and Fall of the Great Powers: Economic Change and Military Conflict from 1500 to 2000*. New York: Random House.

Khan, Taufiq M., and Bergan, Asbjorn. 1966. "Measurement of Structural Change in the Pakistan Economy: A Review of the National Income Estimates, 1949/50 to 1963/64." *Pakistan Development Review* 6 (Summer): 173-91.

Kilby, Peter. 1963. *Development of Small Industries in Eastern Nigeria*. Enugu: Ministry of Information.

Kilby, Peter, ed. 1971. *Entrepreneurship and Economic Development*. New York: Free Press.

Killick, Tony. 1978. *Development Economics in Action: A Study of Economic Policies in Ghana*. London: Heinemann.

Kindleberger, Charles P. 1965. *Economic Development*. New York: McGraw-Hill.

King, Robin A., and Robinson, Michael D. 1989. "Assessing Structural Adjustment Programs: A Summary of Country Experience." In Weeks, pp. 110-15.

Kiondo, Andrew. 1992. "The Nature of Economic Reforms in Tanzania." In Campbell and Stein, pp. 30-46.

Kitching, Gavin. 1987. "The Role of a National Bourgeoisie in the Current Phase of Capitalist Development: Some Reflections." In Lubeck, pp. 27-55.

Klein, Martin A. 1991. "Democracy Revisited." Presidential Address to the African Studies Association meeting, St. Louis. 25 November.

Knight, Frank. 1921. *Risk, Uncertainty and Profit*. Boston: Houghton Mifflin.

Knight, Frank. 1941. "Anthropology and Economics." *Journal of Political Economy* 49(2): 251-69.

Kojima, Kiyoshi. 1978. *Japanese Direct Foreign Investment: A Model of Multinational Business Operations*. Tokyo: Charles E. Tuttle.

Kravis, Irving B. 1981. "An Approximation of the Relative Real per Capita GDP of the People's Republic of China." *Journal of Comparative Economics* 5 (March): 60-78.

Kravis, Irving B., Heston, Alan W., and Summers, Robert. 1978. *United Nations, International Comparison Project: Phase II; International Comparisons of Real Product and Purchasing Power*. Baltimore: Johns Hopkins University Press.

Kravis, Irving B., Heston, Alan W., and Summers, Robert. 1983. *World Product and Income: International Comparisons of Real Gross Product*. Baltimore: Johns Hopkins University Press.

Krueger, Anne O., Arrow, Kenneth J., Blanchard, Olivier Jean, Blinder, Alan S., Goldin, Claudia, Leamer, Edward E., Lucas, Robert, Panzar, John, Penner, Rudolph G., Schultz, T. Paul, Stiglitz, Joseph E., and Summers, Lawrence H. 1991. "Report of the Commission on Graduate Education in Economics." *Journal of Economic Literature* 29 (September): 1035-53.

Krueger, Anne O., Lary, Hal B., Monson, Terry, and Akrasenee, Narongchai, eds. 1981. *Trade and Employment in Developing Countries*. Vol. 1. *Individual Studies*. Chicago, University of Chicago Press.

Kunio, Yoshihara. 1986. *Japanese Economic Development*. Oxford: Oxford University Press.

Kuznets, Simon. 1956. "Levels and Variability of Rates of Growth." *Economic Development and Cultural Change* 5 (October): 1-27.

Kuznets, Simon. 1963. "A Comparative Appraisal." In Bergson and Kuznets, pp. 345-47.

Kuznets, Simon. 1966. *Modern Economic Growth: Rate, Structure, and Spread*. New Haven, CT: Yale University Press.

Kuznets, Simon. 1971. *Economic Growth of Nations–Total Output and Production Structure*. Cambridge, MA: Harvard University Press.

Kuznets, Simon. 1972. "Problems in Comparing Recent Growth Rates for Developed and Less-Developed Countries." *Economic Development and Cultural Change* 20 (January): 185-209.

Lal, Deepak. 1983. *The Poverty of "Development Economics"*. London: Institute of Economic Affairs.

Lal, Deepak. 1990. "The Political Economy of Poverty, Equity and Growth in 21 Developing Countries: A Summary of Findings." Paper presented for the American Economic Association panel on "Economics of Growth and Stagnation." Washington, D.C. 29 December.

Lall, Sanjaya. 1974. "Less-developed Countries and Private Foreign Direct Investment: A Review Article." *World Development* 2 (April-May): 41-48.

Lall, Sanjaya. 1985. *Multinationals, Technology and Exports: Selected Papers*. New York: St. Martin's Press.

Lamb, Beatrice Pitney. 1975. *India: A World in Transition*. New York: Praeger.

Lambert, Richard D. 1963. *Workers, Factories, and Social Change in India*. Princeton, NJ: Princeton University Press.

Lancaster, Carol, and Williamson, John, eds. 1986. *African Debt and Financing.* Washington, DC: Institute for International Economics.

Landes, David S. 1949. "French Entrepreneurship and Industrial Growth in the Nineteenth Century." *Journal of Economic History* 9 (May): 45-61.

Langdon, Steven. 1980. *Multinational Corporations in the Political Economy of Kenya.* London: Macmillan.

Lardy, Nicholas R. 1983. *Agriculture in China's Modern Economic Development.* Cambridge: Cambridge University Press.

Lawrence, Peter, ed. 1986. *World Recession and the Food Crisis in Africa.* London: James Currey.

Lecaillon, Jacques, Paukert, Felix, Morrisson, Christian, and Germidis, Dimitri. 1984. *Income Distribution and Economic Development: An Analytical Survey.* Geneva: International Labour Office.

Lee, Peter Nan-shong. 1986. "Enterprise Autonomy Policy in Post-Mao China: A Case Study of Policy-making, 1978-83." *China Quarterly,* no. 105 (March): pp. 45-71.

Lee, Rensselaer W., III. 1990. "Issues in Chinese Economic Reform." In Feinberg, Echeverri-Gent, Muller, and contributors, pp. 73-102.

Lee, Teng-hui. 1971. *Intersectoral Capital Flows in the Economic Development of Taiwan, 1895-1960.* Ithaca, NY: Cornell University Press.

Lessard, Donald R., and Williamson, John, eds. 1987. *Capital Flight and Third World Debt.* Washington, DC: Institute for International Economics.

Lessinger, Johanna. 1980. "Women Traders in Madras." Unpublished paper, Barnard College.

LeVine, Robert A., and others. 1966. *Dreams and Deeds: Achievement Motivation in Nigeria.* Chicago: University of Chicago Press.

Lewis, Flora. 1988. "Oil Crisis of '73 Wreaking Economic Havoc." *Kansas City Times* (22 November): p. 7.

Lewis, John P., and Kallab, Valeriana, eds. 1983. *U.S. Foreign Policy and the Third World: Agenda, 1983.* New York: Praeger.

Lewis, Oscar. 1968. *La Vida: A Puerto Rican Family in the Culture of Poverty–San Juan and New York.* New York: Vintage Books.

Lewis, W. Arthur. 1967. *Reflections on Nigeria's Economic Growth.* Paris: Organisation for Economic Cooperation and Development.

Lewis, William. 1993. "The Secret to Competitiveness," *Wall Street Journal* (22 October): p. A11.

Lichtenstein, Peter M. *China at the Brink: The Political Economy of Reform and Retrenchment in the Post-Mao Era.* New York: Praeger.

Lippit, Victor D. 1987. *The Economic Development of China.* Armonk, NY: M.E. Sharpe.

Lipton, Michael. 1977. *Why Poor People Stay Poor: A Study of Urban Bias in World Development.* London: Maurice Temple Smith.

Lockwood, William W. 1954. *The Economic Development of Japan: Growth and Structural Change, 1868-1938].* Princeton, NJ: Princeton University Press.

Loxley, John. 1986. "The IMF and World Bank Conditionality and Sub-Saharan Africa." In Lawrence, pp. 96-103.

Lubeck, Paul M., ed. 1987. *The African Bourgeoisie: Capitalist Development in Nigeria, Kenya, and the Ivory Coast.* Boulder, CO: Lynn Rienner.

Lundahl, Mats, ed. 1985. *The Primary Sector in Economic Development.* New York: St. Martin's.

Lyons, Thomas P. 1987. *Economic Integration and Planning in Maoist China.* New York: Columbia University Press.

McClelland, David C. 1961. *The Achieving Society.* Princeton, NJ: D. Van Nostrand.

McClelland, David C. 1964. "A Psychological Approach to Economic Development." *Economic Development and Cultural Change* 12 (April): 320-24.

McClelland, David C., and Winter, David G. 1971. *Motivating Economic Achievement.* New York: Free Press.

MacDougall, G. D. A. 1960. "The Benefits and Costs of Private Investment from Abroad: A Theoretical Approach." *Economic Record* (March): 13-35.

MacEwan, Arthur. 1971. "Contradictions in Capitalist Development: The Case of Pakistan." *Review of Radical Political Economics* 3 (Spring): 42-52.

McGrath, M. D. 1977. "Racial Income Distribution in South Africa." Black/White Income Gap Research Report No. 2. Department of Economics, University of Natal, Durban, South Africa.

McGrath, M. D. 1984. "Inequality in the Size Distribution of Incomes in South Africa." Staff Paper No. 2. Development Studies Unit, University of Natal, Durham, South Africa.

Maddison, Angus. 1971. *Class Structure and Economic Growth: India and Pakistan since the Moghuls*. New York: Norton.

Mahajan, V. S. 1976. *Development Planning: Lessons from the Japanese Model*. Calcutta: Minerva Associates.

Malenbaum, Wilfred. 1982. "Modern Economic Growth in India and China." *Economic Development and Cultural Change* 31 (October): 45-84.

Manakata, Seiya. 1965. "The Course and Problems of National Education." *Developing Economies* 3 (December): 540-59.

Maniruzzaman, Talukder. 1966. "Group Interests in Pakistani Politics, 1947-1958." *Pacific Affairs* 39 (Spring/Summer): 83-98.

Manning, Patrick. 1974. "Analyzing the Costs and Benefits of Colonialism." *African Economic History Review* 1(2) (Fall): 17-22.

Markovitz, Irving Leonard, ed. 1970. *African Politics and Society: Basic Issues and Problems of Government and Development*. New York: Free Press.

Markovitz, Irving Leonard. 1977. *Power and Class in Africa: An Introduction to Change and Conflict in African Politics*. Englewood Cliffs, NJ: Prentice Hall.

Martens, André. 1988. "Structural Adjustment in the Sahel: Beyond the Point of No Return?" In North-South Institute.

Marx, Karl. 1904. *A Critique of Political Economy*. Trans. N. I. Stone. Chicago: Kerr and Co.

Meier, Gerald M. 1970. *Leading Issues in Economic Development*. New York: Oxford University Press,

Meier, Gerald M., and Baldwin, Robert E. 1957. *Economic Development: Theory, History, Policy*. New York: Wiley.

Merton, Robert K. 1972. "Insiders and Outsiders: A Chapter in the Sociology of Knowledge." *American Journal of Sociology* 78(1): 37-51.

Meyer, A. J. 1959. *Middle Eastern Capitalism: Nine Essays*. Cambridge, MA: Harvard University Press.

Mikesell, R. F. ed. 1962. *U.S. Private and Government Investment Abroad*. Eugene, OR: University of Oregon Books.

Miller, William, ed. 1962. *Men in Business: Essays on the Historical Role of the Entrepreneur*. New York: Harper & Row.

Mills, Cadman Atta. 1989. "Structural Adjustment in Sub-Saharan Africa." Economic Development Institute Policy Seminar Report *v* 18. World Bank, Washington, D.C.

Minami, Ryoshin. 1973. *The Turning Point in Economic Development: Japan's Experience*. Tokyo: Kinokuniya.

Mingat, Alain, and Psacharopoulos, George. 1985. "Financing Education in Sub-Saharan Africa." *Finance and Development* 22 (March): 35-38.

Mistry, Percy S. 1991. "African Debt Revisited: Procrastination of Progress?" Paper prepared for the North-South Roundtable on African Debt Relief, Recovery, and Democracy. Abidjan, Côte d'Ivoire, 8-9 July.

Mody, Ashoka, Mundle, Sudipto, and Raj, K. N. 1985. "Resource Flows from Agriculture: Japan and India." In Ohkawa and Ranis, pp. 266-93.

Moore, Barrington. 1966. *Social Origins of Dictatorship and Democracy*. Boston: Beacon Press.

Morawetz, David. 1977. *Twenty-five Years of Economic Development, 1950 to 1975*. Baltimore: Johns Hopkins University Press.

Morgan, Theodore. 1975. *Economic Development: Concept and Strategy*. New York: Harper and Row.

Morris, Morris D. 1967. "Values as an Obstacle to Economic Growth in South Asia: An Historical Survey." *Journal of Economic History* 27 (December): 587-607.

Morrison, Donald G., Mitchell, Robert C., Paden, John N., Stevenson, Hugh M., and others. 1972. *Black Africa: A Comparative Handbook*. New York: Free Press.

Muller, Ronald. 1973. "The Multinational Corporation and the Underdevelopment of the Third World." In Wilber, pp. 151-78.

Munakata, Seiya. 1965. "The Course and Problems of National Education." *Developing Economies* 3 (December): 540-59.

Myrdal, Gunnar. 1957. *Economic Theory and Underdeveloped Countries*. London: Gerald Duckworth.

Myrdal, Gunnar. 1968. *Asian Drama: An Inquiry into the Poverty of Nations*. 3 vols. Middlesex, Eng.: Penguin.

Nafziger, E. Wayne. 1965. "The Mennonite Ethic in the Weberian Framework." *Explorations in Entrepreneurial History/Second Series* 11 (Spring/Summer): 187-204.

Nafziger, E. Wayne. 1969. "The Effect of the Nigerian Extended Family on Entrepreneurial Activity." *Economic Development and Cultural Change* 18 (October): 25-33.

Nafziger, E. Wayne. 1970. "The Relationship between Education and Entrepreneurship in Nigeria." *Journal of Developing Areas* 4 (April): 349-60.

Nafziger, E. Wayne. 1973. "The Political Economy of Disintegration in Nigeria." *The Journal of Modern African Studies* 11 (December): 508-16.

Nafziger, E. Wayne. 1977. *African Capitalism: A Case Study in Nigerian Entrepreneurship*. Stanford, CA: Hoover Institution.

Nafziger, E. Wayne. 1978. *Class, Caste, and Entrepreneurship: A Study of Indian Industrialists*. Honolulu: University Press of Hawaii, 1978.

Nafziger, E. Wayne. 1983. *The Economics of Political Instability: The Nigerian-Biafran War*. Boulder, CO: Westview.

Nafziger, E. Wayne. 1984. *The Economics of Developing Countries*. Belmont, CA: Wadsworth.

Nafziger, E. Wayne. 1986. *Entrepreneurship, Equity, and Economic Development*. Greenwich, CT: JAI Press.

Nafziger, E. Wayne. 1988. *Inequality in Africa: Political Elites, Proletariat, Peasants, and the Poor*. Cambridge: Cambridge University Press.

Nafziger, E. Wayne. 1990. *The Economics of Developing Countries*. Englewood Cliffs, NJ: Prentice Hall.

Nafziger, E. Wayne. 1993. *The Debt Crisis in Africa*. Baltimore: Johns Hopkins University Press.

Nagamine, Haruo, ed. 1981. *Nation-building and Regional Development: The Japanese Experience*. UN Centre for Regional Development Vol. 10. Hong Kong, Maruzen Asia.

Nakamura, Takafusa. 1983. *Economic Growth in Prewar Japan*. Trans. Robert A. Feldman. New Haven, CT: Yale University Press.

Nandy, Ashis. 1972. "Review of *Motivating Economic Achievement*." *Economic Development and Cultural Change* 20 (April): 577-79.

Neary, J. Peter. 1982. "Booming Sector and Deindustrialisation in a Small Open Economy." *Economic Journal* 92 (December): 825-48.

Nelson, Joan M. 1989a. "The Politics of Pro-poor Adjustment." In Nelson and contributors, pp. 100-05.

Nelson, Joan M., and contributors. 1989b. *Fragile Coalitions: The Politics of Economic Adjustment*. New Brunswick, N. J.: Transactions Books.

Nicolson, I. F. 1969. *The Administration of Nigeria, 1900-1960; Men, Methods, and Myths.* Oxford: Clarendon Press.

Nigeria. Office of Statistics. 1963. *Annual Abstract of Statistics, 1963.* Lagos.

Nigeria. Office of Statistics. 1968. *Gross Domestic Product of Nigeria, 1958/59-1966/67.* Lagos.

Nimkoff, M.F. 1965. *Comparative Family Systems.* Boston: Houghton Mifflin Co.

Nkrumah, Kwame. 1970. *Class Struggle in Africa.* New York: International Publishers.

North, Douglas C., and Thomas, Robert Paul. 1970. "An Economic Theory of the Growth of the Western World." *Economic History Review* 23 (April): 1-17.

North-South Institute. 1988. *Structural Adjustment in Africa: External Financing for Development.* Ottawa, Can.: 25-26 February.

Nowzad, Bahram. 1990. "Lessons of the Debt Decade: Will We Learn?" *Finance and Development* 27 (March): 11-12.

Nyerere, Julius K. 1977. *The Arusha Declaration Ten Years After.* Dar es Salaam: Government Printer.

Nyerere, Julius K. 1986. "An Address." *Development and Change* 17 (July): 8-9.

Oculi, Okello. 1987. "Green Capitalism in Nigeria." In Lubeck, pp. 167-84.

Ofer, Gur. 1987. "Soviet Economic Growth: 1928-1985." *Journal of Economic Literature* 25 (December): 1773-787.

Ogbuagu, Chibuzo S. A. 1983. "The Nigerian Indigenization Policy: Nationalism or Pragmatism?" *African Affairs* 82: 241-66.

Ohkawa, Kazushi, and Ranis, Gustav, eds. 1985. *Japan and the Developing Countries: A Comparative Analysis.* Oxford: Basil Blackwell.

Ohkawa, Kazushi, Shimizu, Yutaka, and Takamatsu, Nobukiyo. 1982. " 'Agricultural Surplus' in Japan's Case: Implication for Various Possible Patterns in the Initial Phase of Development." International Development Center of Japan Working Paper No. 19, Tokyo.

Ohkawa, Kazushi, and Shinohara, Miyohei, eds. 1979. *Patterns of Japanese Economic Development: A Quantitative Appraisal.* New Haven, CT: Yale University Press.

Okigbo, Pius N. C. 1961. *Nigerian National Accounts 1950-57.* Enugu: Federal Ministry of Economic Development.

Olorunsola, Victor A. 1972a. "Nigeria." In Olorunsola, pp. 21-36.

Olorunsola, Victor A., ed. 1972b. *The Politics of Cultural Sub-Nationalism in Africa.* Garden City, NY: Anchor.

Olson, Mancur. 1982. *The Rise and Decline of Nations: Economic Growth, Stagflation, and Social Rigidities.* New Haven, CT: Yale University Press.

Organisation for Economic Cooperation and Development. 1985. *Tariffs and Nontrade Barriers.* Paris.

Organisation for Economic Cooperation and Development. 1988. *Historical Statistics, 1960-1986.* Paris.

Organisation for Economic Cooperation and Development. 1989. *Financing and External Debt of Developing Countries: 1988 Survey.* Paris.

Organisation for Economic Cooperation and Development. 1990. *Financing and External Debt of Developing Countries: 1989 Survey.* Paris.

Organisation of African Unity. First Economic Summit of the Assembly of Heads of State and Government. 1980. *Plan of Action for the Implementation of the Monrovia Strategy for the Economic Development of Africa Recommended by the ECA Conference of Ministers Responsible for Economic Development at Its Sixth Meeting Held at Addis Ababa, 9-12 April 1980.* Lagos, Nigeria: 28-29 April.

Owens, Raymond. 1973. "Peasant Entrepreneurs in an Industrial City." In Singer, pp. 133-66.

Oza, A. N. 1988. "Integrated Entrepreneurship Development Programmes: The Indian Experience." *Economic and Political Weekly* 23 (28 May): 47-53.

Pabaney, A. D., Danzig, Elliot, Nadkarni, M. S., Pareek, Udai, and McClelland, David C. 1964. "Developing the Entrepreneurship Spirit in the Indian Community." Small Industries Extension Training Institute and Harvard University, Working Report, Hyderabad, India. 20 September.

Pakistan. Ministry of Finance. 1971. *Pakistan Economic Survey [1970-71].* Islamabad.

Pakistan. Ministry of Finance. 1972. *Pakistan Economic Survey [1971-72].* Islamabad.

Panter-Brick, S. Keith. 1978. *Soldiers and Oil: The Political Transformation of Nigeria.* London: Athlone Press.

Papanek, Gustav F. 1962. "The Development of Entrepreneurship." *American Economic Review* 52 (May): 46-58.

Papanek, Gustav F. 1967. *Pakistan's Development: Social Goals and Private Incentives.* Cambridge, MA: Harvard University Press.

Pareto, Vilfredo. 1971. *Manual of Political Economy.* Trans. London: Macmillan.

Park, Robert E. 1950. *Race and Culture.* Glencoe, IL: Free Press.

Patrick, Hugh. 1967. "Japan, 1868-1914." In Cameron, pp. 239-89.

Patrick, Hugh. 1984. "Japanese Industrial Policy: A Discussion." *Manhattan Report* 5 (April): 1-16.

Patrick, Hugh and Rosovsky, Henry, eds. 1976. *Asia's New Giant: How the Japanese Economy Works.* Washington, D.C.: Brookings Institution.

Pearson, Scott R. 1970. *Petroleum and the Nigerian Economy.* Stanford, CA: Stanford University Press.

Peck, Merton, and Tamura, Shuji. 1976. "Technology." In Patrick and Rosovsky, pp. 525-85.

Pepelasis, Adamantios, Mears, Leon, and Adelman, Irma. 1961. *Economic Development: Analysis and Case Studies.* New York: Harper and Bros.

Pickett, James, and Singer, Hans, eds. 1990. *Towards Economic Recovery in Sub-Saharan Africa: Essays in Honour of Robert Gardiner.* London: Routledge.

Population Reference Bureau. 1990. *1990 World Population Data Sheet.* Washington, D.C.

Population Reference Bureau. 1991. *1991 World Population Data Sheet.* Washington, D.C.

Pound, Edward T. 1990. "Zaïre's Mobutu Mounts All-out PR Campaign to Keep His U.S. Aid." *Wall Street Journal* (7 March): p. A4.

Power, John H. 1979. "Trade Trends in Asia." *Asia Pacific Community* (Fall), pp. 44-55.

Prasad, S. B., and Negandhi, A. R. 1968. *Managerialism for Economic Development: Essays on India.* The Hague: Martinus Nijhoff.

Prebisch, Raul. 1962. "The Economic Development of Latin America and its Principal Problems." *Economic Bulletin for Latin America* 7, no. 1 (February): 1-22 (first published in Spanish in 1950).

Prybyla, Jan S. 1970. *The Political Economy of Communist China.* Scranton, PA: International Textbook.

Rabushka, Alvin, and Shepsle, Kenneth A. 1972. *Politics in Plural Societies: A Theory of Democratic Instability.* Columbus, OH: Charles E. Merrill.

Rake, Alan. 1976. "And Now the Struggle for Real Development." *African Development* 10 (December): 1263-65.

Ramana, Kanisetti Venkata. 1971. "Caste and Society in an Andhra Town." Ph.D. dissertation, University of Illinois, Urbana, Illinois.

Ranis, Gustav. 1955. "The Community-centered Entrepreneur in Japanese Development." *Explorations in Entrepreneurial History* 8(2): 80-98.

Ranis, Gustav, ed. 1964. *The United States and the Developing Economies.* New York: Norton.

Rao, N. A. 1971. "The Commercial Entrepreneurs in Visakhapatnam City: A Survey." Waltair: Department of Cooperation and Applied Economics, Andhra University.

Rao, V. K. R. V. 1983. *India's National Income, 1950-1980: An Analysis of Economic Growth and Change.* New Delhi: Sage Publications.

Rawls, John. 1971. *A Theory of Justice.* Cambridge, MA: Belknap Press of Harvard University Press.

Rhodes, Robert I, ed. 1970. *Imperialism and Underdevelopment: A Reader.* New York: Monthly Review Press.

Riggs, Frederich W., ed. 1971. *Frontiers of Development Administration.* Durham, N.C.: Duke University Press.

Riskin, Carl. 1987. *China's Political Economy: The Quest for Development since 1949.* Oxford: Oxford University Press.

Robertson, H. M. 1959. *Aspects of the Rise of Economic Individualism: A Criticism of Max Weber and His School.* New York: Kelly and Millman.

Robinson, Joan. 1942. *An Essay on Marxian Economics.* London: Macmillan.

Robinson, Sherman. 1971. "Sources of Growth in Less Developed Countries: A Cross Section Study." *Quarterly Journal of Economics* 85 (August): 391-408.

Rodney, Walter. 1972. *How Europe Underdeveloped Africa.* Dar es Salaam: Tanzania Publishing House.

Roemer, Michael. 1985. "Dutch Disease in Developing Countries: Swallowing Bitter Medicine." In Lundahl, pp. 234-52.

Rogoff, Kenneth. 1990. "Symposium on New Institutions for Developing Country Debt." *Journal of Economic Perspectives* 4 (Winter): 3-6.

Rostow, Walter W. 1961. *The Stages of Economic Growth: A Non-Communist Manifesto.* Cambridge: Cambridge University Press.

Rosen, Bernard C. 1959. "Race, Ethnicity and the Achievement Syndrome." *American Sociological Review* 24 (February): 51-52.

Rudolph, Lloyd I., and Rudolph, Susanne Hoeber. 1967. *The Modernity of Tradition: Political Development in India.* Chicago: University of Chicago Press.

Rungta, Radhe Shyam. 1970. *The Rise of Business Corporation in India, 1851-1900.* Cambridge: Cambridge University Press.

Sachs, Jeffrey D. 1989a. "Conditionality, Debt Relief, and the Developing Country Debt Crisis." In Sachs, ed., pp. 275-84.

Sachs, Jeffrey D., ed. 1989b. *Developing Country Debt and the World Economy.* Chicago: University of Chicago Press.

Sachs, Jeffrey. 1989c. "Efficient Debt Reduction." In Husain and Diwan, pp. 239-57.

Sachs, Jeffrey D. 1989d. "Making the Brady Plan Work." *Foreign Affairs* 69 (Summer): 87-104.

Samuelsson, Kurt. 1957. *Religion and Economic Action.* New York: Harper and Row.

Sandbrook, Richard. 1985. *The Politics of Africa's Economic Stagnation.* Cambridge: Cambridge University Press.

Saxonhouse, Gary. 1981. Statement to the Hearings before the Committee on Foreign Affairs and Its Subcommittee on Asian and Pacific Affairs and on International Economic Policy and Trade, House of Representatives, 96th Congress, Second Session, on H. Con. Res. 363, 16, 17, 18, 29 September and 1, 16 October 1980. Washington, D.C.: U.S. Government Printing Office.

Sayigh, Yusif A. 1962. *Entrepreneurs of Lebanon: The Role of the Business Leader in a Developing Economy.* Cambridge, MA: Harvard University Press.

Schatz, Sayre P. 1965. "n Achievement and Economic Growth: A Critical Appraisal." *Quarterly Journal of Economics* 79 (May): 234-41.

Schatz, Sayre P. 1978. *Nigerian Capitalism.* Berkeley: University of California Press.

Schatz, Sayre P. 1984. "Pirate Capitalism and the Inert Economy of Nigeria." *Journal of Modern African Studies* 22 (March): 45-57.

Schatzberg, Michael G., and Zartman, I. William, eds. 1986. *The Political Economy of Cameroon.* New York: Praeger.

Schultze, Charles L. 1983. "Industrial Policy: A Dissent." *Brookings Review* 2 (Fall): 3-12.

Schumpeter, Joseph A. 1939. *Business Cycles.* 2 vols. New York: McGraw-Hill.

Schumpeter, Joseph A. 1950. *Capitalism, Socialism, and Democracy.* New York: Harper and Row.

Schumpeter, Joseph A. 1954. *History of Economic Analysis.* New York: Oxford University Press.

Schumpeter, Joseph A. 1961. *The Theory of Economic Development.* Cambridge, MA: Harvard University Press.

Seers, Dudley. 1963. "The Limitations of the Special Case." *Bulletin of the Oxford Institute of Economics and Statistics* 25 (May): 77-98.

Seidman, Ann, and Makgetla, Neva Seidman. 1980. *Outposts of Monopoly Capitalism: Southern Africa in a Changing Global Economy.* Westport, CT: Lawrence Hill and Co.

Sen, Amartya. 1983. "Development: Which Way Now?" *Economic Journal,* 93 (December): 757-73.

Sender, John, and Smith, Sheila. 1986. *The Development of Capitalism in Africa.* London: Methuen, 1986.

Seshamani, Venkatash. 1990. "Zambia." In Adebayo Adedeji, Sadig Rasheed, and Melody Morrison, eds. *The Human Dimensions of Africa's Persistent Economic Crisis.* London: Hans Zell Publishers.

Sewell, John W., Tucker, Stuart K., and contributors. 1988. *Growth, Exports, and Jobs in a Changing World Economy.* New Brunswick, N.J.: Transaction Books.

Shi Zulin. 1987. "Individual Economy in China." Paper presented to the U.S. People to People Economics Delegation, Beijing, 14 May 1987.

Shigehara, Kumiharu. 1992. "Causes of Declining Growth in Industrialized Countries." In *Policies for Long-Run Economic Growth.* A Symposium Sponsored by the Federal Reserve Bank of Kansas City. Jackson Hole, Wyoming. 27-29 August, pp. 15-39.

Shinohara, Miyohei. 1970. *Structural Changes in Japan's Economic Development.* Tokyo: Kinokuniya.

Shinohara, Miyohei. 1982. *Industrial Growth, Trade, and Dynamic Patterns in the Japanese Economy.* Tokyo: University of Tokyo Press.

Shishido, Toshio. 1983. "Japanese Industrial Development and Policies for Science and Technology." *Science* 219 (21 January): 259-65.

Singer, Hans W. 1950. "The Distribution of Gains between Investing and Borrowing Countries." *American Economic Review* 40 (May): 473-85.

Singer, Hans W. 1990. "The Role of Food Aid." In Pickett and Singer, pp. 178-81.

Singer, Milton. 1972. *When a Great Tradition Modernizes.* New York: Praeger.

Singer, Milton, ed. 1973. *Entrepreneurship and Modernization of Occupational Cultures in South Asia.* Durham, NC: Duke University Press.

Singh, Inderjit. 1990. *The Great Ascent: The Rural Poor in South Asia.* Baltimore: Johns Hopkins University Press.

Sinha, Jai B. P. 1969. "The *n*-Ach-Cooperation under Limited/Unlimited Resource Conditions." *Journal of Experimental Social Psychology* 4: 233-46.

Sklar, Richard L. 1965. "Contradictions in the Nigerian Political System." *Journal of Modern African Studies* 3 (June): 201-13.

Smelser, Neil J., and Lipset, Seymour Martin, eds. 1966. *Social Structure and Mobility in Economic Development.* Chicago: Aldine.

Solow, Robert. 1957. "Technical Change and the Aggregate Production Function." *Review of Economics and Statistics* 40 (August): 312-20.

Sombart, Werner. 1928. *Jews and Economic Life.* Munich: Verlag von Duncker and Humbolt.

Srinivas, M. N. 1962. *Caste in Modern Indian and Other Essays.* New York: Asia Publishing House.

Stedman, Louellen, and Hakim, Peter. 1989. "Political Change and Economic Policy in Latin America and the Caribbean in 1988." In Weeks, pp. 166-74.

Stein, Herbert, and Thurow, Lester. 1983. "Do Modern Times Call for an Industrial Policy?" *Public Opinion* 6, no. 4 (August-September): 2-7.

Stewart, Frances. 1974. "Technology and Employment in LDCs." In Edwards, pp. 80-93.

Stewart, Frances. 1990. "Are Adjustment Policies in Africa Consistent with Long-run Development Needs? Paper presented to the American Economic Association, Washington D.C., 30 December.

Stolper, Wolfgang F. 1962. "The Main Features of the 1962-1968 National Plan." *Nigerian Journal of Economic and Social Studies* 4 (July): 85-91.

Stolper, Wolfgang F. 1966. *Planning without Facts: Lessons in Resource Allocation.* Cambridge, MA: Harvard University Press.

Streeten, Paul. 1973. "The Multinational Enterprise and the Theory of Development Policy." *World Development* 1 (October): 1-14.

Suttmeir, Richard P. 1974. *Research and Revolution: Science Policy and Societal Changes in China.* Lexington, MA: Heath.

Swainson, Nicola. 1977. "The Rise of a National Bourgeoisie in Kenya." *Review of African Political Economy*, no. 8 (January-April), pp. 39-55.

Swainson, Nicola. 1987. "Indigenous Capitalism in Postcolonial Kenya." In Lubeck, pp, 343-81.

Swamy, Subramanian. 1973. *Economic Growth in China and India, 1952-1970.* Chicago: University of Chicago Press.

Swamy, Subramanian. 1989. *Economic Growth in China and India: A Perspective by Comparison.* New Delhi: Vikas.

Tachi, Minoru, and Okazaki, Yoichi. 1965. "Economic Development and Population Growth—with Special Reference to Southeast Asia." *Developing Economies* 3 (December): 497-515.

Takeda, Takao. 1965. "The Financial Policy of the Meiji Government." *Developing Economies* 3 (December): 432-36.

Tan, Jee-peng. 1985. "Private Enrollments and Expenditures on Education: Some Macro Trends." *International Review of Education* 31: 103-17.

Tatanabe, Toshio. 1988. "Helping the NICs Help the World Economy." *Journal of Japanese Trade and Industry*, no. 4: pp. 10-13.

Tawney, R. H. 1926. *Religion and the Rise of Capitalism.* New York: Harcourt, Brace and Co.

"Tax Revenues." *Economist* (21 September 1991), p. 123.

Taylor, Charles Lewis, Hudson, Michael C., and others. 1972. *World Handbook of Political and Social Indicators.* New Haven, CT: Yale University Press.

Tharp, Mike. 1987. "High Schoolers in U.S. Lack Drive of Japan's But Show Spontaneity." *Wall Street Journal* (10 March): p. 1.

Thorner, Daniel, and Thorner, Anne. 1972. *Land and Labour in India* Bombay: Asia Publishing House.

Thurow, Lester. 1984. "Japanese Industrial Policy: A Discussion." *Manhattan Report.* 5 (April): 7-12.

Thurow, Lester. 1985. *The Zero-Sum Solution: Building a World-Class American Economy.* New York: Simon and Schuster.

Tidrick, Gene, and Chen Jiyuan, eds. 1987. *China's Industrial Reform.* New York: Oxford University Press.

Timberg, Thomas A. 1969. *Industrial Entrepreneurship among the Trading Communities of India: How the Pattern Differs.* Center for International Affairs, Harvard University.

Todaro, Michael P. 1977, 1981, 1985, 1989. *Economic Development in the Third World.* New York: Longman.

Turner, Terisa. 1978. "Commercial Capitalism and the 1975 Coup." In Panter-Brick, pp. 166-97.

Truell, Peter. 1990. "Latin American Nations Take Action on Debt." *Wall Street Journal* (21 March): p. A3

Tyson, Laura D'Andrea. 1992. *Who's Bashing Whom? Trade Conflict in High-Technology Industries.* Washington, DC: Institute for International Economics.

Ul Haq, Mahbub. 1966. *The Strategy of Economic Planning: A Case Study of Pakistan.* Karachi: Oxford University Press.

UNICEF. 1985. *Within Human Research: A Future for Africa's Children.* New York.

UNICEF. 1989. *The State of the World's Children.* New Delhi.

United Nations. 1988. *Financing Africa's Recovery and Recommendations of the Advisory Group on Financial Flows for Africa.* New York.

United Nations Development Programme. 1991. *Human Development Report, 1991.* New York: Oxford University Press.

United Nations Development Programme. 1993 *Human Development Report, 1993.* New York: Oxford University Press.

United Nations Development Programme and World Bank. 1989. *African Economic and Financial Data.* Washington, D. C.

United Nations General Assembly. 1986. *Programme of Action for African Economic Recovery and Development, 1986-1990.* New York.

United Nations General Assembly. 1991. *Critical Economic Situation in Africa: Final Review and Appraisal of the Implementation of the United Nations Programme of Action for African Economic Recovery and Development, 1986-1990: Report of the Secretary General.* A/46/324. New York, 6 August.

United States Agency for International Development. 1990. *Annual Report, 1990.* Washington, D. C.

United States Bureau of the Census. 1943. *Sixteenth Census of the United States: 1940.* Vol. E. *The Labor Force: Occupation, Industry, Employment and Increase.* 1, "U.S. Summary." Washington, D. C.: G.P.O.

United States Congress. Joint Economic Committee. 1988. "Gorbachev's Economic Program: Problems Emerge." A Report by the Central Intelligence Agency and the Defense Intelligence Agency presented to the Subcommittee on National Security Economics. Washington, D.C. 13 April.

United States Department of Agriculture. 1980. *Food Problems and Prospects in Sub-Saharan Africa: The Decade of the 1980's.* Washington, DC: U.S. Agency for International Development.

United States Department of Agriculture. 1986. *World Indices of Agricultural and Food Production, 1950-85.* Washington, D.C.

United States Department of Agriculture. 1988. *World Indices of Agricultural and Food Production, 1977-86.* Washington, D.C.

Uppal, Joginder S. 1977. *Economic Development in South Asia.* New York: St. Martin's Press.

Usher, Dan. 1968. *The Price Mechanism and the Meaning of National Income Statistics.* Oxford: Clarendon Press.

Vernon, Raymond. 1966. "International Investment and International Trade in the Product Cycle." *Quarterly Journal of Economics* 2 (May): 190-207.

Vogel, Ezra F. 1979. *Japan as Number One.* New York: Harper & Row.

Wallerstein, Immanuel. 1979. *The Capitalist World System.* Cambridge: Cambridge University Press.

Wangwe, S. M. 1984. "Sub-Saharan Africa: Which Economic Strategy?" *Third World Quarterly* 6(4): 1033-59.

Warner, W. Lloyd, and Abegglen, James C. 1955. *Occupational Mobility in American Business and Industry.* Minneapolis: University of Minnesota Press.

Waterbury, John. 1989. "The Political Management of Economic Adjustment and Reform." In Nelson and contributors, pp. 40-46.

Waterston, Albert. 1963. *Planning in Pakistan: Organization and Implementation.* Baltimore: Johns Hopkins University Press.

Weber, Max. 1930. *The Protestant Ethic and the Spirit of Capitalism.* New York: Charles Scribner's Sons.

Weber, Max. 1958. *The Religion of India-The Sociology of Hinduism and Buddhism.* New York: Free Press.

Weeks, John F., ed. 1989. *Debt Disaster? Banks, Governments, and Multilaterals Confront the Crisis.* New York: New York University Press.

Weisskopf, Thomas F. 1973. "Capitalism, Underdevelopment and the Future of Poor Countries." In Bhagwati, ed., pp. 117-35.

Wheeler, David. 1984. "Sources of Stagnation in Sub-Saharan Africa." *World Development* 12 (January): 1-23.

Wheelwright, E. L., and McFarland, Bruce. 1970. *The Chinese Road to Socialism: Economics of the Cultural Revolution.* New York: Monthly Review.

Whitehead, Laurence. 1989. "Democratization and Disinflation: A Comparative Approach." In Nelson and contributors, pp. 81-93.

Whyte, Martin King. 1986. "Social Trends in China: The Triumph of Inequality?" In Barnett and Clough, pp. 103-23.

Wilber, Charles K., ed. 1979. *The Political Economy of Development and Underdevelopment.* New York: Random House.

Williamson, John, and Lessard, Donald R. 1987. *Capital Flight: The Problem and Policy Responses.* Washington, D. C.: Institute for International Economics.

Wilson, Ernest T. 1991. "Making the Connection: Economic and Political Liberalization in Africa." Paper presented to the African Studies Association meeting. St. Louis. 23 November.

Wolf, Charles, Jr. 1973. "Indian Muslim Muhajirin in the Politics of Pakistan." Paper presented to the American Political Science Association annual meeting. New Orleans.

World Bank. 1971-1991. *World Debt Tables.* Washington, D.C.

World Bank. 1975. *Kenya: Into the Second Decade.* Washington, D.C.

World Bank. 1980a. *World Bank Atlas: Gross National Product, Population, and Growth Rates.* Washington, D.C.

World Bank. 1980b. *World Development Report, 1980.* Washington, D.C.

World Bank. 1980c. *World Tables, 1980.* Baltimore: Johns Hopkins University Press.

World Bank. 1981a. *Accelerated Development in Sub-Saharan Africa: An Agenda for Action.* Washington, D.C.

World Bank. 1981b. *World Development Report, 1981.* New York: Oxford University Press.

World Bank. 1982a. *World Bank Atlas: Gross National Product, Population, and Growth Rates, 1981.* Washington, D.C.

World Bank. 1982b. *World Development Report, 1982.* New York: Oxford University Press.

World Bank. 1983. *China: Socialist Economic Development.* 3 vols. Washington, D.C.

World Bank. 1984. *World Development Report, 1984.* New York: Oxford University Press.

World Bank. 1985. *World Development Report, 1985.* New York: Oxford University Press.

World Bank. 1986. *World Development Report, 1986.* New York: Oxford University Press.

World Bank. 1987a. *World Bank Atlas, 1987.* Washington, D.C.

World Bank. 1987b. *World Development Report, 1987.* New York: Oxford University Press.

World Bank. 1988a. *World Debt Tables: External Debt of Developing Countries, 1987-88 Edition.* 2 vols. Washington, D.C.

World Bank. 1988b. *World Development Report, 1988.* New York: Oxford University Press.

World Bank. 1989a. *Sub-Saharan Africa: From Crisis to Sustainable Growth.* Washington, D.C.

World Bank. 1989b. *World Development Report, 1989.* New York: Oxford University Press.

World Bank. 1990a. *World Debt Tables, 1989-90: External Debt of Developing Countries.* Washington, D.C.

World Bank. 1990b. *World Debt Tables, 1990-91: External Debt of Developing Countries.* 2 vols. Washington, D.C.
World Bank. 1990c. *World Development Report, 1990.* New York: Oxford University Press.
World Bank. 1991a. *World Debt Tables, 1991-92: External Debt of Developing Countries.* 2 vols. Washington, D.C.
World Bank. 1991b. *World Development Report, 1991.* New York: Oxford University Press.
World Bank. 1992. *World Development Report, 1992.* New York: Oxford University Press.
Yamamura, Kozo. 1968. "A Re-examination of Entrepreneurship in Meiji Japan (1868-1912)." *Economic History Review* 21 (February): 148-58.
Yasuba, Yasukichi, and Dhiravegin, Likhit. 1985. "Initial Conditions, Institutional Changes, Policy and their Consequences: Siam and Japan, 1850-1914." In Ohkawa and Ranis, pp. 19-34.
Zheng Guangliang. 1987. "The Leadership System." In Tidrick and Chen, pp. 297-312.
Zhong Jingtai. 1984. "Thirty-five Years: Socialist Construction." *China Reconstructs* (November): pp. 15-24.

## Official Publications and Documents

China. State Statistical Bureau. *Statistical Yearbook of China.* Beijing (annual).
India. Central Statistical Office. Department of Statistics. *Indian Economic Survey.* New Delhi (annual).

## Newspapers and Periodicals

*Africa Demōs.* Carter Presidential Center, Atlanta.
*African Business*
*Economist*
Economist Intelligence Unit. *Country Profile* for various countries. London (annual)
Economist Intelligence Unit. *Quarterly Economic Review* for various countries, London.
*IMF Survey*
*Japan Economic Journal*
*Kansas City Star*
*New York Times*
*Nikkei Weekly*
*Oriental Economist*
*Wall Street Journal*

# INDEX

Abuja (Nigeria)
  statement, of Economic Commission for Africa, 65
Acapulco Summit Meeting of Latin American Presidents (1987) on undermining of democracy by economic crisis, 90
Achievement
  drives, among sons of Protestants, 126-27
  motivation training, 118-19, 123-24
  orientation, 122
Action Group, as political party in Nigeria, 159
Addis Ababa (Ethiopia)
  meeting of ministers of finance and economic planning at, 65
Adedeji, Adebayo
  on support of international community for Africa, 66
Adelman, Irma
  on empirical, historical, and case study evidence, 4
Adjustment
  by Bank/Fund, resistance to, 67
  coordination of policies of, by Bank/Fund and DC donors, 64
  dampening of, in Africa, 60

and democratization, 90
economic, imposed domestically or by the IMF or World Bank, 62
emphasis on longer-term, by Bretton Woods twins, 63
essential for export surplus, 73
with growth, scope for, 71
lack of financing for, 208
loans for, to Africa and Asia, 195
process of, 74
program of, by IMF, 78
programs of, achievement of goals of, 65
programs of, by Africa, 93
programs of, by Bank/Fund, 170, 215
programs of, by democratic governments, 91
programs of, by Sub-Saharan states, 80
programs of, of World Bank and International Monetary Fund, 66
programs of, setbacks to literacy and education during, 200
programs of, temporary suspension of, 89
time for, 209
time horizon for programs of, 92

Administrative
  agencies, lack of information by,
    33
  costs, of performance indicators,
    34
  service, of colonial governments,
    11
Administrators
  maintenance of influence by, with-
    out costs of colonialism, 49
Africa
  bourgeoisie in, weakness of, 87
  economic situation of, 38
  effect of inaction on, 93
  governments in, and capitalist
    development, 81, 84-88
  Leadership Forum, rejection of
    donor biases toward multi-
    party democracies, 90
  long-term development objectives
    of, 64-65
  neglect of agriculture by govern-
    ment in, 49
  roots of food crisis in, 47, 49.
  see also Sub-Saharan Africa
African Alternative Framework to
    Structural Adjustment Pro-
    grammes for Socio-Economic
    Recovery and Transformation
    (AAF-SAP) (1989), 65
African
  capitalism, 81-88
  capitalism, distortion of, 84
  socialism, 51
Africanization
  of civil services, 52
  of jobs, 50
Agarwala, Ramgopal
  on the failure of international
    agencies in Africa, 66
Agnelli, Umberto
  on restrictions on Japanese auto-
    mobiles by Europe, 240

Agricultural
  cooperatives, in China, 167
  experiment stations, in Japan, 196
  export marketing board surpluses,
    54
  exports price, in Cameroon, 55
  exports, revenue from, in Nigeria,
    162
  growth, in China, compared to
    India, 173
  growth, in India, 169
  growth, in Japan, 205
  incomes, compared to industrial
    incomes, 53
  output, drop in, by India, 7
  output, effect of energy crisis on,
    40
  output, growth in, in Indonesia,
    42
  production, less centralization of,
    19
  productivity, slow growth of, 31-
    32
  productivity, as lower than indus-
    trial productivity, in Africa, 88
  real wages, in Japan, 210
  reforms, in China, 189
  research and technology, lack of,
    in China, 182
  sector, producing for village, 212
  sector, transfer of resources from,
    in Pakistan, 157
  surplus, in African countries, 207
  system, based on serfs, 26
  techniques, in China, 180
  underdevelopment, contribution
    of colonial legacy to, 83
Agriculture, capitalist
  in Africa, 85
  collectivization of, 18
  decollectivization of, 31
  incentives in, in Nigeria, 41
  investment in, in Indonesia, 42

large-scale, favoring of, 161
neglect of, in Africa, 49
redistribution of resources from, 155
squeezing of capital from, 206
technical progress in, 211
transfer of resources from, 158
use of oil revenues for, 56
Ahluwalia, Montek S.
on poverty rates in India and China, 178
Aid
consortium for, contribution of, to Pakistan, 149
dependence on, 50
economic, to the Sub-Sahara, 77
financial and technical, China's dependence on, 167-68
link of, to promotion of U.S. exports, 89
military, economic, and technical, 150
official dependence on, for patronage, 86
to Sub-Saharan Africa, 70
as unproductive, 19. *See* Foreign
Alexander, Alec P.
on fathers of Greek industrialists, 132
Alfonsin, Raúl
on current economic conditions, 61
Amin, Samir
on Côte d'Ivoire's transitory rapid economic growth, 83-84
on social development of Africa's peripheral capitalism, 81
Anglo-American
economists, 4, 22-23
development economics, 6
role of, in stable world order, 62
Anyang' Nyong'o, Peter
on origin of ruling classes in post-colonial Africa, 83

Apartheid
support of, by foreign investment, 50
Appreciation
of naira, 55
Apprentice
training, for prospective entrepreneurs, 135
Argentina
as a leading LDC debtor, 67
Aristocracy
landed, political influence of, 207
landed, reduction of power of, 27
Northern ruling, in Nigeria, 149, 153
Armenians
as entrepreneurs, 128
Arusha Declaration (1967)
in Tanzania, 51
Assistance, 6
from government, in India, 112, 113
political, military, and economic, to Nigeria, 151
technical and management, 212
Austerity
African, in face of internal political opposition, 66
years of, in Africa, 60
Australia
average income in, 28
Authoritarian
personality, in traditional society, 124
regimes, compared to liberal democratic regimes, 90
Authority
of managers, in China, 34
Autonomy
in economic affairs, of Japan, 194
Awami League
in East Pakistan, 147
Awolowo, Obafemi, 54

Ayub Khan
  government of, in West Pakistan,
    156
  rule of, 155

Baker, James A., III
  initiative by, 76
  list of severely indebted countries
    by, 61
  U.S. proposal by, 75
  as U.S. Secretary of the Treasury,
    60
Balance-of-payments
  crises, from growing food and
    capital imports, 169
  crises, linked to reducing social
    programs, 62
  deficit, removal of, 209-10
  impact, of oil, 160
  problems, with use of capital-
    intensive technology, 196.
  *see also* International
Balance
  of trade, 208
  on goods and services, 73
Bangladesh
  bid for independence by, 143
  low ranking in HDI of, 39
  slow growth of, 35
  secession from Pakistan of, 39
Bankers
  from U.S., 75.
  from West, 78
Banking
  system, organized by Japan, 195
Banks (commercial)
  concentration of, 205
  credit ratings of African countries
    among, 70
  control of, by large industrial fam-
    ilies, 106
  debt to, 73
  delinking of, to IMF approval, 80

dominance of, by foreign capital,
    151
  insistence on SALs before debt
    rescheduling, or lending by, 63
  LDC debts to, 67
  lending by, 59, 76
  obligations to, by Mexico, 60
  rescheduling of claims by, 61
Baran, Paul
  on agricultural production, 19
  analysis of monopoly capitalism in
    the United States by, 13
  on entrepreneurs, 15-16
  on entrepreneurship, as apologet-
    ics for capitalist exploitation,
    23
  on human nature, 16
  on society with new social ethos,
    18
  on worker and peasant revolution,
    17
Bauer, Peter T.
  clarity of value premises of, 21
  in defense of inequality, 19
Beijing Stone Company
  as producer of electronic equip-
    ment, 32
Belgium
  physical violence in, 28
  sustained growth of, 25
Bellah, Robert N.
  on Japanese religion and eco-
    nomic growth, 127
Bengali
  elite, cooperation of, with West
    Pakistanis, 160
  interests, view of class struggle by,
    153
  upper and middle classes, 162.
Berna, John J.
  on lack of social variables in
    explaining entrepreneurship,
    118

on varied backgrounds of industrialists, 131

Bernstein, Eduard
on ameliorative trends in capitalism, 13

Bettelheim, Charles
on class conflict under actually existing socialism, 13
on new ruling class in the USSR, 19

Bhagwati, Jagdish N.
on "aggressive unilateralism" by the United States in trade, 238

Biafra
balance-of-payments impact of oil in, 160
demand for oil royalties by, 152
gain to, from oil output, 161
unsuccessful attempt to gain independence by, 143

Biersteker, Thomas J.
on managerial control of foreign capital in Nigeria, 84

Bilateral
lenders, and debt, 78

Birth rate
of Japan and Afro-Asia, 210-11

Bolivia
lack of ability of, to service debts, 80

Boomerang effect
of investment by Japanese MNCs in other Asian countries, 239-40

Booming
export commodity, 54

Bourgeoisie
in China, positions of, 134
in coalition with proletariat, 83
indigenous, in Kenya, 84
of Meiji Japan, experience of, 203
native, in British colonies, 145
petty, in Kenya, 87

power to the, 27
weak, in Africa, 85

Brady, Nicholas
plan of, 76, 79

Brahmins
in industrial entrepreneurship, 108, 109, 118

Brandt, Willy
commission of, on IMF policy, 66

Brazil
as a leading LDC debtor, 67
severely malnourished in, 184

Britain (Great Britain)
cancellation of bilateral debt at Trinidad terms by, 77
in construction of India's modern financial system, 204
in the eighteenth and nineteenth-centuries, as model, 8
growth of special interests in, 31
intrusion into Southern Nigeria and East Bengal by, 145
as low performer, 227
sustained growth of, 25. *See also* England, United Kingdom

British
administration
in Nigeria, 82
agricultural policy in Eastern Africa, 83
colonialists, policies of, to meet demands of the nationalist movements, 49-50
colonial rule, India under, 7
creation, of differences among people ruled, 146
diplomats, in Nigeria, 151
economists, in LDCs, 22
government, as majority shareholder in Shell-BP, 152
military power in India, umbrella of, 105
policy, and Indian caste system, 12

private capital, in Nigeria, 149
rule, legacy of, 146
Bruton Henry,
  as textbook author, 4
Buchele Robert,
  on motivation programs, 123
Bukharin Nikolai,
  on decentralized socialism and
    the international class struggle,
    13
Bureaucratic
  class, dominance of, 51
  contacts, as important to Kenyan
    capitalists as production
    knowledge, 86
  leadership, 52
Business
  classes, weaknesses of, 51
  communities, in Pakistan, 132
  cycle index, in DCs, 74
  experience, in Meiji Japan, 87
  families, children from, 19
  houses, in India, 130, 131
  interests by foreigners in Nigeria,
    151
Buyers' market
  in China, 35

Calling
  or secular vocation, 26
Calories, consumption of
  in China, 184
  in China and India, 180, 182
  in Sub-Saharan Africa, 47
Calvet, Jacques
  on restrictions on Japanese auto-
    mobiles by Europe, 240
Cambodia
  slow growth of, 35
Camdessus, Michel (IMF Managing
    Director)
  on adjustment and democracy, 89
Cameroon

growth of, 38
growth of, compared to Nigeria,
  54-56
propensity to flee from additional
  external debt in, 75
terms of trade in 1980 of, 39
Canada
  annual growth rates of real GNP
    per capita of, 30
  average income in, 28
  sustained growth of, 25
Capital
131
  abundant rich countries, technol-
    ogy designed for, 50
  access to, in India, 97, 102, 105,
    106, 112
  access, to indigenization, 87
  accumulation, squeezed from agri-
    culture, 206
  accumulation, by entrepreneur, 16
  accumulation, of capitalist econo-
    mies, 26
  accumulation, prodigious rate of,
    27
  accumulation, rate of, 17
  allocation, in China, 34
  flight, 209
  flight, from LDCs, 75
  flows, 76
  formation, promotion of, 21
  goods, development of, 64
  goods, investment in, in India, 169
  goods, production of, in China, 167
  intensive approaches of the United
    States and Canada, 196
  intensive modern manufacturing,
    212
  intensive technology, emphasis on,
    213
  net transfers of, in Sub-Saharan
    Africa, 70

short world, funds in, 77
stock per person, 75
utilization, political conflict, and
  corruption, 92
*see also* Foreign
Capitalism
analysis of, by Marx, 17
colonial, and rising production of
  consumer goods, 81-82
definition of, 125
as engine for rapid economic
  growth, 28
guided, as model, 201
guided, in Japan, 217
independent of foreigners, in
  Africa, 83
indigenous, thriving of, 88
in Kenya, vulnerability of, 84
growth of, 16
modern, 27
modern economic growth under, 29
modern, entrepreneur as benefi-
  ciary from, 15
modern, growth of, 26
reformed, 18
rise of, 25
rise of, and Protestant Reformation, 126
Capitalist
class, in Africa, 87
countries, dependency on, 148
economic growth, 82
elite, in Pakistan, 150
growth, 81
system, Britain as the center of,
  145
world, Pakistan as allied to, 149
*see also* Foreign
Capitalists
in alliance with political elites, 50
in China, 134
emerging, in Pakistan, 157
support of, by Kenyan state, 86

Carnegie, Andrew
as United States folk hero, 132
Cartel
of debtors, fear of, 75
of international policy enforcement, 195
loan and policy, 80
policy and lending, 92-93
Carter, Nicholas G.
on poverty rates in India and
  China, 178
Caste
concept of, 98-99
differences of, in British colonies,
  146
and *n* Ach, 123
as not conducive to economic
  development, 127
of entrepreneurs, 130
occupational choices assigned by,
  118
of Schumpeterian entrepreneurs,
  131
system of, in India, 12
of workers, 132
Central Europe
death of Marxism in, 12
Cesaire, Aimé, on trampled cultures,
  82
Chenery, Hollis B.
on poverty rates in India and
  China, 178
Chiefs
indigenous, effect of, on nationalism, 145
native, in Nigeria and South Asia,
  11
Child, 124
rearing, achievement orientation
  in, 119
Chile
secondary market prices of bank
  debts in, 59

China
    average food consumption in, 183
    bourgeoisie in, 134
    decontrol of prices in, 31
    development performance of, in
        comparison to India, 38
    development patterns in, after
        market reforms, 186
    disastrous food policies in, 39
    economic performance of, 167
    growth of, 174
    hunger rates in, 184
    individual economy and urban
        reform in, 32
    industrial reform in, problems of, 33
    industry in, planning approach to,
        34
    leaders of, control of industrial
        innovation by, 135
    life expectancy at birth in, 185
    literacy and schooling in, 186
    as medium ranking in HDI, 39
    policy of "walking on two legs" of,
        213
    rank of, on human freedom index
        (HFI) compared to India, 189-
        90
    rapid yearly growth in, 35
    recent market reforms by, 13
    religion in, and modernization,
        127
    revolutionary leaders in, 18
    see also Mao
Chinese Academy of Social Sciences
    on buyers' market effect on
        improving China's industrial
        performance, 35
Chinese Democratic Forum
    as opposition to Chinese govern-
        ment, 32
Civil service
    Africanization of, 52
    salaries in, 50

Class(es)
    antagonism of, after revolution,
        17-18
    associated with commerce, in Pak-
        istan, 147
    composition of, in Nigeria and
        Pakistan, 152
    conceptual matrix not oriented
        toward, 122
    conflict of, crosscutting of, 159
    differences, in British colonies, 146
    discrepancies of, 52
    dominant, lack of desire for ade-
        quate planning machinery by,
        157
    interest of, as basic determinant of
        behavior, 17
    interests and conflict of, Hagen
        and Baran on, 15
    interest of, in ethnic and regional
        enmities, 143
    and n Ach, 123
    origin of, 130
    origins of, of entrepreneur, 129
    ruling and oppressed, 14
    of Schumpeterian entrepreneurs,
        131
    under socialism, 18
    structure of, in Pakistan, 149
    structure of, in Pakistan and Nige-
        ria, 148
    struggle between, international, 13
    struggle of, against encrusted
        bureaucracy, in China, 168
    struggle of, between oppressors
        and oppressed, 51
Clifford, Hugh
    on Nigerian nation, 146
Collectivization
    of agriculture, 18
Collins, Orvis F.
    on income of sample entrepre-
        neurs, 133

on origins of entrepreneurs in
  Michigan, 130
Colonialism
  adverse effect of, 7
  disruption of economies by, 11
  impact of, on the DCs and LDCs,
    6
  legacy, contribution of, to agricul-
    tural underdevelopment, 83
  reorientation of trade during, 8
  roots of food crisis, during, 47, 49
  strengthening of powerful group
    during, 12
  and Western capitalism, 28
Colonial
  burden, policies to ease, 50
  investment, in infrastructure, 82
  factors, in secessionist conflict, 144
  identification, with traditional pol-
    itical entities, 159
  period, continuity through, 49
  period, foreign investment during,
    9
  periods, transmission of class
    standing from one generation
    to another during, 51
  policy, discouragement of indus-
    trial growth by, 148
  possessions, polities and econo-
    mies of, 147
  rule, effect of, on nationalism and
    communalism, 145
  rule, in Africa and Asia, 195
  trade patterns, in Nigeria, 149
  type relationship between Bengali
    elite and West Pakistan, 160
Committee for Academic Freedom
  in Africa (CAFA)
  on academic rights and World
    Bank/IMF policies, 63
Communal conflict
  as feature of modern political life,
    143

competition, for employment and
  business activity, in Nigeria,
  162
competition, for jobs, in Nigeria,
  155
economic competition, 159
nationalism, 146
nexus, in India, 120
Communes
  in China, 167
Communist Party
  of China, 167
  of China, Eleventh Central Com-
    mittee of, 31
  dominance by, of state, 13
  as ruling class in the USSR, 19
Comparative advantage
  based on technological advantage,
    199
  in British industry, 8
Competition
  limitation of, in China, 34
Comprador
  role, of local business in Africa, 84
Concentration
  of export commodities, 71
  of exports, 50
  of land, 11
  of technology, 10
  of wealth, 19
  *see also* Foreign
Concerted
  action, by creditors and debtors, 79
  efforts, by DCs, 80
Concessional
  funds, by IMF, 80
Conditionality
  by donors, 90
  by IMF, 93
Conflict
  economic and political, 18
  between forces and relations of
    production, 14

of interest, between rich and poor
nations, 11-12
of interest, lack of, between
workers and capitalists, 17
between ruling coalition and
masses, 16
see also Interest
Congress Party
in India, 167, 169
Consumer
goods, increase in supply of, in
China, 35
goods, as reward for producers, 32
Corpus Christianum, as all-encompassing religious authority, 27
Côte d'Ivoire
as Africa's most developed state, 84
cocoa farmers in, 18
debt moratorium by, 60
dependence on external aid by
officials in, 86
economy of, open to foreign trade
and investment, 83
integration of, into world market,
82
rapid growth of, 85
secondary market prices of bank
debts in, 59
as severely indebted country, 61
slowdown after 1973 in, 84
strong support for indigenous capitalists in, 85-86
Counterrevolutionary
coalition, common interest of, 17
Creative destruction
of market, 33
Credit
by IMF, 76
rating, of Sub-Sahara, 61
worthiness, lack of, by African
countries, 70
worthiness, of low-income Sub-
Sahara, 68

Creditors
concerted action by, 79
sharing of benefits by, 80
Cultural Revolution (1966-76)
(China)
disruption of production during,
168
disruption of schooling during,
187
management during, 135

Debt
burden, LDC carrying of, 89
cancellation, 77
crises, loss of Latin American presidential elections because of,
90
crisis in Africa, 59-80
crisis, and curtailment of poverty
programs, 50
crisis, as dominant factor in relations between DCs and LDCs,
59
equity swaps, harm of, 79
export ration, 69
overhang, 62
overhang, in an LDC, 78
overhang, in Sub-Saharan Africa,
60, 61
payments, default on, 93
rescheduling of, 76
service, increase in, from oil price
hike, 41
service obligations, in Pakistan,
150
service obligations, in Sub-
Saharan Africa, 70
service ratio, in LDCs, 67
service, reduction in, 76
servicing, in Nigeria, 151
servicing problems in LDCs, 60
servicing, restrictions on, by debtors, 92

writedowns, for Central Europe, 77

writeoffs and writedowns, 75, 76

writeoffs, for Sub-Saharan countries, 80

Debtors
concerted action by, 79

Deficits
external, and need for adjustment, 62
external, of Sub-Saharan Africa, 70
external, reduction of, 63
food, in India and China, 39
international, in Sub-Saharan Africa, 59

Demand labor
increase in, 210
reduction of, under structural adjustment, 63
restrictions on, 208

Democracy(ies)
adverse effect of Africa's debt on, 62
Bank/Fund policies and, 63
lack of, in pre-World War II Japan, 216
LDCs as, 215
in Sub-Saharan Africa, 89

Democratization
compatibility of adjustment and reform with, 90
of Japanese political economy, 223
sacrifice of, 41

Deng Xiaoping
as China's Communist party leader, 31
on China's lagging agricultural research, 182
as China's leader, 168
repudiation of Mao's egalitarian slogans by, 189

Dependence
economic, legacy of, 10
economic, reduction of, by African states, 81
on one to two exports, 56

Dependency
post-colonial, impact of, 7
theorists of, 81, 83

Depreciation
currency, in Cameroon, 55
currency, to solve international payments problems, 66
yen, vis-à-vis U.S. dollar, 215

Deprivation
economic, in ethnic and regional enmities, 143

Devaluation
control of size and timing of, 210
of currency, 62
of currency, as threat to vested interests, 91
effect of, on current account, 208
effect of, on trade balance, 209
under Bank/Fund adjustment programs, 215

Diamond, Larry
on authoritarian compared to democratic regimes, 90

Dickens, Charles
on starvation and destitution, 28

Direct
taxes, in Africa, 74-75

Director's law
on income transfers, 20

Dissenters
in development economics, 3

Distribution
income, 18
income, emphasis on, 21
of income, empirical data on, 129
income, evaluation of, 22
income, for China and India, 177
income, improvement of, 53, 169

of income, in Japan and United
    States, 222
income, lack of trend on, in India,
    189
philosophy of, 20
see also Inequality, Redistribution
Dobb, Maurice
    on capitalism and improved levels
        of living, 28
Domar, Evsey D.
    general synthesis of, by Higgins,
        13
Donor
    biases of, toward multiparty
        democracies, 90
Dore, Ronald P.
    on agrarian poverty and Japanese
        military expansion, 207
Dual economy
    in Meiji Japan, 212
Dutch disease
    effect of, on export revenues, 54

East Asia
    as fastest growing LDC region, 35
East Bengal (Bengal)
    coastal areas of, 145
    generation of foreign exchange
        earnings by, 161
    as hurt by the economic policies
        of Pakistan, 39
    see also Bengali
East Pakistan
    competition with West by, 159
    discontent in, 163 low proportion
        of foreign exchange use by,
        161
    major grievances of, 162
    majority in, neutralization of, 160
    redistribution of income from, 157
Eastern Africa
    British agricultural policy in, 83

Eastern Nigeria
    allocation of oil revenue to, 161
    crude-oil industry in, 162
    discontent of, 160, 163
    resentment of, 159
East Indian Company
    in East Pakistan, 145
East Pakistan
    frustration of younger men in, 154
Eckstein, Alexander
    on Sino-Indian comparisons, 173
Economic Commission for Africa
    African alternative to SAP by, 65
    on Africa's economic condition,
        38
    on holistic alternative to structural
        adjustment policies, 66
    projection to 2008, 49
    recommendation of, on Lagos
        Plan of Action, 64
    rejection of donor biases toward
        multiparty democracies, 90
Education
    in colonies in Afro-Asia and
        Japan, 200
    as component of HDI, 38
    of entrepreneur, and firm survival,
        113
    of entrepreneurs, 102, 105, 108,
        131, 136
    of entrepreneurs, with high pater-
        nal economic status, 111
    in families and communities with
        wealth and position, 98
    improved, for African workers, 82
    and inequality, in Africa, 52
    investment in, by Japan, 216
    in Japan, 228
    and paternal class, 122
    per capita expenditure on, in
        Africa, 65
    in primary schools and higher
        institutions, 53

in science, in Japan, 30
for sons of African elites, 51
of sons from large business fami-
    lies, 107
stress on, by Mao Zedong, 13
*see also* Primary
Egalitarianism
commitment of Tanzania to, 51
Mao's slogans concerning, 189
Egypt
aid to, 77
"debt for war" swap for, 76
Election
boycott, in Nigeria, 155
Elite(s)
African, in alliance with the
    Bank/Fund, 63
African ruling, radical conscious-
    ness directed at, 51
Afro-Asian, 22
civilian political, in Nigeria, 55
compliant political, 11
concentrated business, 201
creation of, by colonial adminis-
    trators, 83
dominant, 123
economic competition among, 143
fathers of, 133
feudal and business, in West Pak-
    istan, 153
governing, in Nigeria, 151
Ibo, attempt by, 148
landed and industrial, in Pakistan,
    152
leader of nationalist movements,
    49-50
of low-income societies, 15
patronage for, 50
political and military, in East and
    Federation, 160
political, bureaucratic, and busi-
    ness, targets of, 5
ruling, and MNCs, 52

ruling, composition of, 56
ruling, communal identification
    by, 144
ruling, control of business by, 156
ruling, development goals of, 3
ruling, diversion of farm land by, 53
ruling, in Africa, bearing of blame
    by, 64
ruling, maintenance of power by,
    150
ruling, of high-ranking politicians,
    military officers, and govern-
    ment administrators, 85
ruling, of Nigeria and Pakistan,
    152, 158
ruling, power and privileges of,
    157
ruling, premises of, 20
ruling, undermining of, 51
ruling, use of overseas expansion
    by, 207
Sub-Saharan, strategies pursued
    in interest of, 62
transfer of, 18
*see also* Ruling
Empire
and development of Europe, 7
Employment
sacrifice of, 41
Engels, Friedrich
skillful propagation of Marxist
    thought by, 13
England
advancement of capitalism in, 125
entrepreneurs of, 128
Industrial Revolution in, 132
landed aristocracy in, 207
physical violence in, 28
political revolution in, 27
*see also* Britain
Enlightenment
as period of great intellectual
    activity, 27

Entrepreneur(s)
assistance by state for, 202
celebration of, 23
as contributors to economic
growth, 117
education of, 136
with high paternal economic status, 113
identification of, 98
independent, in Africa, 84
indigenous, public funds for promotion of, 87
in India, origins of, 97-115
as key figure in technological
advance, 13-14
manufacturing and commercial, of
Pakistan, 150
among marginal communities,
127-28
need for achievement among, 120-
23
planning for, 87
programs for, in Japan, 203
prospective, child rearing of, 119
role of industrial extension centers
in development of, 118-19
socioeconomic class background
of, 134
supply of, 15-16
in United States, 132
Equality
and growth, conflict between, 20
Erbe, Susanne
estimates by, of propensity to flee,
75
Ethiopia
low ranking of HDI in, 39
Ethnic
basis, distribution of benefits on,
51-52
communities, in Nigeria and Pakistan, 159

discrepancies, transfer of potential
hostility to, 52
enmities, 143
model of secessionist conflict, 144
nationalism, growth in strength of,
146
Europe
expropriation of Africa's surplus
by, 81
GNP per capita for, 28
intellectual activity in, 27
squalor and poverty in, 19
trade activity in, 26
European
businessmen, as Protestant, 125
farmers, land transfers from, in
Kenya, 87
oligopolies and restrictions, 82
multinational corporations, in
Kenya, 84
settlers, in Eastern Africa, 83
Exchange
rate prescriptions, validity of, for
Africa, 65
rates, spur of peasant production
through, 49
see also Foreign
Export(s)
of agriculture, 54
of cocoa, in Ghana, 70
commodity concentration of, 71
crops, exclusion of Africans from,
83
by debt reschedulers, 65
dependence on, 56
excessive taxation of, in Africa, 88
expansion of, in Africa, 84
induced development of, 8
international balance on goods,
services, and transfers as percentage of, 73
investment by foreigners in, 82

of maize, other coarse grains, soybeans, and raw cotton, by
China, 31
opportunities for, in Japan, 195
prices of, 55, 60
promotion of, 214
promotion of, from U.S., 89
promotion of, under adjustment
policies, 66
of primary products, 50
purchasing power of, 61
purchasing power of, in Nigeria,
92
trap of, for Afro-Asia, 215
trap of, in Africa, 74
Extended
family, effect on entrepreneurship
by, 135

False
consciousness, creation of, 17
signals to enterprises, in China, 34
Family
background, of Vaishyas, 105
economic status, of entrepreneurs,
102
enterprise, in developing countries, 135
firms, movement from plant to
plant within, 107
milieu of those with low *n* Ach,
122
nexus in India, 120
Famine
in India and China, 184, 185
Farm
population, density of, 211
prices, benefits of, 54
prices, repression of, 71
Farmers, in Africa, supply elasticity
of, 209
burden of tariffs, high consumer
prices, or subsidies on, 50

small, and herders, neglect of, 83
*see also* Peasants
Fascism
in Japan, 223
Federalism
in Pakistan and Nigeria, 147
Fei, John C.H.
model of, unlimited supply of
labor in, 211
Fel'dman
model of, 169
Females
behavior at work by, 137
as industrial wage labor, 210
*see also* Women
Feudal
economy, 26
lords, 27
property relationships, in Japan,
30
Finance
acquisition of, and LDC subordination, 9
concentration in, 205
minister of, from Africa, 78
ministers, in Africa, complaints of,
89
system of, in India and Japan, 204
Fischer, Stanley
on LDCs carrying debt burden
until attainment of political
will, 89
reform and adjustment by debtor
countries, 78
Food
consumption levels, in China and
India, 183
crisis, roots of, 47, 49
deficits, in India and China, 39
demand, rise in, 211
grain output per person, in India
and China, 180, 181, 188

grains in the Sub-Sahara and
India, 47
output per capita, fall of, in Sub-
Saharan Africa, 81
output per capita, in India and
China, 31
prices, in urban areas, 53
prices of, in Japan, 206
production and consumption,
China and India, 182
production in China, 184
production per person in Sub-
Saharan Africa, 47
production, reductions in, 64
Foreign
advisors and teachers, utilized by
Japan, 196
aid and investment, minimal
reliance on, 169
aid, from Consortium, 150
aid, no reliance on, by Japan, 195
aid, potential recipients of, 6
capital, alliances of, 74
capital and technology, import of,
198
capital, entry into Africa of, 50
capital, official dependence on, for
patronage, 86
capital, flows of, 92
capital, power of, 18
capital, power of access to, 51
capitalists, in Nigeria, 158
concentration, reduction of, 52
creditors, loans by, 75
economists, drawing up of Nigerian plan by, 156
direct investment, restrictions on,
197
enterprise, nationalization of, 87
exchange, allocation of, between
East and West, 153
exchange decontrols, to improve
balance of trade, 209

exchange distortions, in Africa, 75
exchange earnings, 73, 161
exchange policy, in Pakistan, 157-
58
exchange price, in Pakistan, 208
exchange price, in Roemer model,
54
exchange prices set below market-
clearing rates, 84
exchange rate equilibrium, in
Japan, 214
exchange rates, repression of, 71
exchange reserves, 56
exchange, to redistribute resources, 155
investment and trade, in Pakistan,
149
investment, as advantageous to
DCs and LDCs, 9
investment, climate for, 14
investment, discouragement of, by
Japan, 194
investment, from west, 50
investment, in Sub-Saharan
Africa, 82
investment, opening of economy
to, 62-63, 170
investment, opportunities in,
decline in, 84
investors, as contributors to high
industrial concentration, 202
investors in Nigeria, during civilian regime, 151
large-scale factory, 212
ownership and management, non-
existence of, in Japan, 204
trade and investment, LDC benefits from, 8
trade and investment, opening to,
83
trade, nondiscrimination in, 213
see also Exchange, Investment

Forrest, Tom
   on growth of Nigerian capitalism with domestic-foreign collaboration, 84
France
   in alliance with African political elites, 50
   family firm in, 135
   political revolution in, 27
   sustained growth of, 25
Franko, Lawrence G.
   on Japanese productivity growth, 225
   on work hours of Americans and Japanese, 233
Free-rider problems
   of bilateral arrangements, 79
French
   colonialists, policies of, to meet demands of the nationalist movements, 49-50

Gandhi, Indira
   election defeat of, 170
   model of, 169
   as prime minister of India, 167
Gandhi, Rajiv
   reduced government industrial regulation by, 170
Garcia Paaerez, Alan
   on debt problem, 75
Gephardt, Richard A.
   on incompatibility of normal trading relationship with Japan, 237
Germany
   annual growth rates of real GNP per capita of, 30
   defeat and occupation of, 31
   as high performer, 227
   sustained growth of, 25
Ghana
   control of discussion and opposition by, 63

dependence on external aid by officials in, 86
   IMF's structural adjustment program in, 92
   independent entrepreneurs in, 84
   as ranking low in HDI, 39
   real wage reductions in, 53-54
   rulers of, squandering of loan funds by, 70
   *see also* Gold Coast
Gold Coast
   transformation of, 47
Gorbachev, Mikhail
   perestroika of, 134
Government
   assistance, to entrepreneur, 112, 113
   discretion, to national monetary authorities, 91
   intervention, to improve welfare, 20
   officials, allied with foreign investors, 50
   officials, local citizens with privileged access to, 86
Gowon, Yakubu
   maintenance of Federation of Nigeria by, 151-52
Great Leap Forward (1958-60)
   in China, 168, 184
Greece
   entrepreneurs in, 133
   industrialists in, 132
   industrialists in, socioeconomic mobility of, 130
   minorities in, as industrialists, 128
Green, Reginald Herbold
   on IMF adjustment programs, 209
Green Revolution
   benefits of, to commercial farmers in West Pakistan, 161
   in India, 47

Group of Seven (G-7)
  failure of, to adopt Trinidad
    terms, 77
  industrialized countries, on resolv-
    ing debt, 60
  meeting, at Toronto, 76
Growth
  in Africa, 38, 51
  in China, 174
  capitalist economic, 82
  capitalist, opportunities for, 81
  constraint of, by external debt, 41
  economic, rate of, xxxii
  economic, slowing of, 31
  entrepreneurs, as contributors to,
    117
  and equality, conflict between, 20
  and income distribution, political
    survival at expense of, 88
  in GNP per capita, in Africa, 85
  in GNP per person in the Sub-
    Sahara, 47
  of GNP, by reschedulers, 65
  in India, in twentieth century, 35
  long-term, use of resources for, 62
  modern, under capitalism, 29
  negative, in the 1980s, 71
  rapid, in China, during liberaliza-
    tion, 168
  rapid, in Pakistan, 150
  rapid, sustained, 25
  before redistribution, 21
  regime survival, and policies of, 49
  slowing of, from oil price shock,
    40
  slowing of, from paying back the
    debt, 60
  slowness of, and inequalities, 84
Gujaratis
  in Bombay, 128
Gurley, John G.
  on China's insurance policy
    against disaster, 184

Gylfason, Thorvaldur
  on economic performance of
    LDCs signing IMF standby
    agreements, 65

Hagen, Everett,
  on Baran's analysis, 15, 16
  on eliteness and manual work, 12,
    23
  on hierarchy of traditional socie-
    ties, 11
  on innovators as protestant dis-
    senters, 127
  on Nonconformists as entrepre-
    neurs, 128
  on rarity of technological innova-
    tion in LDCs, 10
  on socio-psychological changes
    within trading communities,
    118
  as textbook author, 4
  theory of, on technological crea-
    tivity, 124-25
Haggard, Stephen
  on macroeconomic policies of
    democratic and authoritarian
    governments, 90
Hakim, Peter
  on debt crises and external politi-
    cal opposition, 90
Hansen, Alvin H.
  general synthesis of, by Higgins,
    13
Harijans
  lack of Indian entrepreneurs
    among, 99, 105
Harris, John R.
  on expected urban wages, 211
  sample of, of Nigerian entrepre-
    neurs, 132
Harrod, Roy F.
  general synthesis of, by Higgins,
    13

Hausa-Fulani
  community, 159
  nationalism, 147
Health
  of children, 21
  as component of HDI, 38
  improved, for African workers, 82
Higgins, Benjamin
  on borrowing from Joan Robin-
    son and Joseph Schumpeter,
    14
  on competition for capital by
    LDCs, 9
  evaluation and criticism of Marx-
    ist model by, 13
  identification of traditional society
    by, 9-10
  on rarity of technological innova-
    tion in LDCs, 10
  on relationship to political power
    elite, 5
  on secular stagnation, 23
  as textbook author, 4
High-caste entrepreneurs
  survival of firms of, 113
High-yielding varieties of wheat
  in India, 182, 183
Hinduism
  as not conducive to economic
    development, 127
Hirschman, Albert O.
  on democratic government and
    inflationary pressures, 91
Hong Kong
  learning by, from post-World War
    II Japan, 194
Horatio Alger
  model, of entrepreneur, 133
  model, of upward mobility to suc-
    cess in business, 130
Horvat, Bruno
  on socialism as democratic and
    decentralized, 13

Hugenots
  in France, 128
Human Development Index (HDI)
  as index of development, 38
  as measure of human develop-
    ment, 39
Human Freedom Index
  (HFI), 38
  as measure of freedom, 39
  value of, in India and China, 189-
    90
Hungary
  recent market reforms by, 13
Hunger
  in India and China, 180
Husain, Ishrat
  on LDCs carrying debt burden
    until attainment of political
    will, 89
  on reform and adjustment by deb-
    tor countries, 78
Hypothesis
  and data, 4
  and data testing, 5

Iacocca, Lee
  on Japan's "predatory trade," 236
Ibos
  at center of communal competi-
    tion for employment and busi-
    ness activity, 162-63
  community of, 159
  decline in position of, 163
  elite among, 148
  as leading entrepreneurs, 128-29
  in Nigerian nationalist movement,
    147
  ruling, undercutting of, 160
  solidarity of, as guaranteed that
    debts are paid, 135
Ideology
  determinants of, 23-24

Imfeld, Al
  on China's elimination of hunger,
    180
Immigrant
  from North India to Pakistan, 147
Imperialism
  in Africa and Asia, 195
  history of, 7
  in Japan, 223
  Lenin's concept of, 18
  post-colonial, economic impact of,
    6
  post-colonial, and strengthening
    of powerful groups, 12
  of West, toward Japan, 194
  and Western capitalism, 28
  of West, impact of, 82
Imports, agricultural
  in Nigeria and Indonesia, 42
  capacity for, by Nigeria, 91
  from DCs, 71
  of goods and services, 70
  intensity of, 75
  licenses for, national trading cor-
    porations as recipients of, 87
  prices of, 56
  by Sub-Sahara, 61
  substitutes for, protection of, 83-
    84
  substitution for, 66
  substitution for, in Zambia, 92
  substitution for, promotion of, 84
  taxes on, in Nigeria, 158
Income
  distribution and growth, political
    survival at expense of, 88
  gap, in China, 175
  taxes, in Africa, 74
  tax, on agriculture, in India, 208
  tax system, and consumption, 17
  tax rates, in Nigeria, 154-55
  terms of trade, xxx-xxxi, 71, 72,
    73

India
  addressing of food deficit by, 39
  British rule in, 145
  caste system in, and British policy,
    12
  colonial government in, 195
  conflict between Hindu and Mus-
    lim in, 146
  destruction of cottage and work-
    shop industry in, 212
  development patterns in, after lib-
    eralization, 188
  development performance of, in
    comparison to China, 38
  economic performance of, 167
  economic stagnation of, under
    British rule, 7
  entrepreneurship among university
    graduates in, 136
  family nexus in, 120
  food output per capita growth in,
    31
  foreign investment in, under
    colonial rule, 194
  growth in, in twentieth century, 35
  largest private manufacturers in,
    135
  life expectancy at birth in, 185
  literacy and schooling in, 187
  modern financial system of, 204
  no income tax on agriculture in,
    208
  policy fluctuations of, 169
  production of foodgrains in, 47
  as ranking low in HDI, 39
  rank of, on human freedom index
    compared to China, 189-90
  record of, in food output per cap-
    ita growth, 183
  refugees from, as industrialists,
    128
  religion in, and modernization,
    127

slow growth of, 35
subsidies for small-scale industry
in, 213
Indigenization
decrees concerning, 74
laws in the 1970s, 87
in Nigeria, 84
process of, in Nigeria, 154
Indigenous
bourgeoisie, in Kenya, 84
business people, in commercial triangle, 86
capitalism, inhibition of, 83
capitalists, 29
capitalists, in Zambia, Côte
d'Ivoire, Sierra Leone, and
Malawi, 85-86
capital, opportunities for, 85
communities, value on economic
achievement of, 128
counterparts, and commercial success, 10
enterprise(s), 11, 82, 106
entrepreneurs, in Nigeria, 87
personnel, in industrial extension
centers, 123
Indirect
rule, in Northern Nigeria and
West Pakistan, 145
taxes, as high in Nigeria, 154-55
Individual
economy, in China, 32
enterprises, 31
Indonesia
in comparison with Nigeria, 38,
41-42
as prosperous region, 7
terms of trade in 1980 of, 39
Industrial
conglomerates, owned by family,
135
employment growth rate, in
Japan, 211

enterprises, reform of, 32
goods, output of, decline in, 7
growth, in China and India, 189
growth, in China, compared to
India, 173
growth, in Japan, 205
growth, rapidity of, 83
incomes, compared to agricultural
incomes, 53
leader, in United States, 133
positions, in Soviet Union, 134
productivity, relative to agricultural productivity, in Africa, 88
programs, financed by agricultural
surpluses, 54
reform, problems of, in China, 33
reforms, in China, 189
Revolution, innovators during,
132
Revolution, leading entrepreneurs
of, 128
Revolution, poverty and squalor
during, 19
sector, redistribution of resources
to, in Pakistan, 157
Industrialization
beginnings of, 25
burgeoning, 26
Industry
in China, planning approach to,
34
favoring of, 161
growth in, under New Economic
Policy, 18
redistribution of resources to, 155
reforms in, in China, 31
surplus transfer to, 207
transfer of savings to, 158
Inequality
in Africa, 49
and Africanization, 52
in China and India, 175, 176, 179-
80

contribution of multinational corporations (MNCs) to, 50, 74
defense of, 19
effect of zaibatsu on, 202
of income, and class differences, in Africa, 51
of income, in Japan, in 1930s, 223
of income, in Pakistan, 155
in Nigeria, 56
as spur to investment, 20
trend in, 21
Inflation
control of, 90
cost-induced, from devaluation, 209
redistribution of income under, 27
Infrastructure
colonial investment in, 82
inadequate, and supply increases, 209
inattention to, in China, 32
investment by Meiji Japan in, 194
Innovation(s), biochemical
in agriculture, 207
biological and chemical, for Japanese farms, 196
borrowing and adapting of, 198
in Chinese industry, 135
by entrepreneurs, 128, 129
Hagen on difficulty of, 15
mastery and modification of, by Japan, 214
rarity of, in LDCs, 10
resistance to, 134
reward for, 23
technological, freeing of resources for, 31
see also Schumpeter
Innovators
entrepreneurs as, 130-31
"Inside"
perspective, on dependent economies, 3

Institutions
and explanation of political economy, 6
reality of, 4
Inter-American Development Bank, 75-76
Interest
arrears on, in indebted countries, 60
rates of, 78
rates of, reduction of, to debtors, 79
real rates of, 73, 77
Interest(s), 90
conflicts of, 5, 16, 18
harmony of, 12, 144
special and encompassing, 31
vested, opposition from, 91
Intermediaries
dependence of, on external aid, 50
International
balance-of-payments position, in East Pakistan, 161
(see also Balance)
balance of trade, of Japan, 215
balance on goods, services, and transfers, in Sub-Sahara, 73
International Development Association (IDA)
concessional loans from, 78
International division of labor
based on comparative advantage, 8
International Labour Office
on Nigeria's economic loss, 47
International Monetary Fund (IMF)
adjustment programs of, 62-65, 170, 215
adjustment programs of, record of transitional democracies in, 90
Africa Department of, credit outstanding to, 69
borrowing from, beyond initial contribution of convertible currency, 60

conditionality by, 93
concessional funds by, 78
conditionality of, 67
conditions of, 66
in design of adjustment program, 92
discipline of, escape from, 73
emphasis on shock treatment by, 208
as finance minister of the Third World, 63
as gatekeeper for the international financial system, 67
insistence on privatization by, 202
loans of last resort by, 63
model of, resembling that of pre-World War II Japan, 216
neglect of political constraints by, 89
OECD countries as major shareholders in, 195
receipt of net transfers from the Sub-Sahara by, 70
role of, in Brady Plan, 76
"seal of approval" by, 80
stress on devaluation and foreign-exchange decontrols by, 209
technical guidance by, on debt reduction, 79
unveiling of Baker Plan at meeting of, 75
*see also* Multilateral
Intervention
market, by state, 88
state, in Africa, 87
Investment
in Africa, 85
in agriculture, in Indonesia, 42
climate for 9
by colonial governments, in infrastructure, 82
dampening of, in Sub-Saharan Africa, 60
decisions concerning, 33
inducement for, 87
for industry, 205
long-range, in Africa, 93
in "machines to make machines," 169
by Meiji regime, 201
rate of, in China, 167
rate of, in low-income Africa, 216
overseas, 10
in new and productive enterprises, 28
rate of, spurred by inequality, 20
*see* Foreign
Islam
medieval, 26
Israel
aid to, 77
Italy
sustained growth of, 25

Jacobs, Norman
on Japan's ideology and capitalism, 127
Jain
entrepreneurs, in India, 127
Janata Party government
in India, 170
Japan
accelerated growth in, 30
capitalist ideology in, 127
as central capitalist country, 81
defeat and occupation of, 31
exports from, 61
failure of, to adopt Trinidad terms, 77
as graduate from the ranks of underdeveloped countries, 8
as high performer, 227
level of economic development in, 29
as model for development, 193
net commercial bank lending by, 59

as number one, 221
ranked first in HDI, 38
sustained growth of, 25
trade of, with China, 240
as trade-surplus country, 76
as world's fastest grower, 193
*Jati*
concept of, 98-99
Jews
as entrepreneurs, 128
Joint
Action Committee, of Nigerian
major federations, 155
ventures, between MNCs and
state enterprises, 86

Kahn, Herman
on the twenty-first century as the
Japanese century, 221
Kaunda, Kenneth
on multilateral agencies, 92
Kaufman, Robert R.
on macroeconomic policies of
democratic and authoritarian
governments, 90
Kennedy, Paul (Manchester,
England)
on creation of conditions for new
wealth generation by colonization in Africa, 82
as critic of neo-Marxist view on
local business, 84
on emergence of African capitalist
class, 88
on lack of inhibition of indigenous
capitalism from DC-African
relationships, 83
on national trading corporations
in Africa, 87
on reduction on external economic dependence by stronger
African states, 81

on strong support for indigenous
capitalists in Africa, 85-86
Kennedy, Paul (Yale)
on emergence and decline of great
powers, 31
Kenya
as Africa's most developed state, 84
capitalism in, vulnerability of, 84
control of discussion and opposition by, 63
dependence on external aid by
officials in, 86
elites in, distribution of benefits
by, 51-52
emergence of African capitalist
class in, 88
farmers in, prohibition of, 83
grant of tire monopoly by, 86
growth in, 85
integration of, into world market,
82
intermediaries in, dependence of,
on external aid, 50
land settlement in, 87
Kenyanization
of jobs and businesses, 87
Khrushchev, Nikita
on unsatisfactory rate of technological change, 134
Kilby, Peter
on motivational training, 122
Kindleberger, Charles
on intervention into the internal
political and economic affairs
of LDCs, 6
as textbook author, 4
King, Robin A.
on slower export and GNP
growths of reschedulers, 65
Kitching, Gavin
on Marxist underestimation of
variety of capitalist development, 83

promoting capitalist development
with political elite and foreign
capital, 86
on role of African civil servants,
87
Klein, Martin A.
on Bank/Fund and democracies,
63
Knight, Frank
concept of entrepreneur of, 98
on institutional accuracy, 4
Kojima, Kiyoshi
on investment patterns of U.S.
and Japanese MNCs, 239
Komatis
as industrial entrepreneurs, 108
Korea
resource transfer to Japan from,
206
*see also* South Korea
Kuznets, Simon
on average real income, 28

Labor, 91
cost distortions, in Africa, 75
demand and supply, 210
demands of, in West Pakistan, 156
discontent in Nigeria and Pakistan, 154
growth, in Japan, 211
intensive technology, 197, 198, 215
market, in China, lack of, 34
parties, in Nigeria, 159
productivity, growth in, 212
supply elasticities, 216
unrest, from high unemployment
and communal competition for
jobs, 155
using inputs, used in Japan, 198
Laffer Curve
on debt, 78
Lagos
jobs in, competition for, 163

Plan of Action (1980), 49, adoption of, by Organisation of
African Unity, 64
Lal, Deepak
on democratic government as
source of irrational economic
policies, 90
on "trickle down" of growth, 20
Land
appropriation, for large commercial farms, 86
concentration, 11
reform, 21
reform, in India, 176
tax, 205, 206
tax, as financial reform, 204
transfers, from European farmers,
87
Landless
workers, after colonialism, 83
Landlords
as dominant social group, 153
as investors, 202
in Latin America, 207
in Meiji Japan, 205
as part of the elite in West Pakistan, 152
use of tenant rent for capital by,
206
Langdon, Steven
on vulnerability of Kenya's capitalism, 84
Lange, Oskar
model of, of market socialism, 13
Lardy, Nicholas R.
on China's and India's daily per
capita calorie consumption,
180
Latin America
debt-service ratio in, 67
decline of living standards in, 60
landlords in, 207
loans for, held by U.S. banks, 59

with highest GNP per capita, 35
with high inequality, 47
presidential elections in, and
    external debt crises, 90
Learning
by doing, in Japan, 212
by doing, in Pakistan, 150
from experience, 213
technological, 199, 214
Least-developed countries
as recipients of aid, 70
Lebanon
entrepreneurs in, 128
Lenin, Vladimir Ilich
concept of imperialism of, 18
writing of, on monopoly capital-
    ism, 13
Lessinger, Johanna
on women in business, 137
LeVine, Robert A.
on achievement motivation in
    Nigeria, 122
Lewis, W. Arthur
on major weaknesses of planning,
    156
model of, unlimited supply of
    labor in, 211
Liberal democratic
regimes, record of, compared to
    authoritarian regimes, 90
Liberalism
as advocate for self-regulating
    market, 27
Liberalization
in China, 168
effect of, on entrepreneurship, 113
in India, 170, 188
in LDCs, 216
support of, by African elites, 63
of terms for foreign capital, 9
Licenses
awarding of, to newcomers, 153
for capacity, 108

from government, access to, 97-98
for imports, in Africa, 87
for Kenyan traders, 86
for large business families, 106
for large business houses, 107
Life expectancy
in Afro-Asia, 42
in China and India, 185
as component of HDI, 38
in Japan and the United States,
    222
in Malaysia, 38-39
in Sub-Saharan Africa, 35
Linguistic
community, and entrepreneurial
    activity, 98
Literacy
rate, as component of HDI, 38
rate, in China, 186
rate, in Malaysia, 39
Lockwood, William W.
on Japan's income inequality, 223
on "Japan Incorporated," 224
Loxley, John
on restoration of growth and
    external balance, through IMF
    programs, 65
Lubeck, Paul
on African state support of thriv-
    ing indigenous capitalism, 88
on contribution to economic
    growth by integration of Nige-
    ria, Kenya, and Côte d'Ivoire
    into world market, 82
on creation of opportunities for
    indigenous capital, by the drive
    to privatize industries, 84-85
on lack of inhibition of indigenous
    capitalism from DC-African
    relationships, 83
on reduction on external eco-
    nomic dependence by stronger
    African states, 81

on theorists predicting "stagnation, blocked industrialization,
and impotence of bourgeois-
state technocratic alliance," 85
Luce, Henry
on twentieth century as American
century, 221

McClelland, David C.
on achievement drives of Protestants, 126-27
on achievement motivation training, 118-19
on entrepreneur and economic
growth, 129
on high need for achievement and
entrepreneurship, 119
lack of awareness of moral ambiguities when introducing
"change agents" by, 120
lack of conceptual matrix oriented
toward class by, 122
lack of control group by, 120-21
no data on relationship between
class and caste by, 123
*Machismo*
adjustment as exercise in, 78
Macroeconomic
policies of democratic and authoritarian governments, 90
policy, as part of structural adjustment programs, 62
Mahalanobis, P.C.
model of, 169
Major, John
proposal of, at Trinidad, 76
Malawi
control of discussion and opposition by, 63
dependence on external aid by
officials in, 86
intermediaries in, dependence of,
on external aid, 50

strong support for indigenous capitalists in, 85-86
Malaysia
ranking of human development in,
38-39
terms of trade in 1980 of, 39
yearly growth rate in, 35
Malenbaum, Wilfred
on Sino-Indian comparisons, 172,
173
Malnutrition
in Africa, with continued inaction,
92
in China and India, 184
Management
experience, of entrepreneurs, 102,
105, 131
Managers
of enterprises, in China, 34
of family firms, 135-36
high-level, in Kenya, 87
in Japan, scientific and technological background of, 31
of large enterprises, in India, 132
professional, in China, 135
in Soviet Union, 134
task of, in China, 32
worker authority in selection of,
33
Manufacturing
in Africa, 74
entrepreneurs in, in Pakistan, 150
of exports, impetus to, 82
of exports, in Afro-Asia, 215
of goods, in LDCs, 149
percentage of national income in,
in Pakistan, 153
strategy in, for exports in Kenya,
84
tariffs, as benefit for selected
enterprises in, 158
of textiles, in Japan, 213
use of oil revenues for, 56

Mao Zedong
claims by, concerning hunger in China, 180
on classes under socialism, 18
counterattack, on pragmatists by, 168
egalitarian slogans by, 189
leader of China's Communist Party, 167
on "moral incentives," 23
stress on education and indoctrination by, 13
Marginal
individuals, as entrepreneurs, 128-29
productivity of labor, in agriculture, 210, 212
Market, 27, 33, 53
clearing prices, on farm, 54
clearing rates, 84
demand, in China, 35
discipline, inculcated by center states, 85
forces, in China, 34
imperfections, in Africa, 209
interest payments, 77
intervention, by states, 88
rate, of capital, foreign exchange, and labor, 75
reforms, by Hungary and China, 13
reforms, in China, 188
socialism, in China, 31
socialism, in Soviet Union, 18
spur of peasant production through, 49
Marketing
board purchasing prices, 84
board surplus, 54
Maronites
as entrepreneurs in Lebanon, 128
Marwaris
as entrepreneurs, 105, 128

Marxism
analysis of hierarchy by, 15
assessment of, 13
death of, 12
on ideology, 24
of nationalist groups, and threat of class antagonism, 18
as rallying point for discontented people, 17
Marxist
view on local business in Africa, 84
writing, weakness of, in underestimation of varieties of capitalist development, 83
Marx, Karl
brought up to date, 18
on conflict between interests of workers and capitalists, 17
disavowal of movements using his name by, 13
Masoyoshi, Matsukata
as creator of central Bank of Japan, 204
Materialist
interpretation of history, 14
Meier, Gerald
on detrimental effect of colonialism or neo-colonialism, 7
on export induced development, 8
on policies for an inflow of private foreign capital, 9
on Rostow's broader view of human motivation, 14
as textbook author, 4
Meiji
bureaucracy, 87
government, investments by, 194
Merton, Robert K.
on "truths" perceived by insiders, 23
Mexico
inability of, to pay external debt, 60
as a leading LDC debtor, 67

Michigan
  entrepreneurs in, 133
  entrepreneurs in medium manu-
    facturing firms in, 130
Middle East
  entrepreneurial activity in, 128
  with highest GNP per capita, 35
Middle-income countries
  expansion of lending to, 60
Middlemen
  and foreign capital, 50
  between multinational corpora-
    tions and state officials, 86
Migration
  costs of, compensation for, 210
  of entrepreneurs, in India, 110
  of workers, from villages to urban
    complexes, 11
Military
  aid, 77
  coups, and wage reductions, 53-54
  establishment, in Nigeria and Pak-
    istan, 148
  frustration among, 154
  mutiny, in Nigeria, 155
  overcommitment, and economic
    growth, 31
  power, by DCs, 83
  rule, in Nigeria, 91
  spending, in Japan, 223
  support, to Pakistan, 150
Miller, William
  business elite studied by, 133
Mineral
  related industries, in Sub-Saharan
    Africa, 82
Ministers of finance and economic
  planning
  adoption of African Alternative
    Framework to Structural Adjust-
    ment Programmes for Socio-
    Economic Recovery and Trans-
    formation (AAF-SAP) by, 65

Ministries
  economic, discretion by, 91
Ministry of International Trade and
  Industry
  in Japan, 224
Mitsui
  joint venture of, with Stone
    Group, 32
Mobility
  socioeconomic, of entrepreneurs,
    130
  upward, to success in business, 97,
    114
Mobutu Sese Seko
  overseas wealth of, 75
Modern
  economic growth, under capital-
    ism, 29
  economy, of contemporary DCs,
    10
Modernization
  economic, in Europe, 27
  maximization of, 21
  rapid economic, 29
  theorists, 193
Modernized society
  as future of traditional society, 12
Modernizing
  elite, policies oriented toward, 156
  policies, of government, 22
Monetary
  authorities, discretion by, 91
Monopoly
  advantage, of entrepreneur, 129
  advantage, of MNCs, 199-200
  advantage, to families and com-
    munities with wealth and posi-
    tion, 97-98
  return, of large business in Nigeria
    and Pakistan, 157
Monopoly(ies)
  creation of, by government, 86
  of state, 27

Moore, David G.
  on income of sample entrepre-
    neurs, 133
  on origins of entrepreneurs in
    Michigan, 130
"Moral incentives"
  reliance on, by Mao, 23
Morgan, Theodore
  as critic of Baran, 17
  on ideology and values, 23
  as textbook author, 4
Multilateral agencies
  in Baker Plan, 76
  Kaunda on, 92
  lack of debt writedowns by, 80
  see also International Monetary
    Fund, World Bank
Multinational corporations
  (MNCs), 10, 87
  in Africa, 74
  contribution of, to inequality, 50
  creation of factor-price distortions
    by, 198
  from Europe, reliance on, 84
  as international oligopolies, 199
  with middlemen and state officials,
    as commercial triangle, 86
  as partners with ruling elites, 52
  technology of, 75
  in United States, investment
    abroad by, 239
Muslim
  indigenes, in Pakistan, 153
  League, in Pakistan, 147
  nationalism, in India, 152
  nationalism, in Pakistan, 159
Muslims
  in India, protection of, 146
  as industrial capitalists, 147
  as industrial entrepreneurs, in
    India, 109
  as Schumpeterian entrepreneurs,
    130-31

Myanmar (Burma)
  slow growth of, 35
Myrdal, Gunnar
  on eliteness and manual work, 23

Nakasone, Yashu
  abolition of ministry planning by, 228
Nandy, Ashis
  on achievement motivation train-
    ing, 120
  on McClelland and Winter's the-
    ory of personality, 121
Narasimha Rao, P.V.
  as prime minister of India, 170
National Bureau of Economic
  Research
  study by, 214
National Council of Nigeria and the
  Cameroons
  (NCNC), 147, 159
Nationalism
  hampering of, by indigenous
    chiefs, 145
Nationalist
  leaders before independence, in
    Africa, 85
  leaders in India, 168
  leaders in Nigeria, 146
  movement in Nigeria, 159
Nationalization
  of foreign enterprises, 87
Nation-state
  as necessary for larger markets, 27
Need for achievement
  119-23, 129
Nehru, Jawaharlal
  attracted by democratic socialism
    and Soviet planning, 168
  model of, 169
  as prime minister of India, 167
Nelson, Joan M.
  on economic reform and ruling-
    class sustainability, 91

Neoclassical
general equilibrium model, 13
Neocolonialism
as alliance between political elites
and foreign governments and
capitalists, 50
Nepal
as ranking low in HDI, 39
Netherlands (Holland)
advancement of capitalism in, 125
political revolution in, 27
sustained growth of, 25
New Economic Policy (1921-1928)
of market socialism, 18
in the Soviet Union, 13
New Economic Policy (1961-64)
of China, 168
New Zealand
as outpost of western civilization,
28
Nicolson, I.F.
on overstretched colonial administrative machinery, 82
Niefer, Werner
opposition to automobile import
restrictions by, 240
Nigeria
as Africa's most developed state,
84
British administration in, 82
British foreign policy in, 152
British rule in, 145
British support of separate institutions in, 146
capital stock per person in, 75
communal identity in, 162
in comparison with Indonesia, 38,
41-42
control of discussion and opposition by, 63
declining terms of trade by, 92
demands for increased patronage
by, 91

dependence on external aid by
officials in, 86
as dependent on patron nations,
149
drop to low-income country by,
85
economic loss by, 47
elites in, distribution of benefits
by, 51-52
entrepreneurs in, 133
entrepreneurs of, fathers of, 132
federal public service posts in, 52
first development plan of, 1962-68,
20
foreign interests in, 151
growth of, compared to Cameroon, 54-56
high tariffs on inputs in, 158
imposition of ceiling on exports,
60
indigenization in, 84
indigenization decree in, 74
industrialists in, socioeconomic
mobility of, 130
integration of, into world market,
82
interregional contention in, 161
jobs of university graduates in,
136
lack of ability of, to service debts,
80
among major communal groups
in, 159
mutineers in, 148
native chiefs, and nationalism, 11
oil output in, 160
plan of, shortfalls of, 157
propensity to flee from additional
external debt in, 75
as ranking low in HDI, 39
real growth of, 55
rulers of, squandering of loan
funds by, 70

secessionist civil war in, 143
secondary market prices of bank
    debts in, 59
as severely indebted country, 61
terms of trade in 1980 of, 39
thwarting of economic decline by
    traditional political rulers in,
    118
thwarting of industrial export and
    import substitution by colonial
    government in, 195
traditional Northern ruling aristo-
    cracy in, 153
tsetse fly in, 21
weakness and lack of organization
    of labor in Nigeria, 154
Yoruba nationalism in, 147
Nigerian disease
from booming export, 54-56
Nigerian Enterprises Promotion
    Decrees, 74
Nigerianization
as instrument for civil servants,
    military rulers, business peo-
    ple, and professionals, 52
Nkrumah, Kwame
on African socialism as a myth, 51
on transformation of the Gold
    Coast, with self-government, 47
Northern
competition, for positions in busi-
    ness and employment, 163
dominated civilian government, in
    Nigeria, 151
emirs and administrators, 148
dominated civilian government, in
    Nigeria, 149
Nigeria, consciousness and politi-
    cal mobilization in, 159
Nigeria, program for economic
    development in, 157
Nigeria, reaction of, 146
ruling aristocracy, in Nigeria, 153

Northernization
of government and private sectors,
    163
Nowzad, Bahram
on herd behavior, 73
Nurkse, Ragnar
hypothesis of peculiar barriers of, 15
Nutrition
of children, 21
standards of, in Sub-Saharan
    Africa, 47
Nyerere, Julius K.
on Bank/Fund, as usurpers of
    role of finance minister, 63
on egalitarianism and socialism in
    Tanzania, 51

Obasanjo, Olusegun
on petroleum revenue as not a
    cure-all, 41
Official
creditors, Sub-Saharan debt owed
    to, 61
Oil-exporting countries
effect of fourfold increase in oil
    prices in 1973-74 on, 39
growth of, 41
see also Petroleum
Oil-importing countries
effect of fourfold increase in oil
    prices in 1973-74 on, 39
effect of oil price shock on growth
    in, 40
growth of, 41
Oil
industry, in Eastern Nigeria, 162
output, in Nigeria, 160
price shock, of 1973 to 1974, 40
price shock, of 1979 to 1981, 62
revenue, allocation of, in Nigeria,
    161-62
royalties, demanded by, 152
shock, immediate effect of, 41

Okita, Saburo
  as planning minister, 225
Oligopolies
  European, 82
  in Nigeria, 52
Olson, Mancur
  on growth of special interests in
    DCs, 31
Organisation for African Unity
    (OAU)
  rejection of donor biases toward
    multiparty democracies, 90
Organisation for Economic Cooper-
    ation and Development
    (OECD)
  capital, flow of, to Central Europe
    and former Soviet Union, 77
  on commuting by workers in
    Japan, 221
  countries of, on international
    order, 62
  countries of, retention of eco-
    nomic suzerainty in Africa by,
    195
  creditors from, insistence on pri-
    vatization by, 202
  sneezing of, xxx
Organisation of African Unity
  adoption of Lagos Plan of Action
    by, 64
Orthodox
  economic paradigm, and Horatio
    Alger model, 130
  economics, impoverishment of, 22
  economics, hypotheses of, 23
  literature, on Afro-Asian eco-
    nomic development, 4
  literature, on the economics of
    Africa and Asia, 3
  standards of theoretical excel-
    lence, 13
Overvaluation
  of domestic currency(ies), 88, 214

Pakistan
  average material level of living in,
    160
  contribution of economic policies
    of to secession of East Bengal,
    39
  dampening of rise of political dis-
    content in, 162
  as dependent on patron nations,
    149
  development projects of, 150
  disintegration of, 152
  fathers of manufacturing entrepre-
    neurs in, 132
  foreign exchange in, 161
  independence of, Muslim League
    in, 147
  industrialists in, 117-18
  lack of planning machinery in, 156
  military intervention in, 148
  moderate growth of, 35
  planner in, Ul Haq as, 20
  Planning Commission of, promo-
    tion of income inequality by,
    155
  plan of, shortfalls of, 157
  private entrepreneur in, 129-30
  as ranking low in HDI, 39
  refugees from, as industrialists,
    128
  secessionist civil war in, 143
  transfer of savings in agriculture
    to industry, 208
  view of competition in, 159
  weakness and lack of organization
    of labor in Nigeria, 154
Palestinians
  as entrepreneurs, 128
Papanek, Gustav F.
  on fathers of manufacturing entre-
    preneurs in Pakistan, 132
  on inequality as conducive to sav-
    ings, 20

on industrialists in Pakistan, 117-18
on private entrepreneur, in Pakistan, 129-30
Paradigm(s)
dialogue with, 22
dominant development, 4
Pareto
efficiency, 20
optimality, 21
Paris Club
multi-year rescheduling agreements by, 78
negotiation of foreign debts by LDCs with, 60
terms under, 79
Parsi
entrepreneurs, in India, 127
Parti Démocratique de Côte d'Ivoire (PDCI)
as nationalist party, 18
Patents
by mixed and capitalist LDCs, 10
Paternal
class and education in Nigeria, 122
economic status, of entrepreneur(s), 113, 130
Patronage
base in Nigeria, from partnerships with foreign investors, 151
base of, for state officials, 74
dispension of, by officials, 86
disposal of, in Nigeria, 157
expansion of, by Africa's rulers, 71
expansion of, by political elites, 92
expansion of, in Nigeria, Zaire, and Ghana, 70
increase in demand for, in Nigeria, 91
to satisfy interests, 150
Peasants
as absent from politically dominant coalition, 91

compulsion on, to grow selected crops, 83
cross-pressuring of, by class and ethnic identities, 51
diversion of resources from, 88
leaders of, in coalition with bourgeoisie, 16
in Nigeria and Pakistan, consciousness of, 158
prices for, state intervention in, 64
production by, spur of, 49
reduction of farm disposable income by, 206
as revolutionary leaders, 18
revolution by, 17
skepticism and resistance by, 5
tactical power of, 54
see also Farmers
People's Liberation Army (PLA)
learning from, 168
Parasitic capitalism
in Africa, 87
Paternal
economic status, of entrepreneurs, 99, 111-12
Perestroika
of Mikhail Gorbachev, 134
Peripheral
capitalism, in Africa, 81
economies, integrated into world capitalist system, 148
nations, 144
Periphery
archaic economic structures in, and underdevelopment, 11
Peru
lack of ability of, to service debts, 80
secondary market prices of bank debts in, 59
Petroleum
boom from, in Nigeria, 84
as not a cure-all, 41

as single booming export commodity, 54
as share of total energy supply, 40
*see also* Oil
Philippines
loans for, held by U.S. banks, 59
manufacturing entrepreneurs in,
132
as medium ranking in HDI, 39
slow growth of, 35
Pirate capitalism
in Nigeria, 55
Planning
centralized, in China, 167
Commission, of Pakistan, promotion of income inequality by,
155
comprehensive, under Lagos Plan
of Action, 64
for development, in Pakistan, 150
difficulty of, in China, 34
expenditures, in West Pakistan,
161
euphoric, in Nigeria, 55
and implementation, hamstrung
by ruling elites, 156
indicative, in India, 169
long-range by political leaders, 93
machinery of, lack of, 156
as neither integrated or coherent,
33
skilled, in Africa, 87
Poland
failure of, to meet obligations to
European banks, 60
loans for, held by U.S. banks, 59
writedown for, 76
Political
class, antagonistic to worker interests, 51
conditionality, by donor, 90
conflict, 143
discontent, in Pakistan, 162

elite, in Nigeria, 153, 158
elites, in Africa, incurring of debt
by, 92
elites, in Africa, political survival
of, 71
elites, hegemony of, 85
elites, in alliance with foreign
governments, 50
elites, in East and Federation, 160
elites, rents for, in Africa, 86
elites, use of power and wealth by,
19
elites, use of state by, 49
instability, explanation of, 5
instability, in Nigeria, 149
intervention, in Nigeria and Pakistan, 157
intervention, to make economic
decisions, 156
leaders, alliances of, 74
leadership, for rapid economic
modernization, 29
leaders, in Africa, 79
leadership, benefit of, 52
leadership, in Nigeria, 87
leaders in Sub-Sahara, 93
levers, pulled by entrepreneurs,
106
parties, impact of British rule on,
148
parties, in Nigeria, 147
parties, suppression of, 155
power, in Nigeria, 159
support, state policies to increase, 88
survival, and urban bias, 53
revolutions, in England, Holland,
and France, 27
violence, in Pakistan, 152
violence, of Stalin, 18
will, for adjustment, 78, 89
Poor
in Africa, 49
distribution from, to rich, 157

early family life of entrepreneurs
   as, 133
effect of primary education on, 52-
   53
effect of short adjustment times
   on, 209
Population
   growth of, 42, 49, 211
Poverty
   in Africa, with continued inaction,
      92
   of African masses, and revolution-
      ary pressures, 51
   explanation of, in Anglo-
      American development eco-
      nomics, 6
   millionaires trained in, 133
   percentage in, in Sub-Saharan
      Africa, 47
   programs concerning, and adjust-
      ment, 63
   programs concerning, curtailment
      of, 50
   rates of, in China and India, 178,
      179-80, 189
   rates of, in India, 169
   rates of, in 1980s, 71
   rates of, in Sub-Saharan Africa,
      35
   reduction of, 41
   as result of growth collapse, 20
   in rural areas, effect of government
      intervention in prices on, 49
   subculture of, 122
   among tenants and peasants, in
      Japan, 206
   among tenants, in Japan, 207
   uniform, premise about, 5
Private
   capital, from Britain, 149
   enterprise, in India, 167
   industrial entrepreneurial activity,
      in Nigeria, 158

Prices
   in agriculture, 42
   of capital, 75
   of cocoa exports, in Ghana, 70
   decline in, for Zambia, 92
   for exports, in agriculture, 55
   on farm, 54, 71
   for farm commodities, in China,
      31
   for food, 53
   incentives for, 35
   in industry, relative to agriculture,
      86
   of inputs, hike in, 73
   instability of, 50
   for oil, 1979-81, 62
   for petrochemicals, 40
   policies concerning, and fall of
      Sub-Saharan African market
      shares, 88
   setting of, 64
   setting of, in China, 33
   shift in, from nontradable to trad-
      able goods, 66
   as signals, for resource use, 34
   see also Market
Primary
   education, effect of, on equality of
      opportunity, 52
   education, redistributive effect of, 53
   education, uniformity of, 201
   universality of, in Japan, 195
   products, demand for, 73
   products, export of, growth of, 74
   products, export of, 50, 71
   products, export of, expansion of,
      215
   products, in Africa, elasticity of
      demand for, 209
   products, specialization in, by
      LDCs, 81
   products, specialization in, in col-
      onies, 145

Private
assets, flight of, 75
businessmen, sale of government
industrial property to, 201
capitalists, in Africa, 85
enterprise, in China, 32
individuals, decisions by, 25
sectors, African facilitation of, 87
Privatization
favoritism to existing elites in, 202
of industry, 84
of public enterprises, 66
of state-owned enterprises, 62
threat of, to vested interests, 91
Product cycle, 217
model, illustrated by Japan, 199-200
Productivity
differences in, between industry
and agriculture, 53, 88
in manufacturing, in Japan, 222
Profit(s)
as guide to enterprise behavior, 33
in industry, 210
operation of individuals for, 25
retention of, for capital, 34
in Sub-Saharan Africa, 85
Profitable
enterprises, African facilitation of,
87
Progressive
coalition, of bourgeoisie, workers,
and peasants, 16
taxation, effect of, on capital
accumulation, 21
Proletariat
in coalition with bourgeoisie, 83
Propensity to flee
from additional external debt, 75
Property
ownership of, and growth, 21
Protection
effective rate of, by DCs, 215
in India, 106

Protectionism
by DCs, 74
Protestant(s)
entrepreneurs as, 125-26
ethic of, analogies to, 127
lack of Indian entrepreneurs from,
99, 105
Protestantism
spiritual individualism of, 27
"this-worldly" asceticism of, 26
Public
corporations, patronage from, 157
enterprise, privatization of, 66
sector, African bureaucratic facilitation of, 87
sector, growth of, 85
*see all* State-owned
Purchasing power adjustment
to measure GNP per capita, 171-
72
Purchasing power
as spur to capitalist economic
growth, 82

Qingdao Forging Machinery Plant
in China, 33
Quotas
protection of output by African
governments, 86

Radical
economics, hypotheses of, 23
economics, treatment of, 22
Ranis, Gustav
model of, unlimited supply of
labor in, 211
Rationalism
of new science, 27
Rawls, John
first principle of equality of basic
rights and duties of, 21
second principle, 22

Reaganomics
  international application of, 208
Recession
  in DCs, price shocks in Sub-
    Saharan Africa from, 70
  in Japan, 222
  in West, 73
Redistribution
  of income, 22
  of income, from poor to rich, 157
  of income, toward the poor, 53
  and saving, conflict between, 21
Reformed capitalism, 18
Reform(s)
  in China, 31, 188
  in China, emphasis on worker
    authority during, 33
  and democratization, 90
  economic, by African leaders, 92
  economic, by countries, 78
  economic, by new democratic
    governments, 91
  incentive for, by debtor countries, 80
  of market, in Hungary and China, 13
  policy, 62
  protection of vested interests from
    threats by, 63
  in urban areas, 32
Refugees
  as entrepreneurs, 128
Regional
  autonomy, East Pakistani discont-
    ent, and, 156
  community, and entrepreneurial
    activity, 98
  competition for openings and pro-
    motions in military, 154
  differences, in high-yielding grain
    varieties, 161
  economic competition, 159
  economic factors, in discontent in
    Eastern Nigeria and East Pak-
    istan, 163

elite, in Nigeria, 148
elites, in Nigeria, 146
enmities, 143
hegemony, of ruling Ibos, 160
identities and competition in Nigeria and Pakistan, 152
identities, impact of British rule
  on, 148
inequality, in India and China,
  174
revenues, in Nigeria, 162
security of, of Northern Nigeria,
  149
socioeconomic elite, in Nigeria,
  147
struggle, of Bengali interests,
  against Western wing, 153
Regressive
  taxes, in Africa, 74-75
Repression
  against dissidents, in Pakistan, 149
  financial, policies of, 209
  in Nigeria, under military rule, 91
Responsibility
  system, in China, 32
  system, in China, of management,
    33
Revolution(s)
  by workers and peasants, 17
  political, in England, Holland,
    and France, 27
Revolutionary
  leaders, in Soviet Union and
    China, 18
  pressures, exerted on African
    masses, 51
  pressures, in Africa, 85
Risk
  reward for, 21
Robertson, H.M.
  on the accommodation of Purita-
    nism to rising capitalist class,
    126

Robinson, Joan
  Marxian equations of, 14
Robinson, Michael D.
  on slower export and GNP
    growths of reschedulers, 65
Rodney, Walter
  analysis of, on how Europe
    expropriated Africa's surplus,
    81
Roemer, Michael
  on Dutch disease, 54
  on government policy, toward
    booming exports, 55
Roman Catholic
  Christians, lack of Indian entre-
    preneurs from, 99, 105
  Church, asceticism of, 126
  Church, breakdown of authority
    of, 26
Rosenstein-Rodan, Paul N.
  hypothesis of peculiar barriers of,
    15
Rostow, Walter W.
  broader view of human motiva-
    tion of, 14
Rulers
  native, protection of, by colonial
    powers, 49
Ruling
  class, Communist party, as, 19
  classes, insecurity of, 53
  class ideologies, and false con-
    sciousness, 17
  class, reaction to, 85
  class, sustainability of, 91
  *see also* Elite
Rural
  dwellers, organization by, 54
  health service, in China, 185
  poverty and undernourishment,
    208
Russia
  revolution in, 17

sustained growth of, 25
  *see also* Soviet
Russian Revolution of 1917
  and divergent class interests, 19

Sachs, Jeffrey
  on default by major debtors, 78
Samuelsson, Kurt
  on use of Protestantism to legitim-
    ize, 126
Samurai (warrior)
  as industrialists and bankers, 203
  and values conducive to economic
    growth, 127
Sandbrook, Richard
  on authoritarian compared to
    democratic regimes, 90
Sanskritization
  of Sudra *jati*s, 99
Saving(s)
  channelling of, into industry, 204
  domestic, in Pakistan, 155
  increase in, from low real wages,
    210
  inequality as conducive to, 20
  from landed aristocracy, 17
  by Protestants, 126
  rates of, in Japan, 30
  and redistribution, conflict
    between, 21
  reduction in, 211
  smallness of, in Africa, 51
  transfer of, from agriculture to
    industry, 158
Saxonhouse, Gary
  on sale of Alaskan oil to Japan,
    238-39
  on U.S.'s bilateral deficit with
    Japan, 238
Scale
  economies of, of capitalist expan-
    sion, 27

Scandinavia
  sustained growth of, 25
Schatz, Sayre P.
  on Nigerian planning, 55
Schumpeter, Joseph A.
  concept of deviance of, 128
  consideration of Marx's pure the-
    ory by, 14
  on entrepreneurs, as heroic fig-
    ures, 129
  general synthesis of, by Higgins,
    13
  on identification of innovators, 130
Schumpeterian
  entrepreneur, origin of, 130
  entrepreneurs, background of, 131
  innovation, in Japan, the United
    States, and Germany, 199
Science
  applied, 30
  background in, of Japanese man-
    agers, 31
  new, 27
Secessionist
  civil war, 143
  conflict, 144, 152
Sectoral adjustment loans (SECALs)
  by World Bank, 62
Secularization
  of Protestantism, 26
Self-reliance
  for regions, in China, 168
Sen, Amartya
  on famine in India and China,
    184-85
  on food entitlements in India and
    China, 184
Sender, John
  on distortion of African capitalism
    by external forces, 83
  on lack of inhibition of indigenous
    capitalism from DC-African
    relationships, 83

on massive diversion of resources
    from peasants by state, 88
  role of state, in increasing invest-
    ment in Africa, 85
  stress by, on colonial capitalism
    resulting in rising production
    of consumer goods, 81-82
Shell-BP
  British government as majority
    shareholder, 152
Shinohara, Miyohei
  on boomerang effect, 239
Sierra Leone
  strong support for indigenous cap-
    italists in, 85-86
Sikhs
  as Schumpeterian entrepreneurs,
    130-31
Singapore
  yearly growth rate in, 35
Singer, Hans
  hypothesis of peculiar barriers of, 15
Singer, Milton
  on Weber's error in analyzing
    Indian religion, 127
Slave trade
  in coastal West Africa, 7
Small
  industry, environment for, 212
  industry, decline in, 213
  industry, in Japan, 213
  scale entrepreneur, skills needed
    as, 112
Smith, Sheila
  on distortion of African capitalism
    by external forces, 83
  on lack of inhibition of indigenous
    capitalism from DC-African
    relationships, 83
  on massive diversion of resources
    from peasants by state, 88
  role of state, in increasing invest-
    ment in Africa, 85

stress by, on colonial capitalism resulting in rising production of consumer goods, 81-82

Social
factors, as determinants of entrepreneurship, 117, 118

Socialism
centralized, in China, 167
centralized, in USSR, 193
discussion of, by Marx, 17
market, commitment to, by China, 31
market, in Soviet Union, 18
state managed, death of Marxism in, 12
strategies, in Africa, 86

Socialist
approach, of Lagos Plan of Action, 64
economic approach, in Africa, 49
pattern of society, in India, 169

Socioeconomic (economic)
background, of Andhran entrepreneurs, 130
class background of entrepreneurs, 134
class status of entrepreneurs, 132
groupings, strength and position of, 152
origin, of entrepreneurs, 97-98, 99-115
status of entrepreneurs, 105, 123, 133
status of fathers of entrepreneurs, 111

Soft budget constraints
of firms, in China, 34

*Sogo shosha*
in Japan, 213

South Africa
in alliance with African political elites, 50
foreign investment in, 50
as medium ranking in HDI, 39

South Asia
native chiefs, and nationalism, 11
as poorest region, 35

Southern Nigeria
frustration of younger men in, 154

South Korea
exchange rates near equilibrium in, 214
growth and current-account surpluses before democratic transition by, 91
growth in industry in, 214
as high ranking in HDI, 39
income equality in, compared to China, 177
learning by, from post-World War II Japan, 194
*see also* Korea

Southeast Asia
as rapid grower, 35

Southern
elite, in Nigeria, 148

Soviet
advisors, pull out of, from China, 168
model, use of, in India, 169
planning approach, as applied to Chinese industry, 34

Soviet Union
accumulation of capital in, 206
death of Marxism in, 12-13
learning from, by China, 167
new social ethos of, 18
origin of industrial executives in, 134
*see also* Russia, Union

Spillover
effects, 22

Sri Lanka
income equality in, compared to China, 177
as medium ranking in HDI, 39

Stabilization
  programs, and expenditures on
    education, 65
  programs, by fledgling democratic
    governments, 91
Stagnation
  in Africa, 60
  of DCs, 74
  in early 1980s, in Africa, 85
  in Sub-Saharan Africa, 59
Stalin, Joseph
  on deviationism, 13
  violence of, 18
Standardized goods
  comparative advantage in, 199
State, 35
  action by, with economic liberal-
    ism, 216
  allocation by, to cities, 88
  assistance by, to entrepreneurs,
    202
  capture, of resources, 52
  economic planning, in India, 168
  economic policy, levers of, 153
  enterprise, in China, 33
  intervention, in market, as politi-
    cal instrument, 53
  intervention, in peasant price-
    setting, 64
  intervention, to induce investment,
    87
  levers, 22
  levers, by Nigeria's insecure elites,
    55
  monopoly, 27
  officials, 74, 86
  ownership, of strategic and heavy
    industry, in India, 167
  power, and aid, 50
  power, competition for, in Pakis-
    tan, 152
  promotion of social justice by, 169
  protection by, 84

  role of, in increasing investment,
    85
State-owned
  enterprises, 32
  enterprises, privatization of, 62
  organizations, domination of
    international trade by, 87
Statist
  approach, of the Lagos Plan of
    Action, 64
  economic approach, in Africa, 49
  strategies, in Africa, 86
Stedman, Louellen
  on debt crises and external politi-
    cal opposition, 90
Stolper, Wolfgang F.
  against premature preoccupation
    with equity, 20
Structural adjustment loans (SALs)
  under auspices of World Bank, 62,
    76
  and debt rescheduling, new lend-
    ing, or aid, 63
Structural adjustment programs
    (SAPs)
  in Africa and least developed
    countries, 209
  under auspices of IMF, 62
  of Bank/Fund, 64
  effects of, 66
  in Ghana, 92
  integration of, with long-term
    development, 65
Students
  activity of, 156
  political mobilization of, 155
Sub-Saharan Africa
  adjustment programs in, 92
  annual growth of, 38
  Bank/Fund adjustment by, 63
  burden of debt of, 50
  cartel funds for, without condi-
    tionality, 93

countries of, as democratic, 89
debt crisis in, 59-80
efforts at economic adjustment of, 39
foreign investment in, 82
growth in, 47
life expectancy at birth in, 81
market shares of, fall of, 88
as poorest region, 35
unfavorable international environment for, 59
Subsidy(ies)
abolition of, to higher education, 53
alternative to, 22
burden of, 50
to farm inputs in West Pakistan, 161
Subsistence
farming, assumptions about, 5
level, of wages, 210
Sudan
control of discussion and opposition by, 63
lack of ability of, to service debts, 80
as ranking low in HDI, 39
Sudra
range of *jati*s among, 98-99
Suhrawardy, H.S.
as Prime Minister, 153
Supply
leading institutions, in Meiji Japan, 204
response, for cash crops, 209
response, to lending, slowness of, 62
Surplus
capture of, 28-29
employment of, 8
of marketing board, 54
Swainson, Nicola
on world capitalism and indigenous capitalist development, 84

Swamy, Subramanian
data on agricultural and industrial growth in China and India, 189
on higher growth rates for China and India in the 1980s, 188
on Sino-Indian comparisons, 173
Sweden
annual growth rates of real GNP per capita of, 30
Sweezy, Paul
analysis of monopoly capitalism in the United States by, 13
on class conflict under actually existing socialism, 13

Taiwan
as high ranking in HDI, 39
income equality in, compared to China, 177
learning by, from post-World War II Japan, 194
resource transfer to Japan from, 206
Tamil Nadu (India)
industrialists from, 131
manufacturing entrepreneurs in, 118
Tanzania
control of discussion and opposition by, 63
goals of egalitarianism and socialism in, 51
increase in established posts in the civil service in, 52
as ranking low in HDI, 39
Tariffs
burden of, 50
on inputs, in Nigeria, 158
protection of output by African governments, 86
Tawney, R.H.
on effect of socioeconomic change on Protestantism, 126

Tax
  of export resources, 88
Taxation
  progressive, and capital accumula-
    tion, 21
Technical
  activists, among workers, in
    China, 135
  assistance, in Meiji Japan, 212
  change, as prolonged learning pro-
    cess, 198
  change, under colonial capitalism,
    82
  change, scope for, in LDCs, 81
  knowledge, application of, to pro-
    duction, 26
  progress, effect of, on agricultural
    wages, 210
Technicians
  high-level, 87
Technical
  progress, in traditional society,
    124
Technological
  advance, key figure in, 13-14
  advance, during Meiji era, 87
  advantage, 199
  background, of Japanese manag-
    ers, 31
  change, unsatisfactory rate of, in
    Soviet Union, 134
  enclaves, foreign firms as, 151
  gap, between DCs and Afro-Asia,
    213
  learning, through trade, 214
  progress, in agriculture, 207
  see also Innovation
Technology, acquisition of, and
    LDC subordination, 9
  adoption of, from West, 195
  advanced, 74
  appropriate, 197
  capital-intensive, 211

  and factor proportions, 10
  foreign controlled, 18
  improvement of, during Meiji
    government, 194
  of multinational corporations
    (MNCs), 75
  and new spirit of capitalism, 27
  propensity to import, 30
  transfer of, for light industry, 196
Tenants
  distress from, 207
  lack of security of, 83
  reduction of farm disposable
    income by, 206
Terms of trade, 41
  commodity, xxx-xxxi, 39, 71, 72
  decline in, by Sub-Saharan Africa,
    92
  international, volatility of, 67
Thailand
  as medium ranking in HDI, 39
  yearly growth rate in, 35
Thurow, Lester
  advice to M.B.A. by, 231
  on cost of white-collar workers in
    United States, 233
  on industrial policies in United
    States and Japan, 225
  on United States spurring labor to
    take direct interest in raising
    productivity, 234
  on training of American chief
    executive officers, 229
  on United States' lagging produc-
    tivity growth, 222
Todaro, Michael P.
  on expected urban wages, 211
Togo
  relinquishment of policy direction
    by, 66
Toronto
  terms, for debt rescheduling, 76

Tradable
  goods, shift to, 66
Trade
  control of, by Western capitalism,
    29
  elimination of competition in, 158
  entrepreneurs originating in, 118
  with India, by Pakistan, 147
  international, as leading sector, 8
  international, domination of, 87
  international, opening of economy
    to, 62-63
  international, with DCs, 71
  long-distance, 26
  as occupation, before industrial
    entrepreneurship, 108
  pattern of, in Nigeria, 149
  as primary occupation for Pakis-
    tani industrialists, 117
  promotion of, with mother coun-
    tries, 82
  with rich countries, 50
  *see also* East Pakistan, Foreign,
    International, West Pakistan
Traditional
  agricultural society, technical pro-
    gress, 124
  economy, concept of, 10-11
  economy, elites in, 12;
Trinidad
  terms, 77
Trotsky, Leon
  on decentralized socialism and the
    international class struggle, 13
Turkey
  minorities in, as industrialists, 128
Turner, Terisa
  on commercial triangle, 86
Twice-born
  castes, entrepreneurs from, 99,
    102, 105, 131
  Hindu castes, overrepresentation
    of, 130-31

Tyson, Laura D'Andrea
  support of subsidies, duties, and
    market sharing to promote
    U.S. industries in competition
    with Japan by, 237
  support of Super 301 legislation
    by, 237-38

Uganda
  as ranking low in HDI, 39
Ul Haq, Mahbub
  on inequality and growth, 20
Underemployed
  labor, soaking up of, 32
Underprivileged
  background, of family of entrepre-
    neurs, 133
  classes, in "subculture of poverty,"
    122
  groups, entrepreneurs from, 123-
    24
Unemployment
  high rate of, in Nigeria, 155
  increase in Dutch, 54
Union of Soviet Socialist Republics
    (USSR)
  breakup of, and failure of social-
    ism, 193
  disruption among peasants in, 19
  *see also* Soviet
Union(s) (labor or trade)
  fragmentation of, in Nigeria and
    Pakistan, 154
  membership in, in Japan, 224
  strength of, 211
  suppression of, in Pakistan, 155
United Kingdom (U.K.)
  in alliance with African political
    elites, 50
  explanation of slow growth of, 30
  increase in military support to
    Federation by, 152

as major trading partner of Nigeria, 149
*see also* Britain
United Nations (UN)
designation by, of least-developed
countries, 70
on five-year strategy to safeguard
Africa's economic survival, 38
increase in resources of, 80
as international agency to inculcate market discipline by
states, 85
Secretary-General of, recommendation on debt rescheduling, 78
United Nations Children's Fund
(UNICEF)
on adjustment programs and declining educational spending,
200
on adjustment with a human face,
64
on aims of adjustment, 63-64
critique of World Bank and IMF
adjustment, 64
United Nations (UN) Development
Programme
development of two indices of
development by, 38
on public enterprises in Sub-
Saharan Africa, 85
United Nations International Comparison Project
on purchasing power of gross product, 221
United Nations Programme of
Action for African Economic
Recovery and Development,
1986-1990, 38
United States (U.S.)
agencies of, emphasis on, 156
Agency for International Development, consideration of democratization by, 89

in alliance with African political
elites, 50
assistance from, to Pakistan, 149,
151
average income in, 28
Bankruptcy Reform Act of, 79
banks of, saving of, 76
business elite of, 133
business people and farmers in, 73
capital stock per person in, 75, 198
as developed economy, 12
Dutch disease in, 54
economists, in LDCs, 22
as eighth in GNP per person,
1990, 221
entrepreneurs in, 132
explanation of slow growth of, 30
failure of, to adopt Trinidad
terms, 77
growth of special interests in, 31
heterodox views in, 23
industrialists in, socioeconomic
mobility of, 130
on international order that avoids
war, 62
as low performer, 227
military and economic aid pact
with, by Pakistani political
leadership, 148
occupation of Japan by, 193-94
ranking in human freedom of, 39
role of, in creating new capitalist
elite, 150
standards of, 6
sustained growth of, 25
women in business in, 136
as world's second-ranking lender,
59
Unwalla, Darab B.
on income of sample entrepreneurs, 133
on origins of entrepreneurs in
Michigan, 130

Upper
  classes, in Africa, 51
  classes, children from, 19
  classes, as contributors to external
    crisis, 63
  classes, support by, at expense of
    growth and income distribu-
    tion, 88
  class individuals, achievement
    orientation of, 122
Urban
  bias, in Africa, 53-54
  bias, in China, 174
  bias, under Mao, 189
  bias, policies of, 208
  oriented policies, of market inter-
    vention, 88
  reform, in China, 32
  unemployment rates, 211

Vaishyas
  as entrepreneurs, 105, 108
  firms of, 107
Value(s)
  explanation of, 6
  Marxist explanation for origin of,
    17
  presupposition of, 5
Vanek, Jaroslav
  on socialism as democratic and
    decentralized, 13
Varna (caste)
  concept of, 98
Viet Nam
  slow growth of, 35
Visakhapatnam, Andhra Pradesh
  India, 98

Wage
  equilibrium, 210
  increases, by workers, in Pakistan,
    156
  increases, in Nigeria, 155

premium, 211
reduction, in Nigeria and Ghana,
  54
structure, 12
Wallerstein, Immanuel
  on stages of African involvement
    in world economy, 81
Wan Runnan
  and Beijing Stone Company, 32
Waterston, Albert
  on major weaknesses of planning,
    156
Wealth
  concentration of, 19
  inequalities of, 21
  role of, in transmitting class stand-
    ing from one generation to
    another, 51
Weber, Max
  on Protestant ethic, 125-27
  on "worldly" asceticism of Pro-
    testantism, 26
West
  capital in, 84
  as central capitalist countries, 81
  development of, explanation for, 7
  economic contact with, by coastal
    Nigeria, 145
  economic domination of, 8
  exports from, 61
  foreign investment from, 50
  imperialism in, adverse effect of,
    82
  lack of overthrow of capitalism in,
    17
  other economies of, capitalism as
    success in, 28
  Pakistan, as allied to, 149
  success of capitalism in, 26
  sustained growth in, 25
  tariff limitations by, circumven-
    tion of, 214
  treaties by Japan with, 29, 194

upper-and middle-class in the, and
    manual work, 12
values of, 6
West Africa
    slave trade of, 7
    women in business in, 136-37
Western Europe
    average income in, 28
    as developed economy, 12
    rise of strong national states in, 27
Western Nigeria
    jobs in, competition for, 163
    heightening of Yoruba national-
        ism, 147
West India
    business communities in Pakistan
        from, 162
West Pakistan
    assembly of, 153
    competition with Eastern wing by,
        159
    demands of, in, 156
    disparity between, and East Pakis-
        tan, 162
    diversion of foreign exchange to, 161
    industrial and commercial capital-
        ists of, 148
    interests in, 160
    redistribution of resources to, 155
    representation of, 146
    ruling group of, 149
    tactics of, to nullify electoral
        majority in East, 163
    threat to ruling elite in, 157
Wilson, Ernest T.
    on political liberties and economic
        development, 90
"Whipping the fast ox"
    as planning approach, in China,
        34
Whyte, Martin King
    on China's falling income inequal-
        ity under Deng, 189

Winter, David G.
    on achievement motivation train-
        ing, 118-19
    lack of awareness of moral ambi-
        guities when introducing
        "change agents" by, 120
    lack of conceptual matrix oriented
        toward class by, 122
    lack of control group by, 120-21
    no data on relationship between
        class and caste by, 123
Women
    in business, 136, 137
    see also Females
Workers
    authority of, in China, 33
    bonuses of, 34
    burden of tariffs, high consumer
        prices, or subsidies on, 50
    in coalition with bourgeoisie, 16
    cross-pressuring of, by class and
        ethnic identities, 51
    burden of tariffs, high consumer
        prices, or subsidies on, 50
    landless, lack of security of, 83
    and new Soviet ruling class, 19
    in Nigeria and Pakistan, con-
        sciousness of, 158
    pay of, under responsibility sys-
        tem, 32
    as revolutionary leaders, 18
    revolution by, 17
    skepticism and resistance by, 5
    technical activists among, in
        China, 135
    in urban areas, food prices for, 53
Working
    classes, in Africa, 49
World Bank
    adjustment loans by, 67
    adjustment programs of, 62-65,
        92, 170, 209, 215

on buyers' market effect on
improving China's industrial
performance, 35
concessional funds by, 78
data on Chinese-Indian comparisons by, 172, 173
figures by, on India's and China's
nominal GNP per capita, 188
as finance minister of the Third
World, 63
insistence on privatization by, 202
as international agency to inculcate market discipline by
states, 85
on Kenya's protection as "license
to print money," 86
on lack of success in adjustment
by transitional democratic systems, 90
loans of last resort by, 63
model of, resembling that of pre-
World War II Japan, 216
neglect of political constraints by,
89
OECD countries as major shareholders in, 195
on poverty rates, in China and
India, 189
on public enterprises in Sub-
Saharan Africa, 85
reliance on "seal of approval" by
IMF by, 80
report of, on Africa's turnaround,
66
role of, in Brady Plan, 76

SALs by, 76
studies on poverty by, 20
technical guidance by, on debt
reduction, 79
unveiling of Baker Plan at meeting of, 75
*see also* Multilateral

Yamamura, Kozo
on blurring of samurai status, 203
Yorubas
community of, 159
competition of, with Ibos, 162
as leading entrepreneurs, 128-29
nationalism of, 147

Zaibatsu
concentration of, 212
from state assisted entrepreneurs,
202
successor companies to, 223-24
Zäire
debt crisis of, 75
propensity to flee from additional
external debt in, 75
as ranking low in HDI, 39
rescheduling of official debt by, 61
rulers of, squandering of loan
funds by, 70
Zambia
declining terms of trade by, 92
imposition of ceiling on exports,
60
strong support for indigenous capitalists in, 85-86